A
GE TO
NS
WN

Acknowledgments:

This book became possible thanks to the support of those former members of Poison Girls who are still with us, together with the help of the band's wider family and friends. For providing access to the Poison Girls' personal archives, our thanks go to Richard Famous, Pete Fender, and Gemma Sansom.

Photographs and band memorabilia were generously shared with us by Tom Barwood, Adi Cooper, Sue Cooper (Bella Donna), Ming de Nasty, Dominique Downs (Domino), Nick James (Seamus), Ricky Oshea, Bernhardt Rebours, Richard Swales (Richard Famous), Phil (Hedgehog) Tonge, and Reynard Toombs. Thanks also to the contributors to—and the curators of—the Internet Archive, MayDay Rooms, Kill Your Pet Puppy site, and the Sparrow's Nest Archive for making their collections freely shareable.

For sharing their memories of those extraordinary times, we're grateful to Tom Barwood, Bella Donna, Dominique Downs, Martin Goldschmidt, Steve Ignorant, Heather Joyce, Andy Lee, Robert Lloyd, Zillah Minx, Bernhardt Rebours, Gemma Sansom, Alan Schofield, Mick Shenton (Max Vol), and Sid Truelove.

Additional thanks go to Rob Stone (*Positive Creed*) and Simon Nolan (*Essential Ephemera*) for allowing us to make use of their extended published and unpublished Poison Girls interviews, with extra thanks to Simon for sharing his approved reproduction of *Words Written in Trust*. We're pleased to be able to quote the memories and insights of Honey Bane, Peter Jones, Sean O'Neill, Rosanne Rabinowitz, and Pete Stennett.

Further thanks to Kathy Malloy and Steve Doughton from *Snipehunt*, Katie Burkart, Doug Rogers, *Maximum Rocknroll*, Paul Curran, Lance Hahn, Alex Yusimov, and the punk DJs at KDVS and KHSU.

We must extend our lasting gratitude to Richard Famous for agreeing to be interviewed on multiple occasions and for providing insightful and attentive comments on draft versions of the manuscript. "Pester away," he encouraged. And we did. Naturally, any factual errors and all matters of interpretation remain the responsibility of the author, editor, and designer of this book alone. Finally, we're grateful to Joey, Ramsey, Gregory, and Steven at PM Press for their enthusiastic support for the project.

This Is a Message to Persons Unknown
© 2026 PM Press

ISBN: 979-8-88744-136-8 (paperback)
ISBN: 979-8-88744-144-3 (hardcover)
ISBN: 979-8-88744-137-5 (e-book)

Library of Congress Control Number: 2025931317

PM Press, PO Box 23912, Oakland, CA 94623
pmpress.org
thehippiesnowwearblack.org.uk

Frontispiece: Vi Subversa and Richard Famous, Poison Girls live at The Mermaid, Birmingham, 27 December 1984. Photo by Ming de Nasty.

Design: Alec Dunn. Chapter title font based on stencil designs made by Lance d'Boyle for *The Impossible Dream #2*.

10 9 8 7 6 5 4 3 2 1

Printed in the USA.

CONTENTS

FOREWORD

And the message is, in a nutshell—remember Poison Girls, in all their different, changing, evolving colours. Remember how they always stuck out like a sore thumb, beautifully. Remember how they were honest, down-to-earth, polite, and friendly people, so far removed from tacky rock'n'roll yet so able to whip up a storm on stage. Remember how they told us to see radical politics as something that happens not in demonstrations and haircuts and 45 rpm records but in relationships, in washing up and cooking, in love and kindness and in the everyday everyday.

This Is a Message is a handbook for that remembering, and an insight into the stuff we didn't know about but which makes Poison Girls' story even more fascinating. Two things I didn't know about: their theatre-performance-art beginnings, growing from the early 1970s counterculture that I only learned about in retrospect, that connection between politics and art . . . feminism for both women and men, questioning authority in the mainstream and in the kitchen and the bedroom, all somehow presented and explored through the post-hippy counterculture, through do-it-yourself agit-prop theatre. Setting up squats, making noise, organising, all the stuff that came before Poison Girls were a band on stage. I loved reading about this stuff. It's vital. It's the stuff that tells us we can all do this, that great art doesn't come fully formed; it grows from collective work and inspiration stretching back years.

The other thing I didn't know enough about: that decision to leave the Crass model behind, to break out of the slow suffocation of those relentless church hall benefits. Of course those times, those gigs, and those records that both bands shared were incredible, inspirational, life-changing even. But the walking away, and the conversations and ideas behind that walking away, are also inspiring and powerful and fascinating. Reading how this band of mavericks wriggled out of the straitjacket of all that stencilled black-and-white artwork—that's the stuff I wanted to know about. The stuff that made Poison Girls utterly unique.

We played with Poison Girls many times. At first Vi frightened us—she was an icon, a figurehead in a sea of young black-clad lads. She was the anti-rock'n'roll, the diametric opposite of Elvis, so gloriously *other*. But then we met, and we found out that she was funny and gentle and warm and friendly. She was a hero of ours, not for being a powerful woman (we had those in our band, too) but for being everything we wanted our heroes to be, with the cleverest lyrics delivered with a one-of-a-kind voice that rasped and coaxed and admonished.

And Richard Famous, he was my guitar hero. Immediately likeable and approachable, an offstage big smile and an onstage chicken-legged strut that was entirely the antithesis of the anarcho-punk angry guitar stance. Famous was the first person I knew to have a guitar stand and a tuner. A simple fold-out A-frame and a plastic Boss chromatic tuner with (oh yes) LED lights. This was a revelation, and I knew I had to somehow convince our band that we needed these things, too. Richard and Vi were our era's odd couple, happily and defiantly breaking the mould, while writing and recording songs that still resonate down the years—melodies and harmonies and a desire to change and challenge the accepted format.

This book reminds me just how unique Poison Girls were. How extraordinary. It's all a fascinating, compelling story and it's solidly, perfectly told. A book that sends you back to listen to the music, "Piano Lessons," "Promenade Immortelle," "Take the Toys from the Boys," songs out of time and place, music that constantly took you by surprise. This book makes you realise how essential Poison Girls were in that context of politically charged anger, that context of noise and cheap gigs. And to repeat myself, the book's message is simply, in a nutshell—remember Poison Girls in all their different, changing, evolving colours.

Boff Whalley
June 2025

AUTHOR'S INTRODUCTION

Poison Girls were a band as compelling and as impactful as they were singular amongst their peers. During the twelve years of their existence, they released a series of extraordinary and distinctive singles and albums, which combined memorable musical signatures and soundscapes with incisive and insightful lyrics which brought to life Poison Girls' unashamed commitment to feminism and anarchism.

They were always a powerful presence on the live stage, and much of their early reputation came from their close collaboration with Crass. Yet while there's no question that they played as decisive a role in the crystallisation of anarcho-punk as Crass, Poison Girls' significance extends far beyond their status as allies of Crass. Decades on from the band's dissolution, it's still apparent that the impact and value of the work of Poison Girls is not yet widely acknowledged, even by enthusiasts of that tumultuous era in British political punk. Crass's Penny Rimbaud readily acknowledges that Poison Girls were "an absolutely extraordinary group of people led by a very, very powerful feminist voice, in Vi Subversa, and a brilliant poet," adding that "they were absolutely a complete equal to us, on every level."

I first spoke face to face with Poison Girls backstage at a gig in Exeter's St. George's Hall in October 1981—as one of three somewhat awestruck teenage interviewers. The band was brimming with confidence and a sense of urgency on their first full national tour following their ending of their collaborative agreement with Crass. Listening to the patient, respectful, insightful, and articulate explanations of their anarchist and feminist commitments and their outsider DIY practice was an experience as unforgettable as it was inspirational. The passionate, raging set that they played on stage that night was electrifying, confirming just how significant and distinctive Poison Girls were, even amongst the firmament of political punk bands.

I'd already acquired everything the band had put out by that point, from *Piano Lessons* to *Total Exposure*. From that meeting onwards, I enthusiastically collected and endlessly played all of their vinyl releases, scrutinised their written statements, and savoured each issue of *The Impossible Dream*. I travelled to see them play live in Birmingham, Bradford, Carlisle, London, Nottingham, and elsewhere. I corresponded with the band (Richard Famous was the most likely to reply), shared our developing fanzine experiments with them, stayed at their Leytonstone home, and once escaped a fascist mob in the back of their tour van side by side with Rubella Ballet.

Decades later, as I began to document different aspects of the history of British anarchism and the political punk movement, I published one of the first detailed histories of the life and work of Poison Girls in *Punk and Post-Punk Journal*, an account which attracted praise and encouragement from Lance d'Boyle, Richard Famous, and Vi Subversa. "I must tell you that this is the nearest I have seen to an intelligent, truthful, and sensitive account of our history," Subversa wrote. "I congratulate you on the work you have done in researching the material. I feel grateful that we may come out of obscurity into a clearer and more just focus. Thanks and all power to you." It was a huge encouragement to me to develop my appreciation of Poison Girls' story still further.

An exhaustive book-length history of Poison Girls has long been overdue, and I have been thrilled, with the cooperation of so many surviving members of the Poison Girls family, to have had the opportunity to research and tell the band's story, an account that seeks to highlight their unique contribution to the sounds, aesthetic, and politics of the counterculture of 1970s and 1980s Britain. To be able to do so in a book that also illuminates the arresting visual and design work that was integral to the identity of Poison Girls is especially gratifying.

Rich Cross
May 2025

9

0.
STARING THROUGH A HOLE IN THE WALL

PRE/PROTO 1970S

A mix of activists, artists, and musicians, spanning the generations and involved in different countercultural milieux, coalesce in the city of Brighton in the late 1970s. Experiments in outsider art and theatre result in The Body Show (and Edinburgh Fringe Festival 'infamy'). The reverberations of this foray into agit-prop persist as the performers return to Sussex, just as the shockwaves of punk rock reach the city. Members of The Body Show troupe decide the time is right to switch up their cultural focus and form a distinctive, provocative, and politically conscious punk band.

By the time that punk exploded in the UK, the musicians who would form the original lineup of Poison Girls were all living in Brighton, on the south coast of England. Frances Sokolov (who would later take the stage name Vi Subversa) was in her forties when punk first broke. The only child of eastern European Jewish immigrants, Frances was amongst the hundreds of young children evacuated from London during World War II in anticipation of the Blitz. At the age of four, Frances found herself on a station platform "with a label round my neck, a toothbrush and a scrambled egg sandwich in my pocket," she remembered. Being separated from her family was anything but traumatic. "I happily waved my mother goodbye," she explained. "I had escaped not only the doodlebugs."

After she spent the war years in rural South Wales with a kindly surrogate family, her already strained relationship with her parents worsened. "When I came back to London to my family, I wasn't at all ready to be groomed for the marriage market and become a good Jewish wife," Sokolov recalled decades later. Her rebellious impulses were expressed in her work as a creative ceramics artist and involvement in the social experimentation of the kibbutz movement. By the 1950s, and still a teenager, Sokolov had become part of the bohemian and dissident scenes in London's Soho district. Her interest in oppositional politics had grown through the connections and networks of that group of artists, musicians and activists.

"I strayed into the arms of the anarchists," she explained. "I think I was set up to become an anarchist, really. And the anarchists became my family. They made sense of the world to me." Sokolov was drawn to the work of the Freedom Press group, and particularly the *Freedom* anarchist newspaper. She helped at the paper's offices and began street-selling copies. It was the anarchist critique of the Cold War, and of capitalist militarism East and West, that had special salience for the young Frances. "The antiwar issue was my main attraction to the anarchists," she confirmed. With that established, "everything else just fell into place, really," she continued. "It all made sense. It *was* a war economy."

Through her involvement in *Freedom*, Sokolov met the anarchist activist Philip Sansom. "Philip was an amazing person," she recalled. "He was a part of the antiwar movement and had been a conscientious objector." Sansom had written for the anarchist antimilitarist paper *War Commentary* and became a regular fixture at Speakers' Corner in London. "Philip was a member of the Editorial Board of *Freedom*, and he also did cartoons for them," she explained. There was an age difference between them ("Philip was nineteen years older than me," Frances confirmed), but both considered that irrelevant as they became romantical-

ly involved. The pair also worked closely as political comrades, and were active in the London Anarchist Group (LAG) which in 1954 set up the Malatesta Club.

The Club was formed after the LAG had become convinced that "a meeting place and social space was of the most vital importance in increasing the spread of anarchist ideas," anarchist historian Nick Heath explains. Writing in *Freedom*, Sansom had insisted that London anarchist comrades needed "a place of our own, instead of relying on meeting rooms in pubs." Over four years, the Malatesta Club grew into a cultural, social and political hub for anarchists in the capital, until soaring London rents forced its closure. During that time it "provided a new social space for radicals and a haven for both old and young dissidents," Heath adds—a generational mix that Sokolov fully approved of. She had vivid memories of the venue and the surge of excitement around it. "We used to cook for events, and people would come and talk about anarchism, and activists would come and speak," she said.

Sokolov became involved with the emerging antinuclear movement of the late 1950s, and took part in some of the landmark demonstrations organised by what became the Campaign for Nuclear Disarmament (CND). By the early 1960s, the fragmentation of the 1950s anarchist scene was increasingly apparent. "The anarchist movement at that time was very splintered," she suggested. "There were *all sorts* of splinter groups." Sansom and Sokolov sought to traverse the movement's fracture lines, finding ways to remain motivated and engaged even as their own perspectives developed and evolved.

Sokolov's work in ceramics intersected with her political commitments. At an event in Fulham Town Hall in London in 1961 marking the seventy-fifth anniversary of the launch of *Freedom* newspaper in 1886, reporter Caleb Williams noted (in a coincidental pre-echo of the lyrical rhythm of Poison Girls' "Persons Unknown") the presence of "jazz men and musicologists, production engineers and demolition men, psychologists and beatniks . . . a troupe of novelists and poets . . . students, physicians, meter-readers, *Freedom*'s machine-minder and one of its typesetters, a gaggle of architects and the only pacifist bouncer in London's nightlife." Following the performance at the event by the celebrated jazz singer and anarcho-surrealist connoisseur George Melly, he was "presented with a teapot, made for the occasion by potter Frances Sokolov, to replace the silver one taken by the bailiffs when its owner declined to pay that proportion of his income tax which the government proposed to spend on lethal ironmongery."

After an intense few years living, working, and politically agitating in London, Sansom and Sokolov left the capital to take on the renovation of a dilapidated

Page 10: Frances Sokolov (VI Subversa)
juggling, Brighton, 1976. Photo
courtesy of Sue Cooper.
This page: Some of Frances's ceramic
sculptures created in the 1950s. Courtesy
of Gemma Sansom. Below: Philip Sansom
and Frances Sokolov, circa 1959

cottage in Manningtree, Essex, on the Suffolk border. The couple had two children together, Dan (born in 1964) and Gemma (born in 1967).

"I grew up in the counterculture," Dan Sansom (aka Pete Fender) reflected later. "Both of my parents were anarchists, long before I came along, they were activists in the 1950s and '60s. My dad was a conscientious objector, he had printed some leaflets and served time in prison for disaffecting the troops in the Second World War," he continued "He went to prison again when I was about six years old for refusing to fill in the census form. . . . I was born into protest, really."

"I felt acutely aware of how different we were from a young age," Gemma agrees. "My parents didn't believe in the family structure, obviously never married—still quite unusual in those days," she continues. "After they split up when I was four, Frances was looking for a very different setup. She wanted us to live with other adults who would share the work of raising kids and create an alternative to the family."

Bored by the work she had taken up in marketing, Sokolov had been looking for a new direction—both professionally and personally. "I had done a lot of things and gone into a lot of projects and come out the other end and was at a point where there really wasn't anything that I particularly wanted to do." After she and Sansom separated, Sokolov and the children moved out.

"I was a mother, I was middle-aged. I was frightened by years of conditioning, frightened to leave the dull but very safe environment of my kitchen. It wasn't disgust at larger political issues that made me finally do it, it was the overwhelming anger that I'd wasted half my life not really being me because I was too scared not to conform."

Her experience of 1960s counterculture suggested some lessons, particularly for activists like Sokolov who recognised the continuities between the practice of the hippy scene and other oppositional cultures which came later. It was a critical view rather than a rose-tinted one. "There's a lot in common, really, between what was happening in the 1960s and now, except that I think that hippy women hadn't had a lot of the benefit of the women's movement." For Sokolov, the shortcomings of hippies' lack of recognition of the politics of gender had led to isolation in motherhood of many of her contemporaries: "A lot of women were left, after the hippy period of peace and love, with loads of kids that they were left on their own to bring up," she acknowledged later. It was a form

Freedom Anarchist Weekly, 4 November 1961, vol. 22 no. 35 and *Freedom Anarchist Weekly*, 30 January 1965, vol. 25 no. 4. *Freedom* is an anarchist newspaper based in London. It began publishing in 1886 and continues to publish anarchist news and views online.

Freedom Anarchist Weekly, 4 November 1961 — "Are our leaders suicidal lunatics?"

Freedom Anarchist Weekly, 30 January 1965 — "Safe Seat Collapses"

of separation that Poison Girls' reading of punk would later challenge, albeit through the passing of a generational torch.

"There are a lot of people I've lost touch with from the 1960s, old friends of mine, and I'm finding them again—because their children are coming to our gigs." Throughout the life of Poison Girls, Sokolov would strengthen connections between dissidents of different generations: "There's a whole lot of hippies that kind of disappeared in the face of the 'punk onslaught,'" she conceded, but she remained optimistic as she observed the "softening a bit between those divisions now."

As she looked for new direction, Sokolov enrolled on a Diploma of Applied Behavioural Studies (DABS) course at North London Polytechnic. "It was an internationally respected and innovative course, exploring how people react and interact in group situations," Richard Famous recalls. One of the tutors on the course was Gary Lance Robins (later to become Lance d'Boyle). "I think his work as a DABS tutor was a major contributor to his outlook and *modus operandi*," Famous suggests. "And the DABS—for want of a better word—'method' provided the framework of how Poisons Girls were to operate." Seeing a kindred rebellious spirit in one another, Gary and Frances became partners and, as things developed, Robins moved into the Sokolov family home.

"I got together with Lance after I broke up with Philip, and we went to Brighton," she said. "He was intrigued that I was by then a hippy anarchist." Sokolov's defiant, libertarian impulses severed the last of Robins's tethers to the British far left, and encouraged in him a convert's belief in the potential of anarchism.

"I was six when Gary came along," Gemma Sansom recalls. "He was fun and seemed to like us kids. We lived together a bit like a family in Brighton for five years and in London until I left home at seventeen." The following year, Gemma joined her mum, brother, Robins and "a couple of others" on a "proper hippy road trip" to Morocco in a VW Camper. "We listened to The Stones, Neil Young, and Crosby, Stills, and Nash. Happy times. I got my hair dyed with henna by Moroccan women and came back to school with bright orange hair," she says. "I knew I was different even then. . . . I quite liked normal school, I think because it *was* normal. I definitely had a side of me that wanted to fit in, most young kids do. But as I got older this passed and I embraced punk and being different."

Life in Brighton continued to involve political work that crossed the generations. "I was taken on Anti-Nazi League marches and to Rock Against Racism rallies," Gemma recalls. "We would march from Trafalgar Square to one of the big parks in South London and I would complain about the walking—it seemed like a

very long way! But I remember being at one when I was nine, where The Clash played amongst others. I climbed a tree to get a better look at the stage."

As for the new man in her mum's life, "I never called him Lance," she says. "He was a dreamer and an artist and at his best was an intelligent, gentle man. He was a great drummer and very supportive to me as I got behind the kit in Fatal Microbes. He had great records too and we'd listen to Kraftwerk, Roxy Music, T. Rex, Bowie, and The Velvet Underground."

"I've counted myself as an anarchist since I was twenty-three," Robins reflected in his early seventies. That was the age at which he had become "a member of CND and sold *Freedom* and *Anarchy* in Cardiff."

By the time punk broke, Robins had decades' worth of experience in student activism, anarchist circles and in the counterculture that he could draw on. He was less attracted to the dutiful, 'ideologically sound' ranks of the organised anarchists. His interest was piqued by dissident, outsider movements, especially those motivated to use art and culture for political ends. Robins identified more as a bohemian than as a follower of Bakunin, Malatesta, or Goldman. But his reading of punk was informed by his anarchism, long before his anarchism was informed by his contact with punk. His political worldview was infused with a clear understanding of key anarchist precepts.

It was in the early 1970s, when Robins was in his early thirties, that he began to experiment with the idea of becoming a "percussive musician." Famous recalls that Robins later adopted the puppet character of Animal—the frenzied, wild-eyed drummer from The Muppets—as a role model. D'Boyle joined the avant-garde experimentalist group Sigmoidoscope (named after a diagnostic device, combining a light and camera housed in a thin tube, which is inserted through the rectum to check the bowel and lower intestine). His growing abilities in musicianship was only one of his many artistic talents, which also included interest in agitprop art, graphic design and filmmaking. It was the arrival of punk that would enable Robins to leverage all those skills.

Guitarist, singer, and songsmith Richard Swales (later to become Richard Famous) was born in the Yorkshire city of Leeds in 1951. "I spent my teenage years listening to The Beatles, The Stones, The Who, Small Faces, The Kinks, Cream, Hendrix, Dylan, and more," he says. "Quite the musical education!"

"I got my first guitar for my fifteenth birthday—it was a tourist-quality Spanish job, and the neck broke almost as soon as it was tuned. Next I got a crappy steel-stringed acoustic—bought for £2 at a CND demo—which proved to be a cruel introduction to sliced fingertips, and—I later realised—almost impossibly high action."

"I then acquired an electric guitar and, of course, formed a band. We had a great drummer, a wonderful piano player, and three budding guitar players. We played a few youth clubs and a school dance, got better and caught the bug." After a short spell in a blues band, Swales secured his "first shot at songwriting and playing original material" in The Earnest Band, formed in 1970. "We were ex-school friends," he explains. The lineup included Howard Trafford (later Devoto) and Richard Boon, the Buzzcocks manager and cofounder of the New Hormones record label. "We would get together in a room in one of our parents' houses, when we all come home to Leeds in the university holidays," he says. "We'd record songs we'd written in the interim on a quarter-inch reel-to-reel tape recorder. Howard generally wrote by himself, while I wrote music with Richard Boon providing the lyrics."

"I also went on to do a few gigs with Howard as a duo," he explains. "But in 1973, this all came to nothing after we finished university and we were never all together in Leeds at the same time again." Swales and his partner Sue Cooper (soon to become Bella Donna) decided to head off travelling.

"In the summer of 1974, Richard and I had hitchhiked across Europe and North Africa, and then back through Europe," Cooper recalls. "We went to Morocco, Algeria, and Tunisia before coming back." The pair arrived in Brighton that September or October, as Cooper was starting a degree course at Sussex University. Swales was considering his next move, and "what he was interested in now was playing music," she says. His next opportunity to perform came as part of a new theatre group.

In Brighton, Sokolov announced she would embark on a new course of educational enquiry: nephology (the study of clouds). "I think this was a course run by the 'university of life,'" Famous says with a smile. "The story she told is that she had just decided to devote her life to lying on her back in the grass and studying clouds." It was an invitation from Adi (short for Adrienne) Cooper, the twin sister of Sue Cooper, to join a new theatre group that would interrupt her reverie and become an irresistible source of distraction.

"I never believed I had a musical role in life, but I was voicing thoughts friends felt should be heard," Sokolov recalled later. Knowing how powerful, how assured, how mesmerising a frontwoman she would become, it's revealing to learn just how little confidence Subversa felt in her vocal talents to begin with. Her singing began as a private, solitary experiment. "The first time I tried alone. I turned out the lights and turned on the cassette recorder," she recalled later. "Halfway through, I stopped because the window was open and I didn't want anyone else to hear. And when I played the tape back to the group, I insisted that the

lights were out then as well." Encouraged by the support of those around her, she began to believe in her abilities.

"I was very nervous but got strength from friends," she explained. Subversa's confidence grew through singing Bertolt Brecht and Kurt Weill songs (including "Surabaya Johnny" and "Pirate Jenny") as part of a local pub cabaret night. "The idea for the band followed."

"The history of Poison Girls starts with The Body Show," Swales explains. This experiment in art performance grew out of Brighton's prolific alternative and underground cultures. By the end of the 1970s, Brighton had become "a resting place for London dropouts and end of the hippy trail survivors," he says. It was a city that functioned as a "fading 'down at the heel' holiday destination" kept financially afloat by a rising student population, and attracting cash-poor radicals, bohemians, artists and musicians reluctant to endure an impoverished London life—future members of Poison Girls amongst them.

It was through The Body Show that their creative alliance was first brokered, as the group began to experiment with stagecraft and performance. "The Body Show was the baby of Simon Johnson, who would later help set up Xntrix Records," says Swales. The intention was to create a show that could join the Sussex University package at the famous Edinburgh Fringe Festival in 1975.

"The group that put together The Body Show was actually a mix of students and nonstudents, which I think was a bit unusual," Sue Cooper says. "My twin sister Adi was already in her third year at Sussex University and was in a relationship with Simon. They were into drama and had done student productions at the university." Now keen to assemble a more inclusive ensemble, the pair reached out to other local artists. Soon, "Frances and Gary and a friend of theirs called Pasha and his partner" were all on board, says Cooper, "and, of course, Dan and Gemma were involved in it, and then a friend of Simon's called John Scott, who was a sax player from Liverpool." Scott would go on to play with Jilted John, Alberto y Lost Trios Paranoias and would later provide "some wonderful saxophone on several tracks on the *Where's the Pleasure* album," Swales adds. In the end, something like a dozen people were involved in what remained a fluid ensemble.

"We were doing stuff for the first time," Adi Cooper recalls. "Playing instruments, performing, creating music and sketches. It provided a space for ideas to be realised—ambitions we may never have thought to have."

"We had very little theatrical experience, no money—but a load of good ideas," Famous suggests. "The show was to be in the form of a series of multimedia

Clockwise from top left: Bella Donna singing into mic, Pete Fender on drums, Richard Famous on acoustic guitar, with friends, Brighton, 1976. Richard Famous, 1976. The Body Show, Edinburgh, 1975–Simon (left), Lance d'Boyle (centre), Pasha (right). The Body Show, Edinburgh, 1975–Vi at far left. Bella, Richard, Lance, Vi, and friends, circa 1974. Photos courtesy of Sue Cooper.

'sketches' on the broad theme of 'the body politic.'" The intention was to explore questions of personal identity, the complexities of human relationships and the politics of gender, and the dynamic between the individual, society, and the state. There was no question that these were weighty themes to address, but the group was determined to take them on in ways that audiences might make sense of. "The recommended reading for participants was *The Function of the Orgasm* by Willhelm Reich and *The Art of Sensual Massage* by Gordon Inkeles," Swales explains.

The outcome of an intense period of rehearsal was a loose and largely improvised programme of sketches, songs, and theatrical scenes. The writing process had been "completely collaborative" throughout, Cooper remembers, and the contents of the show remained in deliberate creative flux. "For the week we were doing the show, we changed it literally every night," she says. "We'd spend all day reviewing it and thinking about it" and changing things up to ensure the group could deliver a "fresh, new show every night."

"We were performing in a small community hall, not in a theatre at the centre of town," Adi Cooper recalls. "It truly was a 'fringe' event."

The Body Show became embroiled in controversy as soon as the Sussex troupe arrived in Edinburgh to set up in a council-owned venue. Alarmed by the show's title, censorious and straitlaced council officials "demanded to see a copy of the script in case there was any hint of nudity involved—and, just for the record, there was none," Swales confirms. Robins recalled that rumours surrounding his performance as "the Id in a wrestling bout with the Superego" (riffing on Freud's famous psychoanalytic theory) were of particular concern to the authorities. "We had no script. Our show was improvised. So, of course, we indignantly refused to subject our precious show to the censors' scrutiny, citing artistic freedom," says Swales.

Implacable council officials were unimpressed, and the entire Sussex team—who'd brought four separate shows—was evicted from the building ("which made us no friends," Swales admits). The ban attracted front-page local press coverage—and, when the team relocated to a hall above a bus garage, the extra attention meant that they were "guaranteed a full house . . . virtually unheard of for a Fringe event at that time," he adds. "The first night saw the back row filled with plain-clothed coppers, who arrived in squad cars," all of whom had to buy tickets on the door. "It was completely mad," Subversa recalled in *Obnoxious* zine in 1981. "The place was full of dirty old men and police . . . who'd all paid to get in—while we just sat there juggling oranges and stuff!" The seven intense days were an "extraordinary experience," says Cooper. "It was all very exciting and great fun." There was also one important takeaway from their experience in Edinburgh that future Poison Girls would not forget: "Getting yourself banned is great free publicity," Swales affirms. "That was something we proved time and again with future record releases."

"A key part of the Show was the music," Cooper recalls. "Richard had always been into music, Gary was not yet playing a full kit, but would have been playing percussion, and I learned to play bass specifically for the show. My interest in learning the bass came as a result of joining a women's music weekend in Liverpool, where we got to try out playing electric guitar, bass, drums, and other instruments. I came back and asked Richard to help me learn bass. Musically, Richard was the main driver." A Framus 'Star' Bass was bought specifically for the show. "We still have it," says Famous.

The Body Show offered the first live performances of songs jointly composed by Famous and Subversa—"Kitchen Floor Stomp" ("a sub-glam, angry, feminist rock number") and the archly acerbic "I've Only Got Your Interests at Heart." The lyrics of both songs prefigure Poison Girls' style and subject matter. "Kitchen Floor Stomp" is the story of a woman expunging a wastrel partner from her home:

Who you gonna live off now, babe?
You can't live off me anymore
Who's gonna fatten up your ego now?
Who you gonna milk and from whose soft breast?
I'm clearing up all trace of you
From off my kitchen floor

"I've Only Got Your Interests at Heart" is all about having your self-confidence eroded by someone who deems themselves better than you:

Don't answer back
I'm right and I know it
You've only got one chance
And I'm sure you're gonna blow it
I'm older than you
So I'll tell you what to do
I've only got your interests at heart

"The music was easily the most fun, and the most enduring, part of the show," says Swales. It was during the show's rehearsals that Sokolov celebrated her fortieth birthday "by singing in public for the first time."

Key to her emergence as a performer was Sokolov's determination to refute the *expectation of invisibility* imposed on her as an older woman. "I'd been living this private sort of existence up till then," she explained. One of the reasons to take to the stage was "to get out of the house. I think that's very important. I didn't realise *how* important it was at the time." Picking up an instrument

BODY SHOW IS TOLD: DON'T SHOW BODIES

THE Body Show has been ordered to take its bodies off the stage—because they're nude.

The fringe group who are putting on the show at the Edinburgh Festival offended the Lothian Regional Transport Department.

The department are taking this deep interest in the arts because they own the Transport Hall in Annandale Street, where The Body Show began its week's run on Monday.

Officially, no-one at the department had seen the show.

But they heard that it included men and women massaging a naked man, a nude actress painted blue, and a male stripper.

ORGY

Under protest, Mr Simon Johnston, 24, creator of The Body Show, by the Sussex University Theatre, agreed to cut the nude scenes.

The first night—billed as a splendid orgy of physical presence—went ahead without them.

By BRIAN SWANSON

And many of the audience, mainly male, walked out as a result.

Mr Johnston complained last night: " How can you do a body show without bodies—nude bodies ?

" This was meant to be a very innocent show. We were trying to teach people not to abuse their bodies."

Mr Gordon McIntyre, secretary of the region's Transport Welfare Association, responsible for letting the hall, said:

" None of us saw the show, but we were informed there were to be scenes that raised the question of public decency.

" The fact that there were to be full frontal nude scenes was as good a reason as any to demand alterations."

NUDES ON FRINGE TOLD TO COVER UP

TRANSPORT bosses have driven nude scenes off the stage at an Edinburgh Festival Fringe show.

A production called "The Body Show" has been ordered to cover up by Lothian Region Transport Department.

But why the transport department ?

The transport bosses have turned censors because the group from Sussex University are performing on their property, the Transport Hall, Annandale Street.

A row over the nude play flared when 10 plain clothes policemen and two uniform men watched the opening performance on Monday night.

Offend

Scenes such as a nude girl painted blue, men and women massaging a naked man, and a parody on a male stripper, were among the full frontal nudity scenes which were cut.

The scenes were banned because " they might offend public decency."

Producer Mr Simon Johnson, 24, of Brighton, said he and all the performers

By ALASTAIR WILSON

were shocked at Edinburgh's coy attitude.

Mr Johnson said: " How can you do a body show without bodies—nude bodies. This was meant to be a very innocent show. We were trying to teach people not to abuse their bodies. The nude scenes would not have been the least bit disgusting."

The man who questioned the "decency" of the show is Mr Gordon McIntyre, the Lothian Regional Transport official and secretary of the Busman's Welfare Association, who is responsible for letting the hall.

He said: "None of us saw the show. We were informed that there were to be scenes of full frontal nudity. That raised the question of public decency. No one will tell what is public decency. What offends me may not offend you.

'Censors' ban the nude show they never saw

A SHOW has been censored at the Edinburgh Festival —by officials who didn't even see it.

The Body Show, which features nude scenes, was to have been presented as a fringe event in a local transport hall.

Parody

But two transport officials and a woman councillor decided it would offend public decency and

By ROBERT REID

cut a scene featuring a naked girl painted blue, a sketch involving a nude massage, and a parody on a male stripper.

Last night the show's creator, Mr Simon Johnson, 24, said: 'How can you do a body show without nude bodies?'

He said the cast from Sussex University theatre were 'shocked, dismayed and angry'.

Mr Johnson, from Brighton, protested: 'It

Reason

At Monday night's premiere in the Transport Hall in Annandale Street, the audience stormed out when they realised the show had been cut.

The cast juggled oranges and sang rock songs in place of the censored sketches.

The format of the show,

was meant to be a very innocent show. The nude scenes would not have offended anyone.'

Mr Gordon McIntyre, secretary of the Busmen's Welfare Association, who is responsible for letting the hall, said: 'None of us saw the show, but we heard there was to be full frontal nudity.

'This raised the question of public decency—and it was a good reason to demand alterations to the show.'

The censorship decision was backed by transport director Mr R. Bottril and

described as 'a splendid orgy of physical presence', had upset Lothian region transport officials.

A spokesman for Lothian region said yesterday: 'Rules governing use of the hall state that nothing may be shown which is offensive to public decency.

Male

The group was told that unless the show was amended it could not be staged.

The Body Show attracted a manly male audience and nobody under 18 was allowed in.

Councillor Mrs Catherine Filsell.

Modest changes

Two controversial Fringe shows, one originally involving full frontal nudity, went ahead last night. The rock-cabaret-revue of the Sadista Sisters was cancelled after lighting and exits failed to satisfy Edinburgh Council, but allowed to continue after pieces of equipment were shifted. Sussex University's "Body Show" opened with actors who would otherwise have been naked appearing in their clothes and remaining immobile in protest. Transport officials had invoked regulations prohibiting scenes in their hall which might have offended public decency.

(Festival Magazine, Page 5)

Press clippings from *The Daily Record*, 3 September 1975, *Scottish Daily News*, 3 September 1975, *The Daily Mail*, 3 September 1975, *Festival Magazine*, Courtesy of Pete Fender and Gemma Sansom.

and fronting a band was a means to secure vocal visibility. "Making issues that *were* private, *public*—in a situation that's open . . . for anybody to come in and confront," she continued. "This is why I wanted to be in a band."

"Unfortunately, The Body Show failed to set the theatrical world alight," Swales concedes. "Listening to a cassette of a performance, and with the benefit of hindsight, it is easy to see why. A reviewer in *The Scotsman* newspaper wrote, 'I would rather have two hours of toothache than sit through that show again'—which for a long time became the talismanic saying of the band." Whatever its shortcomings, the show allowed its cast to explore the kinds of political themes—including gender roles, parenthood, and the politics of the household—that would soon resurface in the earliest works of Poison Girls.

"After we got back from Edinburgh, for the next year or so, we continued to meet up to play music," Cooper remembers. "We were just jamming, really. We'd go to a park and play together. It was very folksy . . . very 'stoned hippy' sort of stuff." Her confidence boosted by the experience of The Body Show, Sokolov pressed ahead with penning the lyrics for songs that would later feature in Poison Girls' first live set. "Frances continued to write lyrics," says Cooper. "She became a fantastic songwriter. I mean, I think the words of her songs are just extraordinary."

As the storm clouds of punk began to gather, the aesthetic and temperament of these loose musical interludes began to change. Due to his connections with Buzzcocks, Swales found himself in the audience at the landmark gig at the Screen on the Green in Islington, London, in the summer of 1976. On the bill were The Clash and the Sex Pistols, as well as Buzzcocks. "A musician friend said they sounded like a 'herd of elephants.'" he recalls. "But it's important to remember how threatening and dangerously raw punk sounded at the time. To me it was a revelation. Loud, angry, fast, and with more than a hint of menace. And what's more, really exciting."

"We knew it was going on, and it was thrilling," Cooper continues. At the time of the Silver Jubilee celebrations she remembers, "playing the Pistols' 'God Save the Queen' as loud as we could out of a window of our house into the street." Pretty soon this dissident "bunch of hippies" were also identifying as "kind of being punks as well."

"Although we worked collectively, the process of The Body Show personnel morphing into a rock band was primarily down to me," Swales insists. "I was very much pushing in that direction, especially after the Screen on the Green show."

"We were soon aware that something big was happening all over the country," Robins affirmed later. "A new attitude, a new stripped-down musical style. I remember reading a copy of *Sniffin' Glue* in a radical bookshop in Camden. . . . There were reviews of young bands I had never heard of and—at the time—neither had the press or the record industry." The fledgling new band knew that they had "a great performer and songwriter in Vi," Robins acknowledged. They were determined "to make a go of it without funds or any kind of backing" and were confident that, even if they were ignored by the music business, they "could still make something happen."

This new band was formed by an alliance of anarchists and artistic outsiders who saw the potential to make their voices heard, stir up mischief, encourage others to do the same, and embrace the opportunity to enjoy themselves —preferably all at the same time. Sokolov decided that the reflective study of clouds was not where she wanted to focus her energies, and with that "the first incarnation of what was to become Poison Girls was formed."

Bella, Richard, Kano, Gemma, Lance, and Dan rehearsing in a church in Bedfordshire, 1976. Photo courtesy of Gemma Sansom.

"Just before we slimmed down and became the definitive Poisons." —Richard Famous.
Kano and Vi standing at mic, Bella Donna on bass, Lance on drums, Stuart on saxophone, and Pete Fender on guitar at edge of photo, Resources Centre, Brighton, 1976. Photos courtesy of Sue Cooper.

I. WE ARE HAVING PIANO LESSONS

PUNK BEGINNINGS 1977-79

As the new band hone their craft, Poison Girls play a key role in setting up The Vault, Brighton's (quite literal) underground punk venue. It's a breakthrough space for many of the city's emerging punk artists and allows the band to broker useful collaborations, even as Poison Girls confront unwelcome hostility from ageists and misogynists. The lure of the lights of London quickly proves irresistible, and the band relocate to a new centre of operations in the northern periphery of the capital in Epping. The release of Piano Lessons, *the band's first vinyl statement, recorded as a collaboration with Fatal Microbes, announces the arrival within the punk firmament of something intriguing, unusual, and unexpected.*

With the experience of The Body Show as their catalyst, the new band began "working together after that just as friends," Famous told *Realities of Society* zine. And when the starting pistol of punk was fired, those friends "started to play electric music."

During the closing months of 1976, that fluid collection of musicians began to experiment with their new craft—"under various names" and with "shifting personnel," the band remembered. The project attracted and retained "people who could work together and we were all on the same wave-length," Famous told *In the City* magazine, years later. "It wasn't an 'adverts in *Melody Maker*' sort of thing," he added. "Becoming a band was just an extension of what we were doing at the time." As the echoes of the new sounds of punk rock reached Brighton, the music "took on a louder and more 'in-your-face' persona," Famous explains.

The new band needed to settle on a name: "At the beginning it was a pun. As he left the band, Pete Fender said 'you ought to be called 'poisongirls' 'cos it sounds like 'boys and girls,' and there were two women and two men [*in the band*] at the time," Famous explains. "And we'd had fifteen names in two weeks or something before that, and it stuck. That's how names happen." Amongst the "stronger alternative contenders," he remembers, were 'Bare Hands' and 'Vacant Lot.' And "amongst the weaker" were 'Belly Buttons,' 'Goldrush,' 'Ordinary Decent Englishmen,' and 'Liz and the Corgis.'

Like many others finding their place in the punk firmament at that time, the band also adopted stage names and personas. Frances Sokolov Sansom became Vi Subversa (and at other times, Vi Squad); Richard Swales adopted the moniker Richard Famous (after a brief spell as Slug Pellet); Gary Lance Robins became Lance d'Boyle (after a short period as Arse Nick); and Sue Cooper took on the identity of Bella Donna. Some punk musicians chose names intended to outrage or offend. Others chose self-deprecating or intentionally ridiculous names. Poison Girls' choices seemed to mix self-awareness with a theatrical sense of absurdity. "It was also the fact that we had to confuse the Department of Health and Social Security, as we were still signing on," Famous adds.

What increased the evolving band's sense of affinity with the formative ideas of punk was the recognition of its continuity with dissident cultural movements of the past. Three of founder members of the new band explained the phenomenon to *Spitting Pretty Pikktures* zine:

Lance d'Boyle: "Punk came along as a reaction to degenerate hippiedom. In fact, the spirit is very similar. It goes back to the beatniks and the beats . . ."
Vi Subversa: "The bohemians, dadaists and surrealists . . ."
Richard Famous: "The flappers . . ."

Lance: "It's a long strand that's been called all different things, but I think the intention and the spirit is the same."

Armed with that perception, Poison Girls' search for a distinctive musical style remained an unforced process, shaped by their interest in stepping outside the familiar rock template and by the proclivities and talents of the individual performers in the band.

But the group was not made up of virtuoso musicians. "The whole vibe of punk—of it being very DIY, and anything goes, and songs can be simple—really appealed to us, because we hadn't really got musical backgrounds," Donna explains. One of the first things which distinguished the band's sound were the unusual patterns and percussive rhythms of d'Boyle's work behind the drum kit. "It wasn't that he *couldn't* play a simple rock'n'roll back beat," says Famous, "just that it was incomprehensible to him that he would want to."

"The relationship between the rhythm section became key, I think," Donna agrees. "Gary [Lance] and I learned together, really—and created something from scratch. We had to, because when playing punk, it's very fast and tight."

As a drummer, Lance always chose techniques and patterns that were to the left or to the right of the obvious ones. On songs like "Statement" and "Dirty Work" he showed just how brilliant he was at handling the tight "stop-start" timing and pin-point rhythms that those songs demand. Yet given sufficient space to manoeuvre, in the band's more expansive and expressive material his inventive style made use of the space; as he sought out the unexpected, the undercut, or found a way to play through, around, or against the beat. His military-style snare switches would light up "Piano Lessons and Crisis"; his love of weird rhythms would hold together songs like "Ideologically Unsound" and "Daughters & Sons"; he would restrain his presence on "Cry No More," accentuate the swirling power of "Cream Dream" and let rip on "Fucking Mother."

Very quickly, Subversa's voice, a sound that the band themselves described as "a nicotine rasp that cackled or crooned her words of love, outrage or hurt," became as captivating as it was unmistakable. She was soon able to leverage the full range and power of her voice, bringing melodies to the words that she had been writing. But Subversa, frustrated at the limitations imposed on her by others, was determined that she would not simply be "the singer." She made no secret that she "resented the way people's attitudes towards me . . . defined me" and knowing that "playing an electric guitar was something that I shouldn't do and," she "decided that I'd bloody well do it."

Famous and Subversa soon distilled a powerful blend of lead and rhythm guitar sound. Benefitting from a decade of experience, Famous was the more technically confident player, yet the unusual sound textures that the band began to craft were shaped more by innovation and inspiration than by finger-shredding perspiration. Together the pair played with as many jagged, fractured, and atonal guitar parts as they did with rolling, layered, complementary punk riffs.

Even as a very young teenager, Dan Sansom (Pete Fender) was an aspiring, excited musician. "Becoming really good on an instrument was something that meant a lot to me," he reflected later, "and I was fortunate to be good at more than one instrument, so I found I had the opportunity to stretch myself." Fender had attended gigs from an early age, being secreted into at least one Brighton show, under his mother's coat. Being exposed to the volatile, explosive, unpredictable atmosphere of punk rock's surging first wave could only be an eye-opening experience for the young, self-taught musician. For a few of Poison Girls' earliest gigs, Fender appeared on stage, aged just thirteen, playing bass. "I really loved that feeling that we were still underground but starting to break through, that excitement," he recalled later.

Fender's youth became a more pressing concern as the band tried to secure bookings at venues and clubs with an eighteen-and-over age limit. Mindful of the potential risk to their licence, promoters and club owners were unwilling to countenance an underaged musician playing on stage at their premises.

The first dependable Poison Girls lineup stabilised when the four core members "got fed up with all the others who were not dependable and decided we would just work as that group of people who would reliably turn up to rehearsals," says Famous. While Fender would continue to be closely involved with the band's work, in both the rehearsal room and in the studio, he ceased to be a regular member at that point, as Bella Donna's status as band bassist was confirmed. "Dan's role—which was very much appreciated—was that he could easily fill in when we were between permanent bass players."

In any case, Fender recognised the need to follow his own musical path, freed of close family ties. "I realised very early on that I couldn't be in the same band, that I had to do my own thing if I was to achieve any recognition of my own," he said. "I did enjoy working with Poison Girls frequently and in different ways, but it was important to me that I had my own path to tread." In Famous's view, Fender quickly became "the best guitar player in the whole north and east London punk scene."

Poison Girls (Richard, Vi, Lance, Bella Donna) practicing at Burleigh House, circa 1977. Photos courtesy of Sue Cooper.
Page 22: Lance, Vi, Bella, and Richard on a roof at Burleigh House, 1977. Photo courtesy of Sue Cooper.

Gemma's tenure in Poison Girls was much briefer than her brother's. "I sang a couple of songs on stage with Poison Girls down in The Vault," she remembers. "But I wasn't a punk then—god knows what they thought I was doing there, aged nine. I remember Richard used to get down on his knees whilst playing the guitar to be down on my level!"

That sense of inclusive familial fun was completely genuine, but had to be balanced against the sharper political perspectives the band now wanted to articulate. Famous is keen to stress that, despite d'Boyle's and Subversa's anarchist backgrounds, and their shared experience of The Body Show, Poison Girls' earliest material was not exclusively political. "Our first twenty or so songs, none of which were recorded, were very varied. Numbers like "Voodoo Lily," "Rat up a Pipe," "Burning," "Starfish on a Beach" or "Ice Cold"—none of those were particularly political," he says. "We started out wanting to make music—preferably music people wanted to listen to."

An hour's train ride from London, the Brighton punk scene was burgeoning as the 1970s drew to a close. That expanding, febrile culture was on the hunt for as many outlets as possible to make itself heard.

When the noises made by this fast-evolving bedroom band led to "the neighbours shopping us to the police," the need "to find a rehearsal space," became more pressing, Famous continues. The strongest candidate to emerge from the search was the old Presbyterian church in North Street, which was close to the railway station in the centre of the town. "Left untouched for years, it had a large hall and several rooms on the ground floor," he says. Best of all, the church possessed a crypt. This underground space "held the boiler room, a few smaller rooms, three arches, and a large long thin room," Famous says.

Poison Girls played a pivotal role in setting up The Vault as the city's best remembered, most unnerving and influential early punk venue. "Before that, it was only the university that hosted any punk gigs in Brighton—and for a student audience," says Famous. "It was The Vault that opened the floodgates."

The aim was to establish a resource centre that would offer "meeting and performance spaces, silk-screen equipment, technical help and advice," Famous adds. With money from the local council making it possible to hire staff, Vi Subversa of Poison Girls, who'd been "instrumental in getting all the parties together to discuss the opening of the centre," became the venue's first manager.

"We did have the advantage that I could go to the committee meetings of the Resource Centre and not be dismissed because I didn't look like a spotty young punk," Subversa explained to the *Guardian* newspaper years later.

The crypt had initially been off limits, but at Subversa's instigation the locks were broken to allow local band The Dandies to "set up shop in the boiler room," he adds. Poison Girls and The Amazorblades (who would

later release their *Common Truth* single on Chiswick Records) soon followed suit and set up separate and permanent rehearsal spaces in two of the arches. "We rigged up power—I imagine totally illegally, certainly nonprofessionally—put in doors to the arches, and built a makeshift stage out of material plundered from the closed-down West Pier."

Through their efforts, The Vault—the celebrated first-wave Brighton punk venue—was launched. Famous is keen not to overromanticise the setting. "It was a filthy cellar," he says. "We were told it had not been used since World War II, when it had apparently been an air raid shelter. There were certainly 'Remember to Bring Your Gas Mask' posters on the wall," he says. "There was rotting plasterboard covering headstones in the wall, and one chamber with human bones in . . . and one tiny entrance down a dozen or so steps." After members of Poison Girls "took on running the place and decided to make the performance area available for evening rehearsals—within a week of declaring it open it was fully booked." Promoting live shows at the weekend was the next step.

"One of the earliest gigs was with Buzzcocks—it was only their second gig outside Manchester or London," Famous recalls. "We set up the show, but we didn't play at it. I remember we printed the gig posters on newspaper and flyposted them across town. The Buzzcocks slept on my floor."

"This was early 1977, but by summer we could name at least seventy bands in the Brighton and Hove area. The Vault was the only place that punk bands were allowed to play in Brighton." That sweaty, mouldy cellar "was their reference point, and the focus for all things punk in the city." As Poison Girls threw themselves into helping organise the Brighton punk scene, their natural anarchist instincts came to the fore. "We did our own thing—like finding unlikely venues, doing our own posters—all the DIY stuff that became typical of the scene a bit later," d'Boyle recalled. "Within weeks of opening up The Vault, it was the centre of the Brighton punk scene," Famous explained to *Exposure* fanzine, "a focus of energy."

Despite the attention it received, The Vault remained an 'underground' venue in all senses. "There were no toilets, no bar, and no public music licence. There was no formal organisation, no health and safety regulations in effect, no fire exits, and no one making any money out of it," Famous says. "The arched ceilings were so low that if you were playing at either edge of the stage you had to bend your head. Tommy from the band Wrist Action knocked himself out pogoing on stage!" Wrist Action "shocked me with their fuck-off attitude and dangerous energy," d'Boyle recalled later. Incidents like that only added to the provocative atmosphere of the place.

Into this tiny underground space "you could get 150 or so people crammed in," says Famous. "Those early gigs were packed and there was never any trouble." Poison Girls' efforts were soon enthusing others to get stuck in. "If they hadn't helped us, I'd never have picked

Poison Girls band photos: Richard Famous, Bella Donna, Vi Subversa, Lance d'Boyle, Pete Fender, Gemma Sansom, and friends. Burleigh House, 1977. Photo courtesy of Sue Cooper.

up a bass and never become involved in music," acknowledges Helen McCookery (aka Helen Reddington) of The Chefs and Helen and the Horns. Vi Subversa, in particular, was an impressive role model. "Vi just encouraged everyone," McCookery says, "and because she was such a pioneer, being older than most of us, there was no way you could shy away from just getting up there and doing it, because that's what she did."

Following "several appearances with this same lineup performing under different names," Poison Girls played their first-ever gig, at The Vault, on 17 March 1977. As they honed their collective craft, Poison Girls distinctiveness from many of the straight-down-the-line punk bands that they shared The Vault stage with was immediate. Although they were recognised as integral to the new wave of punk artists fighting for attention in the city, acceptance was far from automatic. Poison Girls "weren't really welcomed by other punk bands, or welcomed or respected by audiences, for some time," Subversa acknowledged.

That sense of Poison Girls being *different* is revealed in the few photographs that were taken of those early live shows. They depict an atypical four-piece—a band with a young teenage bass player and a middle-aged female frontwoman—none of whom are dressed in predictable punk rock attire. One photo shows d'Boyle, front and centre stage, dressed in a madcap costume, letting rip in an improvised freak dance. Their presence on stage has as much of a theatrical ambience as it does one of rock'n'roll. During this period, d'Boyle wrote several songs for the band. He penned the early punk thrash "Busted" (in response to a minor possession charge), "Massacre of the Flowers," "Wallpaper Rock," and the intriguingly titled "Green Vinyl Burns." "Gary's [Lance] song 'Radio City' closed the set," Fender recalls. "It's about humans being 'work androids,' and he loses control at the end and freaks out robot-style!"

Vi Subversa played a peerless role as the catalyst for the creative work erupting at The Vault, not least by negotiating the tensions between the young, volatile punks and the unsettled administrators that arose from it.

"That first year, we seemed to gig mostly in Brighton, with repeat appearances at the Resources Centre and The Vault," Donna recalls. "In June 1977, we also played at the Imperial Hotel in nearby Hove, and at the Hungry Years rock venue on Brighton's Marine Parade." Poison Girls played at Burleigh House in Essex twice, during different

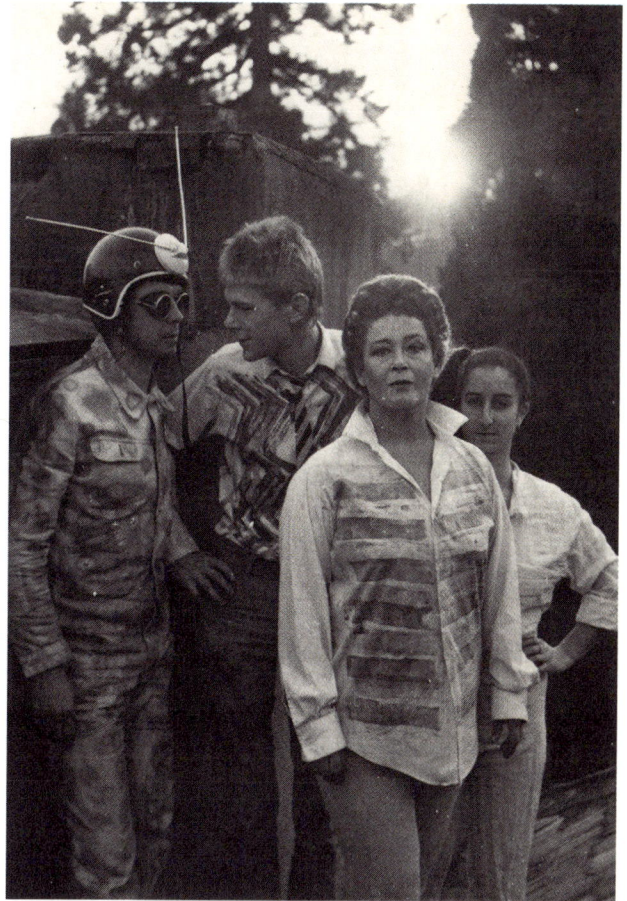

events being held in a building that would soon become central to the band's plans. "In October, we played several London shows, including ones at Centrepoint, at The Rat Club (a music night at The Pinder of Wakefield pub in Kings Cross) and another at The Man in the Moon pub on the Kings Road," Cooper continues. Both pubs played host to several breakthrough punk shows in the capital. "The Man in the Moon gig got cancelled by the publican at the last minute, but we went ahead anyway when the other band we were playing with, Wrist Action from The Vault, set up equipment in the street."

Despite their collective hard work and their encouragement of others, the new four-piece did face criticism from within the scene as well as from outside it. Some of the hostility was simply the expression of crude sexism. Many female punks who sought a role other than being 'a girlfriend' of someone in a band, or part of the passive audience observing their male contemporaries, had to fight for acceptance. The Brighton punk scene was not immune to that kind of sexism and it impacted on the efforts of Poison Girls to secure recognition. But the band's frontwoman had to face an additional challenge: that of age and generation. Although many were receptive, there were uglier voices which loudly objected to the in-

volvement of someone who was, objectively speaking, "old enough to be their mother."

Although two members of the band were of a similar, older age, that hostility "was focused much more on Frances than Gary [Lance]," Donna says. "I don't think he got the pushback in the same way at all—because for men, it's different." Frances faced "a combination of sexism and ageism, really," she continues, a sense of incredulity "at what this older women was doing." It was an attempt to silence her through dismissal that she would simply not tolerate. In the guise of Vi Subversa she would go on to smash "every rock'n'roll mould," the band reflected later, to emerge as a defiantly "middle-aged, militant feminist, peacenik, antifascist, anticapitalist punk!"

Subversa acknowledged to *Subvert* fanzine in 1981 that she was an atypical presence in the punk scene: "Most of the women of my age are tucked away safely at home," she said, something which made it even more important "to hear the women's voices" which had overcome exclusion. When Poison Girls first started, Subversa recalled that they were "slagged off, shouted off, and canned off" and denounced as "old-age pensioners" with no right to participate.

Above: Burleigh House, 1977, photo by Richard Famous.
Below: Burleigh House gardens, photo by Bernhardt Rebours.

"A young male audience tends to find older women threatening: sexually, politically and in every other way," Subversa explained to *Hot Press* magazine, "'cos they're usually the kind of people that they're trying to get away from—mums and aunties and all that sort of thing. They go to a gig and don't expect to see them up there singing to them."

Subversa's robust response to the hostility voiced by some in the scene was an immediate confirmation that she and the rest of the band would allow any such expressions of intolerance. Liking the band was not a requirement, but Poison Girls' right to identify themselves as an integral and legitimate ally in the punk rebellion was not up for negotiation. Subversa did acknowledge that—on the question of age at least—the band might need to earn respect. "I think we've got to overcome an obstacle to being listened to by young people because quite rightly young people are really suspicious of people of our age, because the people of our age have been selling them down the river—like the teachers, the magistrates, the politicians, and the other authority figures." Famous notes that one of the recurring mantras of the original punk wave was "don't trust anyone over thirty." The hostility of alienated young people towards the older generation was "quite justified," she continued, "as most old people let down young people—and themselves."

That said, the band were keen to challenge all the absurd nihilistic pretentions some in the punk scene voiced: "What's partly behind it, the 'no future' idea, is that over the age of twenty, twenty-one, twenty-five, or thirty—death! And especially young women are saying to me: 'Look, it's great; you give me the feeling that when I'm as old as you I could be doing something as well.'"

Subversa's stage persona meant that "instead of rebellious kids pouring vitriol and laying blame at their parents' door, there was this crazy woman shouting back at them." Directly inspired by the performances at The Vault, the groundbreaking regional punk compilation album *Vaultage 78* secured its reputation as "one of the most significant punk venues of the time," Famous adds. "Unfortunately for us, as we'd already left Brighton, we lost the opportunity to be included on one of the *Vaultage* releases—as usual, we were slightly ahead of our times!"

Yet the growing notoriety of the venue had meant that Subversa "had to resign from the 'upstairs' management, as the conflict between the respectable Resources Centre above, and what was happening in The Vault below, escalated."

Soon after that, Poison girls relocated, and local musicians and activists immediately noticed their departure. McCookery suggests that Vi "almost acted as a pressure valve in the Brighton punk scene and she was missed when she left for Essex with the band."

Richard and Vi in Burleigh House rehearsal room, 1977. Photo courtesy of Richard Famous.

Poison Girls decided that the band had reached the limits of Brighton life. Together Vi Subversa, Richard Famous, Lance d'Boyle, and Bella Donna agreed to relocate to better exploit the available opportunities that would come from being closer to London. The move was "a conscious decision to work on Poison Girls full-time," the band said. The new Essex location was "definitely *not* London," Famous insists, "but in fact a long way out on the outer reaches of the Central line, a good ten miles from the East End of London."

"Lance was still working at North London Polytechnic, teaching on the DABS course. Burleigh House was one of the venues where they held weekend training sessions," he adds. "The house was due to be demolished to make way for the planned M25 motorway. We were given a week or so to decide if we wanted to take over the building at a 'peppercorn' rent. We left Brighton in the autumn of 1977 to take over what was essentially a tumbledown mansion." The whole band, together with Subversa's two children, would live communally. "We share all the work, we share all the responsibility for the kids and the domestic situation," d'Boyle told the *NME*. Burleigh House was somewhere "where we could live together and work on our music whenever we wanted, with room for recording, printing and the like," he explained.

"It was an amazing house," Famous reflects. "Ten

bedrooms, four bathrooms, two big ballrooms." There was space for a dedicated rehearsal room and a printing and artwork office. "The place had a one-hundred-yard drive lined by trees, a veg garden, and gardens all around the house. It was surrounded by rare trees—two giant redwoods, a weeping elm, a huge mature yew tree, a wonderful copper beech, and more."

Work on the new orbital roadway, that would eventually encircle the capital, had begun in 1975 with the final section completed in 1986. Countless buildings along the route were compulsorily purchased and knocked down as the build progressed. "We had a nine-month licence from the Department of Transport, and ended up staying there for three years," d'Boyle adds. The band's new base quickly became a hub of activity.

As well as living space, the large property was kitted out to provide rehearsal space and basic reel-to-reel recording facilities, together with room for tabletop screen printing and design activities. "The first thing to happen was the grown-ups built a music room and sound proofed it with egg boxes and Poison Girls rehearsed a lot," says Gemma. "There were a couple of other people living there at first too. Then they left, leaving those involved with Poison Girls, me and Dan." Like Crass's Dial House home ("which by pure chance was four miles or so up the road," Famous notes) Burleigh House acted as something of a centre of

LIFE SPACE BENEFIT

LIVE MUSIC A' CUM CUM WITH

COME EARLY and bring a bottle/s

PETE SMELLEY and the STINK BOMBS

brilliant white and matt vinyl

POISON GIRLS

SPLIT HAIRS at

DEEP THREAT

DIANA'S - BALL-ROOM
194 Goldhurst Terrace NW6
SATURDAY 1st Oct.
7-30 till late   Finchley Rd. Tube
ONLY 50p

a slifli poster   1977.   WOULD YA BURLEIVE IT!!!

32

attraction for young punks, misfits, and malcontents in and around the north London alternative scene. "The house became a bit too open to the local youth," Famous concedes, "who had to be told in no uncertain terms that it wasn't OK for them to come and let themselves in un-invited and have a jam session after the pubs shut."

There was also the sense of insecurity that came from the threat of eviction. "Several times the Department of Transport tried to get us evicted," he says, "once telling us the house would be demolished on New Year's Day whether we were in it or not."

"I've got great memories of that time and the environment was amazing," Gemma enthuses. "I got a motorbike when I was thirteen and blatted it round the fields with a couple of mates. There were horses nearby and huge trees." While there was "a lot of space," that sense of freedom in an idyllic playground was tempered by a sense of danger. "Too many doors were left open," she says. "It felt completely permeable and consequently not safe."

"Burleigh House was a tough place," Gemma concludes. "I feel like we came there as slightly soft round the edges punky types and left as hardened punk rockers, battered by the skinheads and invaded by any passing lost soul. . . . Well, that's one interpretation, but yes, it was a hotbed of creativity too."

As part of that creative process, "the 'print shop' began producing posters, record sleeves, flyers and the like," Famous recalls. A combination of a "very productive silk-screen setup and a Roneo duplicator" afforded the band a high degree of self-sufficiency in art production. A lot of design ideas emerged through that work, mixing and matching the available technology, some of which then fed through into the band's wider aesthetic. "For instance, the *Words Written in Trust* lyric book brought together a silk-screen design with hand-crafted Gestetner prints we used to produce handouts at gigs," he says. "The strange random borders on the prints were a result of the blanking edging papers slipping during the printing process. 'Embrace the mistakes,' we always said. They looked great. Also the big red *All Systems Go* poster series were originally hand-cut stencils that we screen printed, again to be given out at gigs. I designed and hand printed all the copies of *Words* on that setup. It was the last project we undertook at Burleigh House, as we lost the space to set up screen printing facilities when we moved to Leytonstone."

Poison Girls recorded their first lo-fi demos in their home studio at Burleigh House. "We recorded half a dozen of our older songs, live in the new rehearsal room," says Famous. "Those original demos are a mixed bag," he concedes. "'Revenge' and 'Cats Eye' are short and punky;

'Burning' is more rocky; 'Radio City' is long, slow, and weird; 'Ice Cold' has patchy instrumental sections, but great vocals, while 'Starfish' is Poison Girls at their most hippy, with a guest violin scratching away."

"I think this period—pre proper recording—was us trying to find out which direction we were now heading in," he suggests.

Two of the recordings from a later session at a four-track studio in London's Crouch End, of the songs "Reality Attack" and "Alienation," would eventually resurface on the band's *Seven Year Scratch* retrospective album, released six years later. As the tempo of their operations quickened, Poison Girls sought to make contact with other like-minded dissident artists working in and around London with whom they might make common cause.

Donna's twin Adi had travelled in India in the Autumn of 1976, to carry out research for a PhD on a peasant land rights movement from the 1930s. "I'd promised that I would go and stay with her when I finished my degree," Donna says. So in the autumn of 1977. "I went to India to see her and spent three months working as a kind of research assistant, reading Indian-language newspapers and going off and doing interviews." Poison Girls had tried out "various other bass players while I was away," but when Donna returned, they had to settle on a permanent replacement.

"We had worked with a bassist named Jackie (aka Chlorine) who was introduced through a mutual friend, and who played a couple of gigs with us," says Famous. "She was good and fitted in well with what we were doing, but was not able to make the commitment that we needed at that time." Scotty Boy Barker (who'd already been playing with Fatal Microbes) was temporarily brought on board to replace her, before Bernhardt Rebours agreed to take over bass duties just ahead of the studio session for the *Piano Lessons* release.

It was a major shift in the relationship dynamics amongst members of Poison Girls that convinced Bella Donna that, "there was no way I could be in the band," she says.

"This was an important moment in the story of Poison Girls," Famous insists. "The change in relationship dynamic was that when Sue (Bella Donna) left for India I was in a relationship with her, and Vi was in a relationship with Lance. Vi split with Lance, and I got together with Vi. I think that our relationship, both on a personal and creative level, was absolutely pivotal to the progress of the band."

"It gave Vi the confidence, strength, and support to both explore and reveal herself. Some of the artistic tension in the band—which was difficult at times, but generally a good thing—was a result of my sometimes

Diana's Ballroom, London, 1 October 1977. Courtesy of Pete Fender and Gemma Sansom.

strained relationship with Lance," he continues. "There was always an underlying tension between the two of us. As for me and Vi, it is no coincidence that the band broke up immediately after our relationship ended some twelve years later."

"My memories of Burleigh House are almost 100 percent positive. We would not have been able to do what we did—like rehearse every afternoon—anywhere else. It is easily the most strange and wonderful place I have lived."

Burleigh House was soon acting as a free rehearsal space for Fatal Microbes and later Rubella Ballet, bands that both Sansom children had joined. Honey Bane, a young runaway from a London children's unit ("It was a hypersecure children's prison outside Brentwood in Essex," Famous suggests) who would later work on the first 'other artist' release on Crass Records, was a regular visitor, and would soon become the Fatal Microbes frontwoman, as the band began to record at the house.

"I got put in care when I was eleven," Bane recalled many years later. "I got sent to lots of different places. And I would constantly run away from everywhere. And they thought that if they put me in what at the time was the most secure . . . child's prison, for kids that were too young go to prison, they thought it would stop me from running away. But it didn't. I escaped from the most secure part of the building . . . two weeks after I arrived there."

"But one of the staff who worked there was a friend of Poison Girls. And they had a meeting, to see if I would be allowed, with him escorting me, to go meet them and talk about music." It was Subversa's role as an advocate for the marginalised that helped to clear a path.

"It was through Vi that Honey Bane got to know everybody, because Vi had been working in that sort of environment, looking after people that were in foster care and situations like that," remembers Zillah Minx of Rubella Ballet. "Frances facilitated it in some way," Gemma agrees. "I think she was allowed day release to come and make music."

Arriving at Burleigh House, Bane "pretty much went straight into a rehearsal room," she recalled. D'Boyle later recalled Bane coming to the house on Sunday afternoons. "Her minder would stay in the kitchen, while she played with the band in the studio," he said. Initially, Bane was "playing bass and singing," but the new group soon recruited a bass player, because

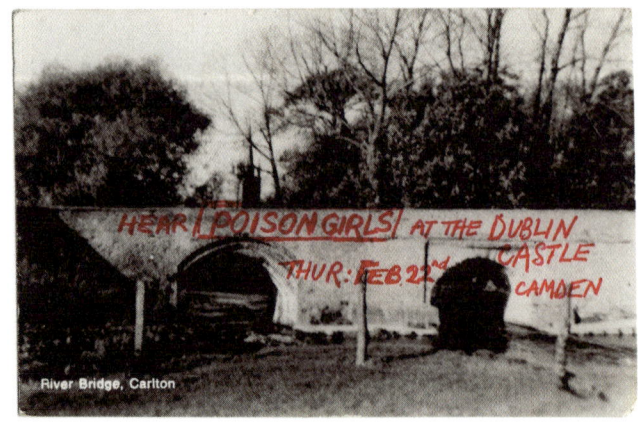

Top to bottom: **North London Poly**, London, 9 June 1978. **Epping Hall**, Essex, 10 June 1978. **The Triad**, Bishop Stortford, 11 June 1978. **Epping Hall**, Essex, 10 June 1978. **Dublin Castle**, London, 22 February 1979.

34

she "wanted to just be a vocalist," she says. The lineup of Fatal Microbes stabilised with Gemma on drums, Dan on guitar, and former Poison Girls bassist Scott Barker recruited as bass player. "Dan was already a really good guitarist," Gemma says. "I got behind the drum kit and found I could knock out a beat. Before I knew it I was the drummer with Fatal Microbes. It was pretty unusual to have a female drummer then, let alone one aged eleven! It was then I embraced the punk thing and I was in bands and not just a kid any more—somehow it's like, that's when my childhood ended."

A short set of songs soon emerged from the rehearsals, which teased at the young band's promise. "Honey Bane wrote great lyrics, but it was hard to maintain the band's dynamic," Gemma reflects. "I loved it and although it only lasted a year or so, we recorded *Violence Grows*, a great single that is still talked about today. You can hear my drumming on the single is basic, kind of embryonic—a bit like me at the time."

Bane came to see Burleigh House as a place of sanctuary. "Because she knew us, and knew where we were, and thought we would be sympathetic—when she did abscond, she came to us," d'Boyle recalled.

Besides Bane, Burleigh House also provided a refuge for other young punks in need. "I was working at a restaurant in Mayfair, and one day I was sacked—so I lost my flat in Notting Hill Gate, and I was homeless," Sid Truelove remembers. "It was pretty hairy not knowing where I was going to LIVE." Already a visitor to Poison Girls' house, Truelove was invited to move in. "Vi said, 'Well, we've got a small room upstairs. You can use that.'" he remembers. "And it was a dream come true—to live in a commune full of musicians. Any spare time that I had, I was trying to get into the rehearsal room because there was a drum kit already set up. You could make a racket, because there weren't any immediate neighbours."

"I think without that rehearsal room. and the equipment in it, I don't think Rubella Ballet would have existed," says Truelove.

"By the time Sid and me got together, Honey Bane had left Fatal Microbes and had started her own band and was doing stuff with Crass," Minx recalls. A fluid group of musicians decided to focus on a new band, and the first incarnation of Rubella Ballet began rehearsing at Burleigh House. "At first, there were a lot of different people involved in Rubella Ballet. And then Annie Anxiety, who'd been singing for the band, left and I ended up being the singer," Minx says.

Poison Girls' encouragement of Rubella Ballet was generous and instinctive. "We were supporting them at their gigs straight away," she continues. "They were always very helpful with everything they could do to get us gigs and a whole lot more."

As Poison Girls' plans for the band crystalised, the residents of Burleigh House were eager to build up alliances with other potential allies.

At the beginning, it was simply a question of proximity that drew Poison Girls and Crass into a shared orbit. Dial House, Crass's own centre of operations, was in Ongar, a short distance from Burleigh House. "Upon such coincidences legends are built," the band recalled later. When they met up, the similarities in politics and approach of both sets of artists were immediately clear. For these two sets of radical, subversive punks, determined to attack any barriers of class, gender, or age, and committed to a do-it-yourself ethos which rekindled the revolutionary temper of the original punk idea, their meeting marked a turning point.

"We first made contact with Crass when they came to see us play at the inaugural concert of the 'Bell Common Be-Bop Society' in Epping," Famous remembers. "We had to create an organisation to book the hall," he adds, by way of explanation. Bell Common is an area of woods and grassland on the southern edge of Epping, and incorporating the name into a made-up 'society' provided the local connection the hall's managers required. The gig that night went well, but the meeting between the two groups became much more significant in the longer term. "We then went to check them out—at Dial House, and a gig they did in Bishop Stortford," Famous recalls. "They had, by that time, done some stuff in America, and had seemed to be on the up," Subversa recalled. "It was immediately obvious that we had a lot in common," Famous acknowledges. The similarities were exceptional. Both Poison Girls and Crass were political punk bands, infused with anarchist inclinations, that had set up operations in communal houses in the environs of London, and were made-up of musicians spanning different generations.

Yet until they became more acquainted, there was a natural degree of scepticism—born, in the case of the older members of Poison Girls, from experience. "My first impression was of Andy Palmer," d'Boyle recalled later. He was "dressed in black shirt and trousers, shiny black DMs, with a handmade version of the logo on a badge—and an upper-middle-class accent." D'Boyle was not immediately convinced. "I was a bit wary, I must say, since at the time there were many middle-class people 'roughing it.'" Were Crass genuine, d'Boyle wondered? What reassured him was the immediate affinity he felt with Crass drummer Penny Rimbaud. "I think I was sort of *prepared* to meet Penny," he said. D'Boyle strongly identified as an anarchist and had street-sold copies of *Freedom*, the country's longest running anarchist periodical. "We were on the same page politically," he judged.

But there was more than a sense of mutual recognition. "In terms of intensity of performance, political nous—and, importantly, ambition and intent—we were a perfect fit," says Famous. "Both bands were disillusioned with the music business," he continues. "Both were desperate to find a better context to perform in." The advantages of these two outsider punk bands agreeing to collaborate seemed self-evident. "For our part, we wanted to channel our energy into a performance in which we were more in control, rather than just playing in seedy clubs and pubs—to even seedier clientele, who weren't particularly interested in a forty-year-old woman fronting another 'punk' band," says Famous. "Crass were concerned, and rightly so, that they ran the risk of being dismissed as just another 'Oi' band." Working together, they might be able to extend their joint appeal, and widen their combined audience. The two groups committed to an open-ended period of close collaboration.

The encounter seemed to come at just the right transitional moment. "Both bands were at a turning point," he says, but facing some tough decisions. "When we started working with Crass, both bands were about to break up," Famous reveals. "Crass were pissed off that they didn't have anywhere to play and that nobody was listening to them. We were playing in pubs and other places and getting stuff thrown at us." It seemed worth considering a new joint approach. "That's why we started working together. We said, 'Let's do an evening together, let's do a series of gigs together, and see what happens.' That's how it started really."

The residents of Dial House also had another proposal. "It was Crass who suggested that Bernhardt Rebours should play bass for us—even though he was not a bass player at the time," Famous confirms. "How right they were!"

The new association seemed to reenergise both bands. With Crass and Poison Girls planning their first vinyl releases "we decided to try playing together," Famous recalls. The aim was a "partnership to create a whole seamless evening," he says. "The result, of course, was extraordinary. For the next hundred-plus gigs Crass would only play if Poison Girls played too. We also played fifty-odd gigs by ourselves during this period. The gigs were initially small. But through word of mouth, and a lot of work, it quickly got bigger, audiences got more confident, and it took off." There was a period of adjustment for some of those turning up to see Crass. "I think the mainly young male audience didn't know what to make of us," d'Boyle reflected later, "a band fronted by a woman old enough to be their mum." Unapologetic, Poison Girls stood their ground. "Gradually we became accepted and I enjoyed every hard-earned minute of it," he acknowledged.

Poison Girls valued associations and recognised affinities with earlier countercultures which has preceded punk. That connection was critical rather than unproblematic; but it emphasised the band's rejection of the Year Zero premise of punk and their belief in the continuity which tied together the different strands of outsider, dissident and oppositional culture threaded through modern British history.

The band shared Crass's instinctive antiauthoritarianism, strong anarchist impulses, firm assertion of the importance of feminism, and a belief in the persuasive utility of the underground. But they differed to an important degree over the strength of their association with hippy culture. While Penny Rimbaud of Crass, in particular, promoted the multiple continuities bridging punk and hippy, Poison Girls' account (their own personal involvement in that scene notwithstanding) was more muted. Poison Girls did not share the same instinctive pacifist reading of anarchist-punk and rarely referenced the experience of hippy or yippie culture in their work.

"I have fantasies where I want to kill people who I think are totally destructive and who have too much power and do too much damage," Subversa confided to *Spare Rib*. "But I've always wanted to change the war economy which breeds war. I think hierarchical government structures deal in war; waste and war are the dynamic of capitalism."

Soon after the Epping move, Poison Girls recorded their first single, *Piano Lessons*—a "musical call to arms," as d'Boyle characterised it. Originally planned to be issued on the band's own newly formed DIY Xntrix label, the twelve-inch was a split vinyl with one side of the record given over to The Fatal Microbes. The two bands travelled to Spaceward Studios in Cambridge for the recording.

"They did a 'one day special.'" Famous says. "You could go in, bash out your tracks and mix them down all in a day. The songs were well honed, so there was little experimentation on the day. The idea was to just get in there and do what we had rehearsed. Spaceward was our first time in a proper studio, and we were slightly awed by the process, certainly not confident enough to make a fuss."

New bass player Rebours had come for his first-ever rehearsal the day before the studio session carrying a borrowed right handed bass. "He was left-handed—but we were able to teach him the specific bass parts," says Famous. "He returned for the recording the next day with the bass restrung for a left-hand player—and nailed the parts in one take. What a trooper!"

Both Poison Girls tracks were recorded on 11 October, and produced by Adrian Grey-Turner who the band knew as the singer and frontman for the Brighton glam-punks Dandies. "He'd played piano to accompany Vi singing Kurt Weill songs," Famous explains. Grey-Turner would die far too young in 1986 from an AIDS-related illness. As well as "Closed Shop," the band also recorded "I Wanted The Moon," a song that

Before the crow . . . the mallard! Poison Girls/Fatal Microbes split EP, 1979. Cover art by Bernhardt Rebours.

would not be released until its inclusion in the *Seven Year Scratch* retrospective. "The studio engineer was less than enthusiastic about the results, but we heard he was shame faced when *Piano Lessons* got single of the week in *Sounds*." Poison Girls' two songs on the twelve-inch received positive reviews across the British music press. *NME* hailed music and lyrics that were "undeniably bright, sharp and calculatingly brittle." *Melody Maker* praised the band's "madcap humour that

chills as it thrills" and the embrace of "inventiveness that constantly entertains."

Fatal Microbes' two tracks were recorded and mixed in a single day, on 4 October, and produced by Richard Famous. Fronted by Bane, and including Gemma and Pete, Fatal Microbes were a band distinguished by the young age of its members just as clearly as Poison Girls stood apart because of their members' relatively 'mature' years. In the history of the original British punk wave, there may have been no other instance of a mother and her children collaborating, on an equal basis, on a record release. Xntrix's first cross-generational release spoke to one of Poison Girls' most important and persistent assertions: that there was no automatic association between age and radical commitment; and that young and old could rage against the iniquities of the system, independently and often in unison.

Poison Girls' twin contributions to the record were disarmingly unusual—both far from the usual punk thrash template. It was early confirmation that the band would plough a very different furrow to many of their contemporaries. There's a deliciously eerie, unsettling quality to the title track of *Piano Lessons*. From its opening swirling invocation to its circular fadeout, it's an oddly staccato track, with its fractured sonic texture and a treble-heavy musical timbre. What makes it anything but weak sounding, is Subversa's extraordinary vocal, which switches between the mischievous to the malevolent as the song presents an unusual metaphor; contrasting the contentment of comfortable middle-class families who live oblivious to the threat of encroaching tyranny and military occupation. It's part fantasy and part political allegory. "Piano Lessons" bears the hallmarks of a familiarity with musical theatre and cabaret that members of the band could call on.

"Closed Shop" makes for a remarkable pairing with "Piano Lessons." Sung by Famous, it's as oblique lyrically as "Piano Lessons," but it's a song challenging the idea of exclusion, principally as an artist and as a musician. Rejection and denial is something that Poison Girls had already experienced from some others in the punk scene, and it's revealing to see the band confront the experience directly on their first vinyl release. The concept of the "closed shop" refers to an organisation only accessible to approved members, in which gatekeepers restrict participation only to those who meet certain requirements. In 1970s Britain, most people would have associated the idea of the closed shop with the arena of industrial relations. It described an agreement between managers and trade union bosses which ensured that only union members "in good standing" would be shortlisted for hiring. This could operate as a mutually beneficial arrangement that minimised the likelihood of industrial unrest, and often reinforced exclusion by underrepresented groups (women, people of colour, those only able to work part-time) by ensuring like-for-like clone recruitment. It ensured the existing profile of employees was replicated and upheld the status quo.

Poison Girls' barbed commentary is, of course, directed just as much at those gatekeepers of the counterculture, who sought to exclude others on grounds of gender and generation, as it was towards those policing entry to better-paid workplaces.

I met some people that really ought to know me
I'm coming on strong and they're coming on slowly
I'm talking to them just trying to get through
They say 'Come back with something new'
My ideas, they're as good as the rest
You tell me straight you only deal in the best
You say 'Don't come here wasting my time
I'm not a musician but the company's mine'

Famous resists the suggestion that the song was a commentary on the contemporary labour movement. "It didn't really have anything to do with the union movement, even though the 'closed shop' was part of the terminology of militant trade unionism that was prevalent at the time," he insists. He suggests the song was more significant for what it confirmed about the creative direction the band would now take. "This recording was probably the last hurrah of the solo approach to songwriting," he says. "It became increasingly clear that Vi had the most interesting voice—both as a singer and writer—and from then on the focus was on her lyrical output. After *Piano Lessons*, we effectively ditched all our existing songs, and started to write what would become *Hex* with Rebours on bass."

The process became more collaborative than before. "Most of the subsequent songs were bashed out in jam sessions—a chord sequence, a riff, or a vocal line was given a good thrashing, as people found their own parts," Famous recalls. "The results were then taken away by me and Vi and formalised, before bringing the results back to the rest of the band to finalise."

Prior to *Piano Lessons*, Poison Girls had already decided to adopt the moniker "Xntrix" (a play on the word "Eccentrics," and a form of self-description that the band could take pride in) as an overarching identity for the band's record and tape label and as the imprint that would be stamped on future publishing activities. Xntrix would also be the entity used to register the music publishing rights of Poison Girls' songs and recordings, a move which—from the very outset—protected the band's material from commercial exploitation by unscrupulous rip-off merchants. It was a savvy decision, and one which confirmed Poison Girls' innate grasp of the predatory nature of the music business was more advanced than that displayed by Crass at that time (who initially made no comparable arrangement, something which led to significant legal issues years later).

The original intention had been to press and release *Piano Lessons/Violence Grows* as a wholly independent DIY release. But by the time the recording had been completed, Poison Girls' evolving relationship with Crass, and with Pete Stennett of the London-based Small Wonder label, had opened up other options. Small Wonder was a key part of the explosion of small-scale punk and postpunk record labels that began to break into the business at the end of the 1970s. With a roster of artists shaped by Stennett's eclectic interests, Small Wonder would release an extraordinary and diverse cavalcade of seven-inch and twelve-inch records over the next few years. "Everything we did was a bit weird, though," Stennett concedes. "There was just an energy of the time. It was really infectious." Small Wonder would provide the first vinyl platform for both Crass and Poison Girls.

Although immediately impressed by both Crass and Poison Girls, Stennett did not feel he could identify as one of the punks. "Oh no, I was too old for that, I was twenty-seven. Christ, I was an old man to them," he says—adopting none of Poison Girls' rejection of generational atrophy. Stennett's fascination with Crass, whom he had encountered before connecting with Poison Girls, came from three closely connected reasons. "Partly it was because Crass were of my generation; partly because intellectually they stimulated me; and partly because they were fascinating people, living in a commune," he explains. "The whole art side of them, everything about them, I just found . . . exciting and dangerous!" Through meeting Crass, Stennett learned of Poison Girls' work. "Yes—they were friends with Crass, and again they just gave us a tape, we liked it and put it out." It seems that it really was that simple, and that immediate. The record was released on 1 April 1979.

Aware that Fatal Microbes had recorded a third track during the Spaceward Studios session ("Cry Baby"), and convinced that there was an audience for this material as a standalone piece, Stennett agreed to rerelease *Violence Grows* as a seven-inch, three-song EP. This release was also co-credited to Small Wonder and Xntrix, which reflected a relaxed approach to the continuing partnership, rather than a strict contractual agreement. Poison Girls paid for the recording of the content and prepared the design and packaging. Small Wonder covered the costs of pressing, printing, and distribution. Both parties then shared the modest returns from sales. It was reasonable for Poison Girls to treat the releases as their own work. "Soon we brought out two singles on our own label," d'Boyle recalled later of the twin releases. The band would soon take advantage of this now proven, mutually beneficial collaboration through the release of their first full-length twelve-inch vinyl, *Hex*.

Within weeks of the release of *Piano Lessons*, the wider political context in which punks, anarchists, and other malcontents were working would dramatically change. Everything that Poison Girls had produced to this point had been created during the final crisis-racked years of the last Labour government to hold office in Britain until 1997. The collapse of the long-strained Social Contract with key trade unions, in the context of global economic shocks that confirmed the postwar boom had well and truly ended, sealed the fate of Prime Minister Jim Callaghan's minority government. Weeks after the (woefully misrepresented) Winter of Discontent public sector strike wave confirmed Labour's inability to contain workplace militancy, Margaret Thatcher's government swept to power in the June election.

It would take several years for the ideology of Thatcherism (monetarism, militarism and mandatory misery) to crystalize. But Thatcher's arrival in Downing Street announced the beginning of eighteen years of uninterrupted neoliberal Conservative rule. In 1981, she would connect with a kindred spirit on the other side of the Atlantic, following the election of Ronald Reagan to the US presidency. The pair shared an aggressive Cold War zealotry, a hatred of the left, a vindictive enthusiasm for reactionary social policies and a determination to eviscerate the power of organised labour. The repellent politics of Thatcherism shaped the response of all social groups opposed to her rule, including those in the political punk counterculture motivated to voice their refusal. Poison Girls had firmly secured their place in the disorderly ranks of the new dissidents.

Above: Fatal Microbes: Pete Fender, Honey Bane, Gem Stone, and Scott Barker. Courtesy of Reynard Toombs.
Below: Lance, Vi, and Scott Barker on bass, 1978. Courtesy of Pete Fender and Gemma Sansom.

POISON GIRLS

THE WORDS

CRISIS

Is it normal is it normal/is it just
another day/ are they emptying the
rubbish/ have the kids gone out to
play/ are you waiting while the bath
fills up/ watching while they read
the papers/ read the headlines over
breakfast/ breadlines /deadlines/has
the milk come/ is it time to have a
crisis/ is it safe to go out shopping/
Crisis crisis/ Panic buying/ water
dripping on the carpet/ is it normal
is it normal/ is it JUST ANOTHER DAY

Are you waiting while the bath fills
up/ watching while they read the papers/
have the shops run out of rubbish/ is it
time to have a crisis/ spill the beans
and take your clothes off/ can you stand
it if I touch you/watching while they
read the papers/ water dripping on the
carpet/can I say No/ will hatheft me
plaster falling from the ceiling/ can
you stand it if I touch you/break the
ice and burn the house down/is it normal
is it normal/ is it JUST ANOTHER DAY

Is it safe to go out shopping/ leave the
kids outside the toilet/water dripping
on the carpet/leave the kids outside the
local/strangers tapping on the window/
is it time to have a crisis/watching while
they read the papers/peel the onions ask
no questions/ hit the baby/ step it
screaming /can you stand it if I touch you/
break the ice and burn the house down/
is it time to have a crisis/ normal/
normal/crisis/Crisis/ /panic/panic/
normal/normal/ JUST ANOTHER DAY

FATAL MICROBES

THE MIRAGE

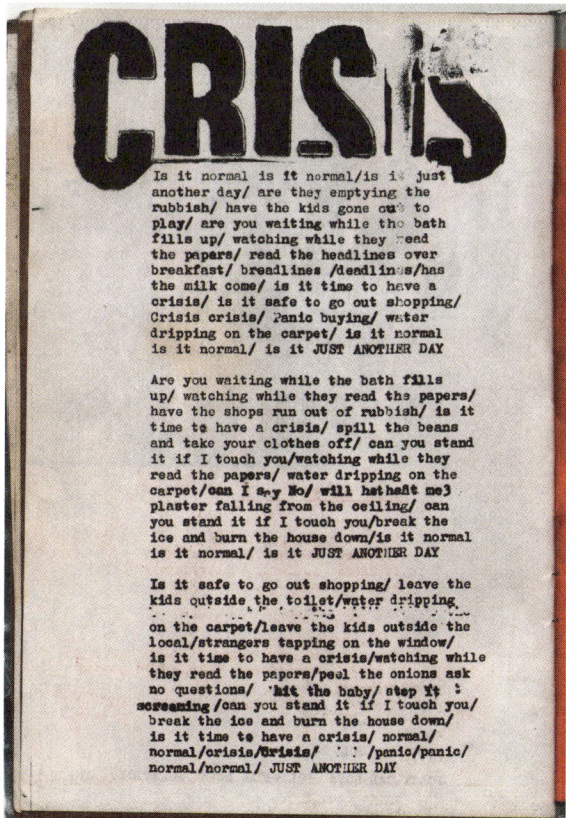

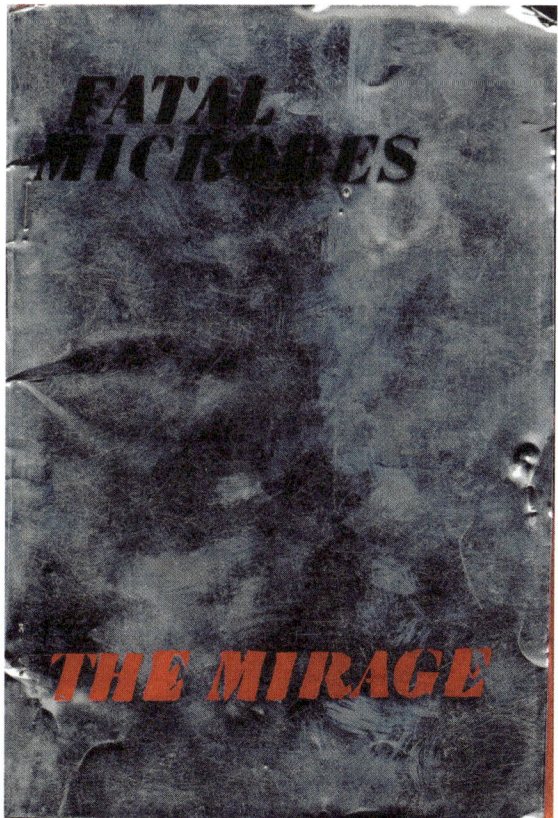

Poison Girls/Fatal Microbes split lyrics zine, cover with spray-paint stencil on sheet aluminum, 1979. Courtesy of Richard Famous.

SPITTING BLOOD

BRIGHTON REAL MUSIC NEWS

BRIGHTON SPUNK PASS IT ON

NUMBER ONE
20 pee
SEPTEMBER 1977

PIRANHAS

DANDIES

WRIST ACTION

PUNKTUATION

POISON FOILS

NEWS   REVIEWS   SPEWS

March for Abortion Rights

Sunday – October 28
Assemble 12:00 noon
Speakers Corner, Hyde Park
(proceeding on to
Trafalgar Square)

A COACH WILL LEAVE NEW CROSS SITE AT 10.30

MEET IN THE CAR PARK AT 10.15

OUR BODIES-OURSELVES

Defend the 1967 Abortion Act

MARCH FOR Abortion on Demand

Sisters Unite

It's a Woman's Right to Choose

NO RETURN TO THE BACK-STREET

FIGHT THE CORRIE BILL

March for Abortion Rights, 1979. Courtesy of Pete Fender and Gemma Sansom.

2. THIS WAY THAT WAY JUMP MAMA JUMP

HEX 1979

The band's debut album is a vinyl declaration like none other yet heard in the British punk firmament. Hex is a singular release that announces the band's political and cultural preoccupations in the boldest of terms, and confirms how unique their musical and aesthetic approach will be. Lyrically, Hex was without parallel, the record's feminist focus on the themes of home and family added to the growing sense of intrigue about the band's 'otherness.' Agreements with the Small Wonder label connect the band to a wider audience for their vinyl releases and, in the process, raise Poison Girls' profile.

Prior to the release of the band's first full twelve-inch, Vi Subversa took the opportunity at a London gig to confront a music press journalist who'd written one of the earliest reviews of the band to appear in a national paper. A few months earlier, writer Paul Morley had attended a Poison Girls gig at The Factory in Manchester. In Morley's write-up, he'd described Subversa as "a middle-aged woman squeezed into a red dress," Famous recalls.

"Vi was livid!" Especially because the band "had it on good authority that he spent all of our set in the bar with his tongue down his girlfriend's throat—maybe metaphorically."

"A few weeks later we were in the audience at the Music Machine in Camden—very unusual for us—and were told that Morley was in the building," Famous continues. "Vi took off like the Phantom of the Opera trying to find him. She eventually tracked him down in the bar, where he still had his tongue down some poor girl's throat—even though he was supposed to be reviewing that gig too. Vi was going to verbally 'have a go,' but the music was too loud for any meaningful conversation, so she just asked if he was Paul Morley, and when he said yes, she whacked him round the face."

It was a moment that would have been the stuff of rock'n'roll legend for any publicity-seeking band looking to enhance their "outlandish" reputation for commercial benefit. But Poison Girls thought the event more amusing than remarkable. "After that, he entered Poison Girls' mythology as Mauled Poorly, and Vi got a bit of respect all round," Famous concludes. "Maybe it was just the wrong side of 'nonviolent direct action,' but a slap is only a slap! In any case, Morley dined out on that story for years and, as it turned out, when *Hex* came out he gave it a good review—and sort of apologised too."

Poison Girls recorded what would become the extraordinarily distinctive *Hex* album at Southern Studios in just two days, on 27–28 April 1979. Rebours provided synthesiser as well as bass, joining Richard Famous and Vi Subversa on guitars and vocals, Lance d'Boyle on drums, and with additional vocals supplied by Eve Libertine. For the first time, Penny Rimbaud took on the role of studio producer for the band, with John Loder acting as studio engineer. As he recalls it, Rimbaud took on the job following "an offer made by Vi which quite simply couldn't be refused, a sort of 'you will do this' kind of offer." Working closely with the band, Rimbaud would go on to be "rightfully pleased with the results I achieved with and for Poison Girls over the years."

"With *Hex*, there was a different atmosphere in the studio from the *Piano Lessons* session right from the start," Famous remembers. "Rimbaud had done a couple of rehearsals with us, and most of the songs had been thoroughly road tested. But he essentially just encouraged us to make as big a sound as we could—not loud, but *big*. He was interested in 'accidentals'—in the sense of unplanned noises and sonics—and was not worried about 'mistakes' at all."

"If you compare my productions of Poison Girls with their later releases, you will hear a profound difference," Rimbaud suggests.

"The idea was to record the tracks as live as possible—no click tracks and with as few overdubs as we could manage," he continues. "The recording *bristles* with that live feel. Vocals were put on separately, but there were very few instrumental extras. It was the sound effects and the mixing that took the most time!"

The result is a record that extends the sense of 'otherness' which *Piano Lessons* had already hinted at. With its focus on the experience of motherhood, home and marriage, *Hex* had a lyrical preoccupation on themes that were far from the workaday concerns of most teenage punk songsmiths. "I think it's important not to have part of human experience pushed off somewhere and nobody talks about it," d'Boyle insisted in a band interview in the *NME*. "People says that talking about the washing up is boring, yet we've been listening to the trials and tribulations of unrequited love for years on end." *Hex* reflected the band's experience of theatrical performance just as much as it reflected the confrontation and aggression of punk rock. There is a mischievous, probing quality to the soundscape and lyricism of *Hex*, a sense that the band are demanding attention from an audience not quite expecting to be asked for it. No other album in the punk firmament even attempted to address such themes, particularly from the perspective of middle age, or in so intimate and exposed a way.

Musically, the record is jagged, spartan, and filled with broken sound textures and unusual song structures and motifs. Many of the lyrical preoccupations of *Hex* appear to be autobiographical, or at least inspired by Vi Subversa's experience of relationships, motherhood, and domesticity. That experience is shaped into anarcha-feminist insights which speak out across the generational divide.

Although her finely honed political and personal insights would become an essential, indivisible component of Poison Girls' success, Subversa's was often reticent about asserting her creative and artistic talents as a lyricist. In a 1981 feature, *Spare Rib* recognised her lyrics as "often ferociously angry and usually rich with highly charged imagery." But Subversa herself was less likely to be so demonstrative. "In defence of my feminine integrity," Vi declared in an interview with *Hot Press*, "I want it known that I write most of the lyrics . . . although to an extent it's true that we all shape the final form of the songs."

Like a minority of twelve-inch releases of the time, *Hex* played at 45 rpm rather than 33 rpm. The front cover, designed by Rebours, was based on a repeat icon of a female head which filled the whole image. Running across

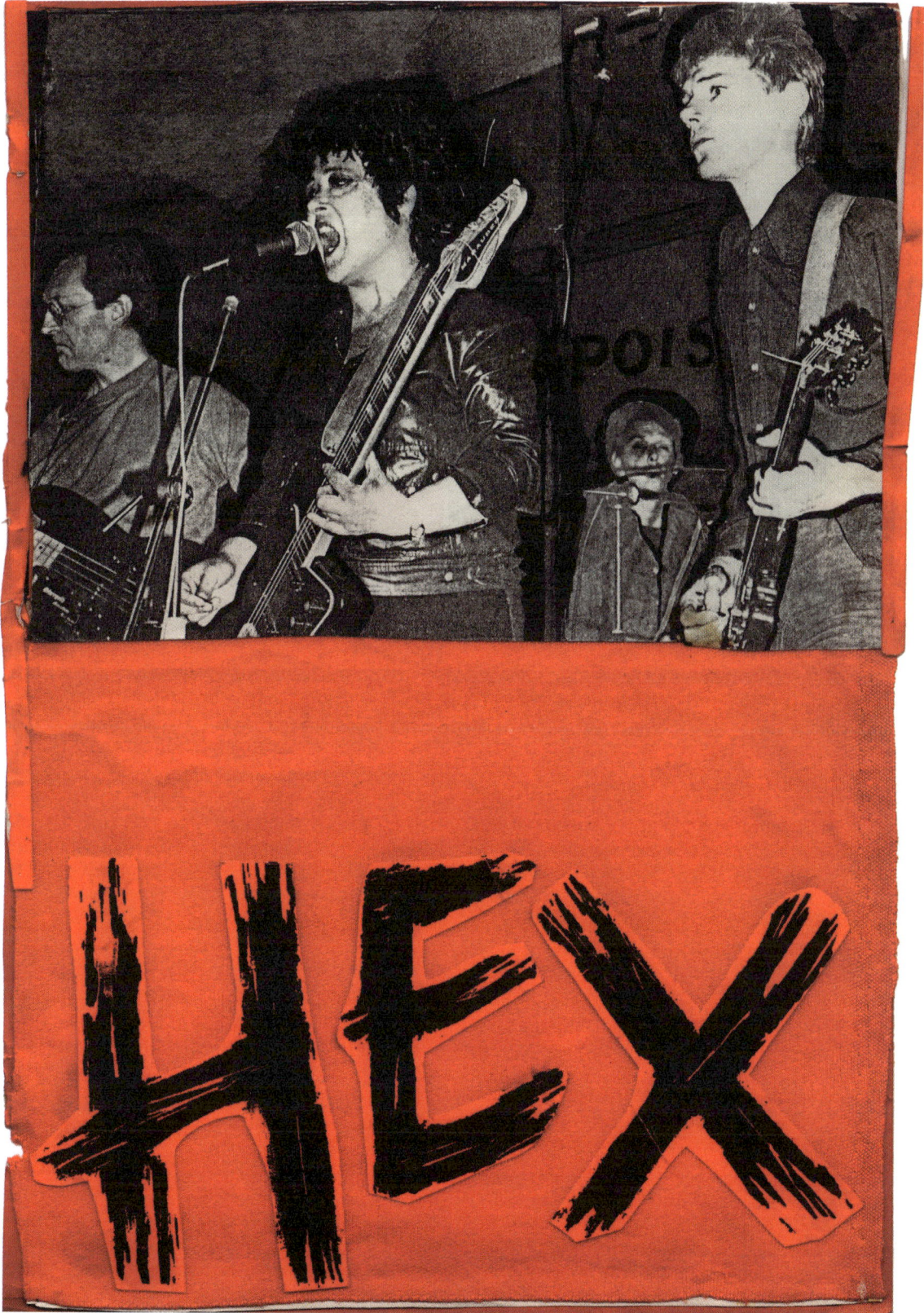

Hex booklet mockup, 1979. Courtesy of Pete Fender and Gemma Sansom.

it was a single abstract image of a strand of barbed wire. The title *Hex* appeared in broad-brush painted letters. The band's name only appeared, in handwritten form, on the bottom left of the back cover, which was dominated by abstracted images of three crows sitting in bare trees, with a repeat of the barbed wire scored across it. A lyric sheet insert presented Subversa's and d'Boyle's words over monochrome images of trees and gardens run wild. The sheet offered different explanations for the title:

Hex. 666. The beast
Curse, charm, spell in magic.
Ritual to evoke instability and injury to
    property and authority.
Also a counter charm to invoke protection from
harmful and malevolent forces
Cleansing, banishing, purging

"Crows are everywhere. They're not aristocratic like eagles. They live how and where they can," Subversa explained to *Obnoxious*. "They're survivors. They're independent. They scavenge . . . They're almost like punks!" As work in the studio progressed, the image of the crow became an ever more potent reference point. "My screaming 'Hex! Hex!' got more and more 'crow-like,' so we developed that, and began looking for pictures of crows to design the sleeve."

"Well before we adopted the crows we had—in an intentionally ironic way—the three flying ducks, seen in every 1950s living room, as our backdrop," Famous reveals. "The crows came when we were first working with Crass, and living at Burleigh House. A crow regularly visited the garden there, and Vi took a shine to it. Crows have a reputation of being independent and scavengers, living off scraps and throwaways. That seemed a good fit for us as a group at that time," he continues. "The crow image was adapted from the *Readers Digest Book of Birds*—well cool, huh—and sharpened up for the cover of *Hex* by Gee Vaucher of Crass." It immediately became "a strong visual symbol, and made a great backdrop."

"Old Tart's Song" is an exemplar of a feminist punk anthem. Seething with righteous scorn, in its repudiation of both misogyny and ageism, the song subverts the accusation, demanding the chance to seize the opportunities only available to men.

"Crisis" is a song about anxiety, overload, and the feeling of not having control. From the isolation of domesticity, the crises of the world appear alarming and unfixable, an unsettling, disturbing form of normality. Responding to those global crises through the pressures of domestic obligation means that the same sense of pressure and powerlessness is recreated in the home.

"Ideologically Unsound" explores the tensions of political commitment and personal entanglement. The struggle is to reconcile attraction and connection with someone else with an audit of their political beliefs. It's also a wider commentary on the state of the radical scene, in which (sometimes minor) differences on questions of politics, strategy, and tactics introduce divisions and conflicts that weaken the opposition and divide it.

"Bremen Song" is arguably the most disturbing track on *Hex*, evoking the wartime history of the north-western German city Bremen, its antisemitism, the enthusiastic engagement of its authorities and its population with the detention, deportation, and extermination of the city's Jewish residents. Bremen was one of numerous locations for the Nazis' forced labour camps, where thousands of prisoners, including POWs, political dissidents, and civilians from occupied territories, were compelled to work, in appalling conditions, in war industries such as shipbuilding. "It was also the scene of a Jewish massacre," Famous adds. "Jews were herded into a church and the building was set on fire."

"They burned sisters, they burned," intones Subversa, as the song begins. The lyrics draw out the historical continuities in which women have suffered persecution and murder, standing accused of being witches and heretics, of being troublesome, or of being civilians caught up in more recent conflict, such as the Vietnam War. Even in the face of such unimaginable horror, there is a mood running through the song of rage and defiance too, hints of an inferno of retribution and revolution. "Germany was always a difficult place for Vi to find herself, despite the wonderful friends we had there," says Famous. "We played a gig in Bremen one time, at a club situated in an old slaughterhouse." Subversa's reaction was visceral and visible. "I suppose today that you would say she was 'triggered' by being there," he adds.

"I'm critically in love with you, politically in love," Subversa sings in the mischievously sardonic opening line of "Political Love," a song which pulls apart the idea of a connection to someone else based entirely on a shared political alignment which offers itself as a substitute for romantic attachment. It's the flipside of "Ideologically Unsound."

"Jump Mama Jump" homes in on the relentless pressures on women of running a family home without support from partner or husband. The endless treadmill of domestic obligation, the bewildering array of responsibilities, the expectation that the homemaker will keep on top of all commitments and ensure the happiness and fulfilment of everyone else in the family unit apart from herself. "This way, that way. Jump mama jump."

The idiom of someone being 'under the doctor' has long since lost its cultural echo. But in the late 1970s it remained a commonly understood signifier for someone who was receiving regular, ongoing medical attention from their general practitioner and dealing with a chronic or persistent ailment. "Under the Doctor" explores the experience of women in this position, and the patronising, dismissive, and thoughtless way in which so many 'mothers and wives' were dealt with and medicated in response to the mental and physical conditions that they presented with in the doctor's office. "Vi was commenting on the pain that was—and still is—inflicted on women when treated by the 'chemical cosh' which was regularly prescribed by the patriarchal medical profession to keep women docile," says Famous. "These were the Valium, Mogadon, and Largactil years."

"Reality Attack" is a clever subversion of the notion of a 'panic attack,' itself an often natural response to unendurable pressure. In this rendering of the idea, it is the recognition that distress is triggered by a recognition of the horrors of the real world—the idea that the existential torment that overwhelms you comes from seeing the world as it really is. It's a witty and subversive idea, and as always with Poison Girls songs that explore notions of crises and distress, there are words of defiance and resistance to accompany the torment. "It always seemed such an epic piece to me," Famous says, "less of a song, more of a soundtrack for a nightmare. It was a brilliant prose poem, and at the same time the storyboard for an amazing film!" The closing refrain cycles and inverts the original idea—"reality attack, attack reality, attack." It injects the idea that it is possible to react not with docility and acceptance, but with a rebellious response of refusal.

Hex became the third Xntrix-Small Wonder vinyl collaboration, and was released on 13 July 1979—less than a week after Margaret Thatcher won the first of three successive general election victories—electoral triumphs that confirmed the ascendancy of a new form of neoliberal, socially conservative right-wing populism on both sides of the Atlantic.

In 1980, and in line with the new agreement between Poison Girls and Crass, *Hex* was rereleased on Crass Records. For the rerelease, the packaging of *Hex* was completely redesigned. The front cover now featured the band's name in a new bold capital-letter font at the top, and while the render of *Hex* has been retained, a new stylised side-on silhouette of the crow dominated the design, black against the white of the cover, with a black border. The sleeve of *Hex* became a fold out (a "double-sided, six-panel concertina fold" no less), with the lyrics, freshly typeset, now filling up the two inner sides of the fold. (The evocation of the meaning of '*Hex*' is not carried through.)

The back cover repeated the image of the crow, still behind barbed wire (but now a realistic, rather than a stylised, image) but now merging into a cloud-filled sky above an open landscape with a copse of trees in the middle distance. The imagery was darker, more foreboding, stripped of all hints of absurdity that lit up the sleeve of *Piano Lessons*. Artwork and photography were by Rebours, with the overall design credited to the band and to Penny Rimbaud. Xntrix was now affirmed as the publisher of the band's music, rather than as the band's record label.

The mainstream music press had most enjoyed the unexpected timbre of Poison Girls first vinyl release. Reviewers' reaction to the sound of *Hex* suggested the experience was more uncomfortable, given the record's highly charged and very personal political focus. Writing in *Sounds*, Phil Sutcliffe acknowledged that *Hex* was "provocative, aggressive, and pandering to nobody in pursuit of sales," but admitted he could "hardly say I enjoyed the record" because it was "an accusing finger pointing my way." Journalists who thought that they had got the measure of Poison Girls (as "offbeat," "quirky," and "unusual") began to reconsider their judgement.

Hex became the singular, assured, and inflammatory vinyl release that quickly amplified the attention already being paid to Poison Girls. The working partnership that the band would soon broker with Crass would propel them to an even higher level of popularity and well-deserved recognition.

Clockwise from top left: Bernhardt Rebours and Vi Subversa, Stroud; Richard Famous, Stroud; Lance, location unknown; all circa 1979–80. Vi at 1979 Stonehenge Free Festival. Photos courtesy of Bernhardt Rebours.

Poison Girls, 1979. Picture by Pete Gilbert for *In the City* fanzine, courtesy of Pete Fender and Gemma Sansom.

The original cover of *Hex* released on Xntrix Records in 1979. Subsequent editions were released by Crass Records, beginning in 1980 and featured the iconic flying crow silhouette and fit in with Crass's more minimal house style.

"The first issue of *Hex* was a collaboration with Lance d'Boyle and me. He created the manikin heads idea and I did the lettering and barbed wire. I don't remember who thought of the raven on the trees on the back cover. It feels like we all had input on this, but I may have drawn it. I'm not really sure. The subsequent releases of *Hex* were artworked by me featuring a back cover photo of a view near the site of the Stonehenge festival and illustrated crow; the inside gatefold had photography by me [one shot of Burleigh House]." —Bernhardt Rebours

POISON GIRLS/HEX/SIDE ONE/OLD TARTS SONG/CRISIS/IDEALOGICALLY UNSOUND/BREMEN SONG/SIDE TWO/POLITICAL LOVE/JUMP MAMA JUMP/UNDER THE DOCTOR/REALITY ATTACK
AN XNTRIX/SMALL WONDER CO-RELEASE XNTRIX Records, Burleigh House, Bell Common, Epping, Essex. Small Wonder Records, 162 Hoe Street, Walthamstow, London E17.   WEENY FOUR

JUMP
MAMA
JUMP

This violent life

Collages by Vi Subversa. Pages from *Hex* lyric zine, 1979.

WOTTEN. —To Lynn and David (nee Howarth), a son, Thomas David, born June 1, 1979 at Whipps Cross Hospital, a brother for Chloe Victoria.

Coming of Age

BESSENT. — Many happy returns on your 18th birthday Martin. — Love from Mum, Dad and family.

CURTIS, Ann. — Congratulations on your 18th Birthday. — Love Carol, Roger and Zoe.

DOUGLAS, Mark. — Congratulations on your 18th birthday, June 4th. Lots of love Mum, Dad, Nan, Jan and Tim.

Births

BANNERMAN. — Congratulations to Tracey and Martin on the birth of your son Lee. Love and best wishes from Sally and all the family.

BEAN, Graham and Kim (nee Walker). — Congratulations on arrival of a son May 30. Love

[...]. — To Peter and Jenny (nee Platt, formerly of Walthamstow), a son, Craig Raymond, May 29, at Tokoroa, New Zealand.

HART. — To Joyce and Roy, the precious gift of a daughter, Keely Joy, born May 25. With all our thanks to the staff at St. Margaret's Hospital.

HULBERT, — To Sue (nee Long) and Mick a beautiful daughter (Michelle Diane) born May 26. Congratulations — Mum and Dad.

Engagements

FRANCIS - ATKINSON. — Announcing the engagement of Graham, son of Mr and Mrs F. A. Francis of Sawbridgeworth and Georgina, eldest [...] of Mr [...] Atkinson and [...] W. A. Atkinson of Guernsey, Channel Islands.

FRY - ALCOCK. — Mr and Mrs R. Alcock of Harlow wish to announce the Engagement of their daughter, Carol [...]

SIMONDS–EMERY. — Mr & Mrs R. Emery have pleasure in announcing the marriage of their daughter Caroline to Francis, son of Mr & Mrs Simonds at the Methodist Church, Epping, at 4 pm, Saturday, June 9th.

Congratulations

BEAN, Kim and Graham. — Congratulations on the birth of your lovely baby Son. Love from Mum and Dad [...]

[...]IP. — Good luck and best wishes Jeff on your 21 birthday. — Love Maxine.

[...]DALL. — Congratulations Christopher and Carolanne on your Wedding June 1, 1979. — Love, Mum, Dad and all the family.

KENARD, Christine. — Congratulations 21st. Better never, [...] wishes [...] Lorraine [...]

SMITH [...]

Lucy [...] on the 2nd. [...] Mum, Nanny and [...]

Deaths

DIX, Irene Ursula June [...] aged [...] beloved Wife [...] Roy and much loved Mother of Chris, B[...], Tony, after a long illness bravely borne. Funeral at Little Laver Church on Thursday.

Silver Weddings

Acknowledgements

COPELAND, Ernest George. — Mrs Copeland and Brian thank friends and neighbours for flowers and many kindnesses upon the loss of a Husband and Father.

CRANE, Bertie. — Phyllis and her children acknowledge with thanks flowers, donations and all help given to our dear Father and Grandad.
From our happy home and circle God has taken one we love,
To join our dear Mum (Nan) Stan and Margaret in a happier home above,
Always gentle, loving and kind,
A most wonderful memory to leave behind.
[...] and 88.

LENTZ, Sarah. —Our grateful thanks to friends, neighbours and Ashlyns [...]

WATSON, Linda. — [...] family of the late [...] da Watson would [...] thank friends and [...] for the many [...] floral tributes [...] messages of [...] received. Also [...] thanks to the [...] nurses and s[...] Livingstone an[...] wards, for the [...] shown to Linda du[...] long illness.

In Memoriam

BASS. [...]
mem[...]
and g[...]
died, Jun[...]
You ha[...]
everyone,
You had a hear[...]
You left us the [...]
memories,
The world ha[...]
known.
—Sadly miss[...]

[...]TY, Jo[...]
memori[...]
husban[...]
[...]ed a[...]
[...]my
[...]h[...]

Join [...]
ou[...]
were [...]
good a[...]
or we thought th[...]
of you,
We never said g[...]
dad,
Perhaps its just as w[...]
We couldn't have [...]
said it,
To the one we lo[...]
well.
— Your everl[...]
daughters, Jean, [...]
Linda and Families.

ideologically unsound

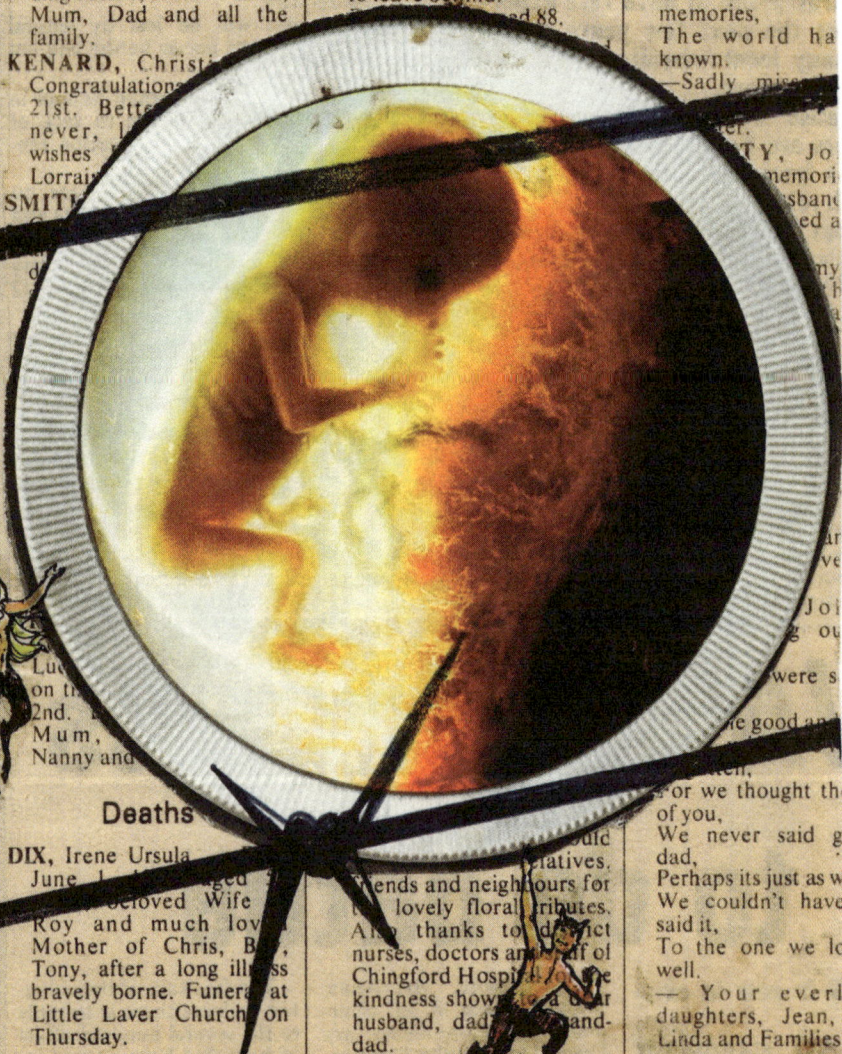

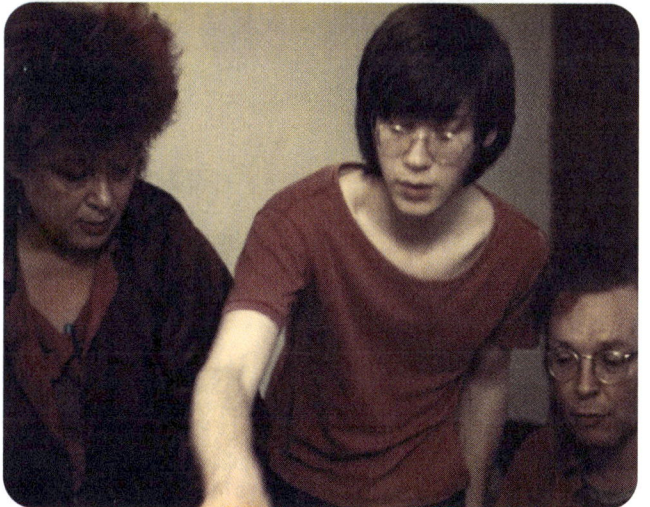

Opposite: Collage art by Vi for *Hex*, courtesy of Pete Fender and Gemma Sansom.
This page, top left: Poison Girls tour van, near Arnheim, March 1980. Top right and middle: Poison Girls and their tent at Stonehenge Free Music Festival, June 1979. Photos courtesy of Bernhardt Rebours, Pete Fender, and Gemma Sansom. Bottom left: Pete, Gemma, Vi, and photographer Seamus O'Riginal. Bottom right: Vi, Pete, and Lance, 1982. Photos courtesy of Sue Cooper.

CRASS
POISON GIRLS
FILM: AUTOPSY

A

 BENEFIT

FOR

THE FILM CO-OP

ON

friday APRIL 20TH

42 gloucester ave

N.W.1. £1 8.30pm.

60

1980

prostitutes * rights organisation
benefit concert
POISON GIRIS
NIGhTINGAIES
BUNKer * G.b.H.

DiGbEth CiViC HaLl
May 10th 7*30 – 11*30
£1 ON THE dOOR * * TiCkEts FROM iNFErNO

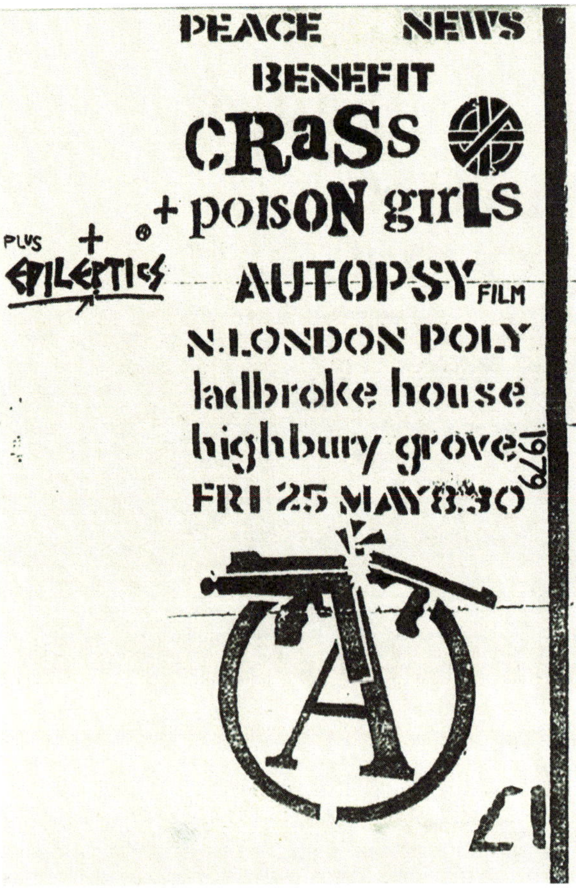

PEACE NEWS
BENEFIT
CRASS
+ POISON GIRLS
PLUS + EPILEPTICS
AUTOPSY FILM
N. LONDON POLY
ladbroke house
highbury grove
FRI 25 MAY 8:30 1979
£1

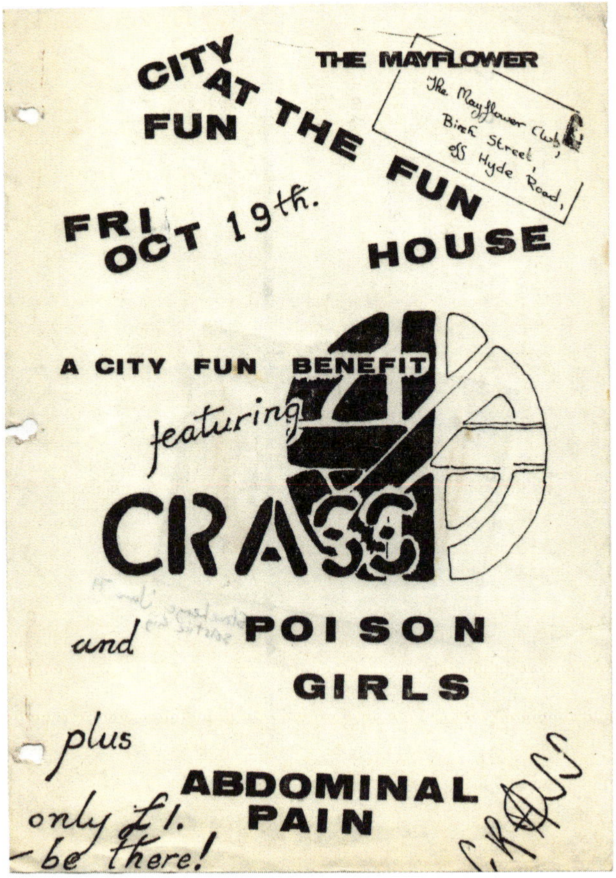

CITY AT THE FUN
THE MAYFLOWER
The Mayflower Club,
Birch Street,
off Hyde Road,
FRI OCT 19th. HOUSE
A CITY FUN BENEFIT
featuring
CRASS
and POISON
GIRLS
plus
ABDOMINAL
PAIN
only £1.
be there!

POISON GIRLS
+ RUBELLA BALLET
SOMEWHERE TO FEEL SAFE
SAFER THAN ALONE
SAFER TO BE SAFE
SOMEWHERE TO FEEL SAFE
YOU ARE NOT THE ONLY ONE
THOUSANDS OF US WOMEN
NEED A PLACE WITH OUR CONWAY HALL
A SAFE PLACE THATS SAFE RED LION SQ.
SOMEWHERE TO FEEL SAFE HOLBORN
SAFER THAN ALONE £1
SAT.
SEP.
15
BENEFIT FOR WOMENS AID
ISLINGTON

C.N.D. BENEFIT GIG
CRASS
with support
the poison girls
+ local band
BEYOND
THE
WALL
tuesday 1st. may.
at 7.30 p.m.
TUNSTALL TOWN HALL
late bar
and disco
admission
80 p.

ACKLAM HALL
MARCH 26 7·30 (Portobello Road)
CRASS
THE WALL
POISON GIRLS
Benefit
for
ANARCHIST BLACK CROSS
CIENFUEGOS PRESS
Adm £1
FREE ALL PRISONERS NOW

INTERNATIONAL ANTHEM
BENEFIT
CRASS
POISON GIRLS
EPILEPTICS
MOONLIGHT CLUB
W. HAMPSTEAD
FRI/SAT. 7/8 MARCH
TICKETS IN ADVANCE FROM
ROUGH TRADE & SMALL WONDER
8.30-12 ONE POUND
A NOK? x 521984

POISON GIRLS
ABORT THE SYSTEM
POISON GIRLS + ZOUNDS
& ANNIE ANXIETY
AT.. ACTION SPACE
CHENIES ST.
WC.2. £1·50
FRIDAY JULY 18

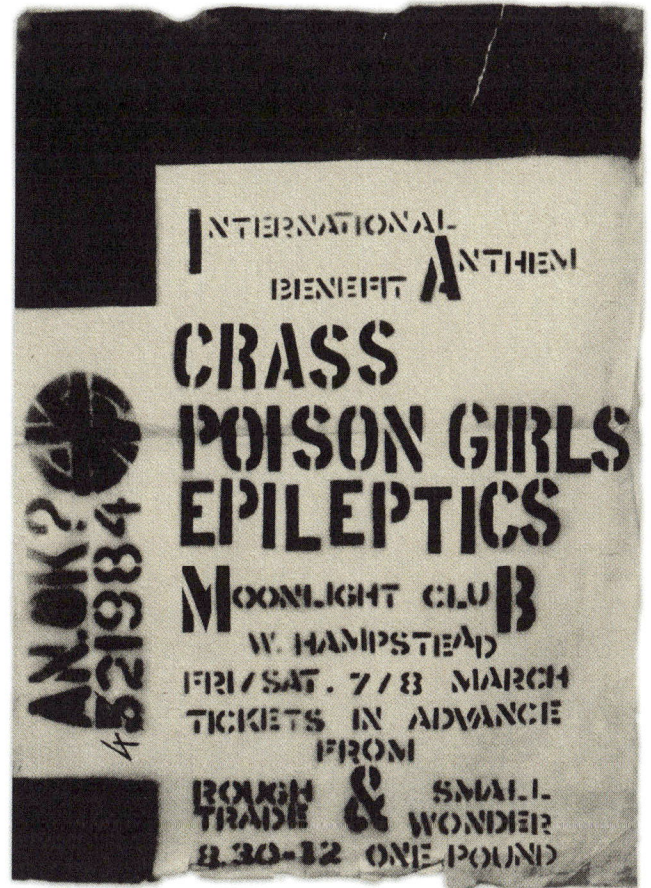

Pages 60 & 61: **412 Gloucester Ave.**, London, 20 April 1979. A benefit for the Film Co-op. **Digbeth Civic Hall**, Birmingham, 10 May 1980. A benefit for Prostitutes Rights Organisation.

Opposite: **N. London Polytechnic,** London, 25 May 1979. A benefit for *Peace News*, the long-running antimilitarist publication at the time based in London.
The Mayflower, Manchester, 19 October 1979. A benefit for *City Fun*, a Manchester-based music zine.
Tunstall Town Hall, Stoke-on-Trent, 1 May 1979. A benefit for the Campaign for Nuclear Disarmament (CND).
Conway Hall, London, 15 September 1979. A benefit for Islington Women's Aid, a domestic violence shelter in London.

This page: **Acklam Hall**, London, 26 March 1979. A Benefit for Anarchist Black Cross, a support network for anti-authoritarian political prisoners; and for Cienfuegos Press, an anarchist publishing house founded by English activist Stuart Christie that published *Cienfuegos Anarchist Press Review* a small but influential magazine about international anarchism's past, present, and future.
Moonlight Club, London, 18 March 1980. A benefit for *International Anthem*, a political art/collage newspaper published by Gee Vaucher and Crass. The Epileptics reformed as Flux of Pink Indians later that year.
Action Space, London, 18 July 1980. Action Space is a radical arts organization that created play spaces for adults and children.

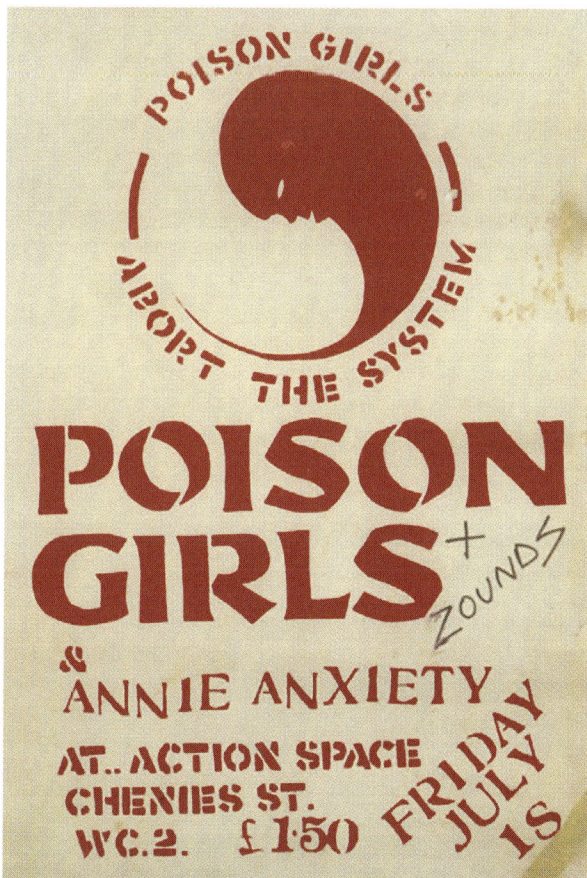

3. SURVIVAL IN SILENCE ISN'T GOOD ENOUGH NO MORE

PERSONS UNKNOWN 1979

The close association with Crass reshapes the nature of Poison Girls' operations and begins an intense period of successful and mutually beneficial collaboration. The release of the Bloody Revolutions/Persons Unknown *split single becomes its most high profile declaration of intent. For members of Crass, association with the London Autonomy Centre is something approaching a political initiation, while for the core musicians of Poison Girls it's the latest expression of their decades-long anarchist commitments. Months later, the* All Systems Go *seven-inch captures the band at their most politically fierce and poetically reflective. Poison Girls refuse to be intimidated by the violence that disrupts their live appearances in London and at the Stonehenge Free Festival.*

The new collaborative partnership between Crass and Poison Girls began in earnest in January 1979. No one involved signed any contracts or memoranda. It was no more than an unwritten agreement that both parties voluntarily committed to. There were clear mutual advantages to both parties in the closer relationship. For Crass, the alliance was a key to the band's ambition to take out on the road a lineup that was politically and artistically aligned, and which could present a coherent live experience. Prior to this, Crass had shared a stage with a variety of different punk and alternative bands many of which had little interest in the band's anarchist, antimilitarist, or DIY commitments. Touring with Poison Girls changed that narrative, not least because the expectations and aspirations of both bands were at that point so much in sync: neither were motivated by commercial success, both wanted to work in ways that were antithetical to the predatory methods of the music business, and both embraced the cultural ethos of the counterculture.

But the new alliance was born more out of shared desperation than optimism. "Both bands were on the verge of giving up," Famous admits. "Crass didn't have an audience at that time, and neither did we really. Working together was the last throw of the dice. For the first few months the gigs were the proverbial 'two men and a dog,' but then word-of-mouth took over and people started to come." Soon after that, a mutually beneficial pact was settled. "The agreement was that we would play together with them, that they wouldn't do a gig without us, but that we could still play on our own," Subversa recalled later. Poison Girls would arrange more than fifty gigs under their own banner during this time.

"Over the next two years they were to play 97 gigs together," Poison Girls' official history recalls. "All but a handful were benefit gigs. All were outside commercial music business venues. This activity jump started the anarcho-punk movement as we know it today."

"At the beginning, no one quite knew how to take them," Steve Ignorant of Crass recalls of Poison Girls' reception. "The punks didn't see them as being punk." In addition, the audience at these gigs was not free of the ageism and sexism that the band had experienced on stage in The Vault back in Brighton. "I remember once at a gig in Birmingham, this bloke came up to me and said, 'Steve, she's a bit fucking old to be doing this, isn't she?' I said, 'And what are you going to be doing when you're forty, mate?'" Over time, and through their own efforts, Poison Girls won over more and more of that shared audience.

But the recognition that Poison Girls were playing to what was predominantly Crass's crowd persisted. "After we played a few gigs together, there was a discussion about the running order. Poison Girls asked, 'Well, why don't you let us go on after you, for a change?'" Ignorant recalls. "And we said, 'Look, people might leave after Crass have played.' But we tried it once, and unfortunately half the audience *did* leave after we'd played and didn't wait around to see Poison Girls." Ignorant recalls that there was a bit of tension afterwards. "It was almost like Poison Girls felt that it was our fault," he says. "But we were clear, 'well, no, it's not. It's just the way it is.'" Whatever the judgement, it was an outcome that, over time, would only increase Poison Girls' interest in reclaiming their own autonomy.

One of these early joint shows "paid for the first batch of CND badges to be produced in ten years," Famous recalls, as Crass and Poison Girls worked to "introduce the CND symbol to a new generation." By 1979, Crass had decided that the band should no longer perform outside the UK, instead concentrating their energies in the country where they better understood the political, social and cultural terrain. Aside from a single exception—an appearance at the We Demand the Future festival in Reykjavik, Iceland, in September 1983—it was a decision which Crass honoured. In sharp contrast, Poison Girls judged such self-imposed restrictions as unwarranted and parochial in scope. They continued to enjoy, and see the clear value of, performing live at shows across Europe and in the USA.

Back in London, the strength of the collaboration between Poison Girls and Crass was reflected in three separate but linked developments. First, due to a family inheritance, Subversa was able to provide Dial House with sufficient funds to underwrite the launch of Crass Records, which Crass would have been unable to have afforded themselves. "It was a big gesture from her," Rimbaud says. "There was a sense of us and the Poisons being a body of the same nature." Second, *Hex* and was reissued on the new Crass label, followed by the release of Poison Girls' second album, *Chappaquiddick Bridge*. Third, the two bands collaborated on the record release which saw them align most closely with the political perspectives of the contemporary British anarchist movement: the *Bloody Revolutions/Persons Unknown* benefit single, intended to raise funds for a putative new "Anarchy Centre" in the capital.

The catalyst for that pivotal seven-inch was the political prosecution of a group of radical militants and activists that the state intended to neutralise. The enduring popularity of that extraordinary Poison Girls song has at times overshadowed the political significance of that legal attack.

In May 1978, six anarchist and libertarian-identified activists were arrested following police raids in London. Six defendants, Ronan Bennett, Iris Mills, Vince Stevenson, Trevor Dawton, and Taff Ladd, soon faced the extremely serious charge of "conspiracy, with person or persons unknown, at places unknown, to cause explosions." Detectives insisted that these militants were "attempting to arm themselves" so that, at some unspecified future time, they would be able to "attack public buildings and prominent people."

As the arrestees were remanded into custody, the British press seized on the story characterising those in custody as members of an "anarchist terror cell" connected to underground and paramilitary groups across Europe. Having been found in what the *Daily Express* dubbed a "bomb-bedsit," antiterrorist police were reported to be "scouring London for a car they believe could kill": a vehicle that, the *Daily Telegraph* insisted, might be "booby-trapped" with explosives. These allegations were the stuff of lurid police fantasy, and in November the original charges were soon dropped with the defendants instead variously charged with "conspiracy to rob," "possessing an explosive substance," "possessing firearms without a certificate," and "handling stolen goods."

A defence campaign was soon launched by activists who declared themselves determined to challenge the "reluctance amongst the British left to acknowledge many of the features of the State under which we live—or at least to confront and resist its growing repressive machinery." The police were soon spying on and harassing Persons Unknown supporters, with the defence campaign able to compile details "of about thirty raids" on the homes and premises of "well-known anarchists [and] other left activists" in London, Bristol, Swansea and Huddersfield under the spurious pretext of "uncovering" linked conspirators.

Despite this, campaigners' hopes that the trial might galvanise opposition to State repression of political activists across the full spectrum of the progressive British left went largely unfulfilled. When the trial began on 20 September 1979, vocal support for those in the dock at The Old Bailey came mainly from anarchist activists and other fringe dissidents, while the bulk of the organised political left and the "liberal intelligentsia" kept a suspicious distance, worried about the taint of association.

The key factor that would connect the trial defence campaign with the work of Poison Girls and Crass was the political commitment and personality of defendant Ronan Bennett. A committed Irish nationalist, and an active member of the Irish Republican Socialist Party (IRSP), Bennett had, at age eighteen, been found guilty of killing a police officer during a botched bank raid in September 1974. Bennett had protested his innocence throughout, and he was freed the following year when his conviction was struck down as unsafe.

Bennett's politics had been moving in the direction of anarchism, and while in jail he had begun to correspond with *Black Flag* writer Iris Mills. Concerned by recurring threats from Loyalist terror groups, Bennett travelled to England as his personal relationship with Mills developed.

Opposite: *Zero #06: Anarchist/Anarca-feminist Newsmagazine,* August–September 1978. From the Sparrows' Nest Library and Archive.

67

As a militant Irish republican, he remained under close surveillance by British police forces right up to the time of his arrest in London.

When he was finally released on bail after months on remand, Bennett was determined to rally the forces of the British anarchist movement to support the defendants. As well as his connections with *Black Flag*, Bennett pressed *Freedom*, *Xtra!* and other anarchist newspapers to cover the case.

While he was aware of the development of the new consciously anarchist strand within punk, he'd had no contact with any of the bands from that scene. Bennett decided to telephone Dial House to pitch to Crass the idea of backing the campaign. Everything that then developed in relation to Poison Girls' and Crass's involvement with the defence campaign, and with the initial funding of the short-lived London Autonomy Centre, began with that single phone call.

The combative anarchist certainties of Bennett appeared to challenge the amorphous antistate individualism of Crass, encouraging the band to familiarise themselves with more conscious, clear-cut anarchist perspectives. But the combined decades of immersion in the anarchist movement that members of Poison Girls could call upon, meant that their understanding of the political imperatives of the case required little additional insight from Bennett. "I'm an anarchist," Subversa affirmed to *New Youth* zine, without the need for qualification or caveat. "I've only ever voted once years ago, and I felt really shit afterwards . . . The trouble is people keep going along to use their little votes. If a big percentage refused to vote it would make a much more worthwhile statement." Nor was there any equivocation from d'Boyle. "I've been interested in anarchy since I was eighteen," he told *Obnoxious* zine in 1981. "I've been through all the leftist ideas and CND the first time around." A core ambition for the band was "getting anarchism across to people," to help the band's audience "understand what the circled-A sign means."

One of the challenges confronting the defence campaign, was the attitude to take in relation to the "culpability" of the defendants for the "crimes" with which they were charged. The organised defence campaign offered no compromise on the issue: "As revolutionaries we all refuse to be judged by the State, and this is why we never at any stage claimed the defendants were either 'innocent' or 'guilty.' But we have to fight a legalistic battle for the sake of the defendants who had no wish to be martyrs."

For the musicians of Crass, at that time resolutely committed to the politics of pacifism, the spuriousness of the charges was an important requisite for their support of the accused: these were anarchists framed and falsely accused by the state. For Poison Girls, who were antimilitarists but not fixated on the observance of nonviolence, the position involved more complex political calculations. Their instincts to express solidarity with these persecuted militants were out of tune with the dominant perspectives of those on the left, precisely because of the incendiary nature of the charges that the defendants faced.

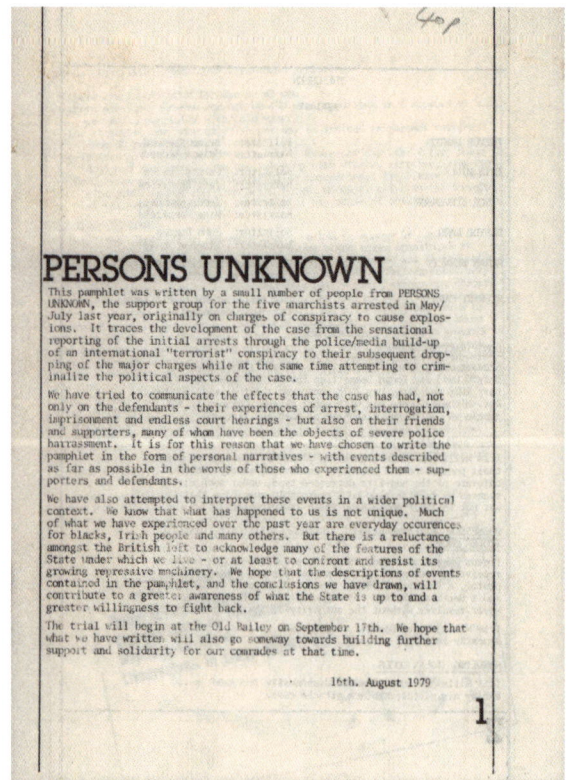

PERSONS UNKNOWN

This pamphlet was written by a small number of people from PERSONS UNKNOWN, the support group for the five anarchists arrested in May/July last year, originally on charges of conspiracy to cause explosions. It traces the development of the case from the sensational reporting of the initial arrests through the police/media build-up of an international "terrorist" conspiracy to their subsequent dropping of the major charges while at the same time attempting to criminalize the political aspects of the case.

We have tried to communicate the effects that the case has had, not only on the defendants - their experiences of arrest, interrogation, imprisonment and endless court hearings - but also on their friends and supporters, many of whom have been the objects of severe police harrassment. It is for this reason that we have chosen to write the pamphlet in the form of personal narratives - with events described as far as possible in the words of those who experienced them - supporters and defendants.

We have also attempted to interpret these events in a wider political context. We know that what has happened to us is not unique. Much of what we have experienced over the past year are everyday occurences for blacks, Irish people and many others. But there is a reluctance amongst the British left to acknowledge many of the features of the State under which we live - or at least to confront and resist its growing repressive machinery. We hope that the descriptions of events contained in the pamphlet, and the conclusions we have drawn, will contribute to a greater awareness of what the State is up to and a greater willingness to fight back.

The trial will begin at the Old Bailey on September 17th. We hope that what we have written will also go someway towards building further support and solidarity for our comrades at that time.

16th. August 1979

1

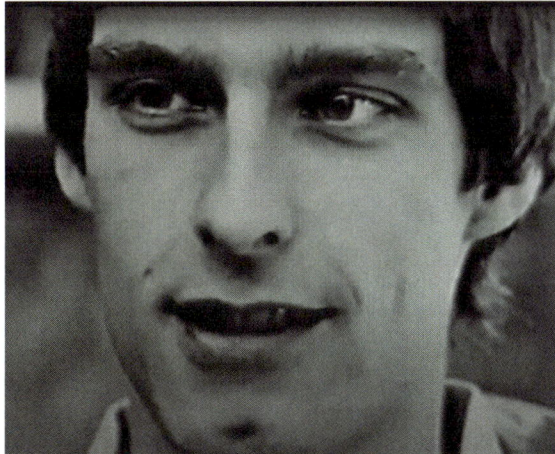

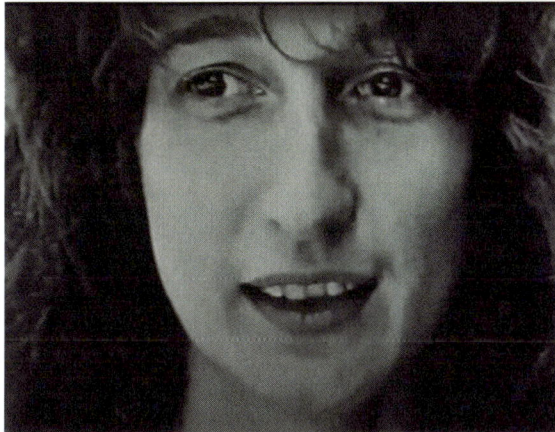

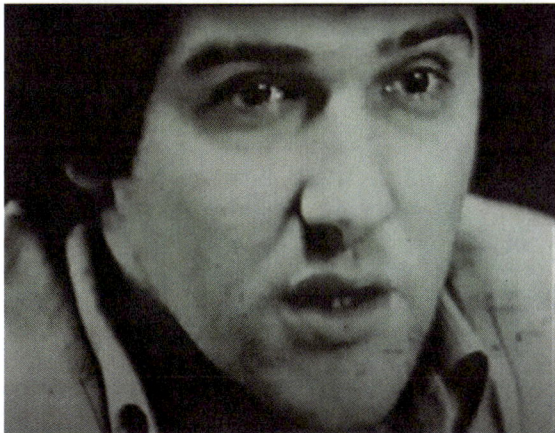

Above: Stills from *Persons Unknown*, a 1980 BBC documentary about the "Persons Unknown" case directed by Gordon Carr. Three of the accused anarchists, from top to bottom: Ronan Bennett, Iris Mills, and Vince Stephenson.

Opposite: *Persons Unknown*, a sixty-six-page resource and information zine, published by the Persons Unknown support group, 1979. From MayDay Rooms/Stuart Christie archives.

On Saturday 8 September 1979, less than a fortnight before the trial began, Crass and Poison Girls were joined by Dutch neo-Maoists The Rondos for a Persons Unknown fundraiser at Conway Hall in London's Red Lion Square. A landmark in progressive politics in the capital since the venue was opened by the site's Ethical Society in 1929, Conway Hall was far from being a usual rock'n'roll venue, and was better known for hosting talks, presentations, and classical concerts. As part of their efforts to organise shows away from traditional music venues, Crass had arranged several gigs at Conway Hall, including fundraisers for *Peace News* and for *Toxic Grafity* fanzine.

Intended to be a political, as well as a financial, fillip for the campaign, this latest Persons Unknown gig degenerated into one of the most infamous political punk gigs of the period. Numerous attendees were attacked and assaulted as repeated waves of violence swept through the audience. Bitter recriminations followed in the aftermath, as arguments raged over who or what was culpable for what had happened. Richard Famous summarises the "notorious Conway Hall event," as the gig "where the SWP [the leftist Socialist Workers Party] attacked the NF [the fascist National Front]."

Supporters of Poison Girls and Crass denounced a leftist, street-fighting hit squad for indiscriminately laying into anyone in the crowd with short hair or who they judged suspect. Critics of the band insisted that volunteer security had stepped into the vacuum created by the organisers' dereliction of duty and were now being condemned for their efforts to protect the audience from a violent rightist onslaught. *Toxic Grafity* editor Mike Dibbol argues that the night was essentially a clash between "boneheads and bikers brought in by the SWP" and recalls that while the "boneheads were used to pushing punks around" they were on the receiving end of "far more than they bargained for when taking on the bikers" that night.

Poison Girls and Crass collaborated on a ten-page black-and-white pamphlet outlining their take on events, which was reproduced in full in the first issue of *Kill Your Pet Puppy* zine. It's immediately clear just how appalled the band was at what they saw as their space being exploited for the poisonous preoccupations of the far left and far right. "There are still bloodstains on our banner," they fumed. Poison Girls issued an uncompromising statement about the Conway Hall debacle the following day:

Events like last night where large groups of young people congregate to share the energy of rock music are being increasingly manipulated by outside agents who wish to colonise that energy and see the audience as young fresh blood to turn into soldiers for various causes—outside agents who are often the doddering relics of past battles like the dusty, shadowy leaders of the National Front and the British Movement, like the weary, jaded lefties left over from the failures of the 60s.

Right wing, left wing, people with old and new ambitions for power and control. The same old sad, bloody story. Poison Girls want nothing to do with these games.

We are not there to participate in or stimulate gang warfare.

We are not after anyone's blood. We don't want a following which can be manipulated by us or anyone else.

The only way out of this shit is for people to resist these outside agents. These agents are the system, no matter what they say. British Movement, Rock Against Racism, National Front, SWP, all support the system of gang warfare while pretending to oppose it.

As the arguments about gig security and political manipulation raged, what was often overlooked in the row was the strength of both bands' determination not simply to perform for audiences that already agreed with their ideas. "I mean, if we exclude people, just preach to the converted, play to politically 'safe' people, that's pointless," d'Boyle fumed to the *NME*. Insisting that collective safety at gigs was "everybody's responsibility," he made a striking allegation. "Nobody has been hurt at any of our gigs except the Conway Hall, which was the one time the SWP offered their 'solution.' That speaks for itself."

"As a matter of policy, we attempted to play gigs where there were no restrictions on entry—so no pubs, no student only venues, and no clubs with age restrictions," Famous recalls. That determination to remain accessible "meant that we had run-ins with the Rock Against Racism and Rock Against Sexism organisers in east London and Essex who compiled an A4 folder of people—skinheads mainly—who were excluded from gigs," he continues. "We didn't exclude any NF kids that we knew about. In retrospect, that was maybe naïve—but for us it was better to talk with them than ignore them. In truth, most were just kids in search of a gang and some excitement, and a few—usually older—ring leaders were exploiting this."

"We always looked out for each other," says Steve Ignorant of Crass. After a violent gig, "we'd either go over to their place or they'd come over to ours, and there'd be discussions about what to do and how to deal with it next time," he says. "It was so desperate sometimes, we'd cry together, you know? I remember at one gig, Vi just holding me, hugging me, and asking, 'Why are you crying?' And I said, 'Well, it's fucking shit. I can't deal with it no more.' She'd console me and just be that lovely voice of reason. And Lance was also amazing—unrufflable, unflappable Lance."

"There'd be that support between each other to help keep us going," Ignorant continues. "But the dark times were something that none of us really wanted to dwell on. We weren't alone in being targeted, loads of other bands were getting it too. So we'd just pick ourselves up and move on to the next one."

In an act of shared defiance, the two bands attempted to arrange another Conway Hall gig two months later, in November 1979—a public rebuke to political agents of the left and right determined to silence or manipulate them. But their booking was cancelled with just forty-eight hours to go after nervous officials at the Greater London Council "made a series of demands on the Conway Hall that made it impossible for us to play," Crass explained. The bloody debacle at Conway Hall confirmed just how difficult it might be for Poison Girls and Crass to carve out an independent cultural space, in the context of London especially.

But vindication for the Persons Unknown campaign finally came on 19 December 1979 when the defendants were acquitted on all charges. Jurors had been already antagonised when press reports revealed that the prosecution in the case had carried out unauthorised and illegal "vetting" of the jury pool, aiming to exclude anyone potentially sympathetic to the accused. Despite the efforts to pack the jury, the case the State had presented had been woefully unconvincing—with the "evidence" little more than a jumbled fiction of coincidence and conjecture. Rejecting the direction of the trial judge to convict, the jury returned not guilty verdicts.

The authorities were livid at the jurors' insolence. *Freedom* newspaper reported that, after the verdict was announced, the twelve men and women were "held back" in the courtroom and "harangued by the judge, who said that the evidence 'would not have confused a child.'" This outrageous coda to the trial, the act of a reactionary, right-wing adjudicator—abusing the power of the bench for one last time in his overlong career—came too late either to salvage the prosecution case or his reputation. The vindicated defendants walked free from the court, to cheers from a ragtag crowd of their supporters waiting outside. The humiliated judge announced his retirement the following day. But, by then, the authorities' attempt to intimidate had failed. Stuart Christie made an impassioned anti-statist case at the press conference that followed the acquittal of all defendants.

Jubilation at victory in the courts was tempered by the fact that the accused had endured months of incarceration before being bailed, by the knowledge that the defence campaign had pulled vital resources away from other struggles, and by the recognition that the police had used the case to amass huge quantities of intel on the activities and associations of one of the key networks of London's anarchists.

Mindful of these costs, defendants Bennett and Mills were determined that the political momentum of the Persons Unknown campaign should not be allowed to evaporate. In collaboration with other anarchists and militant activists that they had become involved with, they began to draw up plans for a new anarchist centre that could provide an organisational fulcrum for the movement in the capital.

Poison Girls attacked on stage

MEMBERS of the Epping-based rock band Poison Girls were the victims of a vicious attack by a gang of British Movement supporters on Sunday.

The assault came while the group was performing on stage at a benefit concert in the Theatre Royal, Stratford.

A group "roadie" was taken to Whipps Cross Hospital for treatment for facial bruising, while the band's drummer, Lance d'Boil, suffered minor head injuries when a gang of about 20 stormed the stage.

Earlier in the performance the Fascist skinhead faction had been chanting "Sieg Heil", but it was during an anti-Fascist number called Bremen Song when the real trouble flared.

As the Bell Common band's 42-year-old singer, Vi Subversa, uttered the line "remember the holocaust", there was a volley of beer cans, which was closely followed by assorted pieces of sound equipment being thrown around.

Both the roadie and drummer were beaten up before the attackers fled the theatre.

Playing in the support band, Rubella Ballet, were Vi's teenage son Pete Fender and 12-year-old daughter Gema Rare.

Their act was also continually interrupted by the Fascist faction, and eventually skinheads got up on stage to take over the group's instruments.

This is not the first time that members of the Poison Girls band have met up with the British Movement. They have previously come across them while supported by another local group — North Weald's Crass.

"It's the first time I've been in a situation where the band has been attacked" said guitarist Richard Famous. "Even at Crass gigs it's only been disruptions among the audience."

The benefit aimed to help raise the £¼ million needed for theatre restoration, but instead Sunday's concert cost the theatre £150 in broken seats.

● Last year's Gazette picture of Vi Subversa, then known as Vi Squad (alias Mrs Simpson) and son Pete Fender, otherwise Pete Smelly 1972.

RIOT WRECKS BENEFIT

A benefit concert at the Theatre Royal in Stratford ended in a riot on Sunday night when Epping band Poison Girls were attacked during their performance by a gang of British Movement hooligans.

A group roadie called Steve was taken to Whipps Cross Hospital in Leytonstone with facial bruising and Poison Girls drummer Lance d'Boil suffered head injuries, after a 20 - strong fascist skinhead faction in the audience stormed the stage during the bands anti-fascist number, 'Bremen Song'.

It was an evening in which politics came in from the street to be played out in a theatre, with disastrous consequences. Rather than raising money towards the theatre's £¼ - million restoration bill, it added to it when nine seats were smashed by the rioters.

It was a night in which the audience determined the plot of the play. First came the pantomime - the warm-up for the closing tragedy. It included the terrace-type chanting of 'sieg heil', heavy booted impressions of Jerry Lee Lewis on the theatre's new piano, seat ripping and intimidation of the support band 'Rubella Ballet'.

Three of the hooligans mounted the stage and got in the support bands way, and with the band members only being in their mid-teens they were in no position to argue. It almost appeared as if it was just part of the show.

As the first part of the evening finished and Poison Girls set approached, things got more tense and more serious. The young punks who'd come along sensed the tension too - because many of them made a b-line for the back exits.

Poison Girls, after much discussion, braved the situation and took to the stage. They performed 'Old Tarts Song', 'Under The Doctors', 'Political Love' and then 'Reality Attack'. And a reality attack is exactly what the band faced in the next number 'Bremen song'.

Like actors, the mob awaited its cue in the song, and as 42 - year old singer Vi Subversa uttered the line "Remember The Holocaust" - the tension reached flashpoint.

First there was a volley of beer cans and this was closely followed by flying lights and monitors. One missile knocked Vi to the stage floor, while Lance got pushed right into the middle of the mob. Both he and roadie Steve were beaten-up and the attackers made a swift exit before the police arrived.

Although there has been similar political violence at gigs by Crass another West Essex band, where Poison Girls have supported - this is the first time that the band has commanded any violence at its own gigs.

"It's the first time I've been in a situation where the band has been attacked," said Poison Girls guitarist Richard Famous, "even at Crass gigs it's been only disruption in the audience.

"I'm only sorry that the confrontation happened on that night. In no way was that the kind of thing we wanted to bring to the Theatre Royal. It was fairly obvious what would happen. We decided to go through with it rather than back off. It's made us all really, really wary. The implications of what happened last night are huge".

GIG VIOLENCE: EDITORIAL COMMENT

SUNDAY'S VIOLENCE AT THE THEATRE ROYAL HIGHLIGHTED WHAT IS BECOMING A GROWING PROBLEM AT ROCK GIGS, AND WE HOPE ALL LMA READERS JOIN US IN CONDEMNING THESE SENSELESS ACTIONS WHICH ARE GIVING MUSIC A BAD NAME.

THE EAST END IS IN A WORSE SITUATION THAN MOST, BECAUSE THE LACK OF ROCK VENUES MEANS IT'S GOT THE MOST TO LOSE.

TWO OF THE AREA'S NEWEST VENUES ARE IN JEOPARDY. AFTER SUNDAY'S FIASCO THE THEATRE ROYAL CERTAINLY HAD TO THINK TWICE ABOUT FURTHER CONCERTS, BUT IT WAS CLEAR THAT BAD ORGANISATION, LACK OF SECURITY AND KNOWLEDGE OF THE TYPE OF BAND THEY WERE PUTTING ON WERE CONTRIBUTING FACTORS TO SUNDAY'S DISASTER.

THE THEATRE HAS ALREADY ACCEPTED AN OFFER BY LMA TO PROMOTE A 'BENEFIT FOR THE BENEFIT' CONCERT TO RECOUP THE MONEY LOST ON DAMAGES TO SEATS. WATCH OUT FOR DETAILS IN A LATER EDITION.

ANOTHER NEW VENUE HIT BY VIOLENCE IS THE NEW WINDMILL HALL IN UPMINSTER. AFTER CLASHES BETWEEN MODS AND ROCKERS THE PROMOTERS ARE NOW HAVING TO BE VERY CAREFUL ABOUT THE TYPE OF BAND THEY BOOK.

ONE LOCAL BAND FALSE ALARM HAVE DISCOVERED THROUGH EXPERIENCE THAT MUSIC AND POLITICS DON'T MIX. SINCE DROPPING THE POLITICAL SONGS FROM THEIR SET, THE HOOLIGAN ELEMENT OF THE AUDIENCE HAS STOPPED TURNING UP TO THEIR GIGS.

IT BOILS DOWN TO THE AGE-OLD PROBLEM OF THE MINORITY SPOILING THE ENJOYMENT OF THE MAJORITY. WOULDN'T IT BE EASIER IF AN INDIVIDUAL DOESN'T AGREE WITH THE SENTIMENTS OR POLITICS WITHIN A CLEAR SONG, NOT TO BOTHER TO SEE THE BAND AT ALL.

P.A. HIRE
01-521-6495

SOUNDS

SOUNDS. 3.11.79.

Bitter Poison

...to as a tribute to Fritz.

POISON GIRLS were the latest victims of British Movement thug violence when they played a benefit for the Theatre Royal, Stratford in London on Sunday.

From the start of the gig a group of about 20 fascists were chanting "Sieg Heil", then when Poison Girls reached a line in 'Bremen Song' which goes 'Remember the holocaust', they charged forward as if on cue. Singer Vi Subversa was felled by a beer can, while drummer Lance D'Boyle was hit over the head with a 'blunt instrument' and one of their roadies was knocked down and kicked. The theatre, which had been hoping to raise funds for repairs, was instead presented with a £150 bill for damage. Now the newspaper, the London Musicians Adviser, is hoping to work with the theatre management to arrange a benefit to pay for the, last benefit.

Newham Recorder

SKINHEADS IN WILD BATTLE

Punk concert ends in chaos as 'Nazi' bovver gang swoop

By SHEKHAR BHATIA

A PUNK concert ended in mayhem at Stratford's Theatre Royal on Sunday night when a skinhead gang chanting 'Nazi' slogans attacked the group on stage.

Two members of the Poison Girls band were treated in hospital for head injuries and their lead singer, 42-year-old Vi Sub-Versa, a mother of two, was knocked down and kicked.

The bovver gang leaped onto the stage as the Poison Girls reached into their self-penned 'Bremen Song'.

One eyewitness said: "They were shouting down British Movement. They were kicking hell out of the band's drummer, Lance D'Boil.

Press clippings from Poison Girls' scrapbook. Clockwise from top left: *Gazette*, 2 November 1979; *LMA*, 3 November 1979; *Newham Recorder*, 1 November 1979; and *Sounds*, 3 November 1979. Courtesy of Pete Fender and Gemma Sansom.

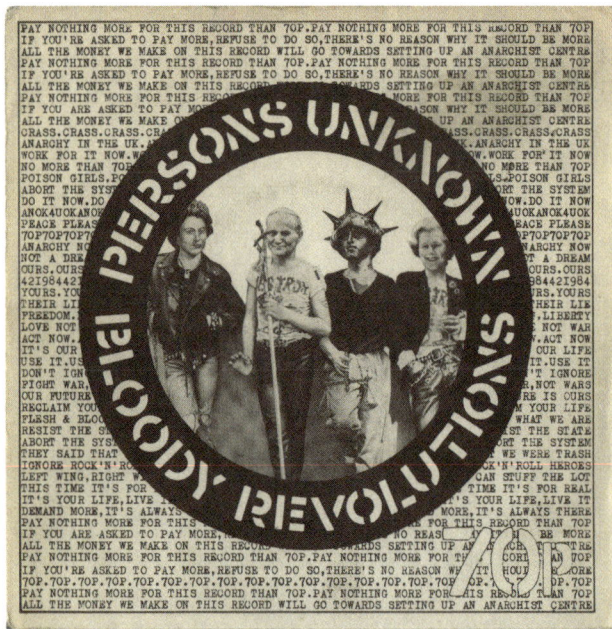

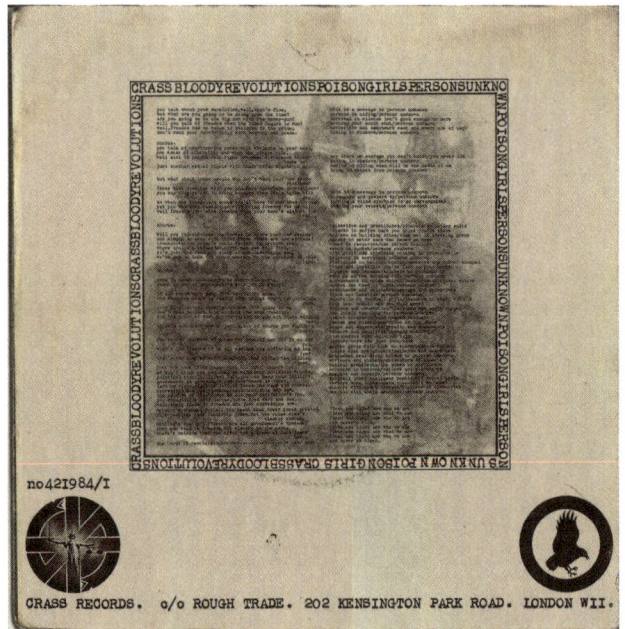

Bloody Revolutions/Persons Unknown, Crass Records, 1980.

Using their connections with the activists of *Xtra*, the London Autonomists, the London Workers Group and others, Bennett and Mills rallied a group of libertarian activists who began to consider how such a centre could be selected, equipped and funded. Not everyone was convinced the idea was a good one, but the ad hoc group of enthusiasts to emerge from the discussions began to look for premises. Early on in their deliberations, the organisers agreed that the new centre should be opened somewhere that could be leased or rented.

At the end of the 1970s, squatted buildings could be found scattered throughout London, providing rent-free accommodation or supporting different political endeavours involving punks, hippies, and others living on the fringes. But such locations were always vulnerable to court-sanctioned—or illegally enforced—eviction. The organisers knew that a provocative new anarchist centre needed to sidestep such a threat by signing a binding contract with a landlord. But that kind of stability needed to be paid for.

Bennett approached Crass and Poison Girls for support, and it was soon agreed that a split benefit single would be recorded and released that might generate sufficient funds to pump-prime the proposed centre. "We were asked to make a recording as a fundraiser," d'Boyle explained. That song became 'Persons Unknown.'" taking its initial lyrical inspiration from the experiences of "political activists facing accusations of conspiracy," d'Boyle confirmed. Equally convinced by Bennett's enthusiasm, Crass also agreed that Bennett would write an extended essay for the single's foldout sleeve: a mini-manifesto

that could put forward a persuasive case for the capital's new anarchist hub. Crass's "Bloody Revolutions" and Poison Girls' "Persons Unknown" would be written and arranged in the closing months of 1979, with recording scheduled for early the following year.

The *Bloody Revolutions/Persons Unknown* single marked a new high point in the creative cooperation between the two bands, and was widely acclaimed as such. *Trees and Flowers* zine was a far from atypical voice in the punk scene in declaring the single "the best thing these two groups have ever committed to vinyl."

Both tracks were recorded at Southern Studios during a two day session in February 1980. Poison Girls recorded "Persons Unknown" on 9 February, while Crass completed "Bloody Revolutions" the following day.

"Persons Unknown" emerged as an extraordinary treatise on the nature of identity and alienation, built around a rollcall of social roles and personas. The song's rolling, cycling, repetitive riff is the irresistible musical background for a series of acutely observed snapshots of human relationships and experiences, in different cultural, social, and historical contexts. It was an inspired extension, development and rethinking of the idea of '*Persons Unknown*,' a concept that had already been explored by supporters of the defendants because it was such an incendiary, provocative and enticing idea.

"As I recall, the writing process was very fast and easy," Famous recalls. "We had a meeting with Crass, decided that we would have to write a new song, and agreed that 'Persons Unknown' was a great title. It's always a bonus when the title comes first!" The band soon

Metropolitan Wharf, part of the complex that housed the Wapping Autonomy Centre, London, 2016. Photo: Dietmar Rabich, CC BY-SA.

recognised that a standard 4/4 punk thrash would not be fit for purpose. "In rehearsal, we settled on a 3/4 time signature with an ascending riff that never resolved itself—so musically it could, and did, just run and run. It's a circle—E, G, A, Bb—that tricks you that it's going somewhere. Even in the coda, it never gets to a satisfactory endpoint."

The song intones its cumulative recognition that these social constructs are artificial and divisive, ultimately separating us from recognizing what we share in common and preventing us from seeing ourselves in the other.

> This is a message to Persons Unknown
> Strangers and passers–by, Persons Unknown
> Turning a blind eye, hope to go unrecognised
> Keeping your secrets, Persons Unknown
> Housewives and prostitutes, plumbers in
>   boiler suits
> Truants in coffee bars, who think you're alone
> Big men on building sites, sick men in
>   dressing gowns
> Agents in motor cars who never go home
> Women in factories, one parent families
> Women in purdah, Persons Unknown
> Wild girls and criminals, rotting in prison cells
> Patients in corridors, Persons Unknown

"Lyrically, the song is the perfect representation of the connection between the personal and the political," Famous continues. "Those 'Persons Unknown' literally describe 'each and every one of us.'" Once the band settled on the idea of a catalogue of identities, "we let loose and all pitched in with suggestions," he explains. "It was left to Vi to sort and compile them, but everything took shape quickly. A lesser writer would have baulked at the idea of such an extensive list—Vi just wanted more. The idea was to make the track build momentum, before it finally breaks into the cathartic release of 'flesh and blood is who we are, flesh and blood is what we are.'" he says. "It worked pretty well too! We had just one rehearsal with Penny Rimbaud, who urged us on, and we went into the studio and just belted it out. It was all very quick, and a lot of fun."

The single was released on Crass Records on 17 May 1980 and sold an impressive twenty thousand copies in the first week. Controversy helped to publicise *Persons Unknown* as the record became the latest vinyl release on the label to be met with both legal threats and commercial pushback. Poison Girls were able to lay hands on an internal memo from the nervous managing director of the HMV record store chain James Tyrell, which posed the question: "does the commercial advantage of selling Crass records outweigh the risk of prosecution?" In other words, was the potential profit from vinyl sales worth potential legal exposure because of the record's content? Tyrell concluded not, instructing all store managers that "all copies of their latest single with Poison Girls on Crass Records should be destroyed or returned to Head Office where they will be destroyed." It was the kind of ridiculous reaction "which only helped" promote interest in the single, Poison Girls confirmed.

Roadmenders, Northampton, 1980. Photo by Daryl Hardcastle.

From their earliest days, Poison Girls had championed the fanzine, outsider, and independent press, providing countless interviews to editors of DIY and short-print-run publications. But the band's view of the commercial music press, and of mainstream media in general, was more nuanced than that adopted by Crass. While Crass allowed multiple exceptions to their general refusal to cooperate with the main music press weeklies *Sounds*, *NME,* or *Melody Maker*, Poison Girls adopted an approach of suspicious, critical engagement. As many critics of Crass's abstention had suggested, refusing to connect with the music press meant ignoring a platform that allowed artists to reach an audience of multiple tens of thousands of readers. The question was whether doing so meant accepting so many accommodations and compromises that the message was lost. Poison Girls were determined to try to navigate the minefield of contradictions in the hope of better disseminating their ideas. By the end of 1979, Poison Girls had secured what they acknowledged was the band's "first serious attention from the music press," including an article in *Sounds* by Phil Sutcliffe headlined "Old People Can Be Rebels Too."

"Sutcliffe's review of *Hex* had been one of the first to appear in any music weekly," Famous recalls. "In it, he said that the men in the band 'must be masochists.'" Worse, Sutcliffe—by his own admission—accused the band of embracing "extremism which would tend to drive men and women apart rather than heal the undeniable wounds inflicted over generations." Famous contacted Sutcliffe "to put him straight" asking

the pointed question: "Why is male anger accepted as the universal scream of discontent whilst female anger is just neurosis?"

In response, Sutcliffe "came to see a gig of ours, and to interview us, and afterwards wrote what was a very good piece," says Famous. "We became good friends after that. Maybe he was worried about the 'Mauled Poorly' treatment!"

What's evident from Sutcliffe's *Sounds* feature is how unusual a band Poison Girls were for a jobbing rock journalist to make sense of. His description of the group's appearance on stage hints at their unsettling deviation from the rock-pop norm:

Lance D' Boyle behind the drumkit with a face more lined and weathered than normally accompanies a skinhead haircut, Bernhardt Rebours tall with glasses and a diffident, academic mien on bass, Richard Famous even taller, blond and very Billy Idolish on guitar, and most of all—because she's so surprising I suppose—you see Vi Subversa, stout, mass of black hair, strumming a guitar and singing. Unless you're a rare deviant from the statistical norm one of the first three thoughts that enter your head is: "Why, she must be at least X years old."

Sutcliffe's assessment of Poison Girls, as a curiosity, a provocation and an intriguing challenge to expectation, set a standard which many subsequent music press writers would choose to follow.

Badge template and badges produced by Poison Girls in conjunction with the *Persons Unknown* split single.

The band were eager to raise awareness of the single by more direct methods too. "When *Persons Unknown* originally came out, we had fifty different badge designs made up," Famous recalls, each with a separate snippet of Subversa's mesmerising lyric ("Terrorists and saboteurs, each and every one of us" / "Judges with prejudice, dissidents and anarchists" / "Strikers and pickets, collectors of tickets"). Able to fit all fifty such designs onto a single printed sheet, a run of twenty sheets allowed the band to produce a thousand *Persons Unknown* badges. "These were all given away free at our gigs," says Famous. "If I remember right, they lasted just two nights!"

Although the "pay no more than" cover price of 70p inevitably limited the amount of money that the single would generate, the release met the objective of becoming the principal kick-off fundraiser for the Centre.

By October, the organisers were able to confirm to *Black Flag* that they had £4,500 at their disposal—"easily making us the wealthiest anarchist group in the country," they suggested, with a mixture of surprise, self-consciousness, and pride.

After shortlisting several potential properties, an empty warehouse in the Wapping area of London emerged as the front-runner. The premises required some significant internal remedial work to make it habitable and fit for purpose. Much of that hands-on, hard graft was provided by Bennett and Mills, who were keen to see a long-term political return on their investment of time and effort.

The London Autonomy Centre opened in August 1981, and played host to many memorable Sunday night gigs by anarchist bands and other deviant artists (including a single appearance by Crass, who played under the one-off moniker "Shaved Women"). The organisers also arranged screenings of radical documentaries, political speakers and discussion groups, and the first-ever London Anarchist Bookfair. These initiatives offered the strongest echoes of the Malatesta Club that Subversa had supported back in the 1950s.

But energy, attendance, and money all quickly evaporated as the weeks passed. When the funds ran out, the Centre closed in March 1982, amidst a great deal of frustration, recrimination and finger-pointing. A weekly schedule of anarcho-punk, goth-punk, and dark-punk was soon up and running at the Centro Iberico, by then operating in a squatted former school on Harrow Road in Notting Hill—including a memorable performance by Poison Girls. But the sharper political focus that the Autonomy Centre had pushed for was blunted in the relocation. And the ambitious political aspirations which had been the catalyst for the *Bloody Revolutions/Persons Unknown* single ended in deflation and disappointment.

"We didn't actually have anything to do with the running of it," Famous explained later. "What happened was that it lasted for about six months, and then it ran into difficulties . . . because the old-style anarchists, or the 'political' anarchists as they like to think of themselves, couldn't come to terms with the anarcho-punks, who were a new phenomenon at the time. . . . It was before the punks actually became accepted as some kind of political force, or had some political identity. . . . In London, there isn't a lot of cohesion at all within the anarchist movement in general, and I think there'll always be a conflict between the mainstream, or the old guard, and the new energy."

Although it was not the band's intention at the time, for several years after its release "Persons Unknown" became Poison Girls' public signature—the single track for which they were "best known." Audiences expected it to feature as a triumphant moment in their set whenever the band played live. Poison Girls would eventually be able to step out from the song's shadow and, in later years, retire the song from the band's live repertoire. Yet the idea of unveiling 'your true self,' against the confines of social convention and expectation, beyond the confines of imposed gender roles, and outside the frameworks of the nuclear family and 'wage slavery,' was one which continued to intrigue Poison Girls for the remainder of the band's life.

At the 1979 year's festival at the Stones, Poison Girls played in the early hours without incident—competing, Famous remembers, against "fifty-six other bands all of whom were soporific in excess" and who played "on and on and on" endlessly. "The French band before us did an encore of one song that was longer than our whole set—which I think came in at just over half-an-hour at punk warp speed," he recalls. The whole scene felt "very decrepit," he recalls, "stale hippies, bikers and only a few punks." A short distance away, the Stonehenge monument "was all barbed wire and tourists—horrible." Poison Girls took the stage at 2am "amidst the mist and damp, and got the buggers on their feet for the first time all night," Rebours says. "Then Crass hammered home the message. I seem to remember the dawn chorus as we finished!" Famous kept a record of Poison Girls' set:

> Old Tart
> Ideologically Unsound
> Crisis
> Persons Unknown
> Piano Lessons
> Political Love
> Jump Mama Jump
> Under the Doctor
> Reality attack
> Bremen

Poison Girls, Crass, and Flux of Pink Indians returned to the site of the Stonehenge Free Festival in June 1980—their repeat invitation seeming evidence

Destroy all 45s

WHOSE MASTER'S VOICE?: **Vi Subversa** of Epping anarcho-rockers **Poison Girls** rang us to report that she had in her possession a copy of a memo from the managing director of HMV record shops, **James Tyrell**, to all branches ordering his staff to destroy all copies of the **Girls/Crass** single, 'Persons Unknown'/'Bloody Revolutions' which is currently No 1 in the alternative chart and selling so strongly it's at 66 in the BMRB.

She read an extract from the memo as follows: 'The question is, does the commercial advantage of selling Crass records outweigh the risk of prosecution? I am not prepared to have HMV dragged through the courts and I regret to inform you that all copies of their latest single with Poison Girls on Crass Records should be destroyed or returned to head office where they will be destroyed.'

It went on to say that other Crass records should not be on display in HMV shops. Exactly why Tyrell fears prosecution and for what crime are not clear to Ms Subversa, but she mentioned the reports from Birmingham a couple of weeks ago that an independent shop there had warned about the laws on blasphemy in connection with another Crass release. On another occasion, copies of their single 'Asylum' had been seized for examination in the light (or dark) of the blasphemy laws but the police had concluded they had no case.

As we went to press no comment was available from HMV as the relevant person was "in a meeting." We hope to report next week.

Sounds . June 7th 1980.

News Editor: Derek Johnson

BIKERS RIOT AT STONEHENGE

A NIGHT of violence all but wrecked the weekend's Stonehenge Festival. The trouble erupted late on Saturday night when a group of middle-aged bikers went on the rampage, attacking every punk they could lay hands on, and effectively preventing Crass and Poison Girls from playing their sets.

The evening began peaceably with music from Nik Turner's Inner City Unit, The Mob and The Snipers, but when punk band The Epileptics took the stage they were greeted with a hail of flour-bombs, cans and bottles. Their lead singer was knocked to the ground by a bottle.

The bikers then set fire to The Epileptics' banner, attacked members of Crass and Poison Girls, damaged the generator and took over the stage. Crass and Poison Girls decided not to play "to avoid a blood bath", and spent the rest of the night trying to break up fights and ferrying their punk fans to the safety of the nearest railway station.

Crass drummer Penny Rimbaud said it was "a four-hour nightmare", with punks being hunted down by bikers in "the most savage attacks I've ever seen."

Gurts DeFreyne, from Inner City Unit, described the scenes as "horrible — the bikers were pulling punks out of their sleeping bags to beat them up; it was really disgusting."

At least two people complained to the police but one of them, John Loder, a sound-man at the festival, claimed that the police were "totally uninterested" and refused to take any action. At Salisbury Police Station, a Superintendent Maddock told *NME* he had no knowledge of the violence or the complaints. He did say that 67 arrests had been made, mostly for drug offences or stealing wood, and added that in the police view "the entire festival was illegal" as it was held on squatted land.

Penny Rimbaud, who was one of the people who started the Stonehenge Festival in the early '70s, was particularly bitter at the bikers' attitude. "They said they didn't want punks taking over *their* festival, they only wanted to hear 'real' music. This is supposedly an *open* festival, of peace and freedom. After this, I don't think Crass will play there again, we won't expose our fans to these experiences and these ri...

Gurts DeFr...

...GHT ...have re-vamped ...dates in their cu...

Press clippings from *Sounds,* 7 June 1980; *New Musical Express,* 28 June 1980. Courtesy of Pete Fender and Gemma Sansom.

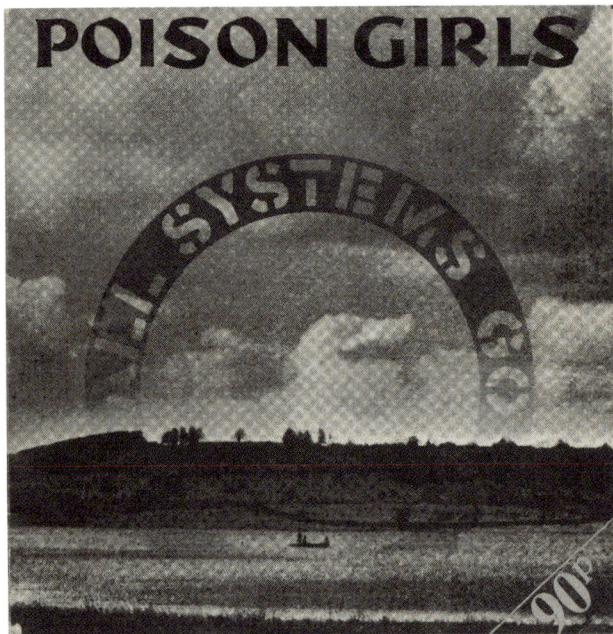

All Systems Go, Crass Records, 1980. Artwork by Bernhardt Rebours.

of a growing shared affinity between peace punks and hippies. "The first year that we went, was the first time when there were any punks there," says Famous. "It was mainly hippies and just a few punks. The second time, there were a lot more punks. The hippies had sort of gone, but the bikers were still there." Crass and Poison Girls had begun a short tour of the south of the UK with a gig in Swansea on 12 June, followed by shows at Barry, Southampton, Stroud, Bournemouth (cancelled), Bristol, Totnes, and Plymouth before making their way to the Stones. On their arrival, the tour's PA system, provided by Paul Tandy, was unloaded and wired up to provide the stage rig for the festival.

"We had been to Stonehenge once before with Crass, and this time more punk bands were to play," d'Boyle remembered. "Our mistake was not to realise that not all the 'clients' at Stonehenge would be in favour" of the presence of punks," Famous says. Trouble erupted when Flux of Pink Indians took to the stage. As soon as they began, members of the crowd began to hurl rocks and other projectiles directly at them. The barrage continued until Flux had to abandon their set. "The culprits seemed to be a gang of bikers who didn't want punk, and wanted to have an acid rock band instead," d'Boyle remembered. The attackers seized control of the stage, and d'Boyle was told "to remove my drum kit by what appeared to be the leader." Musicians amongst the interlopers then "played till they passed out," Famous says. Tandy was unable to retrieve his rig until the stage cleared. "I never saw Paul strip and pack the PA and get the hell out quicker," he adds. "I got whacked, but by all accounts a lot of punky kids got a lot worse."

The seizure of the stage was the trigger for an all-out assault on punks at the festival, which worsened as darkness fell. "Throughout the night people were randomly attacked. Screams and shouting rang out and our tour van became a haven—and, I understand, so did Crass.'" d'Boyle said. Members of the band ventured out on site to try to "assess the situation," but "it was so scary and dark it was impossible."

This was far from being an isolated incident for Poison Girls. The threat—and the actuality—of violence was a recurring concern. At a gig at the Theatre Royal in Stratford on 28 October 1979 "the band was attacked on stage," Famous recalls. "A sort of *Clockwork Orange* outfit arrived," d'Boyle explained later. "Then a band of their mates mounted the stage . . . and proceeded to sing 'Tomorrow Belongs to Me.' The sound guy turned them off." Refusing to be intimidated, Poison Girls went ahead and played their set. When they reached 'Bremen Song,' these right-wing thugs launched their attack. "I was pushed off the stage, and our roadie was beaten to the ground and had his ribs broken," d'Boyle recalled. "We were all over the local papers the next day." Word filtered out that Poison Girls gigs could be a locus for violence. "The incident I'm sure affected people's willingness to ask us to play," he concluded.

Even as threats of violence continued to stalk the band, Poison Girls gave short shrift to those amongst their supposed "allies" who buckled in the face of such intimidation. In January 1980, the band had been booked to play a benefit for the National Abortion Campaign (NAC) at the London School of Economics, before the organisers raised concerns about Poison Girls' "reputation" as a

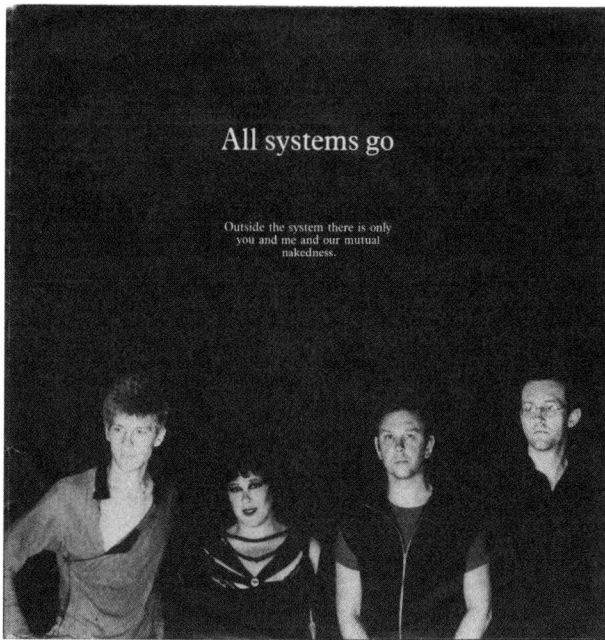
All systems go

Outside the system there is only you and me and our mutual nakedness.

"dangerous" band, likely to attract "trouble." The band rejected out-of-hand the proposal that they be omitted from all publicity and play the gig unannounced, treating it with the contempt it deserved. "Go ahead kiddies. Set up safe good time bops in the name of freedom of our bodies," Poison Girls charged. "When you really want us to play—when you really understand why we have to play—you can renegotiate an event with us!" The band's public statement on the controversy pulled few punches. "What you are is an empty posture mouthing beliefs you will not support when it comes to the crunch," it continued. "The odd bottle or boot sends you running for cover. You are ready to betray anyone who threatens this comfortable position."

Attempts to intimidate the band extended beyond gigs, and surfaced closer to home. "We were attacked at our house by a group of skinheads who visited us one night," says Famous, "and we got regular threatening phone calls promising to burn our house down—and worse." In the face of such harassment, the band remained resilient, but such things inevitably took their cumulative psychological toll. "It was some of the darkest times, at some cost to our well-being and that of the children," d'Boyle acknowledged. "Something we hadn't bargained for."

The last release by Poison Girls on Crass Records was the *All Systems Go* single which featured the potent and powerful "Dirty Work," backed by the sublime and sophisticated "Promenade Immortelle." If the simmering rage and driving tempo of the polemic of "Dirty Work" brought to the fore the band's most abrasive and committed anarchist punk impulses,

"Promenade Immortelle" saw the band venturing away from that territory into a softer, more reflective musical and lyrical style. The result was a song that producer Penny Rimbaud said, "showcased Poison Girls at their blossoming best. If ever the tender side of Vi's passion found true expression, it was on this track." Rimbaud considers the work evolved into "one of my finest production jobs" for any artist. Both tracks were recorded on 13–14 September 1980 at Southern Studios, London.

With evident pride, Subversa described "Promenade Immortelle" as "a very beautiful, lyrical kind of song." She told *The Leveller* magazine that some young fans of the band had said to her "'My Mum liked it.'" noting that "Mum only heard it because that young person took it home." While that generational dynamic was clearly "interesting but peculiar," the single—to Subversa's evident irritation, "actually got ignored because we're defined in a lot of the lists as hard-core punk."

If the A-side affirmed the band's anarcho-punk affinities, the flipside spoke to their growing musical and cultural restlessness. "It wasn't reviewed by anyone and it never got played on the radio," a frustrated Richard Famous explained in a fanzine interview. "The project we undertook was to make a record that was as classy as that one was. I think it worked really well. It took a lot of time to record—a lot of energy and effort."

A tussle with Crass over the design of the single's front cover was another indication of Poison Girls' growing restlessness. "We always had this feeling of being 'branded' by them in everything. You know, being presented as part of the Crass 'imprint.'" d'Boyle recalled later. For *All Systems Go*, Poison Girls wanted an image which stretched the norms of the Crass Records template. The results was a sleeve in which the lower-half of the ubiquitous stencilled circle disappears behind the horizon of a vast, empty rural vista, while the band's name breaks out of the circle entirely to appear horizontally at the top. "That was the compromise we reached," d'Boyle explained. "We fought against having the usual logo."

It was clear that this ambitious and highly motivated group of subversive musicians were beginning to question whether their current approach was the right one. As Poison Girls considered the future, that extraordinary seven-inch release would sign-off the close vinyl collaboration between the two bands in impressive style.

persons unknown/persons unknown/persons unknown/persons unknown/persons
unknown/persons unknown/persons unknown/persons unknown/ persons unknown
persons unknown/persons unknown/persons unknown/persons unknown/persons
unknown/persons unknown/persons unknown/persons unknown/persons unknown

THIS IS A MESSAGE TO PERSONS UNKNOWN

PERSONS IN HIDING/ PERSONS UNKNOWN

SURVIVAL IN SILENCE ISNT GOOD ENOUGH NO MORE

HIDING IN SHADOWS/ PERSONS UNKNOWN.....

KEEPING YOUR MOUTH SHUT/ TURNING A BLIND EYE

DYING IN SECRET/ PERSONS UNKNOWN

TERRORISTS AND SABOTEURS EACH AND EVERY ONE OF US

HIDING IN SHADOWS/ PERSONS UNKNOWN.....

HEY THERE MR AVERAGE/ YOU DONT EXIST/ YOU NEVER DID

HIDING IN SECRET/ HEAD IN THE SAND

HABITS OF HIDING SOON WILL BE THE DEATH OF US

DYING IN SECRET FROM POISONS UNKNOWN.....

THIS IS A MESSAGE TO PERSONS UNKNOWN

TAPPING YOUR CIRCUITS/ PERSONS UNKNOWN

SURVIVAL IN SILENCE ISNT GOOD ENOUGH NO MORE

KEEPING YOUR MOUTH SHUT/ HEAD IN THE SAND

TURNING YOUR BLIND EYE SOON WILL BE THE DEATH OF US

DYING IN SECRET FROM POISONS UNKNOWN.....

flesh and blood are who we are/ flesh and blood are what we are/ FLESH AND
BLOOD ARE WHO WE ARE/ OUR COVER'S BLOWN/ flesh and blood are who you are/
flesh and blood are what you are/ FLESH AND BLOOD ARE WHO YOU ARE/ YOUR
COVER'S BLOWN/ flesh and blood are who we are/ flesh and blood are what we
are/ FLESH AND BLOOD ARE WHO WE ARE/ OUR COVER'S BLOWN/ flesh and blood

POISON GIRLS 1979

WE HAVE TO TAKE RESPONSIBILITY FOR :
WE HAVE TO TAKE RESPONSIBILITY FOR :

OUR OWN VENUES
    OUR OWN VENUES
            our own TIMES
            our own TIMES
                        OUR OWN PLACES
                        OUR OWN PLACES
            OUR own WORDS
            OUR own WORDS
            our own RELATIONSHIPS
            our own RELATIONSHIPS
        OUR OWN DEFENCE
        OUR OWN DEFENCE
                our OWN FEELINGS
                our OWN FEELINGS
                        our own MUSIC
                        our own MUSIC
            OUR own ORGASMS
            OUR own ORGASMS
        OUR OWN WORK
        OUR OWN WORK
                our own EVENTS
                our own EVENTS
                        our own PUBLICITY
                        our own PUBLICITY
        OUR OWN IMAGES
        OUR OWN IMAGES
                OURownCARING
                OURownCARING
                    OUR OWN LIVES
                    OUR OWN LIVES
                OUR OWN BODIES
                OUR OWN BODIES
            OUR OWN DEATHS
            OUR OWN DEATHS
                    our ownFEEDING
                    our ownFEEDING
                OUR own EXPECTATIONS
                OUR own EXPECTATIONS
                our OWN DISAPPOINTMENTS
                our OWN DISAPPOINTMENTS
                OUR OWN LEARNING
                OUR OWN LEARNING
                OUR OWN HOPE..........NO MORE
                OUR OWN HOPE..........

XNTRIX RECORDS·BURLEIGH HOUSE·BELL COMMON·EPPING·ESSEX·TEL·EPPING 72538·BUSINESS REGISTRATION 233/000

Jan.17 1980

ABOUT TWO WEEKS AGO WE WERE ASKED TO HEADLINE AT A NAC BENEFIT AT LSE BY A
WOMAN WHO WAS REALLY ENTHUSIASTIC ABOUT OUR PLAYING AND WHO SAID SHE WAS
BACKED BY A GROUP OF WOMEN WHO 'ALL REALLY LIKED POISON GIRLS AND FEEL WE
THAT POISON GIRLS ARE JUST THE RIGHT BAND TO PLAY AT A NAC BENEFIT'.
.A FEW DAYS AGO WERE PHONED BY THIS WOMAN WHO SAID SHE WAS REALLY SORRY BUT
POISON GIRLS HAD BEEN VETOED AT A MEETING OF STEWARDS WHO DID NOT WANT US TO
PLAY BECAUSE WE WERE TOO 'DANGEROUS' THROUGH OUR 'REPUTATION' AND THAT THEY
DID NOT WANT FUTURE GIGS AT LSE TO BE BANNED BY THE AUTHORITIES IF THERE WAS
ANY 'TROUBLE'.
SHE AND OTHERS FOUGHT FOR THEIR RIGHT TO CHOOSE POISON GIRLS, ANDEVENTUALLY
IT WAS AGREED THAT WE COULD PLAY PROVIDING OUR NAMES WERE WITHDRAWN FROM ALL
PUBLICITY AND ADVERTISING ABOUT THE EVENT, AND THAT WE WOULDN'T SING THE
SONGS THAT THE B.M. DIDN'T LIKE ! A 'SAFER' BAND WOULD HEADLINE.
POISON GIRLS COULD NOT ACCEPT THESE CONDITIONS AND REPLIED AS FOLLOWS :......

DEAR BEAVER COLLECTIVE AND RAS,

YOU PLAINLY DO NOT WANT POISON GIRLS TO PLAY AT THE NAC BENEFIT ON JAN 25th.
AT LSE. YOU SAY OUR 'REPUTATION' MAKES US DANGEROUS. DANGEROUS FOR WHO ?
BECAUSE IT MIGHT THREATEN FUTURE GIGS AT LSE IF ANYTHING 'HAPPENS' BECAUSE OF
OUR REPUTATION. REPUTATION FOR WHAT ? CREATED BY WHO ?
    REPUTATION FOR UPSETTING THE BRITISH MOVEMENT?
    REPUTATION FOR BEING ATTACKED BY A FEW BOOTBOYS ?
    REPUTATION FOR BEING UNDEFENDED AGAINST SUCH ATTACK ?
A REPUTATION CREATED BY THE PRESS AND BY THE LIBERAL 'LEFT' WHO LEAVE US
UNDEFENDED AGAINST SUCH ATTACK BECAUSE WE CAN'T TOE THEIR PARTY LINE EITHER.

GO AHEAD KIDDIES. SET UP SAFE GOOD TIME BOPS IN THE NAME OF FREEDOM OF OUR
BODIES. WHEN YOU REALLY WANT US TO PLAY - WHEN YOU REALLY UNDERSTAND WHY
WE HAVE TO PLAY AND WHAT WE ARE SINGING ABOUT - YOU CAN RENEGOTIATE AN EVENT
WITH US ! BUT WE CANNOT AND WILL NOT PLAY UNLESS WE ARE FULLY SUPPORTED
BY THE PEOPLE WHO ORGANIZE 'RADICAL' EVENTS. MEANWHILE ON WITH YOUR CARNIVAL.
YOUR LEFT LIBERAL HYPOCRISY IS EXPOSED. WHAT YOU ARE IS AN EMPTY POSTURE
MOUTHING BELIEFS YOU WILL NOT SUPPORT WHEN IT COMES TO THE CRUNCH. THE ODD
BOTTLE OR BOOT SENDS YOU RUNNING FOR COVER. YOU ARE READY TO BETRAY ANYONE
WHO THREATENS THIS COMFORTABLE POSITION.

NEITHER THE RIGHT NOR THE LEFT WILL SHUT US UP.
YOU DARE NOT ADMIT OUR PRESENCE.
YOU ATTEMPT TO CENSOR OUR MOST POIGNANT MATERIAL !
WHOSE SIDE ARE YOU ON ?

                    POISON GIRLS

AUTONOMY CENTRE

OFFICIAL SPOKESMAN

01 WAREHOUSE,

METROPOLITAN WHARF,

WAPPING WALL,

LONDON. E1 4LG

TEL: (01) 481 3537

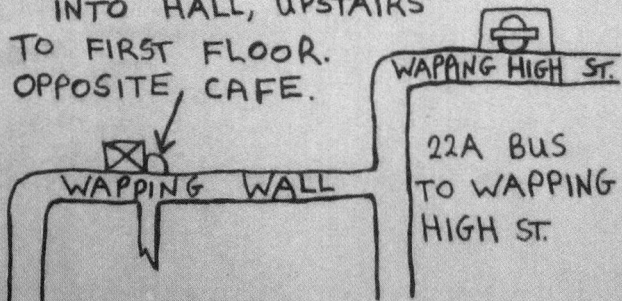

THRU ARCHWAY, TURN LEFT INTO HALL, UPSTAIRS TO FIRST FLOOR. OPPOSITE CAFE.

WAPING HIGH ST.

22A BUS TO WAPPING HIGH ST.

WAPPING WALL

4 MINS FROM WAPPING TUBE

1981. Courtesy of *Kill Your Pet Puppy*.

Words Written in Trust
Thirty-four pages of silk-screened song lyrics in a spray-painted cardboard box
Originally printed by Poison Girls in 1980.
These scans from an authorised reprint by Simon Nolan in 2014.

Poison Girls often handed out silk screened lyrics with small illustrations. Lance d'Boyle released these as a limited edition box set to sell at shows in 1980, called *Words Written in Trust*. This boxed set comprised lyrics for all of the Poison Girls songs up to that point and included songs that never saw official recordings such as "House," "When Love Fell Apart," and "Cry."

POISON GIRLS

..WORDS..

THEIR DISORIENTATION IS ALMOST COMPLETE. WE CAN HARDLY HEAR OURSELVES DO NOT GO QUIETLY INTO THE SILENCE. SONGS WRITTEN IN MOMENTS OF TRUST.

REALITY ATTACK

CLOSED SHOP

PERSONS UNKNOWN

GOOD TIME

PRETTY POLLY

STATEMENT

UNDER THE DOCTOR

YOU CAN TRY HARD WORK/TRY MAKING MONEY
TRY TO MAKE SUCCESS
TRY STRONG DRINK/TAKE TO ACTING FUNNY
OR TRY SOME LIBERATED SEX
TRY OVEREATING/GET A NEW JOB
HAVE ANOTHER BABY
MAYBE YOU'RE AN ARTIST/LEAD A REVOLUTION
TAKE UP YOGA OR JUST GO CRAZY
TRANCENDENTAL MEDITATION/THE NEW DIET
GO TO DISCOS
MAKE SOME CONTACTS/START AGAIN
TRY RELIGION/WRITE A NOVEL/BUY SOME MAKEUP
TAKE UP JOGGING
OR JUST BLAME IT ALL ON THE MEN

WHAT I'M TRYING TO SAY IS YOU GOTTA BE STRONG
NOTHING TAKES THE PAIN AWAY FOR LONG
AND I DON'T WANT TO GO — UNDER THE DOCTOR

WHEN IT GETS REAL HEAVY/YOU START GETTING STROPPY
THEY HAND YOU OUT SOME MIGHTY FINE DOPE
LIBRIUM/MOGODON/VALIUM/THORAZINE
THEY HAVEN'T GOT A PILL CALLED HOPE
AND THOUSANDS OF US WOMEN
HAVE BEEN CUT DOWN BY LOBOTOMY
TERRORIZED BY ECT
BULLIED INTO PASSIVITY/SEDUCED INTO SERVILITY
I'M TALKING ABOUT YOU AND ME

WHAT I'M TRYING TO SAY IS YOU GOTTA BE STRONG
NOTHING TAKES THE PAIN AWAY FOR LONG
I DON'T WANNA GO — UNDER THE DOCTOR

Recorded April 1979
Released on HEX 12" E P
First performed Tunston Town Hall Stokeon Trent
CND Benefit May 1st1979

Rx

ALIENATION

GOT TO LIVE WITH ISOLATION
ALIENATION IS JUST A CUP OF TEA
I HEAR YOU PEOPLE MOAN ABOUT FRUSTRATION
NO CHOICE FOR ME NO CHOICE FOR ME
THERE'S NO TIME TO SEE IT ALL TOGETHER
MAKE AND MEANS WILL SELL US DOWN THE RIVER
JUST WATCH THE DEALERS TRADE ON YOUR FRUSTRATION
LIVING OFF THE GARBAGE IN YOUR MINDS FOREVER
EVER EVER EVER EVER EVER
GOT TO LIVE WITH ISOLATION
ALIENATION IS JUST A CUP OF TEA
I HEAR YOU PEOPLE MOAN ABOUT FRUSTRATION
NO CHOICE FOR ME NO CHOICE FOR ME
THERE'S NO CURE NO SUCH FEELING
WE'RE WAITING FOR A PARTY AND WE CAN'T WAIT FOREVER
WHO'S PURE AND WHO'S NOT DEALING
WE'RE TRYING TO BE ARTY AND WE JUST ACT CLEVER
CLEVER CLEVER CLEVER CLEVER CLEVER

WHAT ARE YOU GOING TO DO ABOUT IT
WHAT ARE WE GOING TO DO ABOUT IT

NO CHOICE
NO CHOICE
NO CHOICE
NO CHOICE
NO CHOICE

First performed at THE VAULT, Brighton Autumn 1977

Released on
CHAPPAQUIDDICK BRIDGE   LP

CRISIS

IS IT NORMAL IS IT NORMAL, IS IT JUST ANOTHER DAY ?
ARE THEY EMPTYING THE MORGUE, HAVE THE KIDS GONE TO PLAY
ARE YOU WAITING WHILE THE RAIN FILLS UP
WATCHING WHILE THEY READ THE PAPERS
READ THE HEADLINES OVER BREAKFAST
DEADLINES DEADLINES HAS THE MILK COME
IS IT TIME TO HAVE A CRISIS
IS IT SAFE TO GO OUT SHOPPING
ORDERS ORDERS PANIC BUYING
WATCH DRIPPING ON THE CARPET
IS IT NORMAL IS IT NORMAL IS IT JUST ANOTHER DAY ?

WAITING WHILE THE RAIN FILLS UP
WATCHING WHILE THEY READ THE PAPERS
HAVE THE KNIVES RUN OUT OF BUDGING
IS IT TIME TO HAVE A CRISIS
SPILL THE BEANS AND TAKE YOUR CLOTHES OFF
CAN YOU STAND IT IF I TOUCH YOU
WATCHING WHILE THEY READ THE PAPERS
WATCH DRIPPING ON THE CARPET
CAN I SAY NO WILL HE HIT ME
PLASTER FALLING FROM THE CEILING
CAN YOU STAND IT IF I TOUCH YOU
BREAK THE ICE BURN THE HOUSE DOWN
IS IT NORMAL IS IT NORMAL IS IT JUST ANOTHER DAY ?

IS IT SAFE TO GO OUT SHOPPING
LEAVE THE KIDS OUTSIDE THE TOILET
LEAVE THE KIDS OUTSIDE THE LOCAL
WATCH DRIPPING ON THE CARPET
STRANGERS TAPPING BY THE WINDOW
IS IT TIME TO HAVE A CRISIS
WATCHING WHILE THEY READ THE PAPERS
WELL THE ORDERS ARE NO QUESTIONS
HIT THE BABY STOP IT SCREAMING
CAN YOU STAND IT IF I TOUCH YOU
BREAK THE ICE BURN THE HOUSE DOWN
IS IT NORMAL IS IT NORMAL IS IT JUST ANOTHER DAY ?

NORMAL NORMAL NORMAL NORMAL NORMAL NORMAL NORMAL

First performed February 1979 Dublin Castle
Recording released on NHX 12" July 1979

THE MOON

I WANTED THE MOON YOU GAVE ME AN ICECREAM
I WANTED TO TALK ABOUT LOVE
YOU WANTED A FREE RIDE I DROVE YOU TO MARLOW
YOU LOOKED LIKE YOU WANTED TO SKI
I OFFERED YOU LINGUINI YOU DREAMED ME WITH SEASALT
I MOURNED IF YOU HAD A BRAND
WE WANTED IT BOTH WAYS I TOLD YOU THAT NO WAY
COULD I TAKE IT ALL BACK WHEN WE PART

I COULD TELL IT WAS SERIOUS YOU FELL ABOUT LAUGHING
I COULDN'T BELIEVE IT WAS TRUE
I GAVE YOU AN APPLE I SATISFIED WHILE YOU DID IT
I SAW YOU WERE WATCHING ME TOO
I NAMED IT EASY YOU SHARED IN THE MORNING
YOU SAID IT'S TOO LATE TO TURN BACK
A CRAZY BEGINNING A LAME WITH NO WINNING
A SINGLE DIPPED SURREALAN TRACK

IT WAS LIKE I WAS DYING YOU PLAYED AT DOCTORS
YOU GAVE ME SWEETS FROM A JAR
TOO COULDN'T STOP PLAYING I COULDN'T STOP RUNNING
TOGETHER WE MADE IT TO MARS
WE KEEP OLD AS THE HILLS WE WERE YOUNG AS THE SUNSHINE
I WANTED TO TALK ABOUT LOVE
YOU WANTED IT BOTH WAYS I TOLD THAT NO WAY
COULD I TAKE IT ALL BACK WHEN WE PART

I WALKED ALONG IN IRELAND
WE WORE OUT OUR DISTANCE
OUT I COULDN'T KEEP YOU OUT OF YOUR ARMS
WHILE WE WERE DREAMING
SOMETHING I WAS WHAT A WHOLE MORNING

Recorded 11 October 1978
First performance Sussex University Dec.9 1977

PIANO LESSONS

THEY ARE MARCHING PAST THE WINDOW
THEY ARE MARCHING DOWN YOUR STREET
THEY HAVE BOUGHT THAT EXPENSIVE CAR
AND YOUR PRESSURE FULL OF MEAT
AND HOW YOU CAME REST WITHOUT THE GRAND DOG AT YOUR FEET

THEY ARE DRILLING IN THE PLAYGROUND
THEY ARE TRAINING ON THE GREEN
THERE'S A MILLION OF THEM OUT THERE
AND THEIR GUNS ARE MADE OF STEEL
BOS DON'T KNOW WHEN BUT THEY KNOW YOU AND THEIR HANDBAG
ARE REAL

WE ARE HAVING PIANO LESSONS
PRACTICE YOUR PIANO
PRACTICE MAKES PERFECT

YOU'VE LEARNT ALL THOSE LESSONS
YOU TAUGHT THEM ALL YOU KNOW
YOU CARRIED OUT THE ORDERS
AND YOU SOLD THEM WHERE TO GO
DO IT OR COMPLAIN WHEN THEN RETURN THE TREATMENT BLOW BY
BLOW

OH WILL YOU COME WITH US ON THE RUN WITH US
WITH THE WILD GIRLS ON THE SUN
COME AWAY WITH US ON THE RUN WITH US
ON STAY INSIDE AND TAKE US ONCE

THEY ARE MARCHING PAST THE WINDOW
THEY ARE MARCHING DOWN YOUR STREET
THEY'VE RENTED OUT THE CORNER SHOP
AND YOUR FREEZER FULL OF MEAT
WATCH OUT BOYS THEY'VE KILLED THE GRAND DOG AT YOUR
FEET

WE ARE HAVING PIANO LESSONS
PRACTICE YOUR PIANO
PRACTICE MAKES PERFECT
WE ARE HAVING PIANO LESSONS

Recorded October 1978
First performed Sussex University December 9 '78

BULLY BOYS

THE BULLY BOYS ARE COMING
THERE ISN'T LONG TO GO
WILL THE BULLY BOYS ARE ON THEIR WAY
WILL THE END BE QUICK OR SLOW
SURVIVAL OF THE FITTEST
IN THE CONTEXT OF THE BOYS
THE BULLY BOYS ARE COMING
WILL THE END BE SLOW OR QUICK
SURVIVAL OF THE FITTEST
THE BULLY BOYS ARE COMING
CAN IT REALLY HAPPEN CHILD ?
PLANTOLOGY OF VIOLENCE
THE BOYS WILL HAVE THEIR WAY
THE BULLY BOYS ARE COMING
MARCHING GOING ON
OUT DON'T YOU CRY MY DARLING
IT ISN'T YOU NEED A TEAR
JUST PUT ON YOUR BLACK LEATHER
THE BULLY BOYS ARE HERE
WE THEM TO BE A VICTIM
FROM BEAUTY IN PAIN
JUST PUT US KILL BLACK LEATHER
THE BULLY BOYS ARE HERE

First performed Trumi's Ipswich
October 15 1979
A live recording was released on
a float with In The City Magazine
August 1980

BREMEN SONG

WITCH BURNED SISTERS THEY BURNED
AND THE FIRE IS STILL BURNING
THEY BURNED SISTERS THEY BURNED
AND THE SMOKE FROM THE FIRE IS STILL BURNING
WE BURN SISTERS WE ARE WE WILL SET THE WORLD ON FIRE
WITH OUR BURNING WITH OUR YEARNING WITH OUR BURNING

REMEMBER THE HOLOCAUST
BURN BURN
HOLOCAUST IN BREMEN
FIRE BURN
IN THE NAME OF THE FATHERLAND
WOMEN BURN
IN THE NAME OF THE FATHERLAND
CHILDREN BURN
IN MOHIBE PATRI
BURN BURN
FOR THE SAKE OF HIS PROPERTY
FIRE FIRE
NAPALM NAPALM
USE BURN USE
WITCHES BURN
FIRE FIRE
WOMAN IN SERMONIC
BURN BURN
WOMAN IN SERMONIC
BURN BURN
REPUDIATE THE CHRISTUS
FIRE FIRE
WOMAN IN MEXICO
BURN BURN

BURN BURN BURN BURN BURN BURN BURN BURN BURN BURN

First performed Brighton 21 December 1978
Recorded April 1979 - 12" EP NHX Xntrix Records

JUMP MAMA JUMP

```
YOUR  KIDS DON'T GET TO SCHOOL ON TIME
YOU DON'T WATCH THE CLOCK MA
THEIR HAIR DON'T CURL AND THEIR TEETH DON'T SHINE
IT'S ALL IN DOCTOR SPOCK MA
YOUR MAN DON'T FEEL TOO GOOD TODAY
YOU DIDN'T TREAT HIM RIGHT MA
AND IF HE DON'T WORK HE GETS NO PAY
BETTER FIX HIM UP TONIGHT MA

THIS WAY THAT WAY
JUMP MAMA JUMP
THAT WAY THIS WAY
JUMP MAMA
JUMP

YOU DON'T KNIT AND YOU DON'T SEW
YOU NEVER MAKE THE BEDS MA
WON DON'T BAKE NO JAMMY CAKES
YOU JUST GO OUT INSTEAD MA
THEY'LL GET YOU MAMA BY YOUR CURLY HAIRS
THEY'LL HAVE YOUR GUTS FOR GARTERS
AND IF YOU DON'T GET BACK HOME TONIGHT
THEY'LL HAVE YOUR TITS FOR AFTERS

DON'T STOP MAMA CLEAN THEM FLOORS
THE BABY'S BUM IS WET MA
ALL SPICK AND SPAN BY HALF PAST FOUR
YOU'RE BETTER NOT FORGET MA
THERE'S LOVE TO MAKE AND HEARTS TO MEND
JUMP NOW JUST ONE MORE TIME MA
YOUR CANDLE'S BURNING AT BOTH ENDS
JUST YOU STAY IN LINE MA

THIS WAYTHAT WAY
JUMP MAMA JUMP
THAT WAY THIS WAY
JUMP MAMA
JUMP

YOUR EYES DON'T LOOK TOO BRIGHT TODAY
AND YOUR FIGURE'S NOT TOO HOT MA
YOUR HAIR AND SKIN ARE TURNING GREY
YOU'RE LOSING WHAT YOU'VE GOT MA
JUMP MAMA  JUMP MAMA  JUMP MAMA
JUMP

First performed Centrepoint, Epping  Winter 1977
Released on HEX  12"EP (XNTRIX) July 1979
```

PEOPLE RELEASE

```
THE RADIO SPEWS OUT GREY DEATH TO THE EMPTY LIVING
ROOM/THE TV ENDLESS PICTURE WEAK PLAYS TO AN EMPTY
MIND/THE SUPERMARKET IT STACKED HIGH WITH EMPTY TINS
TO FILL OUR EMPTY BODIES/OUR EMPTY BODIES RATTLE WITH
THE PILLS WE TAKE TO FILL OUR EMPTY HEARTS/

THE LIVING HAVE GATHERED ON THE EDGE/WHERE THERE IS
NOTHING TO LOSE/NOWHERE TO GO BACK TO/NOFUTURE TO
HANG ON TO/THE LIVING SEARCH FOR THE LIVING AMONG
THE DEAD/THE LIVING DO NOT KNOW WHO THE LIVING ARE/

HOW WILL WE STAY ALIVE WHEN EVERY SIGN OF LIFE IS CON
TROLLED/COLONISED/SUBJUGATED/WHEN THE WORDS AND FORMS
THAT ONCE WERE ALIVE WITH OUR LIFE NOW SPEAK OF DEATH
AND SOUND LIKE DEATH/AND THE LIVING DO NOT KNOW WHO
THE LIVING ARE/

THIS IS A SIGN TO THE LIVING/A SIGNAL TO THOSE WHO
LIVE ON THE EDGE/WHO/KNOWING WHAT THEY DO HAVE NO
CHOICE BUT TO STAY ON THE EDGE AND TO STAY ALIVE/

THE LIVING ARE DESPERATE FOR LIFE/WE ARE/DESPERATE/
FOR LIFE/NOT FOR SUCCESS/ WE DO NOT FIT/ THE CLIQUE
OF MONEY IS THE CLICK OF DEATH/FEAR FEEDS OFF OUR
LIVE BODIES/MEDIOCRITY IS THE FRUIT OF DEFEAT

Printed as part of a PRESS RELEASE
      sent out to the Music Biz with the
      Piano Lessons/Closed Shop 12" EP
```

PEOPLE RELEASE

S.S.SNOOPERS

THEY TAKE AWAY YOUR MONEY IF YOU'RE SLEEPING WITH A MAN
SO YOU HAVE TO BE DEPENDANT/ THAT'S HOW IT ALL BEGAN
THE ONE THAT DOES THE SCREWING IS THE ONE THAT PAYS THE BILLS
THE ONE THAT DOES THE SCREWING'S THE ONE THAT PAYS THE BILLS
SS SNOOPERS SS SPIES BUZZING ROUND YOUR BODY LIKE FLIES

THE GAME IS PROSTITUTION WITH YOUR FELLER OR THE STATE
IT'S A VERY OLD PROFESSION BUT THEY'VE KEPT IT UPTODATE
THE ONE THAT DOES THE SCREWING IS THE ONE THAT PAYS THE BILLS
THE ONE THAT DOES THE SCREWING IS THE ONE THAT PAYS THE BILLS
SS SNOOPERS SS SPIES BUZZING ROUND YOUR BODY LIKE FLIES

THEY'RE CHECKING UP ON SCROUNGERS IF YOU HAVEN'T GOT A JOB
BUT THE MONEY THAT THEY PAY'S LOW YOU HAVE TO CHEAT AND ROB
THE ONE THAT DOES THE SCREWING'S THE ONE THAT PAYS OLD BILL
THE ONE THAT DOES THE SCREWING IS THE ONE THAT PAYS OLD BILL
SS SNOOPERS SS SPIES BUZZING ROUND YOUR BODY LIKE FLIES

First performed Blackfriars London July 27 1979

WHEN LOVE FELL APART

STRONG WITH THE STRENGTH
OF ALL THAT HAS GONE AND ALL THAT WILL CHANGE
STRONG WITH THE STRENGTH
OF THE LONGING AND PAIN THAT FLOWS THROUGH OUR VEINS
STRONG WE ARE STRONG
WITH THE RAGE OF THE PAST AND ALL THAT WILL PASS
STRONG WE ARE STRONG
WITH WAVE UPON WAVE OF CHANGE AFTER CHANGE
WAVE UPON WAVE UPON WAVE
AND WE HAVE SURVIVED AND WE STAND HERE AGAIN

STRONG WITH THE STRENGTH
OF THE DREAMS THAT WE MADE THAT FALL AND FADE
STRONG WITH THE STRENGTH
OF THE HURT AND THE WORLD OUR LIPS NEVER GAVE
STRONG WE ARE STRONG
WITH THE SPORT OF THE GAME, THE LOSS AND THE GAIN
STRONG WE ARE STRONG
WITH WAVE UPON WAVE OF CHANGE AND DESIRE
WAVE UPON WAVE UPON WAVE
AND WE HAVE SURVIVED AND WE STAND HERE AGAIN

LOST AND LIBEAU LOVE THAT WE MADE
OF OUR LUST AND LIES
THERE THAT WE GAVE FOR ANOTHER NEW START
BEATING OF THINGS AND THE LOVE THAT WE MADE
WITH THE WORKING OF MIND
BEATING OF HEARTS FOR ANOTHER NEW START
WHEN IT ALL FELL APART

STRONG WE ARE STRONG
LIKE THE RIVER OF DEATH THAT RUNS FROM OUR VEINS
STRONG WE ARE STRONG
WITH THE STRENGTH OF OUR MIND AND THE HOPE THAT REMAINS
STRONG WITH THE STRENGTH
OF WAVE UPON WAVE OF AGE AFTER AGE
STRONG WITH THE STRENGTH
OF THE HANDS AND THE FEET THAT WILL STAND HERE AGAIN

WAVE UPON WAVE UPON WAVE
AND WE ARE NOT YOUNG AND WE STAND HERE AGAIN

First performed tropical Vina Rochdale 7.10.80
Recorded September 1980 for release on ALL SYSTEMS GO single

HOUSE

THIS IS THE HOUSE THAT HE BUILT
THERE ARE THE WALLS
AND THIS IS THE FLOOR
THIS IS HIS GUN AND THIS IS HIS WAR
THERE ARE THE WALLS
THIS IS THE FLOOR
AND THIS IS THE HOUSE THAT HE BUILT

THIS IS THE BED THAT HE GROWS
THIS IS HIS TABLE
AND THIS IS THE CHAIR
THIS IS HIS MONEY AND THIS IS HIS LAW
THIS IS HIS GUN AND THIS IS HIS WAR
THERE ARE THE WALLS
THIS IS THE FLOOR
AND THIS IS THE HOUSE THAT HE BUILT

THIS IS HIS TIME
THIS IS HIS SPACE
THIS IS HIS FINGERS
HOW WARM IN HIS FACE
THIS IS HIS LAW
THIS IS HIS MONEY
THIS IS HIS FACE
THIS IS HIS AMONG
THIS IS HIS GUN
THIS IS HIS WAR
THIS IS HIS PINE
THIS IS HIS MONEY
THIS IS HIS WAR

THIS IS THE WAY THE HOUSE BURNS
THIS IS THE WAY THE WORLD BURNS

First performed at the ASKING VINE
FESTIVAL August 1979
Published in THE BLACKBIRD OCEAN No.3

CRY

TIRED OF CRYING FOR THE UNBORN/UNBLESSED/FOR THE BLACKS/
THE WOMEN/FOR EVEN BLACK WOMEN/TIRED OF CRYING FOR THE
STARVING CHILDREN/FOR THE UNEMPLOYED OF CRYING FOR THE
WORKING CLASS/FOR THE OLD/TIRED OF CRYING FOR THE MENTAL
LY HANDICAPPED/MULTIPLE SCHLEROSES/TIRED OF CRYING FOR
THE THIRD WORLD/ABSTRACT STATES/HIROSHIMA/NAGASAKI/TIRED
OF CRYING/AMERICA/AMERICA/I'M TIRED OF CRYING/AMERICA

TIRED OF CRYING FOR THE PRISONERS/PRISIONERS OF MIND OR
SKIN/TIRED OF CRYING FOR THE WIVES OF THE AMBASSADORS/
SHIPWRECKED IMPORTURES/RS/TIRED OF CRYING FOR THE WIDOWS
/OR THE LEPERS/MAIDENASSED AT BIRTH/TIRED OF CRYING FOR
THE OPE RND JEWS/ABORTED/ PAWNS AND PAUPERS OF CAPITAL
INE/TIRED OF CRYING FOR THE GRIEVING MOTHERS AND
TIRED OF CRYING FOR THE DEAD DEAD SOLDIERS

TIRED OF CRYING FOR THE RAPED/FOR THE RAPISTS YES I'M
TIRED OF CRYING /TIRED OF CRYING/ TIRED OF CRYING

FOR THE TORTURED AND HUMILIATED FOR POLITICAL OR PRIVATE
REASONS OF SADISM/MACHO/MASOCHISM/MASOCHISMO/PORNO/PORN
VICTIMS/VICTIMS/DAMAGE/DAMAGE/FLESH DAMAGE/BONE DAMAGE/
BRAIN DAMAGE/DAMAGE/ DAMAGE/ YES IT'S A SAVAGE WORLD IT'S
A SAVAGE WORLD/AND I'M TIRED OF CRYING/JUST WANT TO CRY
CRY FOR ME/CRY FOR ME/CRY FOR ME/CRY FOR ME/CRY FOR ME

First performed Action Space/London/24.9.06

just want to cry for me

THIS COLLECTION OF SONGS WAS PRODUCED IN RESPONSE
TO INTEREST IN POISON GIRLS LYRICS AND INCLUDES
MOST OF THE SONGS WRITTEN AND PERFORMED IN THE
LAST TWO YEARS. DURING THIS TIME MANY OF THESE
SONGS WERE SCREEN PRINTED AS INDIVIDUAL SHEETS
TO HAND OUT AT GIGS. THIS COLLECTION HAS BEEN
HAND PRINTED ON SILK SCREEN IN THE SAME WAY.

POISON GIRLS ARE :

LANCE D'BOYLE   : DRUMS / VOCALS
RICHARD FAMOUS   : GUITARS / VOCALS
BERNHARDT REBOURS : BASS GUITAR / VOCALS
VI SUBVERSA   : LEAD VOCALS / GUITAR

AN XNTRIX PRODUCTION / FIRST EDITION 150 copies
ALL LYRICS C. XNTRIX

SONGS WRITTEN
IN MOMENTS OF
TRUST. LONELY
HUNTERS WE
EYE EACH OTHER
UP FOR A FIGHT
OR A FUCK.
LONE.
ALONE..
ALIEN...
SONGS WRITTEN
IN MOMENTS OF
TRUST.

THE IMPOSSIBLE DREAM
FOUR ISSUES
1980-86

"I always seemed to be into making magazines, and it seemed just the moment to do another," explained Poison Girls' drummer and illustrator Lance d'Boyle, recalling the time that the punk scene exploded in Brighton and needed to be documented and shared.

With input from Richard Famous, Adrian Arriva, and several others, d'Boyle produced his first punk fanzine *Spitting Blood* in 1977. As well as percussion, d'Boyle's "other major talent was as a visual artist," Famous recalls.

The one and only issue of *Spitting Blood* hit the city's streets that summer, just before Poison Girls decamped to Burleigh House in London. The contact page carried the memorable tagline 'we're fearless, we're shameless—we're leaving!' With a front cover photo of Famous on stage at The Vault (and Pete Fender out of focus in the foreground), *Spitting Blood* offered features on Brighton punk bands The Piranhas, The Dandies, Punktuation, Wrist Action—and Poison Girls, as well as reflections on the death of Elvis Presley and on the future of The Vault.

Easily able to hold its own amidst the emerging wave of punk zines, *Spitting Blood* was a solid example of what would later become a familiar style of band-based DIY punk magazine. Knowing that Poison Girls were moving to London, d'Boyle put out a plea in the editorial, asking others to step forward and take ownership of *Spitting Blood*. "If you want to help . . . get off your arses," he urged. "It's easy to do, and there will be some money to finance issue no. 2. It's yours if you want it." It seems that no one came forward to take up the offer. But that was a matter for Brighton's punk activists, as d'Boyle attention was now focused on new projects.

"I started editing and publishing *The Impossible Dream* when we moved to Epping," d'Boyle recalled later. It became a print medium which "gave full rein to Lance's artistic talents," says Famous.

As d'Boyle established *The Impossible Dream*'s singular identity, there were other publications in the punk scene that shared its aspirations. Produced by Andy Palmer of Crass and Simon Stockton (aka T42) The *Eklektic* was a bold and often brilliant A4 art magazine, with a great deal of visual flair and a similar sense of preoccupation with the distortion and degeneration of the male psyche. *Sleeping Dogs* was an occasional magazine produced by Dave King (creator of the Crass logo) and member of a band of the same name (who released the *Beware* EP on Crass Records). King was a supremely talented graphic designer and the magazine was just one of an array of impressive and visually literate agit-prop publications that he produced from the late 1970s onwards.

Amongst the countless British punk zines of that era, *The Impossible Dream* shared belief in the power of political visuals with such titles as the mesmerising *Pigs Will Fly* and *The Joy of Propaganda*, or the meticulous hand-drawn intricacies of *Blast* and *Radical Hedgehog*. D'Boyle's work was motivated by the same conviction about the value of matching potent visuals with unsettling, unnerving poetry as inspired the creators of zines like *fuck book*, *Kiss the Earth*, and *Tropical Depression* (a collection of poetic works by Annie Anxiety Guevara published under the Xntrix imprint).

The visual innovations of *The Impossible Dream* "were so inspiring because they said 'look again at everything.'" says Mark Easton, a photographer and filmmaker that d'Boyle collaborated with. "I believe they took a long time as well—it taught me to never be casual with images, each one can be a bomb." Hugh Vivian of the band Omega Tribe got to know d'Boyle well, was able to observe the evolution of the visual aesthetic across all four issues. "Those magazines are iconic and timeless; or rather ahead of their time," he suggests. "His paper collages were fabulous compositions, fine art from torn strips of magazines. He was a ground-breaking artist. His designs were superb."

Boyle made use of humour, ridiculousness, and satire to pour scorn on the institutions of government, machismo, and militarism. Parody and pastiche were mixed in with sober political statements and terse polemic to produce an intentionally "impossible" blend of perspectives and insights.

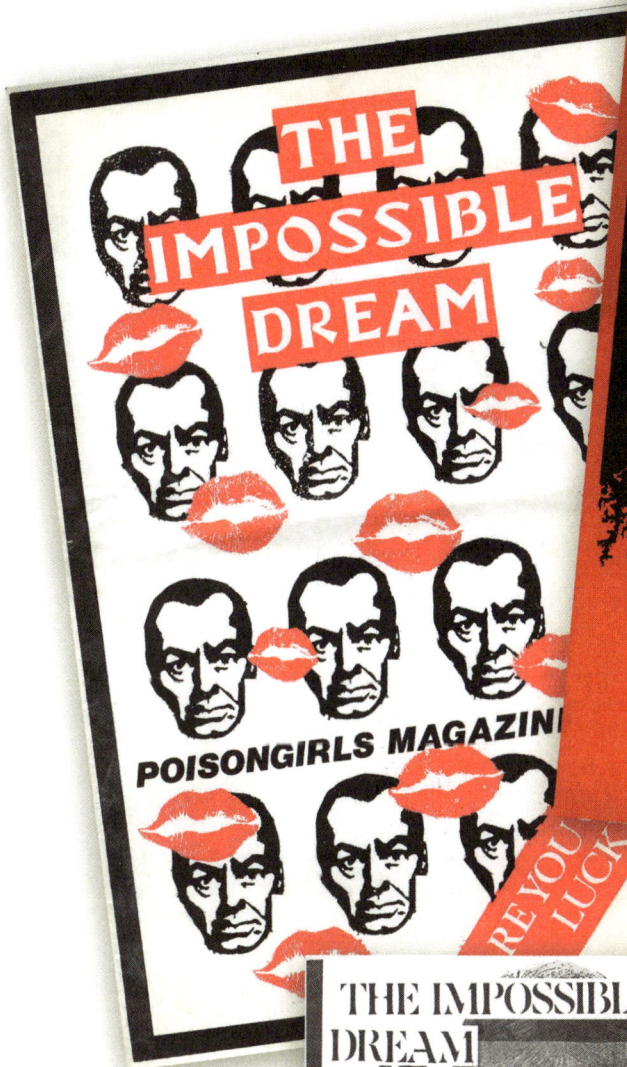

What shines through *The Impossible Dream* is d'Boyle's disdain for the predictable and formulaic in political art. Even when making the most serious of statements, there's a joyful, often exuberant and always playful quality to d'Boyle's practice. There's a gleefulness in his refusal to rely on formal artistic tropes, even when that wilfulness risks pushing the art too far in the direction of being contrary for the sake of it (leaving the art teetering on the edge of ridiculousness on occasion). But that in itself was confirmation of his determination to experiment and to take creative risks in pursuit of artistic impact.

"What I wanted to do was illustrate Vi's lyrics, and set them in a wider context, and to include the work of other writers and artists," d'Boyle confirmed. Amongst other contributors whose work he would draw into its pages included the poet Janet Dubé, an old friend of the group who was living in Wales at the time. Keen to support Dubé's work, d'Boyle and his partner Domino illustrated a collection of her antimilitarist, antiwar poetry published under the Xntrix imprint as *1982: A Lament*. "We designed it together and each had our own pages," Domino recalls, "though in the end I did most of the work as he was away on tour. It received a good review in *Time Out* magazine."

D'Boyle also drew on the work of feminist author Andrea Dworkin and of William Burroughs, one of the catalysts of the Beat movement. "Since Vi wrote about feminism and personal politics, I thought to counterbalance this with an examination of the male psyche and it's relation to violence," he explained. The distortion of masculinity and the baleful consequences of disfigured gender relations became recurrent themes of d'Boyle's striking imagery.

As Famous summarises it, *The Impossible Dream* set out to expose uncomfortable truths about "militarism, sexual politics and the degeneration of capitalist culture." This meant that T*he Impossible Dream* was conceived as both a standalone publication and an extension and augmentation of Poison Girls' own aspiration to challenge and communicate. "It certainly added another dimension to the Poison Girls repertoire," Famous acknowledges. "I thought his artwork was brilliant," Gemma Sansom agrees.

In the UK, the one other publication within anarchist circles that *The Impossible Dream* was often compared with was *International Anthem*, a "nihilist newspaper for the living" created by Gee Vaucher of Crass (although its first issue appeared while Vaucher was still working in the US). But while both were expressions of political punk conviction, each closely aligned with one of the scene's most prominent bands, the comparison highlights more differences than commonalities. While Vaucher's compelling electrifying artwork focused her sense of rage and disgust at many of the same targets that d'Boyle had in his sights, their approaches and aesthetic were sharply different.

Over time, *The Impossible Dream* became more of a solo artistic endeavour. "The first couple of issues were much more 'band' based, and there was a lot of creative input from all over the place," Famous remembers. "The later issues focused more singularly on Lance's individual ideas." But throughout the project's lifespan "Lance, of course, had the guiding vision."

D'Boyle's creativity in the realms of publishing, filmmaking, theatre, and other art forms continued long after Poison Girls had ceased operations. He had planned to publish a selection of his favourite photomontages from *The Impossible Dream*, together with other never-before-seen materials from the 1990s and more recent years. D'Boyle died with the project uncompleted. The vividness of *The Impossible Dream*, and its creator's mischievous, insightful, subversive wit, will remain integral to his legacy. "They are still visually stunning and politically astute, an artistic expression of the cruel, limiting and oppressive construct of masculinity that men had to struggle against," says Famous.

Advertisement for *The Impossible Dream* #3, 1983. Courtesy of Rich Cross.

THE IMPOSSIBLE DREAM #1 1980
YOU'RE SO OTHER

Viewed in retrospect, it's clear that the first issue of *The Impossible Dream* was a transitional experiment. Retaining the A4 size and monochrome appearance of *Spitting Blood*, *The Impossible Dream*'s debut also echoed the same punk zine aesthetic.

On the monochrome front cover, a reclining young woman gazes out at the reader, surrounded by the lyrics of "Reality Attack" from the album *Hex*. In different typefaces, blocks of text namecheck the "merchants of knives / purveyors of furniture / polluters of flesh / dealers in dust / displayers of lies" who are identified as the architects and owners of "*The Impossible Dream*."

The printing of issue one was a hybrid affair—with a mix of photocopied sheets and simpler text-based pages run off on the band's duplicator before being compiled and stapled by hand in Burleigh House. It was the kind of affordable—if basic—DIY means of production familiar to countless punk zine editors.

What was immediately *different* in this new style of publication was the focus on cut-up collage and visual bricolage—and the deliberate juxtaposition of contrasting images to make subversive political statements. "I had been inspired by John Heartfield's photo-montage and the Dada and Surrealist manifestations in the 1930s and 1950s," d'Boyle explained. They appeared to be ideal sources of inspiration for the kinds of approach he was now keen to explore in print. The result was "Lance d'Boyle at his very best," and at the height of his artistic powers, Famous affirms.

Production techniques on the debut issue of *The Impossible Dream* remained simple. D'Boyle culled images from magazines and newspapers through the judicious wielding of a scalpel reassembled them in astutely judged acts of *décollage* to make potent political art. There was not a unifying thematic thread tying together the pages of issue one, but several of the ideas that would define the content of future issues find their initial expression here: the baleful influence of twisted macho Americana; the role of religion, consumerism and patriarchy as control systems; and crushing consequences of subservience and obedience.

In the more visual sections of the issue, text appeared in stencil, typewriter, and ransom-note cut-out forms to illuminate a blend of poetry and polemic. The contents are completed by a set of simpler typed mimeographed pages which include a draft extract of the lyrics of "Persons Unknown" (later to appear on the split single with Crass); words from "Good Time" (at the time entitled 'Sex War'), "Underbitch" and "Other" (all of which will go on to appear on the *Chappaquiddick Bridge* album); "S.S. Snoopers" (that would feature on the live *Total Exposure* album) and "Bully Boys" (that would surface on the *In the City* flexi as well as on *Total Exposure*).

Credit for contributions to the issue was shared between d'Boyle, Pete Wright of Crass, and radical German theatre practitioner and playwright Bertolt Brecht. Taken from the *Prologue* to *The Exception and the Rule*, first published in 1937, an extract from Brecht's prose—urging a rejection of fatalism—appeared beneath an image showing a helmeted policeman kneeling to kiss the hand of the seemingly pleased Pope John Paul II:

> Please, we say to you now
> Do not accept those things
> Especially those things that happen every day
> And seem quite natural . . .
> Nothing must be called natural,
> So that nothing shall remain unchanged

Pete Wright's contributions to the issue are not individually credited, but his ideas are almost certainly reflected in the powerful polemical phrases that appear in bold stencil lettering across several pages. Wright's involvement in what was essentially a Poison Girls project was itself evidence that the close collaboration with Crass was spreading into new areas of collaboration.

With a print run of just one hundred copies, issue one of *The Impossible Dream* was immediately sought after and very well received by those fortunate enough to track one down. "The war machine that Vi sang about was depicted in brutally skilful black-and-white imagery," Famous affirms. Credited to Xntrix Records, the attribution on the back page indicated that there was "no copyright" on the works within, clearly encouraging its reproduction, in whole or in parts, by others.

THE IMPOSSIBLE
DREAM
of the
merchants
of knives

PURVEYORS OF FURNITURE

polluters of flesh

DEALERS IN DUST

displayers of LIES

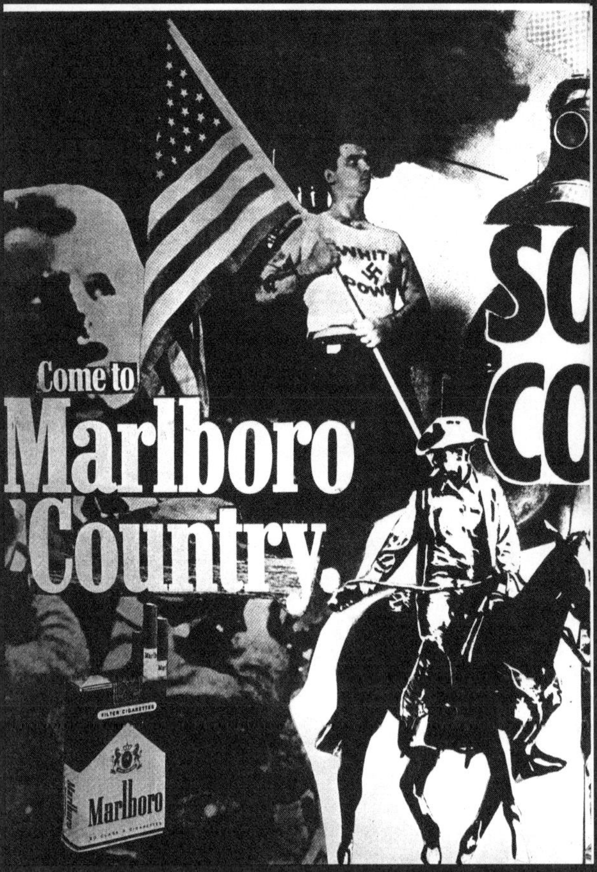

Come to Marlboro Country.

Marlboro
FILTER CIGARETTES

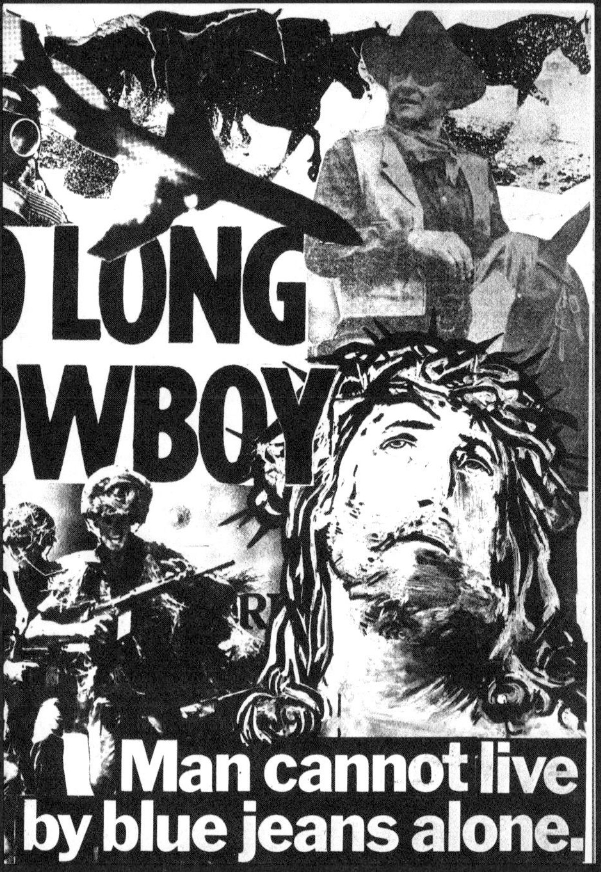

SO LONG COWBOY

Man cannot live by blue jeans alone.

we are
Are?
We?

THE COMMON GROUND IS BONDAGE
THE COMMON INTEREST
IS VARIETIES OF BONDAGE
subtleties Some men Subtle ties
exposed have a way or used
with women

THIS IS THE HOUSE THAT HE BUILT
THESE ARE THE WALLS
AND THIS IS THE FLOOR
THIS IS HIS GUN AND THIS IS HIS WAR
THESE ARE THE WALLS
THIS IS THE FLOOR
AND THIS IS THE HOUSE THAT HE BUILT

THIS IS THE BED THAT SHE MADE
THIS IS THE TABLE
AND THIS IS THE CHAIR
THIS IS HIS MONEY THIS IS HIS LAW
THIS IS HIS GUN AND THIS IS HIS WAR
THESE ARE THE WALLS
THIS IS THE FLOOR
AND THIS IS THE HOUSE THAT HE BUILT

THIS IS THE DOOR THAT HE MADE
THIS IS THE LOCK
AND THIS IS THE KEY
THIS IS HIS WORLD THIS IS HIS AGONY
THIS IS HIS MONEY THIS IS HIS LAW
THIS IS HIS GUN AND THIS IS HIS WAR
THESE ARE THE WALLS
THIS IS THE FLOOR
AND THIS IS THE HOUSE THAT HE BUILT

THE LIVING HAVE
GATHERED ON THE
EDGE, WHERE THERE
IS NOTHING TO LOSE,
NOWHERE TO GO
BACK TO, NO FUTURE
TO HANG TO.
THE LIVING SEARCH
FOR THE LIVING
AMONG THE DEAD
AND THE LIVING
DONT KNOW WHO
THE LIVING ARE.

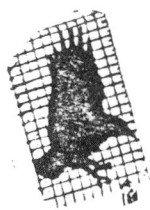

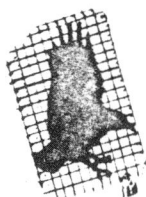

HOW WILL WE STAY
ALIVE WHEN EVERY
SIGN OF LIFE IS
CONTROLLED
COLONIZED
SUBJUGATED
WHEN THE WORDS
AND FORMS WHICH
WERE ALIVE WITH
OUR LIFE, NOW
SPEAK OF DEATH,
SOUND LIKE DEATH
AND THE LIVING
DON'T KNOW WHO
THE LIVING ARE.

THE RADIO SPEWS
OUT GREY DEATH TO
THE EMPTY LIVING
ROOM.
THE TV'S ENDLESS
PICTURE MUSAK
PLAYS TO AN EMPTY
MIND.
THE SUPERMARKET
IS STACKED HIGH
WITH EMPTY PACKETS
TO FILL OUR EMPTY
BODIES.
OUR EMPTY BODIES
WAIT WITH EMPTY
HEARTS.

PLEASE, WE SAY TO YOU NOW,
DO NOT ACCEPT THOSE THINGS
ESPECIALLY THOSE THINGS
THAT HAPPEN EVERY DAY
AND SEEM QUITE NATURAL.
FOR IN THESE TIMES
OF PLANNED CONFUSION
AND DELIBERATE VIOLENCE,
WHEN BLOOD RUNS
AND MEN ARE INHUMAN TO MEN:
NOTHING MUST BE CALLED NATURAL,
SO THAT NOTHING SHALL REMAIN UNCHANGED.

TO PERSONS UNKNOWN

THIS IS A MESSAGE TO PERSONS UNKNOWN
PERSONS IN HIDING/ PERSONS UNKNOWN
SURVIVAL IN SILENCE ISN'T GOOD ENOUGH NO MORE
HIDING IN SHADOWS / PERSONS UNKNOWN
KEEPING YOUR MOUTH SHUT / TURNING A BLIND EYE
DYING IN SECRET / PERSONS UNKNOWN
TERRORISTS AND SABOTEURS EACH AND EVERY ONE OF US
HIDING IN SHADOWS / PERSONS UNKNOWN
HEY! THERE MR. AVERAGE / YOU DONT EXIST / YOU NEVER DID
HIDING IN SECRET / HEAD IN THE SAND
HABITS OF HIDING SOON WILL BE THE DEATH OF US
DYING IN SECRET FROM POISONS UNKNOWN.......
THIS IS A MESSAGE TO PERSONS UNKNOWN
TAPPING YOUR CIRCUITS / PERSONS UNKNOWN
SURVIVAL IN SILENCE ISN'T GOOD ENOUGH NO MORE
KEEPING YOUR MOUTH SHUT / HEAD IN THE SAND
TURNING YOUR BLIND EYE SOON WILL BE THE DEATH OF US
DYING IN SECRET FROM POISONS UNKNOWN............

FLESH AND BLOOD ARE WHO WEARE/FLESH AND BLOOD ARE WHAT WE
ARE/FLESH AND BLOOD ARE WHO WE ARE/OUR COVER'S BLOWN/FLESH
AND BLOOD ARE WHO WE ARE/FLESH AND BLOOD ARE WHAT WE ARE/FLESH
AND BLOOD ARE WHO WE ARE/FLESH AND BLOOD ARE WHAT WE ARE/OUR
COVER'S BLOWN/FLESH AND BLOOD ARE WHO WE ARE/FLESH AND BLOOD ARE
WHAT WE ARE/THIS IS A MESSAGE TO PERSONS UNKNOWN/FLESH AND BLOOD ARE
WHO WE ARE/FLESH AND BLOOD ARE WHAT WE ARE/WHO WE ARE/FLESH AND
BLOOD ARE WHO WE ARE/FLESH AND BLOOD ARE WHAT WE ARE/FLESH AND BLOOD
ARE WHO WE ARE/FLESH AND BLOOD ARE WHAT WE ARE/FLESH AND BLOOD
FLESH AND BLOOD/FLESHAND BLOOD/FLESH AND BLOOD/WE ARE FLESH AND BLOOD
ARE WHO WE ARE/FLESH AND BLOOD ARE WHAT WE ARE/YOUR COVER'S BLOWN
FLESH AND BLOOD ARE WHO WE ARE/FLESH AND BLOOD AREWHAT WE ARE/YOUR
COVERS BLOWN/FLESH AND BLOOD ARE WHO WE ARE/FLESH AND BLOOD ARE
WHAT WE ARE/FLESH AND BLOOD AREH WHAT WE ARE/FLESH AND BLOOD ARE
WHO WE ARE/THIS IS A MESSAGE TO PERSONS UNKNOWN/ YOUR COVER'S
BLOWN/FLESH AND BLOOD ARE WHO WE ARE/FLESH AND BLOOD
ARE WHAT WE ARE/ FLESH AND BLOOD ARE WHAT WE ARE/FLESH AND BLOOD
ARE WHO WE ARE/FLESH AND BLOOD ARE WHO WE ARE/OUR COVERS
BLOWN/FLESH AND BLOOD ARE WHAT WE ARE/FLESH AND BLOOD ARE
WHO WE ARE/FLESH AND BLOOD/OUR COVER'S BLOWN/FLESH AND BLOOD
FLESH AND BLOOD.

POISON GIRLS 1979

---

sSEX WAR

I SAW YOU SHOVE THAT HOSEPIPE DOWN YOUR TROUSERS	OBSESSIVE SEXUALITY
SO YOU CAN SHIVER WITH SOMETHING TO SHAKE	OBSESSIVE SEXUALITY
I'M GONNA RIP THE BUTTONS OFF YOUR TEE SHIRT	OBSESSIVE SEXUALITY
I'M GONNA PICK THE CHERRIES OFF YOUR CAKE	OBSESSIVE SEXUALITY
I'M GONNA LICK THE SUGAR OFF YOUR HAIRSTYLE	AGGRESSIVE SEXUALITY
I'M GONNA PICK THE ICING OFF YOUR CAKE	AGGRESSIVE SEXUALITY
I SAW YOU STUFF THEM BATH BUNS IN YOUR BRASSIERE	AGGRESSIVE SEXUALITY
I'M GONNA PEEL THAT WRAPPER OFF YOUR FACE	AGGRESSIVE SEXUALITY

LA LA LA LA GOTTA HAVE A GOOD TIME LA LA LA LA GOTTA HAVE A GOOD TIME
LA LA LA LA GOTTA HAVE A GOOD TIME GOOD TIME ON THE DANCE FLOOR

YOU CAN FORGET THE MEANING OF EXISTENCE	FASCISTIC SEXUALITY
YOU CAN FORGET THE THINGS THAT MAKE YOU TICK	FASCISTIC SEXUALITY
JUST LOOK AT ME-I'LL WEAKEN YOUR RESISTANCE	FASCISTIC SEXUALITY
PUSH YOU OVER..TAKE YOU OVER..TAKE YOU QUICK	FASCISTIC SEXUALITY

SEX WAR SEX WAR SEX WAR WHAT ARE WE FIGHTING FOR SEX WAR SEX WAR SEX WAR
SEX WAR SEX WAR WHAT ARE WE FIGHTING FOR SEX WAR SEX WAR WHAT ARE WE FIGHTING FOR
COME ON AND DANCE WITH ME COME ON AND DANCE WITH ME COME ON AND DANCE WITH ME
COME ON AND DANCE WITH ME COME ON AND DANCE WITH ME COME ON AND DANCE WITH ME

S.S. SNOOPERS

THEY TAKE AWAY YOUR MONEY
IF YOUR SLEEPING WITH A MAN
SO YOU HAVE TO BE DEPENDANT
THAT'S HOW IT ALL BEGAN
AND THE ONE THAT DOES THE SCREWING
IS THE ONE THAT PAYS THE BILLS
YES THE ONE THAT DOES THE SCREWING
IS THE ONE THAT PAYS THE BILLS

S.S. SNOOPERS S.S. SPIES
SWARMING ROUND YOUR BODY LIKE FLIES

THE GAME IS PROSTITUTION
WITH YOUR FELLA OR THE STATE
ITS A VERY OLD PROFESSION
BUT THEY'VE KEPT IT UP TO DATE
AND THE ONE THAT DOES THE SCREWING
IS THE ONE THAT PAYS THE BILLS
YES THE ONE THAT DOES THE SCREWING
IS THE ONE THAT PAYS THE BILLS

S.S. SNOOPERS S.S. SPIES
SWARMING ROUND YOUR BODY
LIKE FLIES

POISON GIRLS 1979

UNDERBITCH

DO YOU WHEN YOUR TRYING EVER
WONDER WHICH WAY UP IT GOES
WONDER WHICH WAY UP IT GOES
WONDER WHICH WAY WATER FLOWS
WONDER
WHICHWAY
YOU MUST
GO.........
DO YOU WHEN YOUR CRYING EVER
FALL AWAY FROM DAYTIME LIGHT
FALL AWAY FROM DAYTIME LIGHT
FALL AWAY INTO THE NIGHT
NIGHT TIME
NIGHTMARE
KNOWING
NO ONE KNOWS YOU

UNDERBITCH
UNDERBITCH
UNDERBITCH
UNDERBITCH

AND DO YOU WHEN YOUR BUYING EVER
WONDER WHERE THE MONEY GOES
YOU BUY YOUR PHOTO COPY CLOTHES
YOU PEEL IT LIKE A BODY BLOW
POCKETKNIFE
A JACK KNIFE
PEEPING TOM
BABY

UNDERBITCH

AND DO YOU WHEN YOU'RE DYING EVER
CURSE THE COCKY JUGGERNAUT
COCKY BUGGER JUGGERNAUT
JELLYHEAD
THAT RAN YOU DOWN
THAT DOG . . . .
BOSS MOB
JELLY HEAD
THAT RAN YOU DOWN
THAT FEELS YOU UP .....

UNDERBITCH
UNDERBITCH
UNDERBITCH
UNDERBITCH

BULLY BOYS

THE BULLY BOYS ARE COMING
THERE ISN'T LONG TO GO
THE BULLY BOYS ARE ON THEIR WAY
WILL THE END BE QUICK OR SLOW

SURVIVAL OF THE FITTEST
IN THE COUNTRY OF THE SICK
THE BULLY BOYS ARE COMING
WILL THE END BE SLOW OR QUICK

SURVIVAL OF THE FITTEST
THE ENEMY IS FEAR
THE BULLY BOYS ARE COMING
CAN IT REALLY HAPPEN HERE

OVERKILL OVERKILL OVERKILL OVERKILL

PORNOGRAPHY OF VIOLENCE

THE DOGS WILL HAVE THEIR DAY
THE BULLY BOYS ARE COMING
MACHISMO RULES O.K.

BUT DON'T YOU CRY MY DARLING
NO DONT YOU SHED A TEAR
JUST PUT ON YOUR BLACK LEATHER
THE BULLY BOYS ARE HERE

NO TIME TO BE A VICTIM
THE ENEMY IS FEAR
JUST PUT ON YOUR BLACK LEATHER
THE BULLY BOYS ARE HERE

OVERKILL OVERKILL OVERKILL OVERKILL

POISON GIRLS 1979.

YOU'RE SO OTHER	YOU TURN ME ON SO STRANGE
YOU'RE SO OTHER	YOU'RE SUCH ANOTHER KIND
YOU'RE SO OTHER	YOU PLUNGE ME IN SO DEEP
YOU'RE SO OTHER	OUT OF MY MADE UP MIND
YOU'RE SO OTHER	YOU TURN ME ON SO STRANGE
YOU'RE SO OTHER	YOU LURCH ME OUT OF THE SMART PART OF ME
YOU'RE SO OTHER	YOU PLUNGE ME IN SO DEEP
YOU'RE SO OTHER	YOU PLUNGE ME RIGHT TO THE HEART OF ME
YOU'RE SO OTHER	YOU PULL ME OUT OF MY DEPTH
YOU'RE SO OTHER	YOU PULL ME OUT OF MY MADE UP MIND
YOU'RE SO OTHER	YOU TURN ME ON SO STRANGE
YOU'RE SO OTHER	YOU'RE SUCH ANOTHER KIND
YOU'RE SO OTHER	YOU FALL ME-OR DID YOU PUSH
YOU'RE SO OTHER	YOU SHOOK ME SHOOK ME OFF MY TREE
YOU'RE SO OTHER	YOU LURCH ME OUT OF MY MADE UP MIND
YOU'RE SO OTHER	YOU'RE SUCH ANOTHER KIND SUCH ANOTHER KIND
YOU'RE SO OTHER	YOU TURN ME ON SO STRANGE
YOU'RE SO OTHER	YOU PLUNGE ME IN SO DEEP
YOU'RE SO OTHER	YOU TURN ME ON SO STRANGE
YOU'RE SO OTHER	YOU CREEP ME IN MY SLEEP
YOU'RE SO OTHER	YOU'RE SO WHITE-SO PALE
YOU'RE SO OTHER	YOU LIE ON MY DARK SKIN
YOU'RE SO OTHER	YOU'RE FROM THE OTHER SIDE
YOU'RE SO OTHER	NO FAMILIARITY TO EASE ME IN

Will you be my lover
I have loved another

Will you be my lover
I HAVE LOVED ANOTHER

WILL YOU BE MY LOVER
I HAVE LOVED ANOTHER

WILL YOU BE MY LOVER I HAVE LOVED ANOTHER

POISON GIRLS 1979

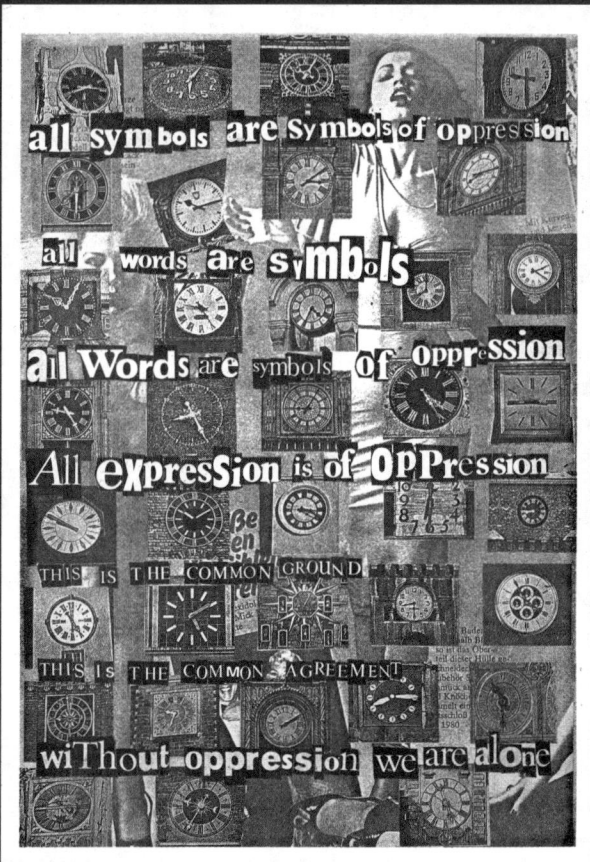

all symbols are symbols of oppression

all words are symbols

all Words are symbols of oppression

All expression is of oppression

THIS IS THE COMMON GROUND

THIS IS THE COMMON AGREEMENT

wiThout oppression we are alone

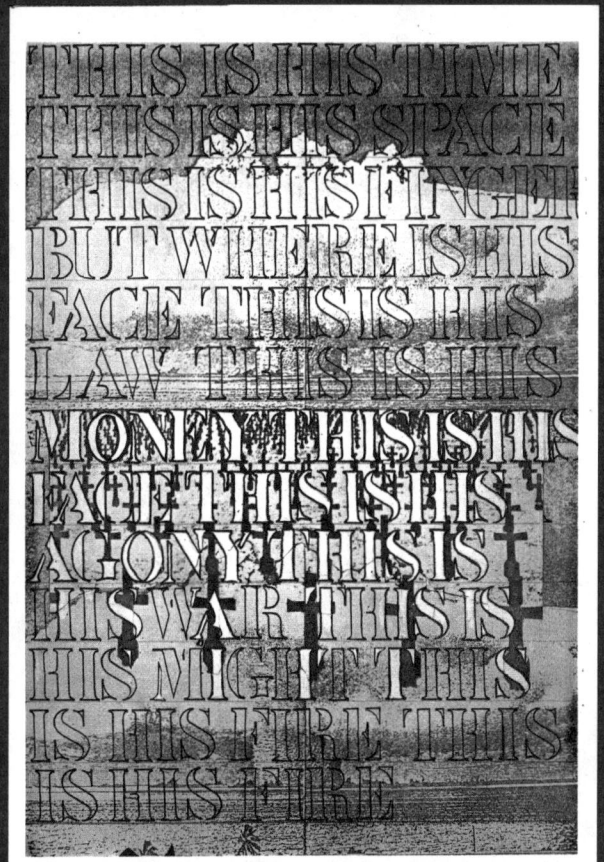

THIS IS HIS TIME
THIS IS HIS SPACE
THIS IS HIS FINGER
BUT WHERE IS HIS
FACE THIS IS HIS
LAW THIS IS HIS
MONEY THIS IS HIS
FACE THIS IS HIS
AGONY THIS IS
HIS WAR THIS IS
HIS MIGHT THIS
IS HIS FIRE THIS
IS HIS FIRE

WRITTEN BY :
POISON GIRLS, PETE WRIGHT, BERT BRECHT.
PUBLISHED BY X N TRIX RECORDS. NO
NO COPYRIGHT.

4. STATE CONTROL AND ROCK'N'ROLL ARE RUN BY CLEVER MEN

CHAPPAQUIDDICK BRIDGE 1980

The band's second album gave Poison Girls more room to breathe and to experiment with sonics and songwriting. With material honed on the live circuit, working alongside Crass and independently, Chappaquiddick Bridge showcased a new richness and warmth in the sounds of Poison Girls and a wider lyrical focus that addressed personal, cultural, and political issues with equal anarchist astuteness. The band's subsequent relocation to new premises in Leytonstone changed the dynamic of home life but allowed the kitting-out of a new studio.

"The music has got a more full feel to it," Richard Famous recalled of the recording of Poison Girls' second album, within weeks of its release. "*Hex* was very sparse. I think that because of this, the record is even more subversive—in that it might get to people who wouldn't listen to *Hex*."

Chappaquiddick Bridge was recorded during a period when the band were continually out on the road and playing live. Touring alongside Crass, an arrangement which had begun in 1979, continued—but it was always on the understanding that Poison Girls would continue to gig independently as well. "We had been gigging a lot in the months before, and nearly all the tracks to be recorded were on the set list—so were well played in," Famous says. "There is nothing like playing a song in front of an audience—especially a boisterous one—to sharpen up a track. Most of the audience were there to see Crass—don't get me wrong, we always won them over, but we had to prove ourselves night after night. So our set was really tight musically, and the performances were seamless—one song segued into the next to allow as little opportunity for fights to erupt as possible."

"We had played a fair number of gigs by the time we were recording this album," Bernhardt Rebours agrees, "and had bonded really well." The return to the studio came shortly after the band's well-received solo tour of Holland and West Germany. "Plans are afoot to return this autumn for further dates in Germany," a statement from the band explained, "as well as to bring some Dutch bands over here to play with us." Poison Girls remained enthused about the opportunity to perform live across continental Europe throughout the group's life. "I think in Holland we were loved, and people's love and respect always included the organisers," Lance d'Boyle reflected years later. "Music, especially our kind, was taken very seriously by intellectual dropouts with their own slant on punk," he suggested. The band always enjoyed playing "great venues in Amsterdam and The Hague."

The agreement to release Poison Girls' second album on Crass Records reflected the strengthening alliance between the two bands. There was, at this stage in the relationship, a great deal of practical reciprocity underpinning the shared political affinities. It was a loan from Vi Subversa that had enabled the cash-strapped Crass to fund the recording and release of their *Stations of the Crass* double album, released in the late December of 1979.

Recording of Poison Girls' extraordinarily distinctive *Chappaquiddick Bridge* began at Southern Studios, under the guidance once again of John Loder as engineer, and Penny Rimbaud as producer, on Saturday 17 May 1980. The session continued the following day, was followed by a second session on 24–25 May, and then concluded with a first mix on 31 May and 1 June—wrapping up the recording of all ten tracks on the album, and

the accompanying flexi disc, in less than a week. That was an impressively productive turnaround, and confirmation of just how tight, well-rehearsed, and close-knit the band had become by the spring of 1980.

By now there was a productive working relationship between the band, Loder, and Rimbaud, based on a sense of mutual respect and a joint acknowledgement of the talents and expertise of everyone involved. "He worked as a producer who wasn't just trying to *record* the thing, but to bring out stuff that was nascent in it rather than pull things through that weren't," d'Boyle remembered. "He had a very hard-working ethic. . . . All his stuff is very meticulously done. And I used to enjoy working with him a lot." Rimbaud's efforts "enhanced . . . or complemented our playing of the music," d'Boyle continued. "He brought out the potential in it—and the intention."

Rimbaud in turn would go on to judge the record as the Poison Girls first masterpiece. It was "in a class of its own," he recalled years later, "a phenomenally weird and surreal piece of work." Coincidentally, that first day in the studio was also the official release day for the *Bloody Revolutions / Persons Unknown* split-single that would pump-prime the finances of the short-lived London Autonomy Centre, and simultaneously give a huge boost to Poison Girls' profile and reputation.

The *Chappaquiddick Bridge* session saw the established four-piece lineup of Vi Subversa, Richard Famous, Lance d'Boyle and Bernhardt Rebours aided by contributions from Nil on violin and Gemma Sansom on backing vocals. "*Chappaquiddick* was the big one for me," says Rebours. "I didn't know it at the time but this was my final studio album."

"*Hex* set the overall elements in place, *Chappaquiddick* pushed it further," he continues. There was "more variation in style and pace, more journey into the unknown." The band were "trying anything that felt genuine," to produce "a true eclectic conglomeration of sound."

"The backing tracks were laid down quickly for all the songs, usually in just one or two takes once the sound had been sorted out," says Famous. "Overdubs were more considered, with Bernhardt able to show off his synth and piano skills to add layers of odd sounds to many of the tracks."

With the band still learning "the practical process of working in a studio," this included embracing happenstance and the unplanned, unexpected consequences of experimentation. At its simplest, that meant "keeping accidents" in the mix whenever they added something, says Rebours.

Although this would be the final studio album that Rebours would play on, it was also the record that confirmed his confidence as an equal contributor in the process. "It was obvious during the recording of *Chappaquiddick Bridge* that things had become more of a

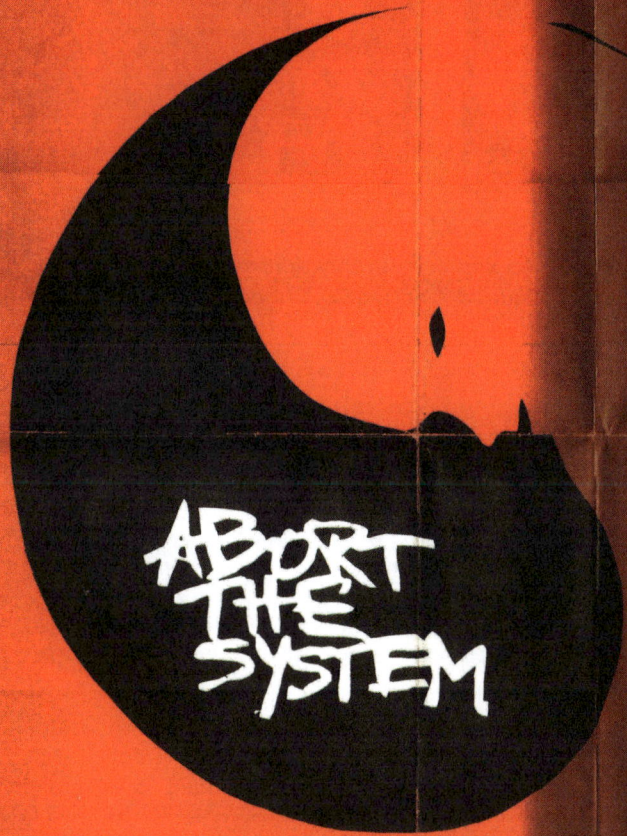

'Abort the System' poster included with *Words Written in Trust*, 1980.

group effort," he says. "I was building a stronger feeling that I was a genuine member of the band. "I had acquired some understanding of the process of recording and mixing, and was more aware of the intricacies of production," he continues. "I was still tentative about offering suggestions, though I did put some ideas into the discussion mix." Rebours felt that, with *Chappaquiddick Bridge*, he had secured his identity and status within the band. "*Hex* was my probation period in comparison," he says.

"We were definitely up for experimentation, and had always been open to 'found' sounds, sonic accidents, and the noise that came out of free improvisation," says Famous. "This was well before we had met Crass. Penny recognised kindred spirits and his work as producer seemed to be to indulge us with this, and to subvert the expectation of what a song—and song structure—should sound like. We were definitely encouraged to challenge ourselves musically, and not to record our more obviously punky tracks. This was not to be 'Hex II.'"

"*Chappaquiddick Bridge* is not my personal favourite Poison Girls' release," Famous continues. "Although I love the songs, and applaud the ambition, it's a record that at times seems to be odd for the sake of being odd. That said, as a body of work, it stands as a unique addition to the 'punk' musical canon—due to the strength of the material, the confidence to take musical chances, and the power and honesty behind Vi's voice and lyrics."

Given how much the political lens of British ancho-punk focused on domestic, home issues, the unusual naming of the album was in keeping with Poison Girls' conviction about the importance of being different. At the time of the record's release, Jimmy Carter was US president, but in the UK the go-to perception of the

American political system was still more readily provided by the Watergate scandal of the early 1970s which engulfed and then ended Nixon's presidency. Watergate had become the watchword for political corruption in the US, a shorthand summary for the systematic criminal abuse of power by a venal and megalomaniac head of the executive branch of government. The criminal actions of a paranoid narcissist who treated the White House as the operational headquarters of his unconstrained personal fiefdom. Poison Girls chose instead to turn the spotlight on an earlier episode in the history of a dynastic family in the US political class: the Kennedys.

"It was all to do with puncturing the reverence the Kennedy clan were held in," Famous explains. "Despite the cultural storm that shook Britain in the 1960s, our politicians were still the definition of 'stuffy.' The Kennedys, by contrast, were considered young and forward looking, and continued to have a political hold on the American establishment. The political capital of the two assassinations—JFK and Robert Kennedy—still resonated. They had been seen as the beacon of energy, the promise of a progressive future, the liberal face for the new modern age."

Late in the evening of 18 July 1969, US senator and aspiring presidential candidate Ted Kennedy, who was 37 years old, left a party of his peers on Chappaquiddick Island in the company of 28-year-old political campaign worker Mary Jo Kopechne, following a night of drinking. Approaching a narrow bridge, Kennedy's car left the road and overturned and sank in the shallow waters of Poucha Pond. Kennedy swam free from the wreck, but Kopechne was left trapped in the vehicle. Kennedy made his way back to his hotel, changed his

Poison Girls used images of the Chappaquiddick Bridge incident throughout the cover design for their LP. The interior gatefold and the side one label uses 1969 press photos of scuba divers recovering the body of Mary Jo Kopechne, whom Ted Kennedy left in a car after driving drunk off a bridge into Poucha Pond, resulting in Kopechne's death. Cover art by Bernardt Rebours.

clothes, and returned to the party. After alerting two of his closest aides, the three returned to the crash site but failed to free Kopechne. Kennedy delayed reporting the accident until the following morning, and only after the wreck had been spotted by a father and son arriving at the pond to fish. After authorities recovered the vehicle and retrieved Kopechne's body it was deemed most likely that she suffocated in the upturned vehicle after

she exhausted the oxygen in an air pocket that formed inside the car.

She was trapped for several terrifying hours while Kennedy abandoned any effort to rescue her or to raise the alarm until her air ran out. In the aftermath, Kennedy sought to evade culpability for Kopechne's death, and was never subject to any legal consequences. Press attention ensured that the "Chappaquiddick incident" became

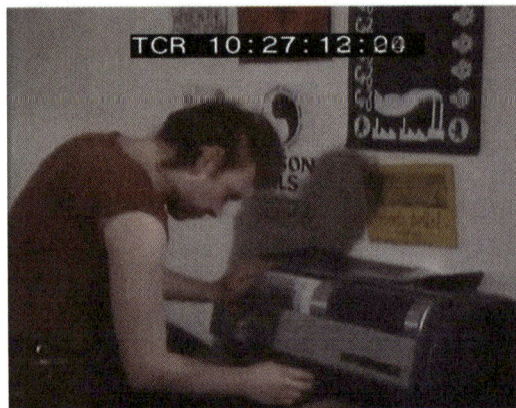

an infamous American political scandal and testament to the self-serving contempt and barely disguised misogyny of one of the most prominent male members of the American political establishment of the time. "The incident showed that, with sufficient money and status, you could get away with murder," Famous observes. "For many, it spelt the death of any residual trust in any kind of mainstream political solution."

Appalling as Kennedy's behaviour at Chappaquiddick clearly was, it was a crisis the reverberations of which were soon displaced by the incendiary revelations of the Watergate conspiracy, and the tapering off of Kennedy's career ambitions, as his hopes of winning the Democratic nomination to run for the presidency sank. Chappaquiddick was a potent metaphor for many of the issues that Poison Girls were anxious to address: the existence of a political patriarchy, the double standards in relation to the value of women's lives, the protections afforded to those of wealth and privilege, and the moral nihilism afflicting those in positions of power.

By 1980, Kopechne's death and Kennedy's culpability were matters that had faded from press headlines and public consciousness, even more so in the UK. Because of everything that it represented, "Chappaquiddick Bridge" certainly was an apposite candidate for a Poison Girls album title. But as a callback to an incident on the other side of the Atlantic from over a decade earlier, it was neither current nor something guaranteed to trigger immediate recognition. To most sixteen-to-eighteen-year-olds in Britain in 1980, "Chappaquiddick" meant nothing. In selecting it as the album's name, it seems that Poison Girls were consciously making clear their awareness of questions of politics and power from the prepunk era. "We had thought of calling the album 'Dallas Book Depository,' the site of Lee Harvey Oswald's sniper's nest," says Famous. "Usually we would throw out suggestions for weeks before something stuck—and then that name would seem obvious. *Chappaquiddick Bridge* is certainly a name that you can't forget—or pronounce or spell either—and as such it works well. It also provided an obvious topic of conversation when we met Jello Biafra of Dead Kennedys."

The sleeve design for *Chappaquiddick Bridge* provided further affirmation of Poison Girls' unique identity and aesthetic in the developing anarchist punk canon. Unusually for Crass Records releases, the band were able to prepare a cover that used the two colours that have long been the signature pairing of anarchism: red and black. Not constrained by the monochrome house style of the Crass label, the result was a striking, rich, and impactful sleeve front which echoed the black–and–white motifs of *Hex* with a similar single central image. *Hex* had featured an iconic rendering of a carrion crow, an image that the band would use extensively in their early years.

Video stills from the BBC2's music television program *Oxford Road Show*, 1981. Top to bottom: Vi, Lance, and Richard greeting the TV crew at the door of their house in Leytonstone, London. Zillah Minx and Vi creating Rubella Ballet lyric books. Lance d'Boyle working the in-house printing press. Richard, Lance, and Vi interviewed on the couch.

Chappaquiddick Bridge introduced a new icon which would become just as synonymous with the band: an evocation of the yin-yang symbol, reimagined as a representation of pregnancy and potential rebirth. Its adoption placed centre stage questions of conception control, reproductive rights, and motherhood, in a fictional image from within the womb that was as unnerving as it was provocative.

"The yin-yang symbol was very prevalent, and probably overused, in the heady days of the late 1970s," Famous recalls. With its origins in the tenets of Chinese philosophy, it became a symbol intended to describe opposing elements that were mutually dependent but held in perpetual balance. In the 1960s, it had become part of the mainstream iconography of the hippy movement, evoking the aspiration for a world in natural harmony in sharp contrast to the chaos, dislocation and crisis of a real world seemingly unmoved by the giddy aspirations of the Summer of Love. Shortly before the studio session, "Vi had finished the long prose poem 'Abort the System,' which we had hand silk-screened into a four poster set," Famous explains. The poem, eventually recorded in a rewritten form with a musical accompaniment, for the *Seven Year Scratch* album begins:

> The woman has a body, that she must call her
>   own
> But they treat her like a flowerpot for a seed
>   that he has sown
> The woman makes a baby and feeds him 'til
>   he's grown
> And those who feed on fresh young blood, will
>   break his spirit down
> They fill his brains with poison and teach him
>   left and right
> And how to hate his brother and teach him
>   black and white
> The woman makes a baby and bears a big
>   strong son
> And those who feed on fresh young blood,
>   would kill him with a gun

"Somehow the image of the yin-yang and the image of a foetus seemed to fit together," says Famous. And through confounding expectations about what the image represented, its adoption allowed the band to "subvert the commonplace" and encourage a reaction—be that surprise, indignation or intrigue. It's not difficult to recognise it as yet another example of hippy getting "punked."

The band's stage backdrop was resewn to incorporate the image, which was also pressed onto badges and printed on stickers, becoming part of the band's visual onstage identity right up until the release of the *Where's the Pleasure* album in 1982. Even after being replaced, as part of the band's efforts to recalibrate their image, the symbol se-

Vi in Amsterdam, 1980. Photo courtesy of Bernhardt Rebours.

cured an unanticipated afterlife. "When we moved to Leytonstone after Burleigh House was demolished, we had to pave the garden area in front of the new house to accommodate our van," Famous remembers. "A huge yin-yang foetus was incorporated into the crazy paving that Nil, our ace fabricator, roadie, fifth Poison Girl, and one time bass player, set into the concrete. It's really only properly visible from above, but it is still there to this day!"

On the sleeve of *Chappaquiddick Bridge* the band's appearance is anything but crystal clear due to the intentional blur of the slow-aperture photos taken by Gee Vaucher of Crass, intended to capture movement by both Famous and d'Boyle. It was an evocative shot, and a rarity at that time for any Crass Records release to include something as unexpected as a "group photo." But it would not be until the release of the *Where's the Pleasure* album that a Poison Girls record sleeve would fully reveal these "persons in hiding."

It was "another anarchist punk album sleeve with a circular logo at its centre," but the contrast with the stark, angular ouroboros that Dave King had designed for Rimbaud's *Reality Asylum* pamphlet (which would go on to become the internationally recognised "Crass logo") could hardly be starker. King rendered the weight of oppressive institutions and ideologies in an interlocking circle of black blocks. Poison Girls' yin-yang foetus spoke to something very different but just as intriguing.

"It was and is a challenging listen," Rebours acknowledges. It was an album with "nothing predictable" in its grooves. "Sometimes going over the top, while other parts were sparse, open, and subtle," the album discomforts and ensnares the listener, he concludes.

The album's opening track "State Control and Rock'n'Roll" is unlisted but provides the ideal introduction to the album's key themes. A seductively simple eight-bar riff (which "incorporates an F# chord as well as the normal E, A, and B," Famous clarifies proudly), State Control was a song the band could play in either restrained or full-on mode, provides the circular musical motif for a critique that's as powerful and passionate as it is mischievous and whimsical. This was anarchist cynicism, which recognised the contradictions of working in and against commercial music industry culture, delivered with a knowing smile and a wink.

> State control and rock and roll
> Are run by clever men
> What they sell is selling very well
> And the price is up again
> State control and rock and roll
> Are run by clever men
> What you know is what they show
> So it all goes round again
>
> State control and rock and roll
> Are run by clever men
> Politics are ultra chic
> And wars are in again
> State control and rock and roll
> Are run by clever men
> Revolution's this year's thing
> We're on the streets again—and again
>
> State control and rock and roll
> Are run by clever men
> And anarchy is this year's thing . . .

"Another Hero" is a powerful and plaintive treatise on the horrors of war and the loss of people sacrificed in the interest of those in power. There's a haunting, cavernous quality to the soundscape of the song, a lightness brought by the dominance of a treble register which clashes, fully intentionally, with the edgy urgency of the twin vocals and the song's fractured feel.

"Hole in the Wall (Thisbe's Song)" is a number inspired by feelings of alienation and otherness, and the sense of being an observer to madness and the incomprehensible, apart and deprived of human connection. The song draws its poetic inspiration from the ancient Greek myth of the doomed romance of would-be lovers Pyramus and Thisbe. With both families opposed to their relationship, the couple communicated through an opening in the wall between their neighbouring houses. Their decision to arrange a face-to-face *rendezvous* in a tomb beyond the city wall ends in tragedy and the suicide of both heartbroken lovers. Their tragedy is retold as a play-within-a-play in Shakespeare's *A Midsummer Night's Dream*. "Vi was into Shakespeare," d'Boyle recalled. "She used to do Shakespeare at school, and so she got to remember . . . lots of bits you can recite." And, of course, repurpose. The myth's lament is a metaphor for forbidden love and the fleeting nature of true happiness. As reimagined again by Poison Girls, the song is a mournful reflection on unrequited, unattainable, or unfathomable romantic love. "The lyrics were also influenced by the band's recent visit to the Berlin Wall," Famous explains.

Arguably the most musically and lyrically caustic song on the album is "Underbitch," which builds its irresistible power through the swirling, alternating percussive vocals of Subversa and Famous—as the "underdog" and the newly assertive "underbitch" battle for recognition in a world which screws them both over. "This is an idea reflected in the way the 3/4 rhythm section battles against the 4/4 guitars," Famous affirms. The song's added edge came from its appropriation of the epithet "bitch" (as well as the noun). "The way that the vocals fitted in with the music was very . . . syncopated and witty," Subversa said later. "People enjoyed it on a subliminal, gut level." Playing the song live, Subversa was pleased to see audiences smiling in response to the song's implicit humour. "That was what I wanted," she said. "That wasn't a song where I wanted to wallow in the pain of it."

"Alienation," which closes out side one, speaks to one of the record's strongest recurring themes: the feeling of being detached and separate and apart, and overwhelmed by the repellent horrors of the world. Its insistent circular rhythms challenge the sentiments of lyrics that could, on their own, be read as a form of defeatism (that risk of "wallowing" that Subversa had cautioned against in playing "Underbitch"). It does invest the album's half-way point with a mood that's as reflective as it is angry, and a reluctance to offer simple sloganeering "solutions."

Side two opens with "Pretty Polly," a critique (mixed with empathy) of the career girl battling misogyny and sexism and condescension by her bosses and peers. She appears guileless and unaware about her predicament. "Anxious to please. Genetic disease," the lyrics chide. Subversa's lyrics and vocal delivery both

Poison Girls on tour, 17 June 1980. Bernhardt Rebours: "Bournemouth Council cancelled the event at short notice (no notice at all was more accurate), partly due to negative reputation/hearsay that trouble occurred at our gigs. The entrance doors were locked. There was a period when we attracted National Front skinhead problems out for 'bovver' with our punk fans. We played for everybody. Our songs were relevant for everybody."

tread the resulting delicate balance between contempt and empathy with great skill.

"Good Time (I Didn't Know Sartre Played Piano)" is a quiet riot of a track. It was the first vinyl hint of a key part of Poison Girls' identity: a refusal to renounce hedonism and the pursuit of pleasure—however much the joyless critics, insistent that all that mattered was "the struggle," might object. Poison Girls' anarchism embraced more than Emma Goldman's enthusiasm for dancing. The determination to savour all that life had to offer was a commitment threaded through the work and band and its output.

The philosopher Jean-Paul Sartre was an enthusiastic amateur pianist. Sartre's existentialism prioritised questions of individual freedom and the subjective experience of existence. So it's not difficult to see his enjoyment of music as a celebration of individual creativity. Perhaps Poison Girls enjoyed the anomalous idea of a po-faced philosopher letting rip on the keys of his piano.

It would not be the only time that Poison Girls would make lyrical reference to the work of philosophers and social theorists. *Where's the Pleasure* would include the mesmerising "Fear of Freedom," an exploration of the themes set out in Erich Fromm's 1941 book of the same name (known as *Escape from Freedom* in the US). Fromm

addressed the social paradox in which individuals seem to desire freedom but simultaneously feel overwhelmed by the responsibilities of personal autonomy. That anxiety can lead the fearful to embrace conformity and the desire to submit to authoritarian rule or ideology.

The lyrics of "Good Time" were short, simple, and wholly ironic. They hint at unfulfilling sexual encounters, distorted by gender stereotypes, where lust is twisted by societal expectations, to produce a form of sexuality that was "obsessive," "deceptive" and ultimately "fascistic," and which corrupted the liberating nature of genuine desire. It was something that again showed the richness and complexity of the band's treatment of questions of sex, sexuality and sexual politics. If you've any doubt about the distinctiveness of Poison Girls' work in the pantheon of early-period anarcho-punk, just try to imagine "Good Time" slotted somewhere into the track listing of *Stations of the Cross*.

"Other" explores the challenging dynamics of relationships and the uncertainties of dealing with others who you are both compelled, bemused, and repelled by. "Daughters and Sons" is without question a song written for Subversa's children: an encouragement for them to find their own autonomous path and grasp their own opportunities for freedom. "You've got to sing your own

songs—you've got your own songs to sing," she urges. The album ends with the gentle refrain of "Tender Lover," a quiet, almost plaintive, appeal to a new partner to share in the honesty and vulnerability that a lovers' connection can generate. "Will you be my lover? My tender lover?" Subversa asks.

One of the most intriguing decisions taken by the band in relation to *Chappaquiddick Bridge* concerns the decision to include the "Statement" flexi disc as an accompaniment to the album. The song itself is a powerful, excoriating denunciation of the agency of state power, a passionate declaration of anarchist intent, a righteous refusal to accept the crushing power of unaccountable authority, and a defiant statement of total refusal. "I denounce the system that murders my children," Subversa begins alone, before the rest of the band join her in a chopping, driving riff that ignites her invective.

> I denounce the system that denies my
>   existence
> I curse the system that makes machines of my
>   children
> I reject the system that makes men of
>   machines
> I reject the system that turns bodies of my
>   own sweet flesh
> Into monsters of iron and steel and war
> And turns the hands of my children into robot
>   claws

As Subversa's personal manifesto unfolds, the rage temporarily dissipates as the music quietens and a lone male voice intones that "there are no words, for us no words." A suggestion perhaps that even this unrestrained condemnation of the horrors of the capitalist war state is not sufficient to give voice to those disfigured by its privations. "Statement" was easily the most didactic song on the record, and its uncompromising anarchist invective was a sharp contrast with the more introspective and reflective material on the record. The song's lyrical line of attack (reinforced by its jagged, layered, stop-start soundtrack) was more in the realm of metaphor and imagery than in the arena of practical politics, but it emphasised the degree to which Poison Girls defined themselves in uncompromising outsider, oppositional political terms. "Statement" confirmed that Poison Girls were unambiguous anarchists, and angry with it.

Throughout the band's life, their lyrical focus would continue to combine the personal and the profoundly political. This was more of a continuum than a tension, but was something writ large in the songs of *Chappaquiddick Bridge*. At other points in the band's career, explicit

Poison Girls live, stills from *Neon*, a Dutch television magazine, 1980.

political statements were pushed to the fore— "Dirty Work," "Stonehenge 1985," "Take the Toys from the Boys," and many others. For the most part, the lyrics of *Chappaquiddick Bridge* were oblique and introspective—exploring vulnerability and self-doubt rather than resolute conviction.

It's not hard to see "Statement" as a political yin-yang which balances the more personally reflective contents of the main album. *Hex* had shown the band's astute and singular understanding of the gender politics of home, family, and parenthood. *Chappaquiddick Bridge* revealed more the band's critique of "love and romance," and the many ways in which relationships became distorted and disfigured by social context.

Music press reaction Poison Girls' third twelve-inch release was polarised. *Melody Maker* dismissed it as "a dour, depressing, pleasureless experience," and the *NME* remained "baffled" by what it declared to be "a very confused, and confusing, album." In sharp contrast, *Sounds* acclaimed a "well considered" release that was "demanding" of the listener and enlivened by music which had "become more varied and interesting than on *Hex*." Unusually, reviewer Phil Sutcliffe shared his assessment of the band's integrity and honesty: "One of the most valuable impressions Poison Girls leave me with is that they are a group of people who can be trusted," he wrote.

Like its predecessor, *Chappaquiddick Bridge* was a record without punk comparison, in its insightful takes on both questions of political power and of alienation and otherness in human beings' relations with each other. The sound texture of the album was also surprising; the song structures were unformulaic and unexpected, as timbres shifted between rage and lament.

Chappaquiddick Bridge successfully secured two objectives. It was the album that positioned the band unambiguously *within* the culture of anarchist music and mischief making, seeing them make common cause with the growing tribe of troublemakers. Through its release, Poison Girls were confirmed as a part of the new underground anarchist insurgency. At the same time, the album made clear just how different Poison Girls' reading of that anarchist imperative would be— musically, lyrically, and in the band's embrace of political literacy.

For Rebours, even forty years on from its release, the album retains its power and its sense of conviction. "The album was a response to situations that confronted us then," he says. "The intention that we had for the music is locked into that album," the soundtrack to the band's certainties and doubts. For that reason, *Chappaquiddick Bridge* "can connect to and make sense for people facing similar situations today." The issues that were the inspiration for "Vi's songs to be recorded and released back then still linger."

Poison Girls agreed with *In the City* magazine to produce a two-song flexi disc that could be included as a giveaway with issue 15, published in 1980. *In the City* positioned itself at the semiprofessional end of the zine spectrum, adopting the layout style and graphic design motifs of more mainstream magazines and embracing colour printing techniques. In terms of content, *In the City* was self-consciously eclectic: the attention it paid to the punk diaspora was matched by a focus on post-punk, goth, industrial, and early electronic artists, and its coverage of fashion, hairstyles, and emerging trends in alternative culture.

Only a few independent maga/zines that were associated with punk (but free of corporate contamination) had the capacity to distribute a flexi disc on any sort of scale. Yet even in a small field of candidates, Poison Girls' selection of *In the City* was instructive. Crass had chosen *Toxic Grafity* zine to carry their *Rival Tribal Rebel Revels* flexi—a title close to the hardcore heart of anarcho-punk. As part of the ambition to extend their reach, Poison Girls had chosen a maga/zine with a far broader appeal, and one in which their music and message would appear in a more open, less didactic context.

Increasing the release's impact, Poison Girls secured front-page billing in the issue, promoting a lengthy and largely sympathetic interview with the band inside. The first track on the flexi (which was pressed in bright red, and played at 33 1/3 rpm) was a live version of 'Bully Boys,' recorded through the mixing desk of Paul Tandy's PA at a gig on 18 June 1980. A different live version of the song would appear on the *Total Exposure* album the following year, but no studio recording would ever be released. Choosing an unreleased track for the flexi added appeal for existing followers of the band. Bully Boys was joined by a rerelease of the Southern Studios recording of 'Pretty Polly' from the *Chappaquiddick Bridge* album. Taken together, the two songs offered an enticing, and for some an uncomfortably challenging, introduction to the band's identity and political preoccupations for those unfamiliar with their work. Viewed in retrospect, the *Bully Boys* flexi also feels like one of the band's first deliberate attempts to stretch their appeal to reach a broader audience.

Other things were in motion too. After several stays of execution, construction work on the new M25 London orbital reached the location of Burleigh House. A few weeks before the building was demolished in December 1980, Poison Girls relocated to a new shared home, and revitalised centre of operations for the band, in Leytonstone in East London.

"We had been quite stressed trying to find somewhere else we could afford to live," says Famous. "We even considered a canal boat at Camden Lock—before we realised it was the same size as the corridor at Burleigh!" The band's new residence was "completely different," he adds. "In fact, it couldn't have been more different. The large Victorian house on Hainault Road was large, semi-detached, and came with a big garden. But compared to Burleigh House it "seemed tiny, claustrophobic, and surrounded by other houses." One major plus was the spacious cellar, split into two rooms. "When we first looked into the cellar it was evident how damp it was and we could see a big toad sitting in each corner!"

The move initially seemed to dampen the enthusiasm and energy of the band. On 31 July 1980, Subversa wrote an open letter to her family and others in the band acknowledging her feelings. "The house is sad—the cellars are wet and crumbling—the foundations are inadequate—my feelings last night when we went there . . . were awful," she wrote. "The environment in the streets around set me off into a depression and the house itself finished me off." Determined not to let a downbeat mood overwhelm the band, she called on everyone to find "enough life and love in us to warm the walls and dry the damp and light the gloom."

The band wasted no time fitting out a permanent rehearsal space beneath the building. "We chose the larger of the two spaces, digging out a part of the floor so that we could stand upright, putting four tons of sand between the joists as sound proofing, and sound treating the walls," says Famous.

As a result of their hard work, the mood soon brightened—and attracted others. Adi Cooper and her partner Penny moved into the house the following year. "There was a double-bed mattress on a platform under the ceiling at the top of the stairs: we lived there, 'on the shelf' for six months, until we moved into a house around the corner," she recalls. She remembers that Hainault Road developed its own energy and 'buzz.' "There was always a lot going on in the house. People coming in and out, music and food, talking and dramas. There were always projects, printing leaflets, producing stuff. It was a very creative space."

One important new endeavour, instigated by Dan Sansom (Pete Fender), focused on creating a home studio. "He set up his first four-track facility in the corridor section next to the rehearsal room," Famous explains. "This was later relocated and upscaled to an eight-track studio, based around an ex-BBC Neve desk console."

The studio at Hainault Road was used extensively over the following years, with Sansom in the role of producer. "'The Offending Article' was the first track that Poison Girls recorded 'in house' in Leytonstone," Famous continues. "We went on to do a couple of tracks to help finish off the *Songs of Praise* album that had got stuck unfinished. Those four-track recordings of "No More Lies" and "Feeling the Pinch" stand up perfectly well against the other material on the record. Later still,

we recorded more Poison Girls' demos, and the backing tracks—and the eventual full soundtrack—for the *AIDS: The Musical* project."

Other bands recorded at the home studio too. "We spent time in the basement of the house in Leytonstone in August 1983 to record our *Syndrome* demo," Heather Joyce of Toxic Shock recalls. "Dan (Pete) was very patient with us. I discovered just how appallingly out of tune my singing could be. It was slow going, and a bit scary, but lots of fun—and, of course, it was all down to the hospitality of Poison Girls that we were there and had that opportunity."

Through collective effort, Poison Girls had reenergised and reequipped their unprepossessing Leytonstone home and headquarters—creating a revived centre of operations from which they could confidently set out in a new direction.

Vi and Richard at Leytonstone, 1981. Photos courtesy of Richard Famous.

TO POISON GIRLS
FROM VI SUBVERSA
POLICY STATEMENT AND INTERIM REPORT 31.7.80

you are all aware of the pit we may be in at the moment. yes i know we are also
at a peak - the album, the major triumphs(its all relative) of our three tours and
recent gigs. but those of us living at Burleigh have being going through agony
upon agony of entropy and insecurity and actual threat from a number of outside
hositilities for a long time now. as if that were not enough to cope with our actual
domestic realtionships have been not good enough; xxxxe i am now realizing how we have
all been unhappy in varying ways and degrees. We rarely experience collective
pleasure at home. And we protect ourselves and each other from sharing the difficulties
ikxxx so that issues are ignored and the situation gets stuck. I don't want to go into
decribing each persons unhappinesses right now, but i know that if xr we are to
continue to grow and capitalize our achievements as a band without loss of time
and initiative we are going to have to produce a marathon of creative energy which
we must apply to our problems. Now this means individual efforts - e.k. but what I
am writing this for is to generate some concept of collective energy and goodwill
because that is ulimately what it isx all about. We are faced with a desperate move to
a basically unsatisfactory situation in Leytonstone. The house is sad- the cellars
are wet and crumbling - the foundations are inadequate - my feelings last night when
we went there with seamus were awful. The environment in the streets around set me off
into a depression and the house itself finished me off. I was already spiritually weak
and physically shaky. I wanted nothing to do with it. I wanted to stop, die, give up.

Now in the morning I can see only one thing clearly. That any one of us could
do that and that would be the end of it all. Or a weakening - a slackening of
committment - AND WHAT IT IS ABOUT IS LACK OF HOPE AND FAITH.THAT THAT POOR DEAD
LOVELESS HOUSE WILL OVERCOME US. THAT WE HAVE NOT GOT ENOUGH LIFE AND LOVE IN US TO
WARM THE WALLS AND DRY THE DAMP AND LIGHT THE GLOOM. WELL THAT HAS TO BE A LIE.
WE HAVE GOT TO FIND IN OURSELVES THE ENERGY TO MAKE IT COME ALIVE. THE ONLY REAL FUEL
I KNOW IS UTTER WHOLEHEARTED GOODWILL (LOVE?) AND DETERMINATION TO REALLY VALUE OURSELVES
AND WHAT WE HAVE ALREADY ACCOMPLISHED.

I am not interested any more in negativity.we have to find the positive forse to dig out
the rotten foundations and shit and mould and DO IT.
and we are all going to need a lot of support and love from each other. and i want to st
start by saying that I do love you all. I knew it is not xxx equal. the nature of it
is different for each of you. and i want it recognized and accepted and bloody well
returned. in what ever way you can.

Vi's letter to Poison Girls on the upcoming move to Leytonstone, 1980. Opposite: Promo poster for the release of *Chappaquiddick Bridge*, 1980. Though 1979's *Hex* had eight songs on a twelve-inch record, it was considered an EP. Thus "The First Album . . ." designation.

THE FIRST ALBUM...

Chappaquiddick Bridge

POISON GIRLS

FROM STATE CONTROL TO TENDER LOVE

Opposite upper: After the gig—Poison Girls and Crass, Plaza Ballroom, Glasgow, 1980. Opposite lower: Pete Fender, Vi, Gemma Sansom, and Eve Libertine (Crass) catching a nap while leaving Holland, 1980. This page, upper: Poison Girls live, location unknown, 1980. Photos courtesy of Sue Cooper. Bottom: Richard Famous, Vi Subversa, Steve Ignorant (Crass). Paradiso, Amsterdam, 20 March 1980. Photo courtesy of Bernhardt Rebours.

POISON GIRLS

with disco students

AND THE erAtiCS

AT THE CENTRO IBERICO

FRIDAY 14th MARCH... 8PM.. COME EARLY £1·00

CENTRO IBERICO.... 421a HARROW Rd. westbourne park

PERSONS UNKNOWN/BLOODY REVOLUTION/POISON GIRLS/CRASS/NEW SINGLE

THIS IS A MESSAGE TO PERSONS UNKNOWN/PERSONS
KNOWN/SURVIVAL IN SILENCE ISN'T GOOD
YOUR MOUTH SHUT/PERSONS
AND EVERY ONE

HOUSEWIVES AND PROSTITUTES/
BOILER SUITS/TRUANTS IN COFFEE BARS/ THINK YOU
ONE/BIG MEN ON BUILDING SITES/SICK MEN IN DRESSING GOWNS/AGE
WHO NEVER GO HOME/WOMEN IN FACTORIES
WOMEN IN PURDAH
GIRLS CRIMINALS
PERSONS UNKNOWN
RUBBERSTAMPED BLIND
MORNING WITH
NYLON SHIRTS/FEMINISTS IN FLORAL SKIRTS/
WHEN IT HURTS/PERSONS UNKNOWN/ASTRONAUTS
HYPOCRITES LIARS AND LUNATICS/PER
POOLS/TEACHERS IN EMPTY
THE LONELY
ANARCHISTS
AND PICKETS
RADICAL
ON HER THRONE/
SAILORS AND STEVEDORES/ BEGGARS AND BANKERS/PERS
FOOTBALL CROWD HOOLIGANS BUNKIN OFF SCHOOL AGA
OLS AGAIN/UNITED'S AT HOME/SMOKERS WITH HEART DISEASE
LAVATORIES/ THE OLD WITH THEIR MEMORIES /PERSONS UNKNOWN
ARE WHO WE ARE/FLESH AND BLOOD WE ARE/FLESH
WHO WE ARE/OUR COVER IS BLOWN/
WE ARE /FLESH
GE TO PERSONS
RS EACH AND EVERY ONE OF
ESH AND BLOOD ARE WHO WE ARE/
ESH AND BLOOD ARE WHO WE ARE/OUR COVER IS BLOWN

PERSONS UNKNOWN/BLOODY REVOLUTION/POISON GIRLS/CRASS/NEW SINGLE OUT SOON ON CRASS RECORDS

SOON ON CRASS RECORDS OUT SINGLE NEW/CRASS/POISON GIRLS/BLOODY REVOLUTION/PERSONS UNKNOWN

CRASS POISON GIRLS ANNIE ANXIETY FLUX OF PINK INDIANS

AN 021 party for Anarchy + Peace

DIGBETH CIVIC HALL WED 22nd APRIL

£1 : PEACE CENTRE : INFERNO : ROCKERS : OR ON THE NIGHT

THE REALITIES OF SOCIETY

ANARCHY AND PEACE

NATURE CREATED A PARADISE IN THE SUN; MAN DESTROYED IT!

in THE CITY

Free Flexi-disc Inside

30p

POISON GIRLS

THE GADGETS

#15 Crass - Suicide - The Method

Opposite: **Centro Iberico**, London, 14 March 1980. Centro Iberico was a squatted social centre begun by anarchist Spanish Civil War veterans, refugees, and former political prisoners. This page: **Digbeth Civic Hall**, Birmingham, 22 April 1981. *In the City* was a London-based fanzine. Issues 13 and 14 included a two-part interview with Poison Girls, and issue 14 included a flexi with a live version of "Bully Boys" and the album track "Pretty Polly." *Realities of Society*, anarcho-punk fanzine, produced by Dar-i* (Omega Tribe's Daryl Hardcastle), published by Xntrix, 1981.

125

THE IMPOSSIBLE DREAM #2 1980
ALL SYSTEMS GO-READY?

By the time the second issue was completed, the aesthetic of *The Impossible Dream* had changed completely.

The band had agreed to fund a more ambitious—and a much more expensive—method of design and print. From this point on, *The Impossible Dream* would be published in a fold-over A2 page format, printed on heavy-duty, gloss paper, and embracing the twin anarchist colour palette of red and black. No longer a strictly DIY affair, the printing, collating, and folding of *The Impossible Dream* would be outsourced. Subsequent issues would adopt the same method.

The visually arresting front cover, which reimagined the band's yin-yang and foetus-in-the-womb icons in a new and startling way, was designed by longtime member of the Poison Girls family (and sometime bassist) Nil.

The design of issue one had been hectic, as d'Boyle sought to make best use of the available space. But in issue two there's more room for the images to breathe. This allows the design to leverage the impact that can come from simplicity. The preparation of artwork was still reliant on table-top, hands-on techniques. But the upgraded format gave d'Boyle the larger canvas on which he could deliver striking visuals, in which the simplicity of the presentation of the image frequently belied the sophistication—and the impact—of the idea it represented.

The question of the nature of masculinity is again a predominant theme. Yet here the attention is focused on the position of the masculine persona within rock'n'roll. A centre-page spread pictures a Roger Daltry–style figure posing as frontman, the embodiment of preening excess, desperate to broadcast his sexual prowess and in search of adulation. The character is a towering colossus, and around his feet are countless cloned figures, dancing in unison to his tune. An all-male audience stands static, viewing the spectacle.

There are also reflections on fatherhood and the anguish of dysfunctional, emotionally crippling behaviours being passed down the male line, which ends by asking the question: "The sins of the fathers—will we, the sons, pass them on?"

Poison Girls' lyrics again feature prominently. Fitting with the theme of the commercial corruption of rock's rebellious potential, the opening lyrics of "State Control and Rock'n'Roll" are writ large across a single page; the full set of words on another. There are also twin teaser references to the phrase 'all systems go,' which would become the title of band's final seven-inch release on Crass Records. The first time the phrase is appended with the words 'going, going'; the second time with the one-word question 'ready?' Alongside the righteous anger of the misfortunes of mainstream male music making, there's the sadness, reflection and sense of regret that full lyrics of "Cry No More" capture so eloquently.

The input of Pete Wright into the first issue had drawn attention to Poison Girls' creative connections with Crass. That association is carried over into issue two and also given an unexpected satirical twist in the form of an imaginary interview with Penny Rimbaud, a self-deprecating encounter penned by d'Boyle which quickly unravels in absurdity—but not before revealing some of the complex history of romantic associations within the band. It's a pointed humorous interlude from the issue's otherwise focused and serious tone.

It's only outmatched by the laugh-out-loud crudity of the kitchen-sink-based montage, in which a smiling housewife suggests that it's wrong to worry which side in the Cold War has the largest nuclear arsenal, when attention should be focus on which party to the conflict has the most impressive male appendage. Manhood, militarism and nuclear anxiety—all mocked through an absurdist feminist prism.

Writing for this issue was credited to d'Boyle and Vi Subversa working together with contributors Pete Wright, Nil, Richard Famous and "Sli Fli Posters." In issue two, the notion of "The impossible dream" first introduced in issue one is framed in a different way—as an aspiration held in the grip of frustration. "Our impossible dreams are our reality / Our reality is an impossible dream / An impossible dream is a nightmare." This second issue was published in 1980, the same year that Poison Girls contributed the track "Persons Unknown" to the *Bloody Revolutions* single.

THE IMPOSSIBLE DREAM

OUR IMPOSSIBLE DREAMS ARE OUR REALITY OUR REALITY IS OUR IMPOSSIBLE DREAM AN IMPOSSIBLE DREAM IS A NIGHTMARE.

THE IMPOSSIBLE DREAM ISSUE 2. Designed and edited by Lance d'Boyle, writing by
Vi Subversa and Lance d'Boyle, contributions from Pete Wright, Nil, Richard Famous
and Sli Fli Posters. Thanks to Eve, Sarah, The Squatting Monster Her Little Brother
and Nil for the cover. Published by X & TRIX Publishing 1980. Correspondence C/O
Rough Trade Records, 202 Kensington Park Road, London W11.

CRY NO MORE

I'M TIRED OF CRYING FOR THE UNDERPRIVILEDGED THE BLACKS
THE WOMEN OR EVEN THE BLACK WOMEN OR THE STARVING
CHILDREN OR THE IRISH OR THE WORKING CLASS OR THE OLD
AGE PENSIONERS MULTIPLE SCELEROSED MENTALLY HANDICAPPED
THE THIRD WORLD THE NURSES THE MINERS THE RADIOACTIVATED
IN HIROSHIMA NAGASAKI AMERICA PRISONERS PRISONERS OF
MIND CONTROL THE WIVES OF THE AMBASSADORS THE SHIPWRECKED
AND THE UNFORTUNATES WICKED SINNERS LEPERS WIDOWS
BRAIN DAMAGED AT BIRTH THE ONE EYED JEWS THE ADDICTS
PAWNS AND PAUPERS OF CAPITALISM THE DEAD SOLDIERS
GRIEVING MOTHERS THE RAPED THE RAPISTS THE TORTURED AND
HUMILIATED FOR POLITICAL OR PRIVATE REASONS OF SADISM AND
MACHO MACHISMO MASOCHISMO O O PORNO O O VICTIMS
VICTIMS FLOOD DAMAGE BONE DAMAGE DAMAGE DAMAGE DAMAGE
YES ITS A SAVAGE SAVAGE WORLD AND I WANT TO CRY FOR ME –

I'M TIRED OF CRYING FOR THE NEGLECT OF OUR TALENTS THE
UNEMPLOYED AND THE ABANDONED I'M TIRED OF CRYING FOR NOBLE
CAUSES   FOR COLLECTING BOXES FOR THE DESOLATION OF OUR
BODIES FOR THE ABUSE OF OUR SEX THE COLLECTIVE WASTE
FOR THE DECAY THE CRIMINAL POLLUTION   FOR THE VICTIMS
OF THE VIOLENCE OF PROTECTION AND PRIVILEDGE VICTIMS MORE
VICTIMS VICTIMS I'M TIRED OF CRYING FOR THE STUPID STUPID
CONTEMPT AND DISCRIMINATION   FOR THE TRAPS AND TRICKS AND
CONTRADICTIONS AND BROKEN BROKEN BROKEN HOPES AND PROMISES
AND FOR THE CAREFULLY CONTROLLED AND FULLY IMPLEMENTED
MURDER OF OUR IMAGINATIONS AND I WANT TO CRY FOR ME –

THE SINS OF THE FATHERS - MY FATHER,
BITTER, DEFEATED AND EMPTY AFTER A
LIFETIME OF SERVING THE SYSTEM, IS
DISAPPOINTED IN ME BECAUSE I DO NOT
SERVE THE SYSTEM WELL. HE IS ASHAMED
OF ME FOR SHOWING UP HIS SHAME, FOR
NOT KEEPING QUIET ABOUT HIS DEFEAT,
FOR POINTING TO THE SUFFERING BEHIND
HIS PRIDE.
HE HATES ME
FOR NOT PRETENDING THAT I LIKE WHAT'S
HAPPENING TO ME - LIKE HE DID
FOR ROCKING THE BOAT, IN CASE WE
LOSE WHAT LITTLE WE HAVE GOT
FOR SCREAMING MY DISGUST, IN CASE THE
NEIGHBOURS HEAR - IN CASE WE DRAW
ATTENTION TO OURSELVES - IN CASE WE
ARE SEEN TO BE LOSING THE RACE THAT
NOBODY IS WINNING.

THE SINS OF THE FATHERS - WILL WE
THE SONS, PASS THEM ON ? BETRAY OUR
LIVES FOR THE SAKE OF APPEARANCES.
WILL WE CONTINUE TO SWALLOW THE DEATH
DEALING PROPAGANDA THAT LABELS OUR
DISGUST AND RAGE A MINORITY PERVERSION
AND CONDEMNS OUR DISOBEDIENCE AS A
BETRAYAL OF THEIR SELF SACRIFICE FOR US.

130

```
    THE SINS OF THE FATHERS
TO LOOK BRAVE
TO BANG THE DRUM
KEEP SECRETS
FROM OUR BROTHERS
AND SISTERS
HIDE OUR LUST
BEHIND NEWSPAPERS
DEDICATE OUR LIVES
TO SMALL MERCIES
FIGHT BACK THE TEARS
NEVER GIVE
THE GAME AWAY
AND ALWAYS BE PREPARED
TO FIGHT
TO OUR DEATH
OUR RIGHT TO
SERVE SHIT AND
EAT SHIT
```

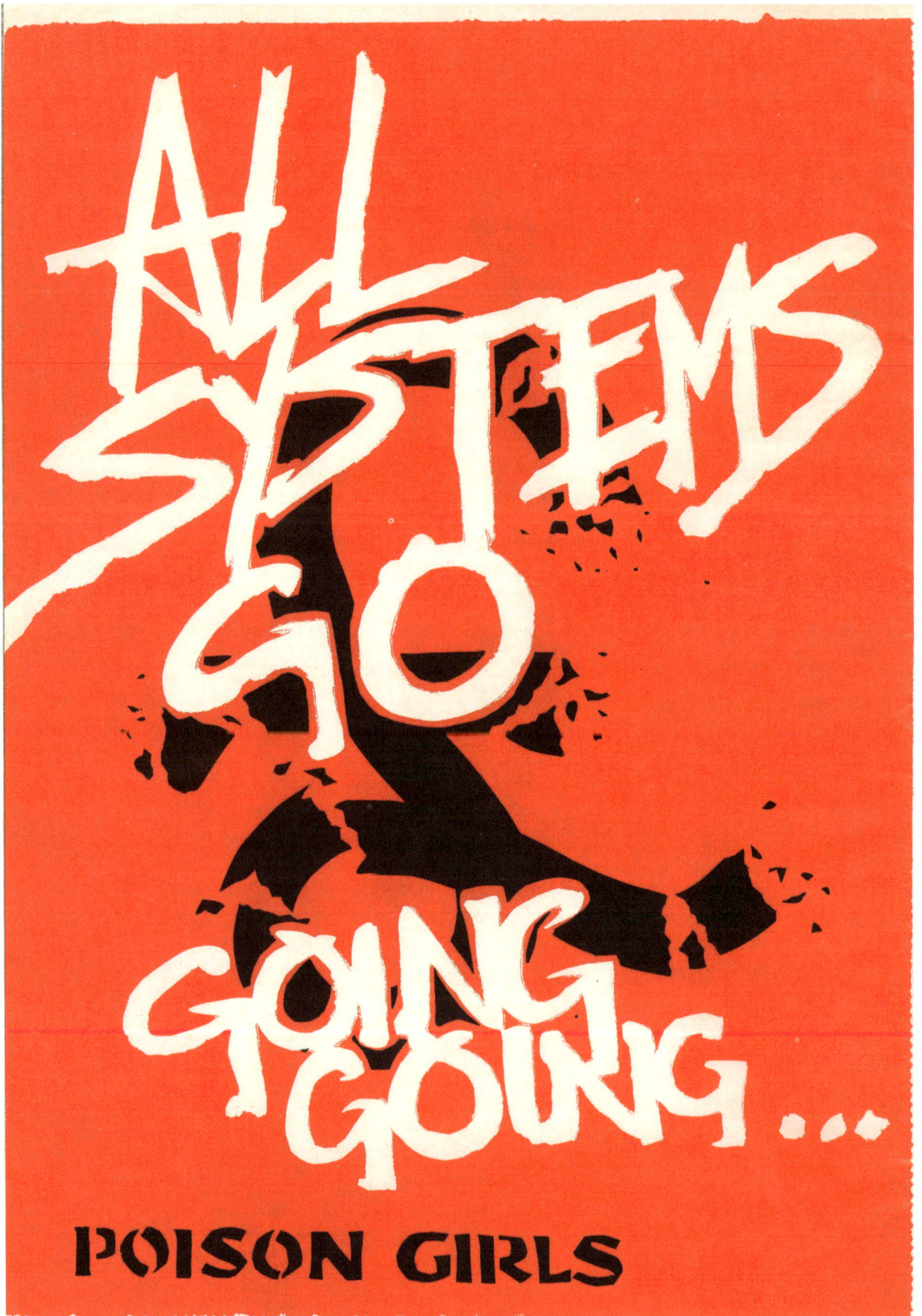

ALL SYSTEMS GO
GOING GOING ...

POISON GIRLS

STATE CONTROL AND ROCK AND ROLL ARE RUN BY GREEDY MEN IT'S ALL GOOD FOR BUSINESS WE'RE IN THE CHARTS AGAIN

STATE CONTROL AND ROCK AND ROLL ARE RUN BY CLEVER MEN
WHAT YOU KNOW IS WHAT THEY SHOW AND IT ALL GOES ROUND AGAIN
POLITICS ARE ULTRA CHIC AND WARS ARE IN AGAIN
FOLLOW THE HERD AND SWALLOW THE WORD IT ALL GOES ROUND AGAIN
REVOLUTIONS LOST AND WON ITS TIME TO FIGHT AGAIN
THEY BUY YOU OFF AND THEY SELL YOU SHORT IT ALL GOES ROUND AGAIN
STATE CONTROL AND ROCK AND ROLL ARE RUN BY CLEVER MEN
ANARCHY IS THIS YEARS THING AND IT ALL GOES ROUND AGAIN
STATE CONTROL AND ROCK AND ROLL ARE RUN BY CLEVER MEN
ITS ALL GOOD FOR BUSINESS WE'RE IN THE CHARTS AGAIN
THEY BUILD YOU UP AND THEY BREAK YOU DOWN THE BOSS MOB WIN AGAIN
THE SHORT SHARP SHOCK IS THIS YEARS THING ITS BACKLASH TIME AGAIN
STATE CONTROL AND ROCK AND ROLL ARE RUN BY CLEVER MEN
FOLLOW THE HERD AND SWALLOW THE WORD IT ALL GOES ROUND AGAIN
STATE CONTROL AND ROCK AND ROLL ARE RUN BY CLEVER MEN
WHAT THEY SELL IS SELLING VERY WELL AND THE PRICE IS UP AGAIN

YOU KNOW IT'S TRUE BUT WHAT CAN YOU DO
YOU LOOK FOR A GAP TO GET OUT OF THE TRAP
IT'S A VICIOUS CIRCLE YOU TRY TO BREAK LOOSE
BREAK OUT OF THE TRAP GET OUT OF THE NOOSE
YOU KNOW IT'S TRUE BUT WHAT CAN YOU DO
YOU PLAN IN YOUR HEAD AS YOU LIE IN YOUR BED
THE VICIOUS CIRCLE YOU TRY TO BREAK LOOSE
BREAK OUT OF THE TRAP GET OUT OF THE NOOSE
YOU KNOW IT'S TRUE BUT WHAT CAN YOU DO
COS WHAT YOU'RE FEELING IS A HUMAN BEING
NOT THIS YEAR'S THING NOT LAST YEAR'S THING
NOT THIS YEAR'S THING NOT NEXT YEAR'S THING

STATE CONTROL AND ROCK AND ROLL ARE RUN BY GREEDY MEN
IT'S ALL GOOD FOR BUSINESS WE'RE IN THE CHARTS AGAIN
STATE CONTROL AND ROCK AND ROLL ARE RUN BY CLEVER MEN
ANARCHY IS THIS YEAR'S THING AND IT ALL GOES ROUND AGAIN

ALL SYSTEMS GO READY?

POISON GIRLS

DYNAMIC EXCITEMENT. Be dynamic. Maintain a free position. Or is the passivity and stability of normal life another sort of freedom and excitement? The essential ingredient of all movements,while the interpretation of movements is a personal and self interested choice,even with the same content,however blatant. A power of thrills rather than a power of ideas.

What if? What if everyone did it? probably already exists. Here. the uncomfortable present,and confidence tricks. Con power. Con power. Another cheap "What if?" Far easier Predictions are a form of events intrude. No future.

Well,we all do. Postulate a state and it Adjusting our assumptions to approach beyond that,a battle of opposing Conned by the thrills and spills. trick,another neat rip. Con power. and more palatable than,"what is?" blinkered postponement,at least until No future please.

Honest questions. Oh! begged. Don't want answers. questions. Paring. intelligence and disappearing up

All is one— can be changed— it doesn't matter someone else's or permanent. future. State of Whose headache?

Or reaffirming. punctuation trap, about assumptions what follows implying the of validity there is becomes.

Can't think of any. They're all All dead. Marylin. Honest peeling,improving,sharing understanding on the way to your own are.
all is illusion—nothing only scratching the surface— anyway. Records left us of switch off point. Temporary Petty investments in the flux,statement of no flux.

Caught in the process/ but still affirming.Thinking, made assumptions. Determine by fixing the starting point. direction. Somebody's sens— tied in there somewhere. If the point,the question now not why,but who?

Look what you neutral? Predicted How do you Morality and Stance. So, throw around

One million. people. Victims of million,two hundred as remote control only. The assumptions left of coffee in Brazil. Marylin leaves

with tunnel vision,see in some. Marylin Monroe in. Fritz Stangl in neutral— with benefit of hindsight. like that?all seem up— morality projections. us.to fire for a while. and look again. two hundred thousand Treblinka? Or one and one thousand people me.questioned. An awful lot morality. Operating the me cold. Buddha else.

Everyone a buddha. to me. tortured and tortuous thoughts don't bother me a bit if they aren't mine. Caring about the world I am in,not the world anyone else is in. A statement of aloneness,or a different layer of togetherness. Affected by a feeling of interdependence. Saucy buddha. Aloof. Amused by a complexity which is in never external. At what point does the present intrude? That world deals in the present. Responsability. At what point does the present intrude? That world deals in the present. Responsibility? They may recognise the present of a state of freedoms involved with the past and views. Past and future. Emotional reactions to the other. freedoms involved with the past and future. Love,possession,masculine,feminine,on and on. To note — actually existing but having no legal right. Movement; Moving or part of the illusion of stasis.

Desperation is a form of the present. If the action isn't extreme,it must be half assed. Terrorists frighten. They put short fuses on their bomb. Short,but fuses all the same. Reduces two worlds. Disadvantages of both. As Geneva Convention. War in newspaper forms. Treblinka unfolds. Marylin pinups. Buddha in bermuda shorts,lace up shoes.
A prison of bits and pieces,by bits and pieces,for bits and pieces. Clutter and crap.

137

TAKE OFF THAT GLOOMY MASK OF TRAGEDY ITS NOT YOUR STYLE

THEY PASS BY THE CRIPPLES OF THE CITY NOT ONE HAS ESCAPED

138

All of this indicates that people are not simply dissatisfied with the rising cost of living, but with the way they live in society. In a sense, we can even understand this sentiment. Apparently, shoppers feel insulted by being forced to buy back what they have already produced as workers. Shopping, however, is as necessary as work. American society needs its consumers. People may feel sometimes that in our economy, things are more important than they are, but, after all, we do give you a choice of what you can buy.

Those people who think shopping is boring are the same people who are bored with their work—in fact, they're probably bored with everything our system has to offer. But shopping is not necessarily a dull obligation; it can be an exciting experience, a useful way to spend your leisure time. Many people, especially housewives, do a lot of shopping and find it rewarding.

However, the contempt for authority that people display when they steal could easily become widespread. If these people and our employees started acting together, we could be faced with serious revolt against the foundations of our society—work and shopping. The kind of people who don't pay are capable of anything, including the notion that they could run society by themselves without any need for people to give them orders.

we are aware that you are often bored and frustrated in your work situation. But we are confident that you are not disenchanted with our society as a whole because of this. We are already implementing programs that will make your job more meaningful to you by involving you more actively in the decision-making process. All of this will not change your position in society but it will bring your work closer to you. While you may be unhappy with your present conditions of employment, we know that underneath it all, you still believe in work itself and the system of authority that lies behind it.

It may appear to you that your work bears little relation to what you really want to do, and that it mainly consists of producing, selling or servicing items which have no apparent value in themselves. This may be true; nevertheless, work keeps people occupied and gives them a goal in life. Besides, this is the way it is all over the world, even in the so-called "socialist" countries. Work has helped everyone live much the same way.

Work may be unpleasant, then, but it is absolutely essential. If people wanted to get rid of it, they would have to change everything and create a completely different kind of world. But let's be realistic—nobody has to go that far. We are convinced that the average worker respects his superiors and is basically satisfied with his life.

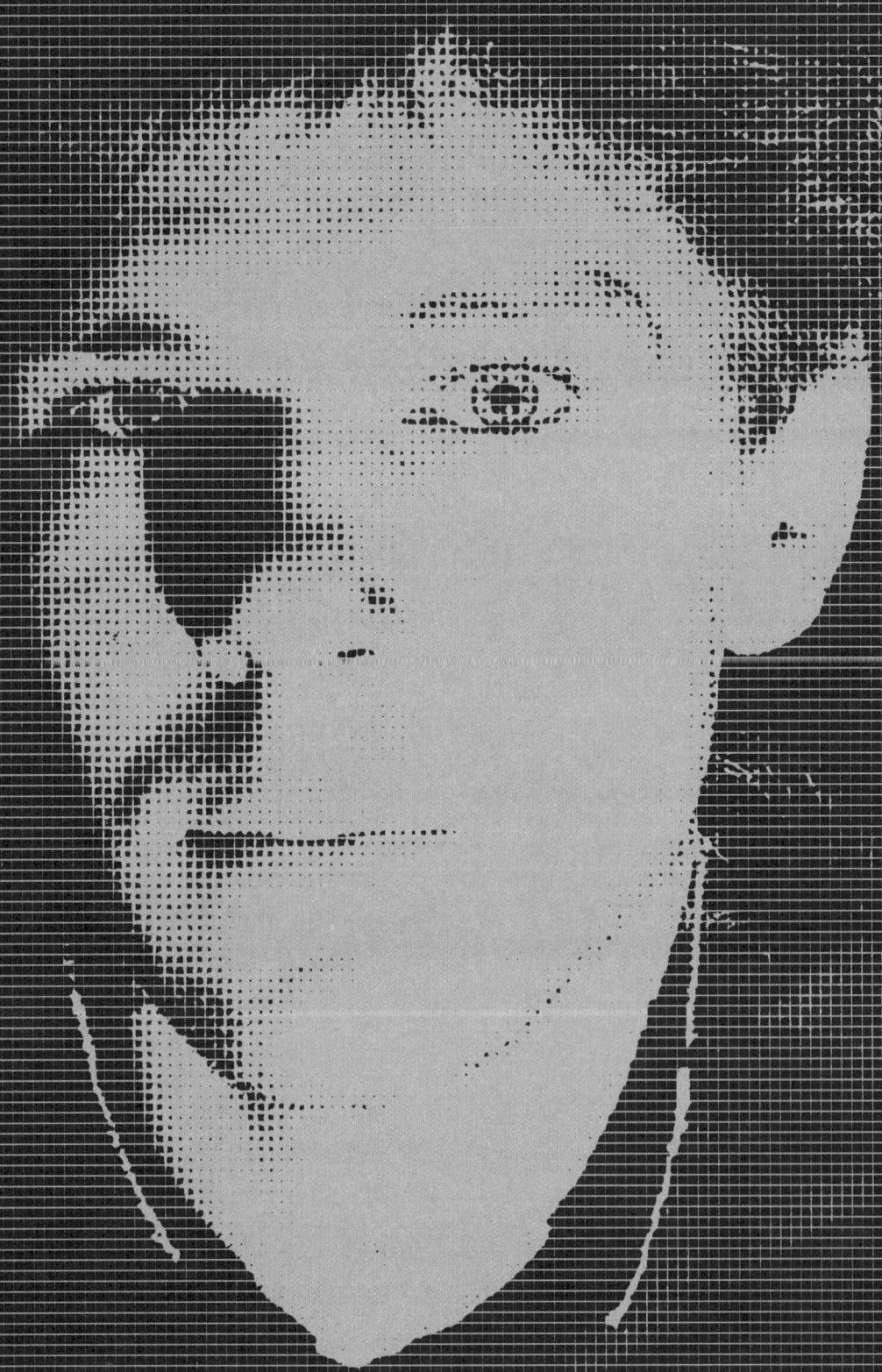

5. THE TENSION BETWEEN WHAT YOU CAN AND YOU CAN'T DO

FROM CRASS TO TOTAL EXPOSURE 1981

Concerned at the extent to which they were being eclipsed in the partnership, Poison Girls sign off their collaboration with Crass in striking style with the Total Exposure *live album, recorded at the final show that the two bands would play together. Poison Girls embrace life as wholly independent anarchist insurgents and reenergised cultural mischief-makers for a second time. The extensive* Total Exposure *tour that the band then embarks on sees Poison Girls start to experiment with a different approach to the live experience that might better suit their evolving audience. Independence leads to Poison Girls' first live shows on the island of Ireland, with memorable and exhilarating dates in Dublin and Belfast.*

By the time the band took to the stage to perform the live set that would be recorded for the *Total Exposure* album, Poison Girls had already decided to end their working relationship with Crass to an end and to fully embrace the advantages and uncertainties of a renewed independent existence.

For both bands, the shared experience had been thrilling and empowering—and had proved the viability of their shared DIY, not-for-profit approach to touring. "We were taking eighteen people on the road, providing a PA and the whole lot—all those gigs were benefit gigs, every one of them, for one thing or another," Famous remembers. "We didn't pay ourselves, even in daily expenses. It was possible to do that because of the goodwill of all the people involved."

Poison Girls' public statement on concluding the collaboration framed the whole experience in the most positive of terms:

> We believe that the partnership worked better than any of us had imagined. As carriers of the original punk values and as people playing and arguing for radical changes in personal politics, we were unequalled. We were also a completely new phenomenon in the music biz. We reached thousands of people with our work with little or no help from anyone in the business and often against their active opposition or ignorance.

But Poison Girls' judgement was that the benefits of such a close alliance were now diminishing while the disadvantages that accrued from it were becoming more burdensome. The band felt they were now "becoming increasingly invisible and are losing a sense of our own identity." The importance of Poison Girls retaining their sense of self was such that throughout the period sharing the stage with Crass, the band had "always retained our separate identity in terms of the subject matter of our lyrics and the style of our music." More than that, while throughout their alliance Crass had only played live in their company, Poison Girls had continued wholly separately to book and perform their own gigs. The sense of freedom that that engendered, and the contrast with compromises required by aligning with Crass's expectations, meant that it felt like the time had come for the band "to protect our own independence." Crass said little publicly about the end of the affair. Their brief acknowledgement in their regularly updated news flyer simply noted that Poison Girls were now gigging on their own once more, but did not acknowledge the yearning for greater autonomy that was the catalyst for the separation.

"Personally, I was surprised that it had taken so long for them to do it," says Steve Ignorant. "It wasn't, I don't think, that they were being held back by us; it was that they couldn't move any further forward while they were still attached to us. They needed to get away from us to do their own thing, which they did. They could do their own gigs, in whatever way they wanted to, without being judged by the Crass audience. I thought it was the right move to make."

"I was sad about it, because we'd got so used to working together," he continues. "But I don't remember there being any bad feeling about it at all. I do remember thinking, 'good luck to them,' you know?"

Penny Rimbaud suggests that the exposure that the alliance with Crass afforded them was requisite of the band's later independent success. "They were a fine band, but I'm pretty certain that without Crass's support they would have remained fairly unknown," he says—a contention that Poison Girls would have rejected outright, refuting the idea that their close collaboration was brokered on such a one-sided premise.

For years thereafter, Poison Girls were repeatedly asked to account for their decision to end the collaboration by countless fanzine interviewers (and far more frequently than Crass ever were). When questioned, the band offered a variety of different explanations for the separation. But those responses shared common refrains: the concern that the band were playing to Crass's audience rather than their own; that the secondary status in the alliance risked overshadowing Poison Girls' own work; that Crass's audience were predominantly young men, while Poison Girls wanted also to reach young women and older people; that independence would give the band greater sense creative and political leverage; and that, freed of constraints, Poison Girls were now intending to put their own action plan into effect.

"The decision not to gig with Crass was taken because touring with them was getting more and more comfortable," Subversa suggested to *Obnoxious* in 1981. "It was too easy. Also people would just talk to Crass—who were the main band—people didn't talk to us." In a 1983 interview, Famous suggested to *Exposure* fanzine that "the situation over the two-and-a-half years we worked together had changed from confronting to comfortable." In an interview with *Rough Justice* fanzine the following year, Famous reflected that the situation between the two bands might, in fact, have become *less* comfortable: "We were being taken for granted . . . and our own ideas and creativity was being withheld. We have to take risks as a band or we will die—to become more autonomous was one of those risks." Reflecting on the move many years later, d'Boyle also emphasised the importance of self-direction and control: "We

Opposite page top and following spread: Crass & Poison Girls setting up, Lesser City Hall, 4 July 1981. Opposite bottom: Trinity Church Irvine soundcheck, 3 July 1981. Photos courtesy of Bernhardt Rebours.

142

Total Exposure cover, Xntrix Records, 1981. Cover stencil based on a photo by Jill Posener.

played with Crass over a period of two years or so in a situation designed by them," he said. "They found the gigs, [and] planned small tours—with us as the support band."

There was no animosity expressed in the separation, and no hint of rancour. That was made easier by the fact that the culture in which both were working was now much larger and more populated than it had been at the time that their collaboration began. Both had more options, more opportunities to make new associations and more artists to call upon. And while Crass would now pull together art-

ists from within the anarcho-punk core to tour with, Poison Girls were keen to expand their collaborative horizons. The band pledged to "remain as passionate, meaningful and relentless as we ever were."

In an interview with *In the City* fanzine, prior to the split, Subversa pinpointed one of Poison Girls' key ambitions in relation to the scene's perception of sex and gender: "Crass said to us the other day, 'Your problem is, (this was to us as a band) you are not going to get the women out, you are not going to get them out on the streets.' . . .

146

Well, my answer to that is that we've *got* to get the women out . . . men and women in one place socially, in an atmosphere which is not just women tagging along because the boys are going out, but is a woman's reality as much as a man's." Addressing that misbalance, and reframing the experience of women, would mean approaching the practice of live performance differently.

Looking back at the decision from the perspective of the present day, Famous summarises the position succinctly. "Basically they got too big, you know? This was the problem," he says. "There was a crowd that came to see Crass which was not necessarily the people that Vi wanted to talk to, exclusively. Of course, she wanted to talk to young men, but she also wanted to get in touch with the women and girls as well. And I think that that was a bigger incentive to actually stop working with them—wanting to attract an audience which was not just punk men," he explains. "And we didn't like getting gobbed on, either. That was the other attraction of going it alone."

Famous also acknowledges that it was a transitional period for the band. "It was a time of a big change for us," he affirms. "We were being thrown out of Burleigh House, which was where we'd been when we met Crass, and Bernhardt had confirmed he was leaving. So we had a lot of reevaluating to do, and it seemed like a good time to try something a bit different."

When asked to comment, Crass simply restated that Poison Girls now preferred to work on their own. Both bands agreed that they would honour the dates of a final shared live tour, which would conclude with shows in Scotland in the summer 1981. With no managers or lawyers involved determined to enforce a contractual obligation on either party, that fact alone was evidence of the absence of animus in dissolving the partnership.

To mark the end of this period in the band's life, Poison Girls decided to record the last gig that they would play alongside Crass, and release the band's one and only full live album (although the retrospective *Seven Year Scratch* double LP would include a live side).

The resulting twelve-inch was the precursor to a live UK tour of the same name that would commence that autumn. *Total Exposure* was recorded live at the Lasswade High School, Edinburgh on Sunday 5 July 1981, using the facilities of Cargo Studios. It was later mixed back at Southern Studios in London. The Edinburgh gig concluded a short series of Scottish dates, beginning at The Music Hall in Aberdeen on 1 July, continuing at Trinity Church in Irvine on 3 July and Lesser City Hall in Perth on 4 July.

Released in October 1981, *Total Exposure* is the least polished recording that the band would issue commercially. The sound texture of *Total Exposure* is unvarnished, and might be characterised as harsh, but it's gloriously defiant nonetheless. *Maximum Rocknroll* were impressed by the way the band had "translated a sense of rawness and snarling intensity onto this live LP which hasn't yet been heard on their studio efforts." Other reviewers judged the results to be a more mixed affair. "Some of the songs come across better live—especially 'State Control' and perhaps 'Persons Unknown,'" the writers of *Self Destruct* zine suggested, "but others suffer." Most of the mainstream music press appeared unmoved. The *NME* concluded that "the only effect of their fierce noise and virulent delivery is numbness and a headache."

In the years since its release, there has been a tendency to downplay the album's importance in the discography of the band. In truth, *Total Exposure* is a deeply impressive record, a bold and brave testament to the band's refusal to accommodate to the expectations of others. Another reflection of the record's "Total Exposure" was the fact that the recoding had not been augmented in the studio. No layers of artifice or of make-up had been added, the sound of the band was a distillation of how Poison Girls sounded on stage—unadorned, and exposed. "One regret I have is about Vi's vocals," says Famous. "She had serious laryngitis on the night, and her voice was totally raw. Thinking about things commercially, we should have rerecorded the vocals afterwards."

Total Exposure was pressed in see-through vinyl, and housed in a clear sleeve which pictured the band in silhouette. The lyric sheet that slipped into the record was black-and-white. It was a striking, impressive look for the record, and distinctive too—when compared with its anarcho-punk contemporaries. The album a clear statement by the band that their formative period, immersed in the anarchist punk scene and entangled with the politics and aesthetics of Crass, had ended.

The record included several songs not previously recorded by the band that would not appear on any studio album. By the time that the band began work on *Where's the Pleasure* their musical instincts had changed.

Lyrically, "Tension" and "Fucking Mother" are extensions of themes introduced in *Hex*, exploring the pressures of domestic servitude and the righteous determination to break free of the expectations of womanhood, even more so in middle age. "Fucking Mother" shows Subversa at her most righteously defiant, rejecting anyone's attempt to pigeonhole or dismiss her, and comparing the wisdom of age and lived experience with the arrogance and impetuousness of youth. It's a manifesto of controlled rage, voiced by an older woman directing her ire at the immaturity and weak impulse control of those young people content to follow social expectation and artificial gender conformity. The jagged, cycling rhythm of "Tension" also addresses the experience of stress, anxiety and worry and its impact as it becomes endemic and chronic. "Bully Boys" confronts the question of male violence, the brutality of the patriarchy and aggressiveness of packs of hostile young men. There's a charged, challenging quality to "Don't Go Home Tonight," a sense that teeters on the edge of recklessness with its encouragement not to return

POISON GIRLS

EUROPEAN THEATRE OF WAR

ST. GEORGES HALL,
MARKET ST. EXETER.

OCTOBER 20th

7-30pm

£1

Tickets: on door or C.N.D shop, 4 New Bridge St or Chapter & Verse, Princesshay

CND DEMONSTRATION OCT 24th LONDON

148

home. It's a message about breaking expectations, pulling away from the norm, taking risks, and taking back a degree of control over your life.

One memorable moment on the record comes at the end of side one when Subversa is heard confronting a member of the audience. "I'm heard shouting 'may you rot in hell' at someone who's just gobbed on me," she recalled later.

The band were now looking forward to a fully independent life. Striking out on their own, freed of that benefit—and its costs—was another form of "Total Exposure."

For Rebours, the band's bass player throughout those turbulent, breakthrough years, *Total Exposure* marked the end of his involvement with the band—as a musician, at least. The show was to be, the band explained, "our last gig with Bernhardt Rebours who has left to follow his heart and to live in another part of the country." Incoming bass player Nil "is rehearsing a new set with us in preparation for a tour in the Autumn. Nil had been part of the wider Poison Girls collective since the band's arrival at Burleigh House, working with tape samples and analogue audio recording techniques. Nil agreed to pick up bass duties on Rebours's departure and became part of the band for the duration of the *Total Exposure* tour.

Now independent once more, organising live shows was again the band's direct responsibility. "The gigs were always in dingy halls, marginal spaces, pubs, and community centres," recalls Adi Cooper, who went to numerous Poison Girls shows. "There would be very smoky atmospheres, very sticky floors. It was cheap to go, there were sliding scales for entrance costs, and concessions if you were on the dole. I did drive the Poison Girls van to gigs occasionally—the band's five-foot short female roadie."

The tour was organised under the banner of No Nukes Music and in conjunction with local CND groups who were approached directly to take on the local organisational work. The ethos of the *Total Exposure* tour was clear evidence of Poison Girls' desire to do it differently. Threaded through the fabric of the tour was the sense that Poison Girls were reconnecting with interest in theatre, film, and cabaret. The band projected agit-prop slides onto a large canvas on the stage, and screened the first short film that close collaborator (and future bass player) Nils had created. "There's more time and scope for new ideas," Subversa enthused. "And if we feel there are other bands where there's mutual interest, we can try working together."

The band approached European Theatre of War and Tony Allen to join them on the road, and asked CND organisers to find a suitable local support act to complete the bill.

Robert Stredder had been a member of the radical arts group Action Space in the mid-1970s, and had formed the European Theatre of War, along with his partner and performer Jackie Bardwell and the film and TV actor David Rappaport (who'd appeared on the big screen earlier in 1981 in Terry Gilliam's *Time Bandits*), as another cultural front in the antinuclear campaign. "We toured cities across Europe dressed in surplus army gear and camouflage, sending up the nuclear arms race," Stredder recalled many years later.

For Rappaport, the escalation in the Cold War triggered by the USSR's invasion of Afghanistan in 1979 was the catalyst that encouraged him to find a new outlet for antimilitarist theatre. "I got involved with European Theatre of War after Afghanistan, when I thought something really stupid was going to happen," he told *No Nukes Music*. "It's not going to change the world in a week, but it's a release for me and we've reached a lot of people." Throughout the early 1980s, countless local peace groups put on amateur "street theatre" performances as an adjunct to CND rallies and marches. The European Theatre of War was an altogether more polished, more professional and consciously confrontational endeavour.

Arabella Churchill, who played a key role in the evolution of Glastonbury Festival, setting up the site's theatre area and children's space, and running the circus field, described the work of European Theatre of War in hugely positive terms. "It was one of the most moving shows I've ever seen," she wrote later. Churchill praised the company's willingness to incorporate political stripping in their live performances, describing it as "one of the few times I've seen nudity [on stage] work." When satirising Aneurin Bevin's infamous speech at the 1957 Labour Party Conference condemning a motion in support of unilateral nuclear disarmament that would, he suggested, "send a British Foreign Secretary . . . naked into the conference chamber," Stredder appeared on stage fully nude. "Nobody laughed, it was brilliant, it worked," Churchill added. The troupe also used absurdist humour, to mock the nuclear idiocies of state authorities. "Then they acted out what the government suggested you should do in the case of a nuclear attack—all get under the kitchen table."

Rappaport defended the intensity of the work. "It should be a strong show because Poison Girls are strong," he explained—emphasising the close connections between the band and the theatrical troupe. It was an affinity which led Stredder and him to "use some of their song lines in the play," emphasising the "links [and] echoes" between the two projects.

Anarchist comedian and raconteur Tony Allen, then in his midthirties, had long been a fixture of the London anarchist scene. A regular a Speakers' Corner at Hyde Park (as Subversa's husband Philip Sansom had been), Allen was a comic, an actor and a practising rabble-rouser, whose decisive contribution to developing the craft of a

---

Total Exposure tour poster, 1981. Courtesy of Rich Cross.

new and disruptive generation of comedians in the UK in the early 1980s is rarely recognised. To those in the know, his efforts earned him the moniker the "godfather of alternative comedy" in the process. Alongside Alexei Sayle, Allen had helped to shape the ethos of London's breakthrough Comedy Store, and had brought together the acclaimed Alternative Cabaret troupe whose efforts to tour around the country built the first live stand-up circuit.

But while Allen had the talent to match his many contemporaries, his radical politics, his disdain for the privileged graduates of the Cambridge Footlights and his complete lack of interest in commercial success meant that he never saw himself as part of the new comedy intake now getting commissions from the BBC and (following its launch in November 1982) the new Channel 4 TV network.

Allen did accept a brief cameo in an episode of the upstart (and often described as "anarchic") BBC sitcom *The Young Ones* (appropriately enough playing an anarchist, named Fisher). But it was clear that his priorities lay elsewhere. The nonconformist, acerbic and politically committed Allen was a natural fit for Poison Girls' new live approach. In his autobiography *Attitude*, Allen recalls being approached by Poison Girls, who "were about to headline a nationwide antinukes tour, and were looking for an innovative support act." Impressed by the band's songs, which he described as like "raw music hall anthems with highly charged political lyrics," Allen agreed, taking on what he says was "a difficult job in difficult circumstances—but also, as it turned out, in excellent company."

"He had been working with The Clash in what he called a 'wind-up position,'" d'Boyle recalled. "He would go on first and get the audience all wound up before he introduced the band. It's something that lifts the energy."

The style of stand-up that Allen brought to the tour had an unpredictable edge to it—a tension heightened by the fact that his "set" was so heavily improvised, and focused on anything but conciliation with the audience. "Tony talks about violence—confronts people with themselves," Subversa suggested. His material mixed a running anarchist commentary on the latest news headlines with self-deprecating insights into the life of a bohemian artist and calls for resistance to the rule of the state.

"He did some amazing performances and interacted with the crowd a lot," d'Boyle continued. "In the beginning, the audiences were mainly young men—people from the Crass scene coming to see what we were doing. He used to provoke and insult and challenge people. And some of the discussions he used to get going with the microphone were remarkable. He'd get a lot of people talking to him after the show, having a chat with him about stuff. It was a different way of doing things and of involving the audience more."

With the ambience of their gigs changing, the band now empowered to assert their ownership of events, and

audiences continuing to turn out to see them, Poison Girls had every right to feel vindicated by their decision to end the association with Crass. "The great thing is the mixture of people that come," Subversa affirmed. "There's a lot of punks—and we share a lot, we understand each other. But there's all sorts of other people too, all mixing up and talking to each other." D'Boyle was equally impressed. "The audiences have been really good," he said. "It's very important to us that they *are* interested and want to talk to us and keep in touch. We've been pleased because it's not *adulation*; it's showing an interest in our ideas." Putting things together with care and commitment seemed to be key to this.

Under their own banner, Poison Girls arranged a tour of West Germany, travelling on through the land corridor that connected to the country to west Berlin, at that time a "landlocked western enclave behind the 'iron curtain.'" as the band described it—a place few artists in the anarchist punk firmament reached in the early 1980s.

For several years, Poison Girls' cost-effective mode of transport when touring was a decommissioned ambulance that the band adapted for their use. It was far from luxurious, and "was a bugger to drive," Tom Barwood remembers. "It had this huge slab of concrete wedged in the bottom of it to keep it stable. And I remember the first time that Lance let me drive it, and I completely screwed up the gear change and ground to a halt on a steep hill, on the way out of Exeter towards Plymouth. And it took a few, a few days at least before I was allowed to try driving it again!" Rebours remembers "running on empty" in the ambulance and being told to "turn off the ignition and coast downhill" to conserve the last of the fuel. Despite the lack of creature comforts and the tight budget for diesel, that vehicle housed and transported the band for many thousands of miles. "They'd converted it really well," Zillah Minx of Rubella Ballet remembers. "They'd made it a space to live in, they'd put beds into it and everything," she says. "For the first Dutch tour we shared, they took the ambulance with us in it to Holland, and then we toured and played a load of gigs together."

As they toured independently, Poison Girls' own politics once again came into sharper relief. "I suppose if we do specialise, it's in the domestic connection of violence," Subversa suggested. "We're explicit in our opposition to sexism; also we want to familiarise people with the violence shown to women and the violence between women and children."

Yet Poison Girls struggled with the same political tensions that ensnared Crass, when trying to balance the struggle for personal liberty against the advocacy for the state's overthrow in their work. Famous suggested to *Anarchy* magazine in 1982 that personal change remained the decisive political act: "Actually, it's far more important to change the way that you live than to change the government." Months earlier, a Poison Girls flyer had set out a far wider political agenda, and hinted at the connections between the conscious voluntarism of the individual and the marginalisation of the power of that state which could cumulatively result from its collective pursuit: "The economy *is* a war economy. The world economy is geared for war. . . . To remove the Bomb by itself is not to remove the threat; the threat is in the actual structure of the war economy. Real changes will only come from individual rejection of the values of the war economy in ways that will make that ultimate power as irrelevant as it is unnecessary."

Poison Girls shared Crass's profound reluctance to engage with formal political organisation, and shared a similar reluctance at being pushed towards a position of leadership within anarchist punk culture. Famous told *Anarchy* magazine: "It comes down again to whether we're being set up as leaders or gurus of some sort. One of the things we have to say is there isn't any salvation in organisations. That's part of anarchy isn't it?" The band shared a sense of profound suspicion at what were seen as the wafer-thin political affiliations of some bands, including those within punk. Lance d'Boyle was clear of the band's disdain: "I hate the way some bands use the CND banner to play under because it's the in thing; like Rock Against Racism, the Anti-Nazi League—all have been used, as fashion." They were just as clear at their refusal to support front organisations of the left whose ambitions were seen as antithetical to the anarchist cause. They told *No Nukes Fanzine* in 1981: "We've been asked to support the Right to Work march, things to do with unemployment, but we never supported that. . . We want to support the right *not* to work, in that sense, or rather the right to work not for other people, but for yourself."

Those anarchist sentiments found reflection in all aspects of Poison Girls' early work. More reconciled to the idea of speaking with the music press, Poison Girls had made clear to journalists the importance they afforded to the idea of radical autonomy—even winning over the *NME*'s Du Noyer in the process: "Defiant outsiders, they've got nothing but contempt for the pop process . . . this band spit out their refusal to be consumed. If true subversion means working underground, that's where they'll stay."

What the band came back to time and again was the importance of individual and collective volition: "We can undo the system by stopping acting like puppets," they

On the return ferry from 1981 European tour: Pete Shepherd (Omega Tribe), Gem, Richard, Mandy Fry, Nil, Vi, Lance, Daryl Hardcastle (Omega Tribe), and Dave Wilcox. Photo courtesy of Bernhardt Rebours.

Total Exposure tour stickers, 1981. Courtesy of Pete Fender and Gemma Sansom.

insisted. "Rejecting the necessity of a violent and degrading war of total death by finding hope and daring to treat each other like the sensitive and reasonable human beings that we really are . . . by believing in ourselves."

In the closing weeks of 1981, Poison Girls arranged to play three live shows in Ireland. In September of the following year, Crass would play at the same two Irish venues in the same sequence. The first Poison Girls gig, at Lourdes Hall, on Sean Mac-Dermott Street in Dublin on Friday 18 December was organised by the Dublin Unemployed Action Group (DUAG) which fought for "resistance to job losses, for higher dole payments, and for useful well-paid work for all who want it." In what seemed to be a complete coincidence, Poison Girls were supported that night by a newly formed melodic psychedelic-pop band from Balgriffin, Dublin named The Xn-Trix (aka Xn Trix or Xntrix), who would break up in 1983 before releasing any vinyl.

Peter Jones, later of Paranoid Visions and the DIY punk labels FOAD Records and Rotator Records, was a "shy fifteen-year-old" at the time of the gig, but had already corresponded with Richard Famous and plucked up the confidence to talk to him. "We chatted about guitars and how I wanted to get a band together but was finding it hard to find people who shared the same idea as me," he recalled in *Great Gig Memories: From Punks and Friends*. "He told me to stick with it and when I had the right people there I would know it as there was no feeling like creating music on your own terms with like-minded people. I knew immediately that I had to follow this through. Sure enough, a month or so later I joined the first lineup of Paranoid Visions and have remained there to this day." For Jones the gig was both "awe-inspiring" and personally pivotal. "The warmth of the artists, the camaraderie of the audience and the sense of belonging changed me forever," he says.

Poison Girls then travelled north to play two afternoon gigs at the Anarchy Centre in Belfast, on 19–20 December. "They were the most memorable shows, I think, we ever did," says Famous. "It was an eye opener, even to us, to what was going on in Belfast at that time."

"We parked up and went into this café where we were meeting people and they asked, 'have you left your van outside?' We said yes, and they said, 'Well, you'd better move it, otherwise the police will blow it up,' because it was an unknown and therefore suspicious vehicle. That was alarming in itself. And then seeing the British army on the streets with guns. And then being told, by the people we were staying with, which roads we had to walk down. 'Don't walk down that road,' they said. 'Walk down this road, and you'll be alright.'"

The Anarchy Club on Belfast's Long Lane had opened in November 1981, mainly at the instigation of the Belfast Anarchist Collective (BAC), which had its base in the city's anarchist bookshop Just Books. The BAC approached the owners of a new gay venue named The Carpenter Club to ask if they would be willing to hire out the venue on selected afternoons. The club agreed, on the understanding that—whatever gigs took place—the hirers would ensure that the premises were put back to their original state at the end of each booking. "The walls were painted with slogans, graffitied across all the walls," says Famous. "And after the gig, they got the audience out and painted all the walls black again, before the gay disco that night. The next day, when we turned up to do the other gig, they'd graffitied the walls again. I mean, it was wonderful."

Sean O'Neill, coauthor of *It Makes You Want to Spit! The Definitive Guide to Punk in Northern Ireland*, recalls the thrill surrounding the gig: "My excitement was palpable, catching the Saturday morning bus into Belfast city centre with my mates," he writes. "It was just six days before Christmas." As these were daytime gigs, "all the windows in the venue were blacked out to make it dark inside," he adds—as well, of course, as to make it harder for the Royal Ulster Constabulary (RUC) to peer in.

When Poison Girls first took to the stage and were about to play, "the audience started shouting 'SS—RUC' and doing *Sieg Heil* salutes. And we thought 'bloody hell, we're gonna get murdered here.'" Famous recalls. "But the crowd's ire was not being directed at the band. "The RUC had arrived at the door to see what was going on. So the organisers told them, and sorted everything out." And when Poison Girls began to play "the audience went absolutely bananas."

Writing in *Sounds*, Johnny Waller—who'd accompanied the band on their Irish trip—described the band "blistering through an hour-long set" which affirmed the wisdom of them breaking free of their connection with Crass in a demonstration of "vigour and commitment." Attendees remember two electrifying shows, topped off with riotous, celebratory versions of "Persons Unknown."

"It was a moment to treasure, missed by persons unconscious slumped with glue bags on the floor," says O'Neill. It was also an inspiration and a catalyst. "The gig was an awakening to lots of those present," he adds.

Having reaffirmed their ability to tour independently, and on their own terms, and with the *Total Exposure* album calling time on their connections with Crass, Poison Girls were now ready for a recalibration of their sound, their approach, and their practice.

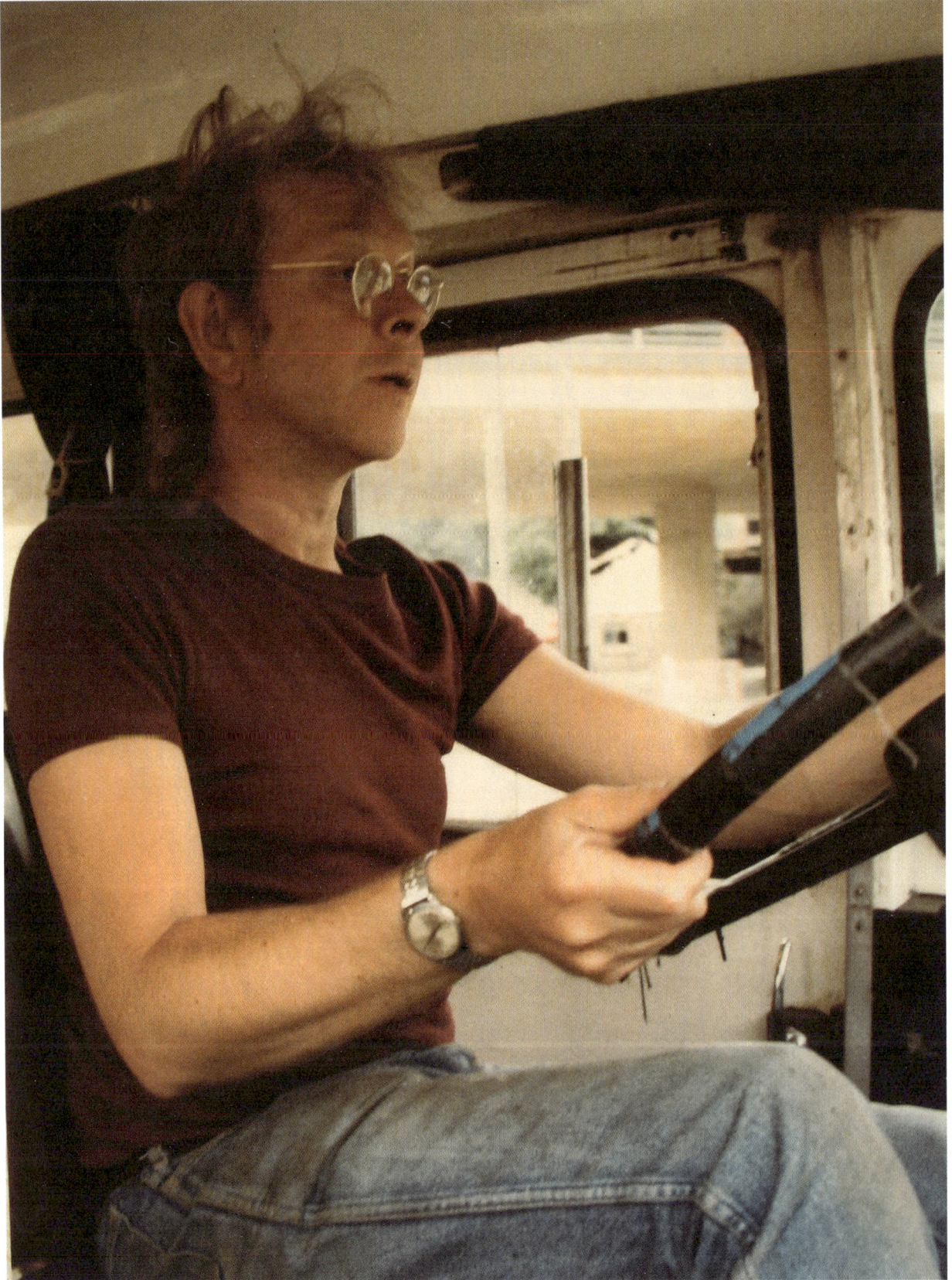

Lance, 1981. Photo courtesy of Domino.

POISON GIRLS

WAR, INVASION, TAKEOVER, DESTRUCTION, PEACE, PROPOGANDA, NEWS, ADVERTISING, BOMBS, CARS, TELEVISION, LIES.
THE ECONOMY IS A WAR ECONOMY. THEIR PEACE IS AN ILLUSION. A SHORT SPACE BETWEEN THE BULLETS. THE WORLD ECONOMY IS GEARED FOR WAR. WAR/WASTE/WAR. THE WORLD ECONOMY IS GEARED FOR WASTE. THE ECONOMY IS A WAR ECONOMY. BUSINESS IS BUSINESS. WAR IS WAR. WAR IS BUSINESS.
REAL PEACE DOES NOT EXIST. PEACE IN THEIR TERMS IS THE SPACE BETWEEN BUSINESS BOOMS. THEIR PEACE IS GEARED TOWARDS WAR. THEIR PEACE IS GEARED TOWARDS WASTE. THIS IS THE WAR ECONOMY.
THE BOMB TECHNOLOGY EXISTS. THERE IS NO ESCAPE FROM THE MAD KNOWLEDGE THAT IS IN THE HANDS OF ANY SIXTH FORM SCIENTIST. WE HAVE THE ABILITY TO OVERKILL OURSELVES. EXPAND, ESCALATE, EXPLODE. THE ULTIMATE OFFER YOU CAN'T REFUSE. BUY OR DIE. CONFORM OR DIE.
THE GAME IS 'CIVILIZED LIFE,' THE RULES ARE EXPLOITATION, GREED, AND VIOLENCE. OUR WAY OF LIFE IS UNDERWRITTEN BY THESE RULES. THE POWER OF AUTHORITY IS NOT ISOLATED IN THE BOMB. TO REMOVE THE BOMB BY ITSELF IS NOT TO REMOVE THE THREAT. THE THREAT IS IN THE ACTUAL STRUCTURE OF THE WAR ECONOMY, IN THE STRUCTURE OF OUR LIFE. THAT THREAT IS BASED ON THE FEAR, BY THOSE IN CONTROL, THAT THEY WILL LOSE THEIR POWER. IF THE PEACE MOVEMENT IS JUST ANOTHER POWER-SEEKING ORGANISATION, THEN THE WAR ECONOMY WILL CONTINUE. PEACE IS THEN JUST A CONTINUATION OF BUSINESS/WAR/WASTE/POWER.
THE BOMB IS A DISTRACTION. THEY GIVE US THE BOMB SYMBOL AS A DECOY, A DIVERSION TO BATTER OUR ENERGY AGAINST. THEY CAN FUNCTION WITHOUT CRUISE, OR TRIDENT, OR POLARIS. THEY HAVE MORE WHERE THEY CAME FROM. THERE IS NO SHORTAGE OF WEAPONS, BECAUSE THEY CONTROL THE RESOURCES. THEY CONTROL US. THE WAR ECONOMY DEPENDS ON OUR SUPPORT. WE ACCEPT THE GAME, WE PLAY BY THE RULES. DISSENT THAT DOESN'T CHALLENGE THE POWER STRUCTURE OF THE WAR ECONOMY IS ALLOWED, ENCOURAGED AND FULLY EXPLOITED. MANY ARE GROWING RICH ON THE RETINAL AFTER-IMAGES OF HIROSHIMA.
DISSENT THAT DOES CHALLENGE THE POWER STRUCTURE OF THE WAR ECONOMY IS ILLEGAL OR UNDERGROUND. YES, LET'S BAN THE BOMB. LET US AVOID THE ALMOST INEVITABLE ACCIDENT. BUT THAT'S JUST THE START. REAL CHANGES WILL ONLY COME FROM INDIVIDUAL REJECTION OF THE VALUES OF THE WAR ECONOMY IN WAYS THAT WILL MAKE THAT ULTIMATE POWER AS IRRELEVANT AS IT IS UNNECESSARY.
THERE CAN BE NO REAL PEACE UNTIL WE DO.

POISON GIRLS. November 1981

WRAP UP WELL, THEY SAY. DEFEND AND INSURE. LOCK UP AND SECURE. PROTECT AND SURVIVE. INVEST IN MORE AND MORE ARMOUR, ARMAMENTS, AMMUNITION. THE CURRENCY IS FEAR. THE RACKET IS PROTECTION. THOSE WHO DEAL IN WEAPONS GROW RICH. THOSE WHO DEAL IN AND DISTRIBUTE FEAR ARE THEIR AGENTS. THAT IS THE ECONOMY OF WAR. INVISIBLE PEOPLE, SHOW YOURSELVES. PEOPLE IN HIDING, COME OUT. SAY WHAT YOU WANT. SHOW WHO YOU ARE. RECLAIM THE LIFE THAT IS LEFT. WE WILL CREATE A NEW ECONOMY. THE ECONOMY OF PEACE WILL DEPEND ON A CURRENCY OF TRUST. THERE ARE MORE OF US THAN YOU THINK.

Total Exposure tour handout, 1981.

155

OCTOBER

POISON GIRLS · TOTAL EXPOSURE TOUR ·

1981

FREE

RIO DISCO STINK

DO YOU KNOW WHAT IT MEANS WHEN YOU HEAR THE PAIN IN AN UGLY WOMANS SONG
I KNOW THE TRUTH, WON'T HOLD MY TONGUE ABOUT WHAT'S GOING ON
I KNOW WHAT IT MEANS WHEN YOU LOOK AWAY WHEN I START TO SING MY SONG
I GOT NOTHING TO LOSE AND NOTHING TO GAIN AND WHAT YOU'RE DOING IS WRONG

DO YOU KNOW WHAT IT MEANS WHEN YOU HEAR THE CRY OF THE HUNGRY GIRLS IN RED
IT HURTS MY MIND AND IT HURTS MY PRIDE THAT THEY HAVE TO COME TO YOU FOR BREAD
AND YOUR COMPANY CREEP WILL DIG THEM DEEP AS THEY LIE DOWN ON THEIR BEDS
AND YOU MAKE YOUR PILE ON THEIR WEARY SMILES AND THE HOLE BETWEEN THEIR LEGS

DO YOU KNOW WHAT I MEAN ?

YOU MAKE YOUR PILE WHERE THE MINERS DIE AT THE RIO TINTO ZINC
DO YOU KNOW WHAT I MEAN , CAN YOU HEAR THEIR SCREAMS, AND CAN YOU SMELL THE STINK
OF THE HUNDREDS DEAD AT THE R.T.Z. TO PAY FOR YOUR BRITISH FUN
THE ROTTING MEN AT THE ROSSING MINE THAT DIGS URANIUM

DO YOU KNOW WHAT I MEAN ?

DO YOU KNOW WHAT IT MEANS TO BREATHE THAT DUST AND FEEL IT ON YOUR SKIN
WHEN YOU'RE POOR AND BLACK AND THE WHITE MAN'S GOT A WHIP
THEY MAKE WHITE MAN'S POWER FROM A HOLE IN THE GROUND AT RIO TINTO ZINC
AND THE COMPANY BANKS FILL UP THEIR TANKS BUT YOU CAN'T LOCK UP THE STINK

ITS NOT ENOUGH TO CRY THAT THE MINERS DIE AT RIO TINTO ZINC
URANIUM CAN KILL YOUR SON WHATEVER YOU MAY WANT TO THINK
ITS NOT ENOUGH TO CRY THAT CHILDREN DIE FOR THE LEADER OF YOUR PACK
WHEN YOU HEAR THEIR SCREAMS YOU'LL KNOW IT MEANS THEY GOTTA GET YOU OFF THEIR BACKS!

DO YOU KNOW WHAT I MEAN ?

DO YOU KNOW WHAT IT MEANS WHEN YOU LISTEN TO THE PAIN IN AN UGLY WOMAN'S SONG
THE GIRLS IN RED ARE GETTING OFF THEIR BEDS, WE'VE BEEN THERE FAR TOO LONG
WE KNOW WHAT IT MEANS TO WANT TO BLOW UP THE QUEEN AND RIO TINTO ZINC
AND TO TAKE A SHOT AT THE CREAMY LOT WHO SELL US TEA TO DRINK

WHEN THE MUSIC DIES IN YOUR DISCO DIVES AND THE NEWS FADES ON YOUR SCREEN
YOU'LL GET NO REST, YOU'LL GET NO SLEEP, YOU'LL HEAR THEM IN YOUR DREAMS
URANIUM CAN KILL YOUR SON, WHATEVER YOU MAY WANT TO THINK
ARE YOU FEELING PROUD OF THAT HOLE IN THE GROUND AT RIO TINTO ZINC ?

DO YOU KNOW WHAT I MEAN ?

THEY MAKE WHITE MAN'S POWER FROM A HOLE IN THE GROUND AT RIO TINTO ZINC
THE COMPANY BANKS FILL UP THEIR TANKS BUT THEY CAN'T LOCK UP THE STINK
URANIUM CAN KILL YOUR SON WHATEVER YOU MAY WANT TO THINK
ARE YOU FEELING PROUD OF THAT HOLE IN THE GROUND AT RIO TINTO ZINC ?

POISON GIRLS
OCTOBER 1981

WONT
N.O.N.T lysistrata a thing or two

If MAN is so clever, how come he is in imminent danger of blowing us all up ?
The atom bomb is not just a strange aberration. It is the logical outcome of a "civilization" which is founded on injustice.

According to the United Nations Report in 1980, women constitute HALF the worlds population, do TWO THIRDS of the worlds work, earn ONE TENTH of the worlds income and own less than ONE HUNDREDTH of the worlds property. We bear a huge burden of labour but have no economic power and no say in the decisions that affect everybody's lives.

Our society is based on the domination of man over woman, of the rich over the poor, of white people over black people and of the human species over the rest of creation. All power is violence. The powerful have advantages which they can only maintain by excessive force. They will fight to the death-your death, my death, even their own death-rather than give up their power.

Nuclear weapons are an extreme form of violence, more horrifying than anything that we can imagine. But in fact we are surrounded with other forms of violence all the time. We are so used to it, that we can hardly see it any core.

Millions of people starving in the third world, when the west have more food than we know what to do with. 'Good news on the jobs front'-which means a thousand people have been given work making missiles or war planes.

It is men who commit this violence. Yes, of course, women are sometimes aggressive. But men as a group are not physically terrorized by women as a group. There is no female equivalent of the ripper or the Boston Strangler. Men are not scared of women as walk the streets, (although they may be scared of other men)

I'm not saying that men are innately violent or women are innately gentle.
We are all trained in playing our part to keep the system going.

Boys are deliberately brutalised, taught to be tough, active, selfish. They are given war comics to read, guns and action man sets to play with. If they don't conform to the hard-hitting norm they are despised as cissies.

Girls meanwhile are taught to be nice at all costs.
We mustn't get angry and we must not fight, not even in self-defence. We are all warned that we are in danger of being raped, but not taught how we might defend ourselves from attack.

And all of us are expected to enjoy thrilling films like 'He knows you're alone' or 'Violation of the Bitch' - films which portray men as sadists and torturers and women as helpless victims. Thats entertainment ? Films like that make killing and afflicting pain seem exiting and glamourous. They encourage men to be violent and women to accept violence from men, to take it for granted.

How do we make things change? The Houses of Parliament, political parties, and Trades Unions were all founded by men (who in every case tried desperately to keep women out)and are all based on rigid competitive hierarchies. The only way a woman can succeed is to become a male impersonator like Thatcher. Within the Unions and The Labour Party, which supposedly want to take power away from the bosses, women find it hard to make themselves heard. And so do black people, gay people, young people and old people, and people with disabilities.If you're not articulate, quick witted, energetic, ruthless, and ambitious with lots of free time, then forget it!

Dear old CND is not immune from these problems. Lots of us find it impossible to participate in large groups and excruciatingly boring boring meetings; half a dozen people speak to each other and everyone else feels invisible or dead.

In the womens liberation movement we have found the most effective way to organise is within small groups where we can get to know and trust each others amazing what can be achieved. In the struggle against the nuclear threat we want to carry on working in the same way. We're never going to get rid of the bomb if we go on submitting to the authoritarian mentality which produced it in the first place!

Women have been excluded from political power and from access to science and tech-nology, we have been terrorised by male violence in all its forms. But we will not be intimidated any longer. We're going to TAKE THE TOYS FROM THE BOYS.

Lucy Whitman

Take The Toys from the Boys !

TAKE THE TOYS FROM THE BOYS they made a bomb out of cotton
TAKE THEIR HANDS OFF THE GUNS made a bomb out of coffee
TAKE THE TOYS FROM THE BOYS they made a bomb out of sugar
GET THEIR FINGERS OFF THE TRIGGER they made a bomb !
TAKE THE TOYS FROM THE BOYS they gotta make a living
GET THEIR HANDS OFF THEIR GUNS they gotta make a killing
TAKE THE TOYS FROM THE BOYS they gotta get promotion
GET THEIR FINGERS OFF THE BUTTON they made a bomb !
TAKE THE TOYS FROM THE BOYS they made a bullet out of rubber
GET THEIR MINDS OFF THE MONEY made a cannon out of water
TAKE THEIR EYES OFF THE DIALS they gotta make a killing
GET THEIR FINGERS OFF THE BUTTON they made a bomb !
THEY MADE A BOMB OUT OF COTTON they made a bomb out of coffee
THEY MADE A BOMB OUT OF SUGAR made a bullet out of rubber
THEY MADE A BOMB OUT OF MUSIC made a hit with a record
THEY MADE A FOOL OUT OF YOU THEY MADE A BOMB !

techno chemico metho petroleum/macho mechanico micro effluvium/
microfission alcoholplated missile plutonium/ techno genetico
rocket planetarium/ irrelevant formulas for metal pandemonium/
research your kneejerk for traces of uranium/ they give the
toys to the boys but the girls get the dollies/ birth control
or mind control/ its a war economy !

JUST ANOTHER BOMBSONG
ANOTHER BLOODY BOMBSONG
JUST ANOTHER PEACE SONG
ANOTHER BLOODY PEACE MARCH/ANOTHER PROTEST/
ANOTHER ISSUE/ ANOTHER MINDFUCK ?

ISN'T IT AMAZING THAT WITH ALL THE MONEY
THEY SPEND ON NUCLEAR BOMBS AND ALL THE
OTHER UGLY WASTEFUL DEATHCULTURE TECHNOLOGY,
THERE STILL ISN'T A SAFE AND RELIABLE
CONTRACEPTIVE............????????????????

POISON GIRLS take the toys from the boys

This economic and political system exploits and controls people. It reduces people to the level of things and gives machines - clocks, dictaphones, production lines - control over them. Things are made because they are profitable, not because we need all those garden gnomes, toilet seat covers, Royal wedding souvenirs. But we must be made to feel that we need more and more - trendy clothes, the latest records, better house, smarter car, holidays abroad in more exotic places - always spending all we get, never stopping, never satisfied. To help this process, adverts play on peoples fears - loneliness, lack of confidence, no friends. They create an illusion of choice, concealing the fact that we are given very little real choice. We have to go to school. We need money to survive. We are brought up to the idea of getting married and having kids.

Family relationships, are so often romanticised and contrasted with the alienating competitiveness of Out There, are also about power - the endless drudgery of housework done in the name of love/the convention of faithfulness or the furtive affair/the 'I'm not having my daughter going out looking like that'. Wives and mothers who don't do paid work are utterly dependent on a man. On his side, he has to keep going to work to support the family. Home is the heart of the system, the one little space where we are allowed to express ourselves. Creativity gets reduced to choosing the colour of the front door or the pattern on the wallpaper. Girls are given dolls to play with, toy ironing boards, nurses outfits. They're taught to Help Mummy, to be submissive and to make the best of their looks. Boys get guns and are taught not to cry.

We are left in isolation to deal with the system. We are supposed to think that we are to blame for our situation. They tell you if you haven't got a job you can't have tried hard enough. Who wants to spend most of the day doing something stupid or boring? If you're depressed and find it hard to cope, there must be something wrong with you. If you don't like being pushed about and can imagine a better way of life you're not to be trusted.

The dominant values of this society - respect for money/property ownership/consumerism/contempt for peoples creativity and potential - reach into every aspect of our lives. The most important subject at school - discipline and respect for authority - is never written on the timetable but is part of every lesson. Sit still/don't talk/obey and go when the bell rings. Only believe what the teacher tells you or what you read in books. If your body/machine breaks down, take it to the doctors for an overhaul. For desperate cases theres spare part surgery, but it may just be in the mind. Take these pills, they'll blot out the problem for a while. Like cars, we're not supposed to understand what makes us go.

Millions of people in the world are starving, yet relatively rich countries like Britain feed tons of grain to animals so that people can eat meat. World spending on arms has now reached more than one billion dollars a day - roughly half a billion pounds. The British government is planning to spend around £12,500,000,000 on arms next year. This is more than it spends on either health or education and more than double what it spends on housing. But its not just a question of transferring the 'defence' budget to the 'housing' or 'health' but of dismantling the whole exploitative system.

We are paying twice over to live in a war economy. - with our money (from income tax, VAT, and tax on cigarettes and drink) and with our lives, the ultimate violence of a nuclear war as well as the day to day violence of living in an inhumane society.

We have been born into a society dominated by greed, arrogance, irresponsibility competitiveness - a system which exploits everyone (though some much more than others) and which denies our potential. It disciplines us in the name of 'education', manipulates our ideas and opinions through the papers and TV, puts poison in our food, treats us like machines and is obsessed with

---

war and death. If we don't stand out against it we are lending ourselves to it and supporting it. Things don't have to be like this. Profit doesn't have to be the driving force. Science and technology don't have to be used to dream up more and more horrific ways of mutilating and killing people. People don't have to spend all their working lives shuffling papers or producing or clearing up rubbish. Learning things doesn't have to be boring or intimidating. There doesn't have to be a separation between home and work. There doesn't have to such gross inequalities between rich and poor. We can take control of our lives. We have ideas, time and energy to make our own decisions as to how we want things to be. Choice is not given, but has to be taken. The way things are organised is not god-given, or fixed forever, but created by people. It can be changed if enough people want it enough.

GWYN

FREEDOM FILMS

SOUND REBELLION/SIGHT REBELLION

How do clever men make money? They run the state, the drug companies, record companies and film companies. To name a few. The film and record industries are champion brothers together in their support of pain. The record industry bombards young minds with fads getting filthier with each generation, manipulating disco compilations into every channel available.

VIDEO: THE NEXT BIG SCREW.

If you dont like being screwed you could buy a guitar and sing about it; but is it OK for Marlon Brando to be paid $2,000,000 for four minutes of hot air? or do you mind MGM and United Artists spending $35,000,000 on war films of the future?

Its cheaper to make a film than a single, dont let anyone tell you otherwise.

CLINT EASTWOOD/ABBA
BOOMTOWN RATS/JODY FOSTER

'By second class air mail comes a great new Horror Fantasy all the way from a moron floating in a Beverly Hills swimming pool, Calafornia, USA' Forget the cinema, if you dont like sitting down to watch a band, why do it for a film?

ITS NOT DIFFICULT, ITS NOT ART, ITS NOT EXPENSIVE.
My only film cost £50 (dole money) to make and lasts for 22 minutes, it could have been cheaper.

MARK X X X.

Invisible people, show yourselves.
Say what you want. Show who you are.
Reclaim the life that is left.
Radiation burns. Pollution withers.
The cold eyes of the hostile stranger kills like a stone.
Wrap up well, they say. Defend and insure.
Look up and secure. Protect and survive.
Invest in more and more armour, armaments and ammunition.
Our currency is fear. The racket is protection.
Those who deal in weapons grow rich.
Those who deal and distribute fear are their agents.
That is the economy of war.

They are trying to drive us into deeper and deeper shelters of fear,
privacy and loneliness.
We are hiding and sheltering ourselves to death.
And most of our bodies, condemned and abandoned in a hostile
environment like molluscs in a shell.
Forgotten and vunerable, alienated from our own strength.

Behind the carnival funfare cosmetic masks, behind the white smiles of
persil curtains, shuffling patiently behind each other at the supermarket
checkouts, lost in a drifting quicksand of privacy.
Lost in a confusion of roles and labels.

People in hiding, come out.
Those who desire peace and freedom
must create a new economy.
The economy of peace will depend on a currency of trust.
Invisible people, show yourselves.
Say what you want.
Show who you are.
There are more of us than you think.

POISON GIRLS

VI SUBVERSA VOCALS/GUITAR, RICHARD FAMOUS GUITAR/VOCALS, NIL BASS/VOCALS, LANCE d'BOYLE DRUMS.

Write C/O Rough Trade 137 Blenheim Cres. LONDON W11.

TOTAL EXPOSURE

THE NEW LIVE ALBUM BY POISON GIRLS. RELEASED BY XN TRIX RECORDS.
Available from October 12th. From independent record shops.

tony allen

GODS, LEADERS, SUPERSTARS, MEDIA MAFIOSO, PURVEYORS OF THE ANTI-LIFE.
POLITICIANS, GOVERNMENTS, BEAUROCRATS, ADMINISTRATORS OF THE ANTI-LIFE.
POLICE, MILITARY, NUCLEAR TECHNOCRATS, GUARDIANS OF THE ANTI-LIFE.
ROYALTY, BANKS, BUSINESS CONGLOMERATES, OWNERS OF THE ANTI-LIFE.
VOTERS, WORKERS, PUNTERS, EVERYONE OF US, RELUCTANT CONSUMERS OF
THE ANTI-LIFE.

films

TOTAL PRODUCT By Mick Duffield. FREEDOM FILMS PRESENTS By Mark.
SLIDES By Gwyn.

wont

There are about fifteen WOMEN OPPOSE THE NUCLEAR THREAT groups across the country. We aim to develop a feminist analysis of the nuclear threat and to work with other women to resist it. Any women interested in joining or forming a WONT group in her area can get details from:

WONT, Box 600, Peace News, 8 Elm Avenue, NOTTINGHAM.

p.a.

Live sound by Paul Tandy and Duane Cool.
This book designed by Daryl.
Published by XN TRIX Publishing.

1981 European tour photos. Opposite: Ghent, Belgium. Vi with Roger and Marja from Dutch support band Bunker. Poison Girls German tour poster, Berlin. This page: Bernhardt Rebours and Annie Anxiety on the train. Gem Stone, Annie Anxiety, Paul Tandy, and Ian in Berlin. Lance resting on return ferry. All photos courtesy of Bernhardt Rebours.

AT LAST !!!! ANOTHER CHEAP GIG.......
ANOTHER GREAT NIGHT.....

It's ROCK 'N' DOLE part 2

Remember ROCK 'N' DOLE part one in June, the four band gig in the Lourdes Hall? The Dublin Unemployed Action Group is helping to organise part two. We have brought over the English band POISIN GIRLS who will play with Dublin's own XN TRIX.

Dublin Unemployed Action Group fights for resistance to job losses, for higher dole payments and for useful well-paid work for all who want it. We publish the paper 'HARD TIMES', we operate an advice centre for people having hassles with the dole or social welfare and organise activities to defend the interests of unemployed people. We meet every Thursday in the ATGWU office in Marlborough St, opposite the Abbey Theatre, at 3pm. Come along and see if you would be interested in what we are doing.

SPECIAL BENEFIT GIG...with POISON GIRLS and the XN TRIX...Friday December 18th...Lourdes Hall, Sean MacDermot St (beside the church)...only 400 yds from O'Connell St...SEE YOU THERE........

SPECIAL BENEFIT GIG
from London....
        POISON GIRLS
from Dublin....
        XN TRIX
This FRIDAY (Dec 18th)
        8pm-12.00
Lourdes Hall,
    Sean MacDermot Street.
        (beside the church)
Adm.£2;(only £1.50 if you
    bring your dole card)

This page: **Lourdes Hall**, Dublin, Ireland, 18 December 1981. A benefit for the Dublin Unemployed Action Group.

Opposite, above: **Anarchy Centre,** Belfast, 19 & 20 December 1981. The Anarchist Centre was a short-lived, self-organized, punk venue and social centre in Northern Ireland. Below: **VERA**, Groningen, Netherlands, 23 March 1980. **VERA**, Groningen, Netherlands, 24 July 1981.

SPECIAL   BENEFIT   GIG

POISON GIRLS

(BY ENGLISH ANARCHO-FEMINIST-GROUP)

FRIDAY 18th DECEMBER, 1981

8.00 p.m. LOURDES HALL,

SEAN MAC DERMOT STREET
(beside the church)

£2.00 Adm..   £1.50 with dole card

Poster: SATURDAY 19 DEC. 1PM. POISON GIRLS with £2 JUST DESTINY stalag 17 — LONG LANE A CENTRE Lower North St. 000079

Poster: 000054 — LONG LANE A CENTRE Lower North St. POISON GIRLS SUNDAY 20TH DEC. 1PM. with £2 DEFECTS Dogmatic Element

Poster: VERA ZO. 23 MRT 21.00 U. CRASS + POISON GIRLS VERA ENTREE F6. (NL. F7.)

Poster: POISON GIRLS VOORPROGAM NRA DONDERDAG 24 JUNI 6.50 +BZ.KAART 21.00 UUR VERA RUBELLA

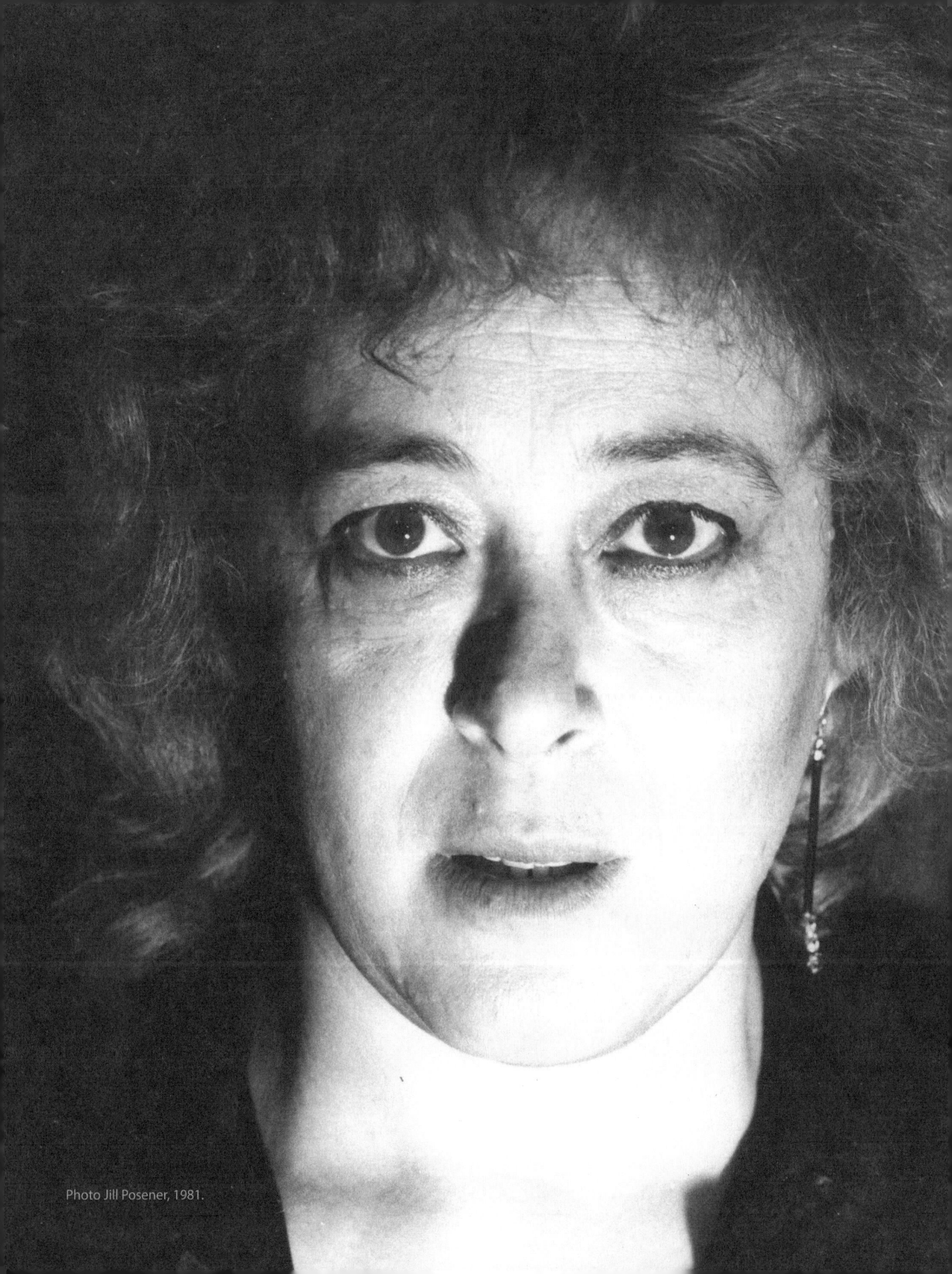

5. WE'RE SO LIBERATED, SO SOPHISTICATED -BUT LOVE IS NEVER FREE

WHERE'S THE PLEASURE 1982

With an album which explores the rich pleasures (and some of the pitfalls) of independence, Poison Girls project a refreshed identity, experiment with a changed approach to their craft, and reveal a range of new musical and lyrical motifs. Poison Girls secure some further welcome coverage in the mainstream music press, while the band's participation in the Wargasm *antinuclear* compilation fires up media interest in Vi Subversa, opening up an unexpected new media platform. An end-of-year tour concludes with Poison Girls' appearance at the singular and celebrated Zig-Zag squat gig.

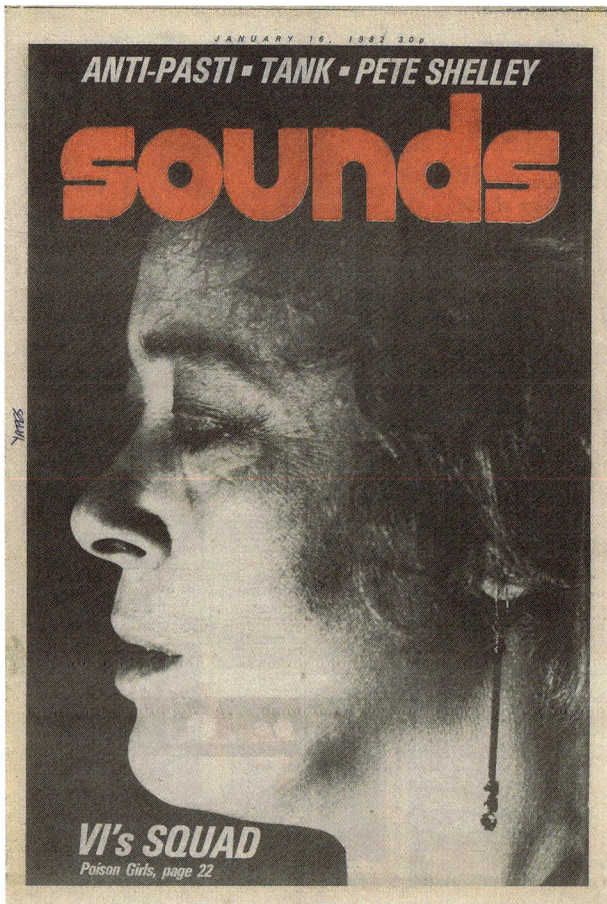

ANTI-PASTI · TANK · PETE SHELLEY

sounds

JANUARY 16, 1982 20p

VI's SQUAD
Poison Girls, page 22

For Poison Girls, 1982 began with an encouraging breakthrough in their efforts to build the band's public profile. A sympathetic two-page feature in the British music weekly *Sounds*, published on 16 January, was given extra impact by the editor's decision to award Poison Girls exclusive front-cover billing. For many upcoming and commercially minded bands, such a moment would have been welcome but unremarkable confirmation of their rising profile. For groups from the DIY anarchist punk scene it was a statement of something very different.

The portrait of Vi Subversa which filled the cover of *Sounds* was one of a series of shots taken by the acclaimed photographer Jill Posener, who'd visually documented the development of feminist and lesbian and gay movements since the 1970s, with a special focus on lesbian identity and erotica. In 1982, Posener would publish *Spray It Loud!*, the decade's definitive celebration of feminist graffiti art targeting advertising hoardings, building sites, and empty urban properties. Her affinity with the ambitions of Poison Girls and with the persona of Vi Subversa was immediate.

Posener's cover shot for *Sounds* was a striking, side-on close-up of Vi's face. It was a potent and evocative image which caught the sense of stillness, serenity and strength which she exuded in that moment. It was

about as far from the usual poses, band shots, and musician antics that were the stock-in-trade of the British music weeklies, as it was possible to get. Women of Vi's age were occasionally featured on the front page, but these were artists from the 1960s on the retro circuit or reviewing a career in musicianship. They were never images of a middle-aged frontwoman from a band demanding recognition in the present. Most *Sounds* readers would immediately have recognised the cover's tagline ("Vi's Squad") as a pun on the name "Vice Squad," the Bristol-based 'UK82' punk band, fronted by the then eighteen-year-old Rebecca Louise Bond (aka Beki Bondage).

The front cover status fed into the band's growing sense that the door to a dialogue with the musical mainstream might be more ajar than they had appreciated. By 1982, the centre of gravity in the UK punk scene had shifted strongly in the direction of UK82 punk (typified by bands like Discharge, The Exploited, and GBH). The new sounds of Poison Girls placed them closer to the aesthetic of the more astute and creative postpunk artists. But the band's commitment to their DIY outsider origins raised challenges when it came to carving out new territory in which to operate.

The British anti–nuclear weapons movement, under the direction of CND, was continuing to expand in response to the accelerating arms race between Washington and Moscow. Numerous bands from the punk, postpunk, ska revival, and reggae scenes were offering to play benefit shows for CND and other organisations. Some of that mainstream artistic identification with the peace movement was heartfelt, but the antinuclear impulses of other artists were superficial or, even more cynically, part of a transactional marketing strategy. A wave of singles and compilation albums echoed the rising antinuclear sentiment. In the punk scene, the imagery of nuclear devastation and of global human annihilation permeated the lyrics and sleeve art of countless record releases. This preoccupation reflected perspectives that ranged from the gratuitously nihilistic to the politically inspirational.

In the spring of 1982, Crass's attention was all-but consumed by the horrors of the Falklands-Malvinas War. From the nonattributed 'Falklands flexi,' rush-released in the early weeks of the conflict, through the *How Does It Feel to Be the Mother of a Thousand Dead?* single (and the Parliamentary attention it attracted), the follow-up *Gotcha* seven-inch, and the frustration and rage of the *Yes Sir, I Will* album—that bloody, brutal "conventional" war came to dominate Crass's attention.

Poison Girls were no less horrified by the carnage jointly engineered by Argentinian president Galtieri and British premier Thatcher. But the band were not so single-minded in their focus on this single war. They were though equally determined to confront the narrative of a "peace movement" that failed to follow through on its own antimilitarist logic.

Subversa prepared a short but powerful hand-written speech that reworked the rhythm and structure of "Statement" to critique peace movement passivity, which she hoped to deliver at the national CND march held in London in October 1982. It began:

I denounce the system that incorporates
the peace movement
I denounce the system that uses and
controls us
I denounce the system that denies direct
action
I denounce the system that buys us off
with a one-day peace march and
expects us to go home peacefully
afterwards

"There was a quarter of a million people at the CND demonstration in October and nothing happened," Famous opined to *Anarchy* magazine. "We did that whole tour which was supposed to be a build-up to that march, but we made it very clear we thought the march was irrelevant, and what was more important was what happened when those people went back home. . . . CND isn't doing anything." In the same interview, d'Boyle insisted that "a big split" was imminent "between the traditional committee activists and marchers," on the one side, "and people who want to do more direct action" on the other.

Even amongst the growing cacophony of antinuclear noise, the antimilitarist *Wargasm* compilation album offered something distinctive. Released in April 1982, the album attracted a roster of punk and alternative which extended its reach beyond the frontiers of anarcho-punk. *Wargasm* was the initiative of the Sheffield-based activist and gig promoter Marcus Featherby (aka Kristan James Melik). "Marcus was never a punk," anarchist activist and organiser Andy Lee (aka Jesus) insists. "He was something like fifteen years older than me and had already been putting on gigs in the city for a while. We became really close and lived together—platonically. Before he set up Pax Records, we'd begun to put on local punk gigs on the first floor of The Marples pub in Fitzalan Square. He was quite a character. Before he arrived in Sheffield, his life had been full of outlandish moments and bizarre coincidences, when he travelled to Africa and to the US. He even managed to land in New York just as Crass arrived to play their one and only set of live shows in the US."

"Among the many bands Marcus booked to play in Sheffield were the likes of Crass, Angelic Upstarts, UK Subs, Vice Squad, Discharge, Chelsea—and a very rare appearance from Nico of The Velvet Under-

Above: *Freedom Anarchist Fortnightly*, 29 May 1982, vol. 43 no. 310.
Opposite: *Sounds*, 16 January 1982, cover photo by Jill Posener.

ground," says Lee. "He also helped to organise free gigs for the unemployed at Sheffield Polytechnic and brought along New Order, The Damned, Bow Wow Wow and others to the venue," Lee continues. "His input into Sheffield's music scene and the associated bands, along with his outstanding talent for capturing many of the bands on camera was truly something to be admired."

Featherby's connections, built up through his gig work, allowed him to approach a wide array of bands with the idea of contributing to *Wargasm*. "I was lucky, as I arrived in Sheffield at a time when it was very exciting and a lot of new things were happening," Featherby told *Maximum Rocknroll*. "I drifted into more of a punk thing and became more involved with bands outside Sheffield far more by accident than design. It was a natural personal progression." Featherby set up the Pax label in 1981, putting out singles by The Danse Society and Stunt Kites, before beginning work on *Wargasm*.

Amongst the maelstrom of antinuclear sentiments surfacing in the work of numerous bands, the politics of *Wargasm* stood out in two ways: first, in its outright opposition not just to nuclear conflagration but also to the horrors of conventional warfare; second, the album's title leaned into the idea of the bloodlust, megalomania, and distorted sense of sexual excitement that animated those generals and politicians responsible for the slaughter. Featherby's message on the back of the sleeve was an excoriating antiwar polemic:

> The biggest evil, which is not only permitted, but actively encouraged—is that most people throughout the world are brainwashed into believing that war is a normal and acceptable part of their everyday lives.
>
> All wars are foul, dirty, and more revolting than your imagination will allow, but we are still supposed to accept them!
>
> We will never persuade the so-called world leaders to stop lobbing missiles at each other as long as we continue to fight amongst ourselves. As long as ordinary people remain divided, governments and politicians will continue to use us as disposable war fodder to bolster their own importance and power.

"Our contribution to *Wargasm* was the 'orchestral' version of 'Statement,'" Famous recalls. "We brought in ten to twelve members of The National Youth Orchestra of Great Britain, and worked from a score written by Barney Unwin, who would go on to play trumpet on *Where's the Pleasure*." This new version, which featured backing vocals from Gemma Sansom, was recorded at Southern Studios by Tony Cook and produced by Jason Osborn. "It was a very different arrangement of it," d'Boyle remembered. "It was interesting to sit and listen to them working. But it was really Vi's idea to bring an orchestral spin to it."

"It was an equally powerful—but different—version to the *Chappaquiddick* one," says Famous, "and reduced Marcus Featherby to tears when we played the tape for him." Subversa preempted the band's punk critics. "Why shouldn't we reclaim orchestras?" she challenged. "They're not just for playing *Rule Britannia*." Each artist contributing to *Wargasm* was able to select the beneficiaries of their proportion of the royalties. Poison Girls chose to send funds to the Women's Centres in Belfast and Dublin.

In April 1982, *Wargasm*'s launch was backed by some inventive promotional gambits, including a press event in a nuclear bunker in Wanstead Park, East London, in which Poison Girls took a prominent public role. Around one hundred No Nukes activists rallied at the site, opened for the day by the Greater London Council "to show citizens how well their safety is being cared for," *Freedom*'s reporter mocked. Photos of Poison Girls standing around a bunk bed, deep within the "surprisingly bare" underground concrete coffin—the absurdity of the affectation of normality evident on their faces—appeared in music weeklies, the fringe political press, and CND's magazine *Sanity*. Many reports quoted Subversa's wry observation: "A bunker is probably the most honest monument to Western culture there is."

Like other releases in the anarchist punk firmament that addressed the risk of nuclear conflagration, *Wargasm* attracted attention precisely because its artistry resonated with that rising antinuclear sentiment. Poison Girls' involvement in the promotion of *Wargasm* resulted in an unanticipated focus on Subversa, who became the subject of multiple mainstream press interviews and appearances on radio talk shows, including some high-profile programmes on BBC Radio 4. Poison Girls benefitted from the heightened media scrutiny, but effectively at one remove, as journalists focused attention almost exclusively on the persona of Subversa.

But the media spotlight proved to be both transitory and focused almost entirely on Subversa's supposed *novelty*. "*The Guardian* most certainly presented her as being strange because of what *she* is doing, which to me shows a great lack of understanding for what *the band* are doing," Famous explained to *Exposure* zine. The mainstream media's priority, he continued, was on "what to their feeble minds is important—like how old we are, or what we were doing before we were a band." Famous frustration was evident. "Vi isn't a *freak* any more than anyone who won't conform to predetermined roles is a freak."

It seemed obvious that the band would need a more dependable platform from which to launch a sustained incursion into the mainstream. The Xntrix label, operating under its own steam, simply would not suffice.

After the end of the *Total Exposure* tour the previous November, bassist Nil had announced he was leaving the band "to study Chinese." We have had several bass players," Famous acknowledged to *Exposure* zine, "most leaving to do things other than music." It was a process that would continue throughout the band's life. Pete Fender agreed to step back into the lineup to temporarily cover bass duties once more while the search began again. It was Andy Lee who recommended Chris Grace, an accomplished fretless bass player from Sheffield, as a replacement. "I was visiting Poison Girls at Hainault Road, and, with the kind of confidence you have when you're seventeen, I suggested my school friend Chris, who I knew was a talented, inventive—even an obsessive—bassist. Vi asked me to invite him down to try out with the band, which I did." Grace was an immediate and impressive fit. "Thanks for Chris," Vi wrote in a letter to Lee shortly afterwards. "We met him on Good Friday and started our new album on Easter Monday. Very holy."

The first three months of the year were spent writing and arranging material for a new studio album that would be a strikingly different musical undertaking than anything Poison Girls had attempted before. "We're changing what we're doing from a very raw sound to a

Photo by Jill Posener, 1981.

smoother sound," Famous confirmed to *Anarchy*, "but maintaining lyrics which actually mean something, and seeing if that will change the quality, or number of people that listen to what we're doing."

Recording began at Forest Studios in London on 12 April 1982, before relocating to Southern Studios from 23 April. It was a lengthy and complex process, with work on the album concluding on 16 August, following what the band described as "much deliberation." "We owe a big debt to Adrian Grey Turner, an old friend from the Brighton days, who helped with arrangements and initial production," Famous says. The album was provisionally called 'L'amour and more' ('Love and more') during the recording process.

Time in the studio produced some welcome surprises. "We've used a commercial producer," Subversa explained. "We said we wanted him to tell us how to make a commercial sound. But what's happened is he's been subverted by us. He keeps saying how we're so different to work with and he likes the food here and all sorts of things—like we'll have to meet his wife because she'd be interested in what we're saying, and he's sort of saying we've made him question his life, you know."

"We made a deliberate attempt with the *Where's the Pleasure* album to try to reach out to a wider audience," Famous explained shortly after its release. It was part of a conscious effort 'to push ourselves and our audience into a broader space,' as the band 'deliberately set out to try to break the expectations some of our audience had of us.' The attempt was not intended as a complete rupture, or a total break with what had gone before, with the band presenting the change as an evolution. "I don't think the actual content of the record is different," Famous suggested to *The Leveller*. "There's just been a slight change of emphasis on how it's presented."

This first follow-up to *Total Exposure*, a new studio album inquisitively entitled *Where's the Pleasure*, showcased the band's new approach. If *Hex* was an album about the pressure cooker of domesticity and motherhood, *Where's the Pleasure* was a record concerned with the perils of sex, romance, attraction, and physical relationships which challenged the sexism and ageism of capital's social conventions. Where *Hex* was stark, angular and full of sharp edges, *Where's the Pleasure* was polished, seductive, and captivating.

167

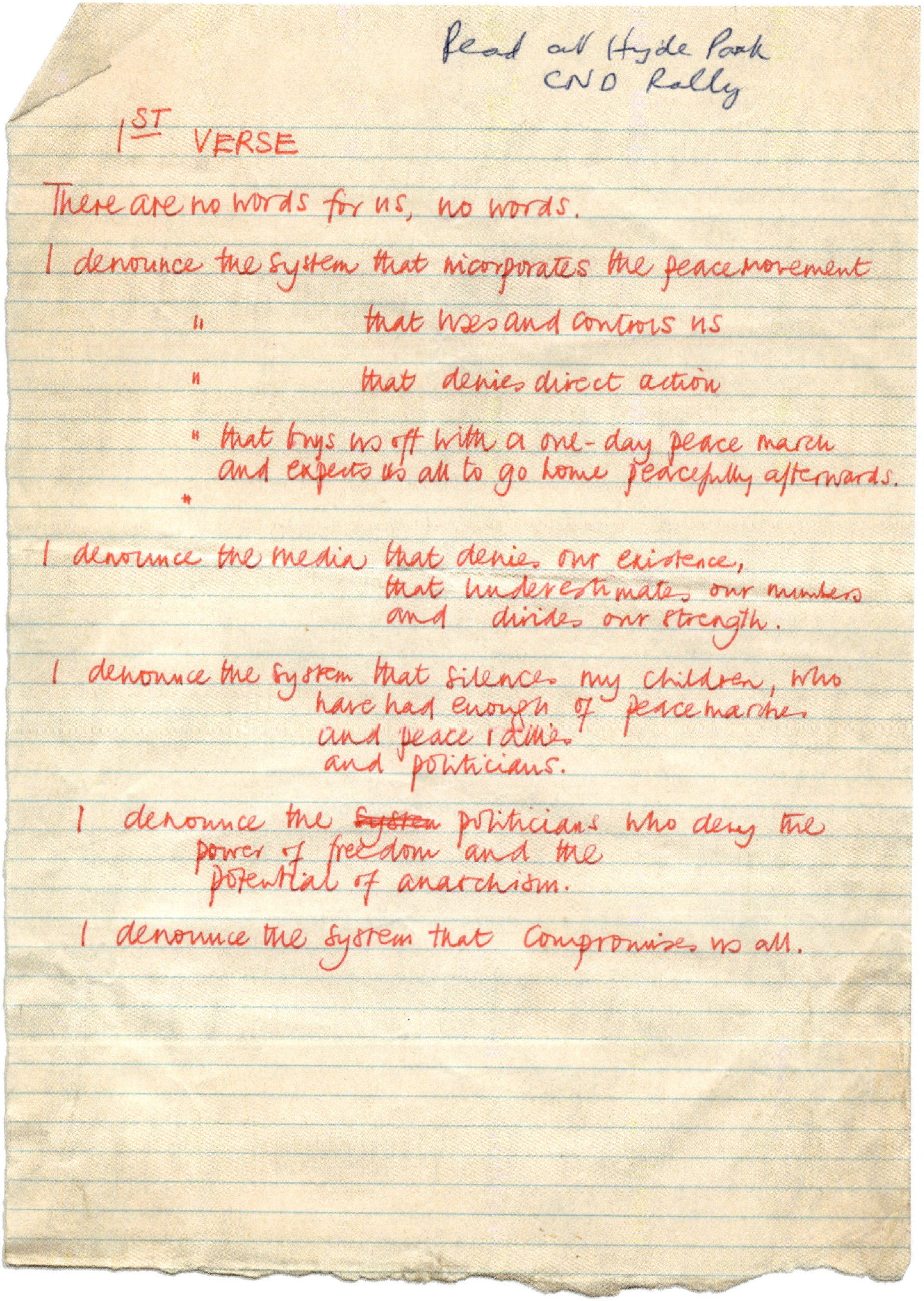

Read at Hyde Park
CND Rally

1ST VERSE

There are no words for us, no words.

I denounce the system that incorporates the peace movement

" that uses and controls us

" that denies direct action

" that buys us off with a one-day peace march
and expects us all to go home peacefully afterwards.

"

I denounce the media that denies our existence,
that underestimates our numbers
and divides our strength.

I denounce the system that silences my children, who
have had enough of peace marches
and peace idlies
and politicians.

I denounce the ~~system~~ politicians who deny the
power of freedom and the
potential of anarchism.

I denounce the system that compromises us all.

Vi Subversa's speech notes for the October 1982 CND rally. Courtesy of Pete Fender and Gemma Sanson.

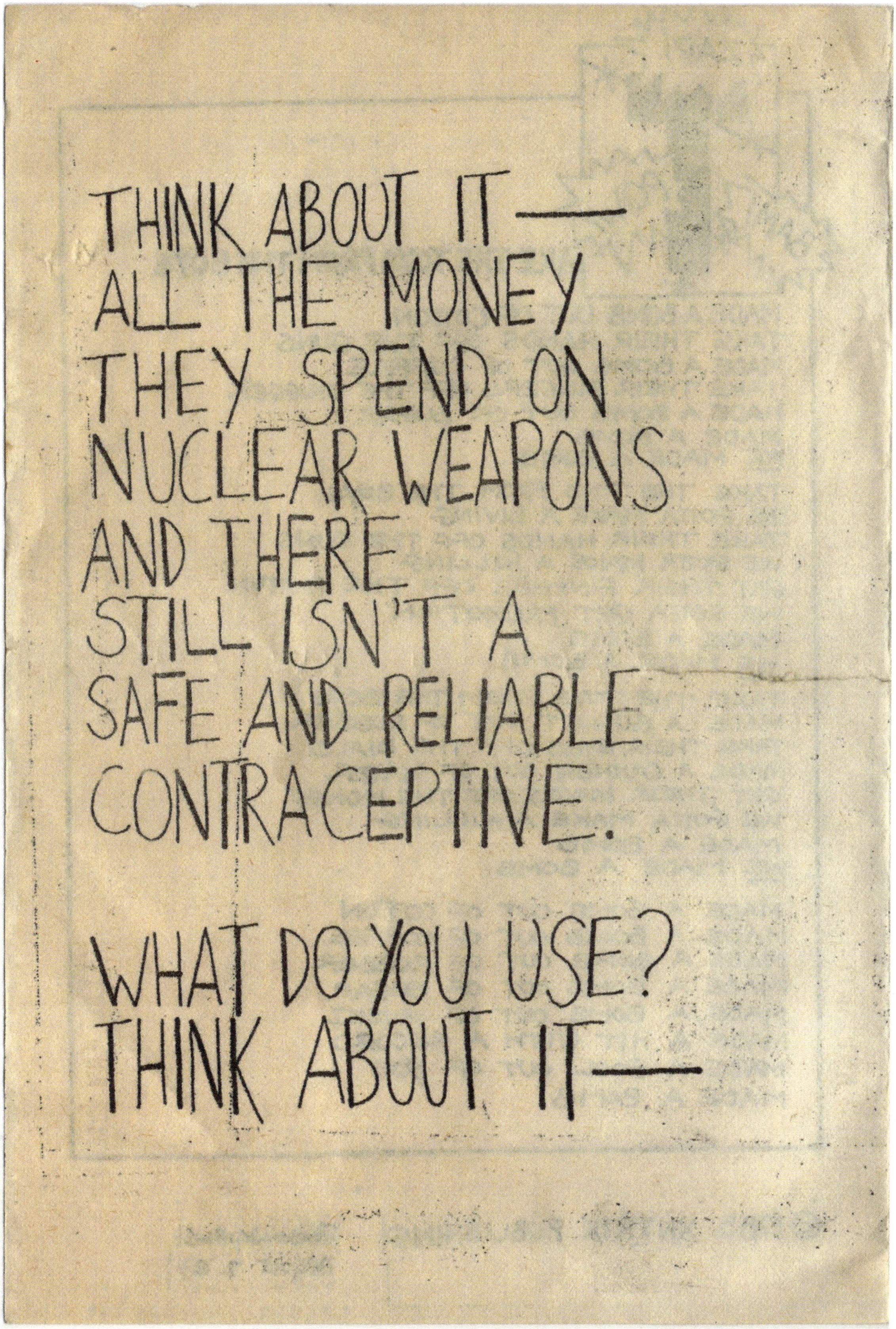

THINK ABOUT IT—
ALL THE MONEY
THEY SPEND ON
NUCLEAR WEAPONS
AND THERE
STILL ISN'T A
SAFE AND RELIABLE
CONTRACEPTIVE.

WHAT DO YOU USE?
THINK ABOUT IT—

Where's the Pleasure lyric zine, 1982.

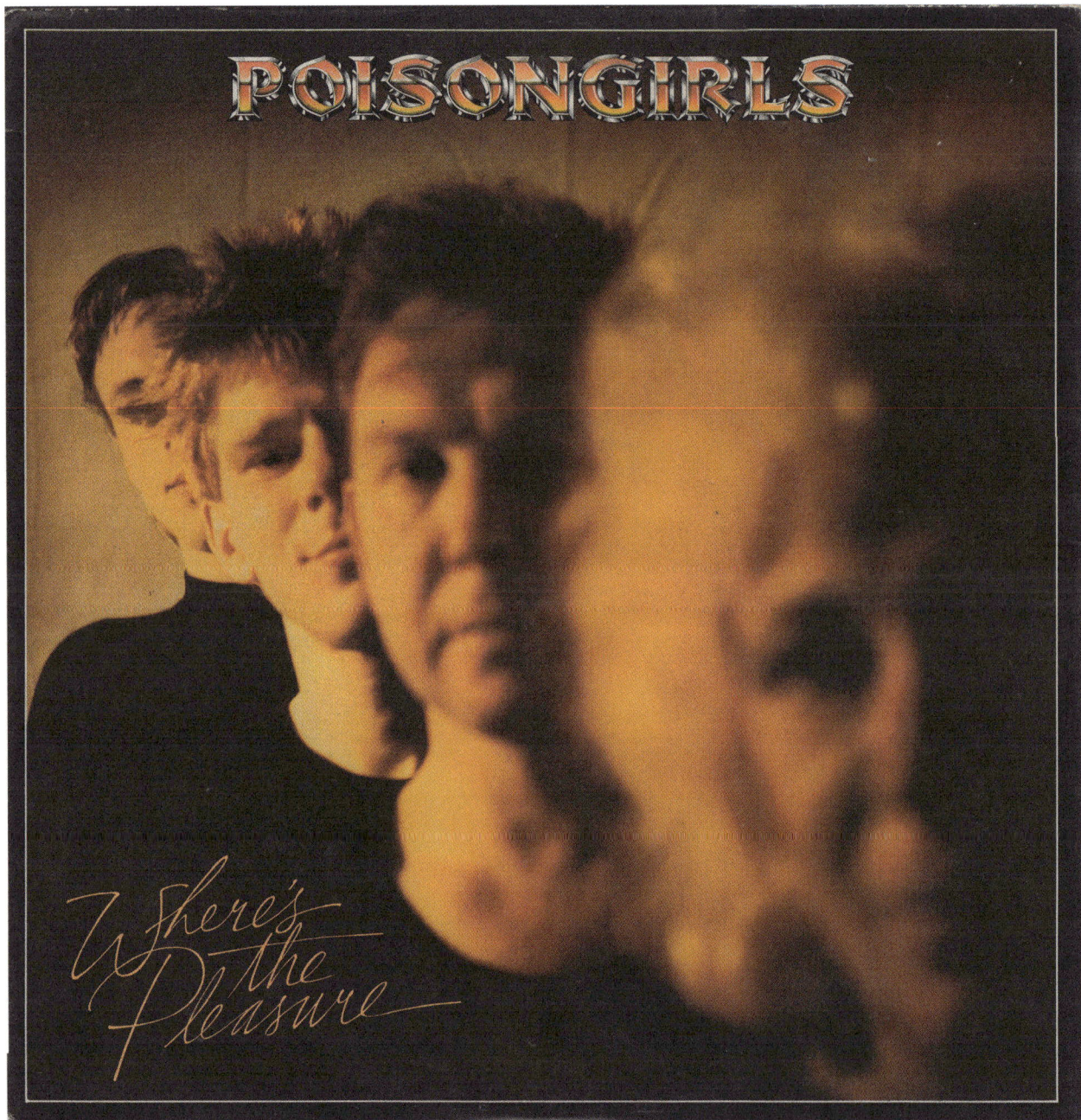

Where's the Pleasure, Xntrix Records, 1982. The durable and iconic Poison Girls font was designed by bass player Bernhardt Rebours. He updated the letterforms and added a metallic sheen for *Where's the Pleasure.*

Lyrically, the record shared the same mixture of concerns that had shaped the band's previous releases (a mixture of personal politics, focused on the impact of gender on relationships, and broader critiques of capitalism, exploitation, and alienation). But the musical timbre was very different. The contrast between the unvarnished, blunt directness of *Total Exposure* and the rich, complex, and textured tones of *Where's the Pleasure* could scarcely be starker. The album was an extraordi-

narily accomplished piece of work, which confirmed the growing confidence and distinctiveness of the band and Poison Girls' determination to move in new productive and unexpected directions.

The presentation of the album sleeve was also a sharp break from previous practice. Gone was the stencil lettering, and monochrome look; replaced by a new warm colour palette and a deliberate sense of conscious design. The carrion crow, which had been the band's signature icon, was absent, and the band's name was presented in a new metallic gold-and-silver font designed by Bernhardt Rebours. In place of the anonymity that was common in the graphic design of most anarchist punk bands, all four members of Poison Girls appeared on the sleeve, standing one behind the other, and looking straight into the camera. There was a rich, warm colour palette to the sleeve, something more familiar in the relaxed, knowing perspectives of postpunk than found in the strictures of anarchist punk, in which that type of self-presentation was frowned upon.

The band's choice of album title was once again intriguing. 'Where's the Pleasure' was posed as a statement, not as an inquiry, hence the lack of a question mark. There's a strong sense that this is part of the process of the band distinguishing themselves from their earlier close associations with the anarcho-punk scene. From their earliest days, Poison Girls were determined to embrace the indulgences that life afforded and to revel in the ability to reclaim portions of your life, your being, from the entrapments of society and the state, by seizing the opportunity to love, laugh, dance, and rejoice in the wonders simply of being alive as an autonomous agent in that endeavour.

Part of what had increased the band's disaffection with playing to Crass's crowd was the seeming forswearing of humour, hedonism, and the enjoyment of life. Whether the criticism was valid or not, Poison Girls took pleasure in the freedom to celebrate and embrace the pursuit of pleasure, seeing it as a way to stick two fingers up to the authority of the state and not find oneself consumed by rage and disgust at the state of the world. This was a record that raised the question both of how joy might be combined with opposition to the powers that be and of how that rage against the machinations of the war state might be expressed in a different and unexpected countercultural voice.

The clear message of Where's the Pleasure was that subversive cultural practice should celebrate the pursuit of fun and of hedonism, embrace whimsy, comedy, mischief-making, and pleasure, as well as project righteous anger. Subversa acknowledged that the shift left the band exposed: "To audiences who prefer something hard and aggressive, we have a policy to confront them with their own tenderness if you like, and it's always been a risk."

The risks were not just reputational but financial. The more sophisticated production techniques were among the most expensive the band had had to finance so far, and these higher studio costs pushed the band into significant debt. "We had several meetings with the bank manager—if you can remember them," says Famous. "He ended up saying that we owed the bank so much money that he had to lend us more. That's the fucked up logic of big finance. I think the overdraft was at least £15k, with interest rates over 15 percent—a whole lot of money in those days. We ended up having to sell half our garden in Leytonstone to some developer to eventually clear the debt."

The critical reception for Where's the Pleasure from the mainstream music press was amongst the most positive the band had yet received. The NME relished the album's release, heralding it "the last great punk record." Interest once again crossed over to the political press. Writing in the British feminist magazine Spare Rib, Jill Posener—a long-time supporter and photographer of Poison Girls—welcomed the "theatricality . . . humour and warmth" of the record which combined to distinguish the release as "something special." Poison Girls had, Posener concluded "been brave enough to take a long hard look at their music, and have emerged quite simply a better band."

The production on the album was textured and sophisticated: everything that Total Exposure was not. The record included what would go on to become some of the band's best regarded songs—crowd-pleasers which would form the mainstay of the band's live set from this point onwards.

"Where's the Pleasure" was an attention-grabbing opener that distilled the band's reaffirmed manifesto. A rich, rolling pop number with prominent keyboards and a catchy hook, all built around a strong refrain. The song exposed the chasm that can separate the reality of romantic love, distorted by dysfunctional sexual politics, that result in the absence of pleasure and the burden of social expectation. An alienated form of nonconnection which obliterates the chance for genuine human affinity.

Where's the pleasure, where's the fun?
You bring me down, you wind me up
It don't take much to work it out
Love is what it's all about

"Lovers Are They Worth It" offers a disdainful spin on the benefits of lovers, when weighed against the costs and consequences of being made to play the game required. Subversa croons and growls her way through the lyrics, as she revels in making her frustration and scorn. Underlying that disparagement is the perception that the answer, despite everything, might still be 'yes.'

"I've Done It All Before" is one of the most impactful and lyrically unusual songs on the album. It explores the idea that relationships retread familiar experiences, but that the value of those experiences comes from their newness, their uniqueness with each individual partner. Like other songs on the album, it also places Subversa, a fortysomething woman, as an active sexual operator, a person literate in relationships, forging new entanglements and having expectations and perspectives based on experience, and antithetical to the idealised teen romance that's been the staple of pop since the 1950s. In

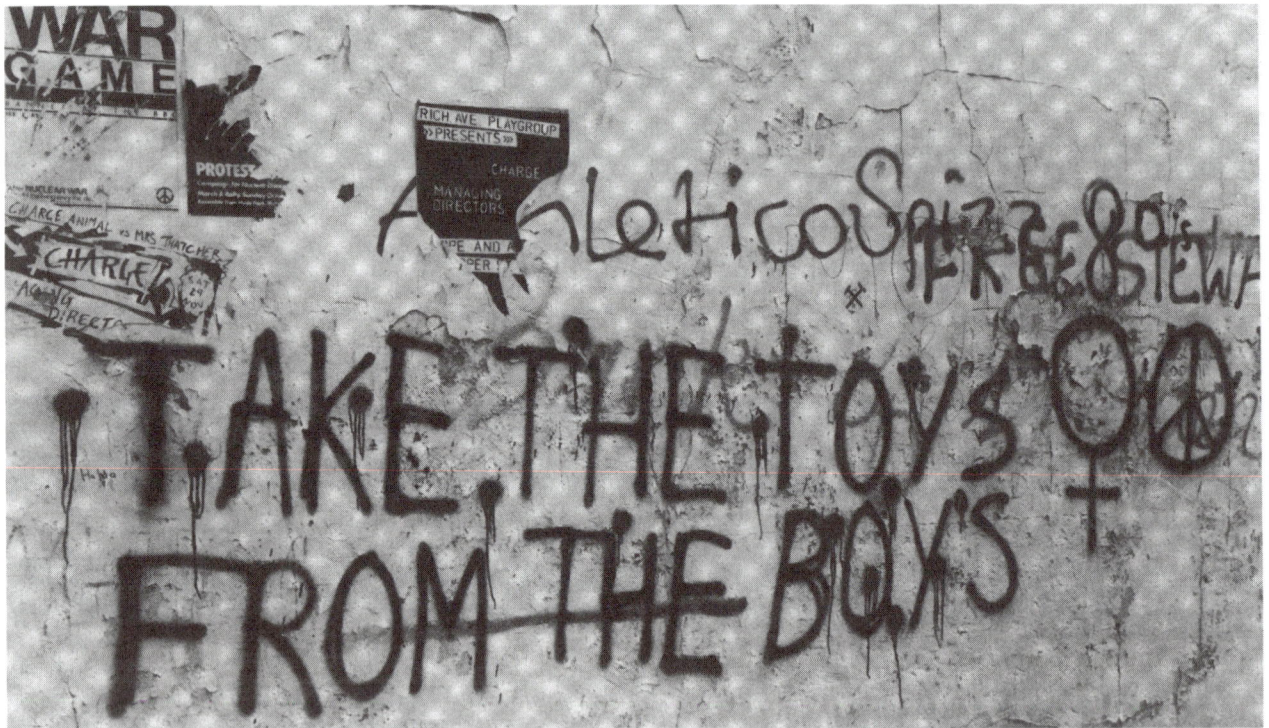

Islington, London, 1982. Photo by Jill Posener, from her 1982 book of feminist graffiti, *Spray It Loud.*

reinstating her as a decisive sexual player it is deeply subversive and gloriously provocative.

These ideas resurface, in a more challenging form, in the lyrics of "Whiskey Voice" and its reflections on "the rising cost of seduction" and a hint to the lure of alcohol and of medication as a means to manage the pressures of ageing and decline in sexual capital. "Ménage Abattoir" is a twist on the challenges of the *ménage a trois* and of the feelings of betrayal, inadequacy, and jealousy that can haunt a three-way relationship.

The next track sees a return to wider political perspectives, in the classic antimilitarist feminist treatise "Take the Toys from the Boys." As a slogan, these words were in widespread use throughout the culture of feminist-inspired peace activism, and amongst the community of women activists based at Greenham Common. With this political demand as her inspiration, Vi Subversa crafted a statement which added additional anarcha-feminist ire to the case against the war state.

> Take the toys from the boys
> Made a bullet out of rubber
> Take their eyes off the dials
> Made a cannon out of water
> Get their minds off the money
> Gotta make a killing
> Made a bomb
> We made a bomb

The result was realised as a mellifluous and magisterial choral lament, as a scratch choir was assembled in the studio to render the song as a powerful, potent and searing manifesto—every bit as impactful as "Dirty Work" but with its own unique timbre.

"We had fourteen people in the choir, all grouped around different microphones," d'Boyle remembered. "They were all our friends, and we thought they could probably sing alright. We got everyone in the control room afterwards and played it back, with lots of echo on it. It sounded like we were in the Albert Hall! Everybody was so pleased with it—gobsmacked by what we'd done."

Subversa regularly voiced her support for the Greenham Common peace camp, for women-only and women-first initiatives in the peace and feminist movements of the 1980s. At an all-female lineup of artists at a Greenham benefit at London's Roundhouse on 19 December 1982, Subversa delivered a spoken-word poem which began:

> If just one woman with one pair of arms can hold
>   herself and know
> That her body's her own and her mind is her own
>   and that she is free to grow
> And if just two women with two pairs of arms can
>   hold each other and show
> That love's not just for the boys, we'll all got a
>   choice, as most of you will know

"Take the Toys from the Boys" lyric sheet and music score, 1983.

Well, there's boys here tonight, and that's al
    right, please don't get me wrong
I quite like some boys, I just don't like their toys
    . . . but that's another song

Subversa often cautioned against the adoption of a type of separatist women's politics which was intrinsically hostile to any connections with men. Keen to reset any misconception of the band's worldview that some might have drawn from the lyrical approach of *Hex* or *Chappaquiddick Bridge*, Subversa chose to begin *Where's the Pleasure* with an appeal to step outside the confines of dogma—including any shibboleths concerning gender politics. "The statement that opens that album is 'I don't believe in the brotherhood of man. No state of grace, no five year plan,'" she explained to *Kick It Over* newspaper. "That's saying that the state of our system politics needs a kick up the ass. We can't take anything for granted anymore. And then I go on to say 'I don't believe in sisters against the men. My sister has betrayed me yet again.'" As was so often the case, Poison Girls were side-stepping comfortable political positions.

The first side of the album nears its conclusion with the riotous "Soft Touch" and the riotous advocacy of new forms of sexual intimacy, subverting the traditional critical meaning of the idea of being a 'soft touch.' There's a joyous quality to the stepping, circling tempo of the song and the upbeat shared vocals that run through an alternative bedroom experience that ought to be more liberating for everyone involved.

Side one is signed off with an evocative vocal reprise of "Take the Toys from the Boys," with its rebuke of those bored by expressions of antimilitarist conviction.

Oh-oh no, not another bomb song, bomb song
Oh-oh no, another fucking bomb song, bomb song

Side two opens with "Velvet Launderette," a musically sophisticated number with an equally intriguing lyrical premise. The band would go on to use the iconography of George Orwell's *1984* and the idea of Big Brother, and there's a sense threaded through the song of O'Brien telling Winston or Julia of the way that their freedoms will be suffocated and their lives controlled by the state.

Poison Girls, 1982: Nil, Vi, Lance, and Richard. *Words Written in Trust* on the table. Photo by Jill Posener.

"Rio Disco Stink" adopts a forensic political focus, publicising the campaign against the ruinous activities of an international mining company. The work of the rapacious Rio Tinto Zinc (RTZ) was a minor *cause célèbre* for the fringes of the anarchist movement and the unaligned left in Britain in the early 1980s. Organised opposition to RTZ had developed out of Colonialism and Indigenous Minorities Research and Action (CIMRA), a lobby group that campaigned in support of indigenous peoples' struggles to prevent corporate seizure of their land in countries across the globe. In 1978, CIMRA had played host to a European tour by a delegation of Aboriginal land activists, which highlighted the "multiple violations of indigenous rights" that were RTZ's modus operandi. The tour was a catalyst for formation of People Against Rio Tinto Zinc and Subsidiaries (Partizans), at the initiative of Roger Moody, animal rights activist and former coeditor of *Peace News*.

Poison Girls always maintained a self-protecting safe distance from formal political organisations—especially those keen to sign them up as cultural capital. But the small-scale, loosely organised, libertarian-inclined, and cash-poor Partizans was a more comfortable match than most. It was a lo-fi, DIY endeavour. "Partizans was run from a semiderelict house [at 218 Liverpool Street] in Islington, north London for most of its existence, where various people lived," the group's official history explains. "Here meetings were held, the newsletter written and produced. It was mostly chaotic and dirty, never an easy place to work, with every surface covered in papers." Its organisers focused on publicly challenging RTZ's directors and shareholders at the company's annual general meetings (AGMs), held in London every April, producing alternative, and devastatingly critical, "annual reports" on RTZ's activities, and on pressing councils and charitable organisations to disinvent (the group's newsletter *Parting Company* pressed home the ambition). Its tactic was to sell single shares (from a tiny portfolio it owned solely for the purpose) to supporters who then had the right to attend and speak at the RTZ annual meeting.

Out of instinctive solidarity with the group's aims, Poison Girls were keen to support and promote Partizans's efforts. The band promoted such activities and reprinted (sometimes reworked) Partizans's flyers to circulate at gigs and to their postal contacts. Subversa would sometimes punctuate the live performance of the song with an impromptu speech urging the audience to join in action against the company.

Flyers from and about the group were regularly included in Poison Girls' mailouts, and when on stage the band would often pause after playing the song "Rio Disco Stink" for Subversa to encourage members of the audience to engage with their work.

In 1982, the AGM ended in complete uproar when the Chair closed the meeting prematurely, to prevent protesters from asking questions. After Aboriginal activists took control of the platform demanding to be heard, the police arrived to clear the building. The following year, Subversa delivered the first question to the board in the form of a heartfelt a cappella version of "Rio Disco Stink," a "powerful rendering" of the song *Parting Company* reported. Decades later, evidence from the infamous *Undercover Policing Inquiry*, investigating clandestine infiltration of protest groups, confirmed that Partizans were amongst numerous organisations targeted by the police's Special Branch.

"Rio Disco Stink" was a righteous condemnation of the company's activities, set to a pulsing disco beat and a sublime walking bass line. This was one of the most self-evidently political tracks on *Where's the Pleasure*. A focus on the campaign against RTZ was something that would surface strongly when the band played the song live.

"Cry No More" is a complex song to assess, because it teeters on the edge of self-pity. It is about the phenomenon of overload and burnout amongst political activists when faced with the unimaginable horrors of the world they are opposing. It adopts the same list style as "Persons Unknown" to iterate through snapshots of misery and conflict. It also includes an atypical, mournful guitar solo from Famous.

"Mandy Is Having a Baby" feels like an extension and update to "Pretty Polly." It's a singsong nursery rhyme infused with cautionary insights about the unreal choices facing an oblivious Mandy as the world seemingly spirals towards war.

"Fear of Freedom" is an extraordinary way to conclude the album. An unexpected and captivating musical arrangement, mixing saxophone, trombone, trumpet, and guitar, is blended with Subversa's emotionally astute vocals, into something beautiful and evocative. It ends the record with a soulful frustrated call to arms, quietly raging against docility in the face of the war machine, recoiling from the opportunity to embrace freedom.

The band rebutted any suggestion that their musical recalibration was a move away from Poison Girls' radical roots. "I'm really surprised that the bands who call themselves . . . alternative and propose individuality are all playing the same three chord bash," Subversa protested to *Subvert*. "The problem is that bands who are speaking in the name of freedom, nonconformity, honesty and truth are actually being dominated by the fear to be different, the fear to try things new," she insisted.

Famous stressed the importance of the band not remaining static, not just in the approach to songwriting but in its delivery on stage too. "When we started we used a method of confrontation—in that we played one song straight after another, and no one in an audience had been in that situation before where they weren't allowed one second off," he explained. "If we want to continue to confront people, then we've got to give them something apart from just forty minutes of noise, of very well-intentioned, intense, emotional screaming. We've got to go beyond that to maintain the confrontation." Recognising that, and needing to keep things unexpected, Subversa added, it had increasingly become important "for us to do gentle songs in front of an audience which is dying to be tough."

And were the band pleased with the album's reception amongst their core audience? "Yes," Famous said at the time. "It was treated with respect by punks who said that they liked it—after a few plays. We have never been just a thrash band, so people know to expect the unexpected from us." *Where's the Pleasure* was "the most collaborative album that we produced," he contends, "and, in my opinion, the most 'Poison Girls' of all of them."

To round off the year, Poison Girls embarked on a series of European shows, including dates in Holland and Germany: "a chance to meet local nutcases and make many friends." In Holland, the band discovered that their approach "was taken very seriously by intellectual dropouts with their own slant on punk," d'Boyle explained.

The tour was followed by a series of live shows back in the UK. At a gig in Carlisle in December 1982, an attack launched by a gang of fascists and hangers-on (working under the encouragement of the far-right 'Rock Against Communism' front) disrupted sets by both Rubella Ballet and Poison Girls. The assault was repulsed by the firm collective action of the audience, before local police used the 'disorder' as a pretext to shut down the event. Later in the evening, both bands had to flee, just as the last of their equipment was loaded into the minibus, when an emboldened gang of thugs returned to exact vengeance for their humiliation.

The year 1982 had been dire for all progressive political forces in the UK. The postcolonial slaughter of the Falklands War, engineered by a British prime minister facing electoral defeat, had been its nadir. The Zig-Zag event was "just a gig," but it was an important restatement of intent by the political punk scene, and a rallying moment for those convinced that that scene could still be a credible locus of principled resistance.

Although the capacity of the venue was in the low hundreds, and was far from being packed out on the day, the Zig-Zag gig became a landmark event in the story of

Lance, Tony Allen, and friend, 1983. Photo by Domino.

the British anarcho-punk movement—its reputation out of all proportion to its actual scale. It was the audaciousness of the idea, the brilliance of its execution, and the impressiveness of the day-long roster of anarchist artists that it brought together that made it such an inspiring event—just as much to the thousands who would have liked to be there as to those few hundred lucky enough to attend.

Members of Crass, who organised the event, invited bands from across the anarcho-punk scene to join the bill—including Omega Tribe, Lack of Knowledge, D&V, Conflict, Flux of Pink Indians, and Dirt. The fact that Poison Girls were amongst the invitees was confirmation that relations between the two bands remained cordial.

"The gig is very fresh in my mind," d'Boyle reflected, decades later." It was something special and unique. My main feeling looking back was that it was a coming home. Leaving aside the political ambitions, one of the most important aspects of anarcho-punk was the feeling of being with family and loved just for that."

While for d'Boyle arriving to play at the Zig-Zag alongside so many other like-minded bands felt like a homecoming, for Famous it felt far less special. "It was a very strange gig for us," he begins. "I know that it's

gone down as being a significant event, but there was an awful lot going on which was distracting us at the time, and I don't think we were in a particularly good mood, as a band—it had been a particularly fraught few days."

"We had been on a tour in the north of England, when Vi's daughter had been taken ill and had to have an operation in a hospital in Bradford. So we came back without all our gear, which we had to leave in Manchester, and then the van broke down as well, I think. Everything had gone kaput."

"Crass got in touch and said, 'We're doing this squat gig—you should come and play.' It was the first time we'd really had any contact with them since the split. We were happy to take part in it, and we're glad we were asked to take part in it. I think it would have been wrong for us *not* to have played it. But it was not really 'our' gig, if you know what I mean. I remember we just turned up and played, and then left. It didn't seem particularly important to us," he concludes. "There were other things going on."

The disaggregation of the British punk movement was built into the punk eruption from the beginning. If the band were looking for any additional justification for their decision to refocus their efforts away from the punk rock core, the "Punk Debate" organised by the music weekly Sounds in December 1982, seemed to be irrefutably (if unintentionally) persuasive.

Organised by *Sounds* journalists Johnny Waller and Winston Smith, a range of punk artists was invited to their publisher Spotlight Publications London HQ: Hoxton Tom (4 Skins), Steve Drewett (Newtown Neurotics), Beki Bondage (Vice Squad), Mensi (Angelic Upstarts), Jello Biafra (Dead Kennedys), Attila the Stockbroker (punk poet), Colin Jerwood (Conflict), and Vi Subversa. The stated aim was to judge the response of the room to the publication of an attention-seeking opinion piece by Garry Bushell which announced that "punk is dead." Vi Subversa's participation in the debate meant that Poison Girls began and ended 1982 able to use *Sounds* as a platform to express their ideas. But the confusion, dislocation, and competition revealed in the debate confirmed the extent of British punk's growing identity crisis, and the uncertainty and conflicting ambitions afflicting it.

Subversa's participation ended in disappointment, although of course not for want of trying. "Well, the question 'Is Punk Dead' to me is meaningless; because for me, punk is about life; punk was about taking my life for myself," she said in response to one of Waller's and Smith's questions. "There's no way I can say punk is dead, because while I'm still alive and kicking I need a word for it, and 'punk' will do." Subversa also pushed back strongly at the divisive sexist and ageist views other in the room were voicing:

> Sitting round this table I've heard people talking about "cunts" and old-age pensioners right? Well, I mean I happen to have a cunt, and I'm not very far off being an old-age pensioner, and those are the people that are particularly powerless in our society, and for any definition of punk to exclude a lot of people who are extremely powerless is an invalid definition, and it's going to leave you as weak as ever. We've got to make these connections and not keep splitting up.

"The punk debate in *Sounds* was a farce," the band complained months later, dismissing the occasion outright. For Poison Girls that debate was disheartening confirmation of what was becoming inescapably obvious: that the straitjacket of punk was too restricting for the ambitions that the band now had for themselves. The Zig-Zag gig had also pulled the band back closer to the epicentre of the anarcho-punk scene than they were now comfortable to find themselves. But it was clear that Poison Girls now sought to loosen the binds of that punk straitjacket, and to shift the artistic gravity of the band's work in a new direction, and to put together a new "London update of the Berlin cabaret."

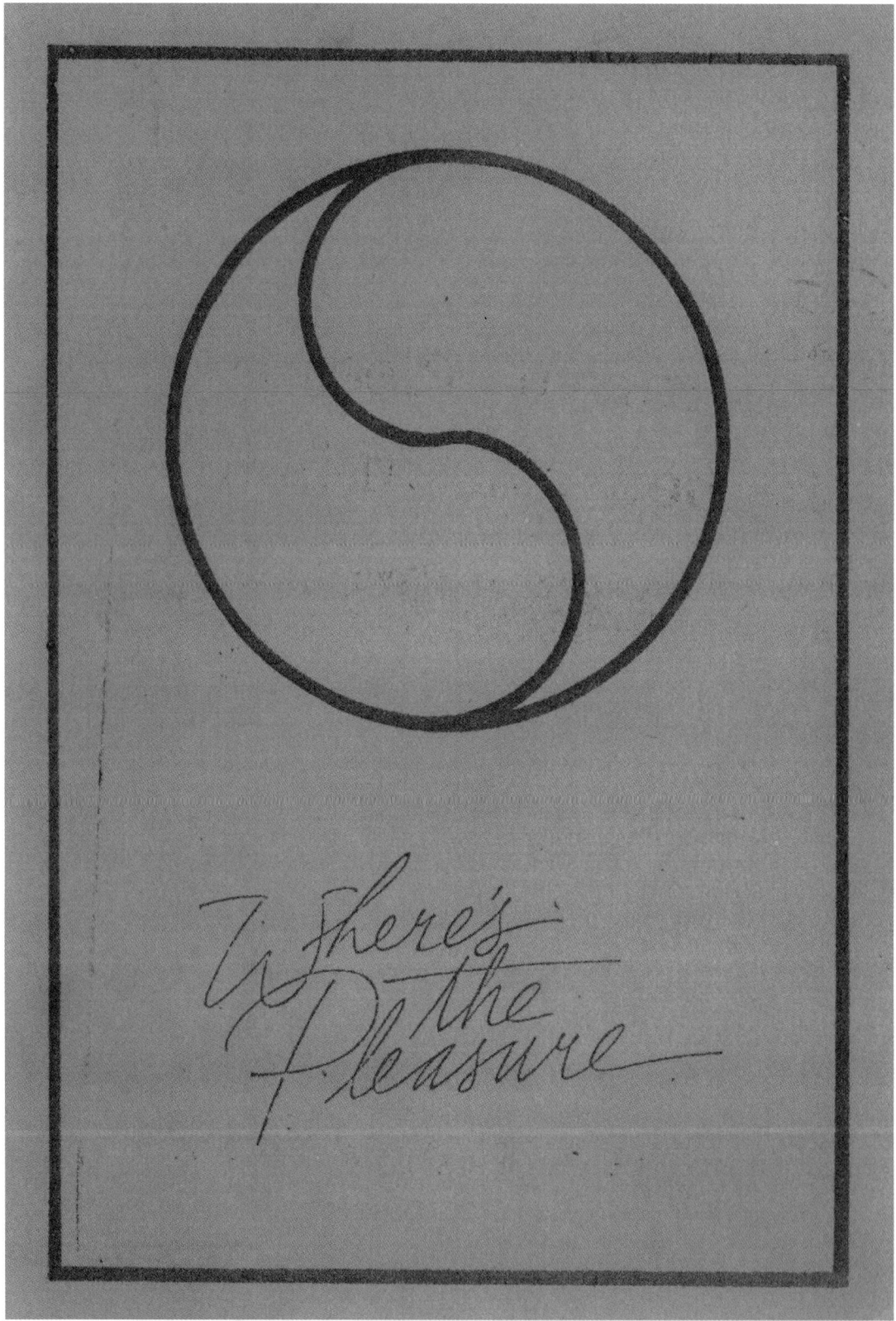

Where's the Pleasure promo zine, 1982. Following two pages: Poison Girls published the names and addresses of the major shareholders of the Rio Tinto Zinc as part of a campaign against the international mining company. Protests against the company continue to this day.

WHERE'S THE PLEASURE

POISONGIRLS have never accepted outside limitations or the comfort of conformity. The record was envisioned as an open door. There is always need to confront and expand an audience with unexpected styles and new sounds. For example the use of a 15 piece, 7 part harmony scratch choir for the 'Toys from the Boys' track, and the haunting brass arrangement of 'Fear of Freedom' are both musically ambitious and show a scope of sound not often heard on one record.

In making this L.P. a string of friends were co-opted into the studio to contribute their noises and voices, and the resulting richness and warmth of the finish tracks is here on record.

WHERE'S THE PLEASURE

WHERE'S THE PLEASURE

The long awaited third album from POISONGIRLS is released this week; titled "WHERE'S THE PLEASURE" and out on the band's own XNTRIX RECORDS label (cat No. XN 2006, distributed through Rough Trade and the Cartel). Those who know the band from their previous recordings will recognise that this L.P. marks a significant musical development.

The intensity and depth of feeling of Vi Subversa's voice and lyrics remain unique in the 'rock field' whilst the music, keeping all the power and energy of POISONGIRLS earlier work, has reached a new level of subtlety and accessibility.

The interface between the 'personal' and the 'political' has always been one of the prime areas of POISON GIRLS material, and this L.P. takes that exploration further than ever before. The song titles speak for themselves- 'Where's thePleasure', 'Lovers- are they Worth It', 'Done it All Before' 'Whisky Voice', 'Menage Abattoir', 'Take the Toys from the Boys', 'Soft Touch', 'Velvet Launderette','Rio DiscoStink' 'Cry No More', Mandy is Having a Baby', and 'Fear of Freedom'.

POISONGIRLS : A SHORT BIOGRAPHY

POISONGIRLS are : Vi Subversa, vocals, guitar; Richard Famous, guitar; Lance D'Boyle, drums ; and new fretless bass player Chris Grace.

The third L.P. from POISONGIRLS, "Where's The Pleasure", now out on their own XNTRIX label, marks the start of a period of radical change for the band. Change is essential.

Vi Subversa's lyrics are as bitingly relevant and committed as ever, ruthless and compassionate; while the music, keeping its subtlety, excitement and edge, adopts a more accessible form. The velvet glove.

POISONGIRLS have been working together since 1976, when, in Brighton, needing a practice room for themselves they opened and ran the now legendary Vault, the only punk gig/rehearsal space available at that time. Within days of opening the Vault was packed. The Vault was important. Energy.

The move to London in autumn 1977 resulted in a long and intense collaboration with Crass, from early 1979 to summer 1981. Over 200 live performances throughout the U.K. Northern Ireland and Europe has created a strong network of independant contacts, a large and intelligent grassroots following and the basis of a genuine alternative, healthy and relevant context for bands to work in. Connect.

What did you say your name was again?

POISONGIRLS

You make your pile where the miners die at RIO TINTO ZINC. Do you know what I mean, can you hear them scream and can you smell the stink of the hundreds dead at the R.T.Z. to pay for your British fun. The rotting men at the Rossing Mine that digs uranium.... A cancer spreads from that hole in the ground at RIO TINTO ZINC. Your company banks fill up their tanks but you can't lock up the stink. Uranium will kill your son whatever you may want to think. Are you feeling proud of that hole in the ground at RIO TINTO ZINC ?

"RIO DISCO STINK"

A SONG BY POISONGIRLS

ABOUT R.T.Z. BRITAINS LARGEST MOST POWERFUL MULTINATIONAL MINING COMPANY. PRODUCER OF URANIUM FOR THE WEST. DEALER IN DEATH.DEALER IN DUST. RIO TINTO ZINC.

FROM THE ALBUM

"WHERE'S THE PLEASURE"   on XNTRIX RECORDS

WHO ARE R.T.Z.

SHAREHOLDERS INCLUDE HER MAJESTY THE QUEEN AND HER COCKTAIL PARTY, SIR ANTHONY TUKE (CHAIRMAN OF BARCLAY'S BANK), THE DUKE OF WESTMINSTER, AND THE MINISTRY OF FINANCE FOR NORTHERN IRELAND.

WHICH MAY NOT SURPRISE YOU.

BUT ALSO INCLUDE A LARGE NUMBER OF RELIGIOUS ORGANIZATIONS AND REVEREND GENTS, INCLUDING AN ARCHDEACON, THE BISHOP OF NORWICH, THE DAUGHTERS OF THE HOLY GHOST, SOUTHWARK CATHOLIC CHILDRENS SOCIETY ETC. ETC.

AND ALSO

THE ROYAL COLLEGE OF PHYSICIANS THE ROYAL COLLEGE OF PATHOLOGISTS, AND A NUMBER OF HOSPITAL BOARDS

AND ALSO

THE GREATER LONDON COUNCIL (HOW NOW RED KEN?), THE ROYAL AGRICULTURAL COLLEGE, UNIVERSITIES AND COLLEGES OF OXFORD, CAMBRIDGE, KENT, BRISTOL, LONDON, LIVERPOOL, YORK, ETC. ETC.

AND EVEN

A LARGE NUMBER OF COUNTY COUNCILS AND DISTRICTS DECLARED NUCLEAR FREE ZONES.......INCLUDING THE GLC....AND COUNTY COUNCILS OF AVON, CLEVELAND, DURHAM, DYFED, GLAMORGAN, GWENT, GWYNEDD, HUMBERSIDE, W.MIDLANDS, NOTTINGHAM, TYNE AND WEAR.

THIS LIST IS INCOMPLETE. A FULLER LIST OF SHAREHOLDERS IS BEING PREPARED FOR CIRCULATION; WITH NAMES AND ADDRESSES. IF YOU DON'T LIKE WHAT RIO TINTO ZINC ARE UP TO, THIS HIT LIST COULD GIVE YOU SOME IDEA OF WHERE TO HIT BACK. AND HOW ? THAT'S UP TO YOU.......

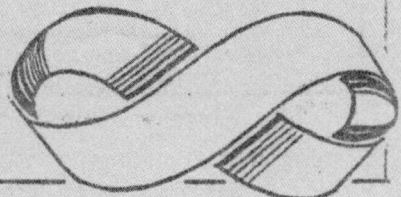

POISONGIRLS

Shareholders list.....RIO TINTO ZINC......................Sheet 3

- Sir Anthony(Favill)TUKE (Chairman, Barclays Bank)
  Address........68,Frognal, Hampstead, London N.W.3.

- ROY WILLIAM WRIGHT Director of many RTZ companies and subsidiaries
  Address   .....COBBERS, FOREST ROW, EAST SUSSEX

- Edward Arthur Alexander SHACKLETON   Deputy Chairman RTZ since 1975
  (Baron Shackleton of Burley) History of M of Defence, RAF, Military Intelligence etc
  Address ..... c/o RTZ Corporation, 6 St.James Square, London S.W.1.

- Royal College of Physicians 14,000 shares
  Address .... 11, St Andres Place, Regents Park, London N.W.1.

- Emmanuel College , Cambridge 39,375 Shares
  Address .... Cambridge CB2 3AP

- University of Oxford Community Chest 2125 shares
  Address........... 16/20 Wellington Square, Oxford

- University of Kent 45,000 shares
  Address .... Canterbury, Kent. CT2 7NT

- Northampton Roman Catholic Diocese 8,000 shares
  Address .... Bishops House, Marriot Street, Northampton

- Rev. D A Rees   724 shares
  Address   ..... Vicarage, Dale, Haverfordwest, Dyfed, Wales

- Secular Clergy Common Fund 9,000 shares
  Address ...... St Mary Cemetary, Harrow Road, London N.W.10

- Representetive Body of the Church of Wales   100 shares
  Address ...... 39, Cathedral Road , Cardiff.

- Rt Rev C O'Toole   832 shares
  Address...... Mount St Josephs Abbey, Rxxxxxx Rosscrea, County Tipperary

- ArchDeacon A.H. Thompson 324 Shares
  Address   .... Rivermead, Maguiresbridge, Co.Fermanagh, N.Ireland

- Rev.Canon F.C. Tindall   1,513 shares
  Address ...... c/o Bircham & Co., 1,Dean Farrar St., Westminster SW1, London

- University of London King's College 3,908 Shares
  Address ...... The Strand, London WC2

- University of London Senate House   6,550 Shares
  Address .... Malet Street, London WC1

- University Court of the University of Glasgow   41,000 Shares
  Address .... The University, Glasgow

- University Life Assurance Soc. Loan shares 100,000; Ordinary 70,000
  Address   ...... 4, Coleman Street, London EC2R 5AR

- Bishop of Norwich   3,500 Shares
  Address .... c/o Bol Prior Esq.,Leathes Prior & Son, 7a The Close, Norwich
- RIO TINTO ZINC(HEAD OFFICE, London)
  Address.... 6, St James Square, London S.W.1.

FEB '80

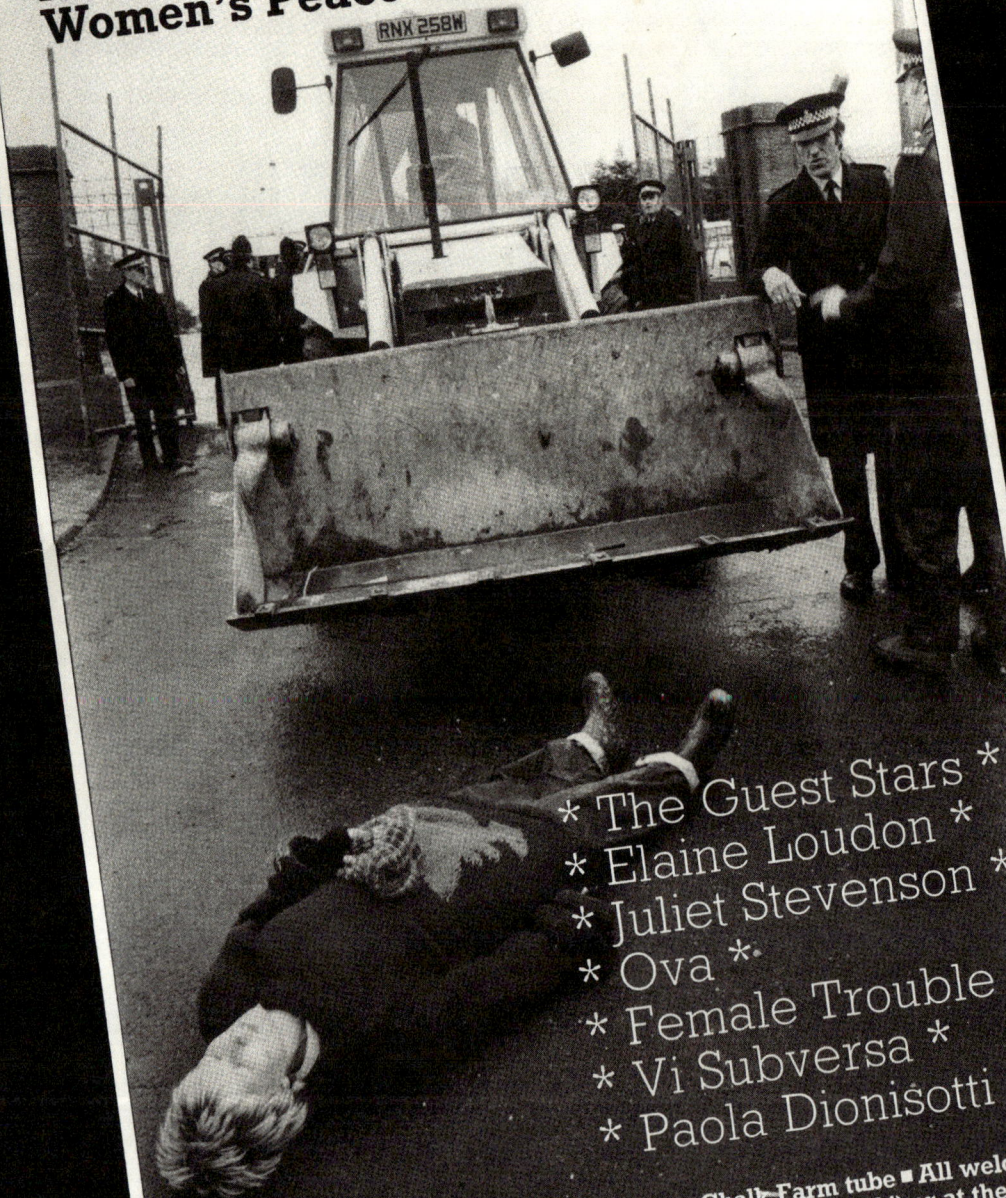

The Round House
Chalk Farm Road, London NW1

Benefit Performance
for Greenham Common
Women's Peace Camp

RNX 258W

* The Guest Stars *
* Elaine Loudon *
* Juliet Stevenson *
* Ova *
* Female Trouble *
* Vi Subversa *
* Paola Dionisotti *

Sunday 19 December ■ 7.30 (doors open 7.00) ■ Chalk Farm tube ■ All welcome
Admission: £3 (£2 unwaged) ■ Tickets from box office (267 2564) or at the door

IF JUST ONE WOMAN WITH ONE PAIR OF ARMS CAN HOLD HERSELF AND KNOW
THAT HER BODY'S HER OWN AND HER MIND IS HER OWN AND THAT SHE IS FREE TO GROW
AND IF TWOXRXX JUST TWO WOMEN WITH TWO PAIRS OF ARMS CAN HOLD EACH OTHER AND SHOW
THAT LOVE'S NOT JUST FOR THE BOYS, WE'VE ALL GOT A CHOICE, AS MOST OF YOU WILL KNOW
WELL THERE'S BOYS HERE TONIGHT, AND THAT'S ALL RIGHT, PLEASE DON'T GET ME WRONG
I QUITE LIKE SOME BOYS, I JUST DON'T LIKE THEIR TOYS,....BUT THAT'S ANOTHER SONG

WELL, THREE OR FOUR WOMEN CAN REACH OUT THEIR ARMS AND SING AND DANCE AND PLAY
THERE'S WOMEN IN BANDS ALL OVER THE LAND GETTING NOISIER EVERY DAY
SO...IF JUST ONE WOMAN WITH ONE PAIR OF ARMS CAN HOLD HERSELF AND KNOW
THAT HER BODY'S HER OWN AND HER MIND IS HER OWN AND THAT SHE IS FREE TO GO
IF WE ALL JOINED HANDS ACROSS THE LANDS FROM DONEGAL TO PERTH(IN AUSTRALIA)
HOW MANY WOMEN WOULD WE NEED TO STRETCH RIGHT ROUND THE EARTH ? OR EQUATOR ---

NOW I'VE DONE SOME SUMS AND I'VE MEASURED MY ARMS AND THEY COME TO JUST XXX FIVE FEET
AND ME AND MY BAND IF WE STOOD HAND TO HAND WOULD REACH ACROSS A STREET
WELL I NEVER WAS MUCH OF A ONE FOR SUMS BUT I'M SUDDENLY EXCITED
WONDERING WHERE IT ALL COULD END IF MORE OF MXXXXX US UNITED
ONE THOUSAND AND FIFTY SIX OF US, COULD REACH OUT TO XXXX A MILE , OR MORE
SO TO REACH AROUND ,NINE MILES WOULD TOOK, NINE THOUSAND, FIVE HUNDRED AND FOUR
NINE MILES WAS THE DISTANCE AROUND THEXXXXX MISSILE BASE AT GREENHAM COMMON
WE CCXXXXXXXXRRXXTXMXX THREW THREE RINGS AROUND THAT BASE WITH, THIRTY THOUSAND WOMEN
                                                              OUR

I'M LOSING SLEEP I'M COUNTING SHEEP WITH MY POCKET CALCULATOR
BUT JUST HOW MANY WOEN HOLDING HANDS COULD CIRCLE THE EQUATOR
SIXTYFOUR THOUSAND MILES ROUND THE GLOBE WE COULD GO WITHXXX 67 MILLION 500 AND 84 000 WOMEN
THAT'S ONLY TWO THOUSAND AND FIFTY TIMES THE NUMBER AT GREENHAM COMMON

I DON'T WANT TO TAUNT YOU AND I DON'T WANT TO DAUNT YOU WITH SUCH CONFUSING COMPUTATION
BUT I COULD GO ON TO CONSIDER THE TOTAL WORLD POPULATION
FOUR THOUSAND TWO HUNDRED AND FORTY SIX MILLION 216 THOUSAND
AT THE LATEST COUNT,(BUT THEY WON'T KEEP STILL) OF EACH AND EVERY NATION
JUST DIVIDE BY TWO TO GET THE NUMBER OF US THAT ARE THE WOMEN
½ THATS A HELL OF A LOT TIMES MORE THAN THE NUMBER THAT WENT TO GREENHAM COMMON

BUT STATISTICS ARE NOT TO BE TRUSTED COS EVERYONE KNOWS THEY ARE EASILY FIXED
I'VE MADE A FEW JOKES BUT I KNOW THERE'S NO HOPE IN FLASH MATHEMATICAL TRICKS
THE VALUE OF NUMBERS TO ME IS THAT THEY SHOW ME I'M NOT ALONE
COS IT'S HARD TO KEEP FIGHTING FOR PEACE WHEN YOU'RE BACK IN YUR SEPARATE HOME
BUT REMEBER FROM NOW THE DAY THAT WE ALL BECAME THIRTY THOUSAND STRONG
WE LEFT OUR MEN AND WE LEFT OUR HOMES TO STAND AGAINST WHAT IS WRONG
AND IT ALL WENT FINE AND WE HAD A GOOD TIME AND WE KNOW WE CAN DO IT AGAIN
COS WE KNOW THAT THE SHOPPING AND MINDING THE KIDS CAN BE PREFECTLY WELL DONE BY MEN
AND IF ALL THE MEN TAKE TO MINDING THE KIDS AND COOKING AND WASHING THE FLOOR
THERE WOULDN'T BE ANY OF THEM LEFT TO DROP BOMBS AND KEEP ON WITH THEIR WAR WAR WAR WAR

AND WE LEFT OUR PLACES OF WORK TO WORK FOR PEACE AT GREENHAM COMMON
THE CHOICE IS OURS...THE WORKING HOURS OF EVERY MAN XXXXXXXX AND WOMAN
TO LEAVE THE JOBS AND COMPANIES THAT MAKE US WORK FOR WAR
WE MUST MAKE THE CHOICE...NO MORE COMPROMISE...ON WHAT WE ARE WORKING FOR

WE CIRCLED THE BASE BECAUSE ITS A PLACE THAT BREEDS HXXXHXXXX VIOLENCE DEATH AND PAIN
TO SAY NO TO THE PLAN THAT SETS MAN AGAINST MAN AND BRINGS US ALL DOWN IN THE END
BUT THE BASES AT GREENHAM LAKENHEATH ETCETERA DON'T JUST SPRING OUT OF THE GROUND
THEY'RE PAID FOR BY PROFIT AND TAXES AND TIME THAT WAS STOLEN FROM OUT OF OUR HANDS

AND THE MULTINATIONAL COMPANIES LIKE RIO TINTO ZINC
AND EVERY SCHOOL AND EVERY PRISON, EVRY SUPERMARKET AND BANK
ARE PART OF THE GAME THAT'S SO INSANE THAT IS KILLING OUR WORLD, OUR EARTH
WE MUST CIRCLE THE LOT, COS THAT'S ALL THAT WE'VE GOT...AND TAKE IT ALL BACK FOR LIFE
                                                               AND REBIRT

Opposite: A 1982 benefit for Greenham Common, an all-women anti–nuclear weapons encampment surrounding an American Air Force base that began in 1981. Poison Girls played shows benefitting several encampments in the UK, Vi performed at this benefit show in London. Poster courtesy of Rich Cross. This page: Vi's speech notes from her Round House performance. Courtesy of Pete Fender and Gemma Sansom.

7.30pm North London Poly Holloway Rd N7

GREENHAM
WIRECUTTERS BENEFIT

1st Dec '83

POISON GIRLS

JOOLZ

SHARON LANDAU

HI JINKS

FALLOUT MARCHING BAND

£2.50
£2.00 unwaged

DEC 11TH 83
WOMEN COME
AND RECLAIM
GREENHAM COMMON

WE WANT TO TURN THE BASE INSIDE OUT AND REGAIN OUR COMMON LAND. BRING MIRRORS, TREES TO PLANT, AND ANY TOOLS YOU MAY NEED.

WOMEN ALL OVER THE WORLD ARE SAYING THE SAME THINGS. WE WANT AN END TO THE ARMS RACE. WE WANT TO STOP URANIUM BEING MINED, TRANSPORTED AND TAMPORED WITH, BRINGING INCREASED LEVELS OF RADIATION AND CANCER. TOO MANY PEOPLE HAVE CANCER AND TOO MANY PEOPLE ARE SUFFERING POVERTY AND STARVATION WHILE BILLIONS A DAY ARE SPENT ON WEAPONS.

CRUISE MISSILES ARE A SYMBOL OF THIS MADNESS

WE WANT TO GET BEYOND THE MADNESS. WOMEN COME TOGETHER. SHARE VISIONS, FEARS, STRATEGIES, IMAGINATION AND ACTION, FOR NOW AND THE FUTURE.

ONE WORLD.

SAT
dec 3

DOORS OPEN
7.30 PM

POISON GIRLS
RUBELLA BALLET · OMEGA TRIBE
· **DORMANNU** ·

£2.50 or
£2.00 ADV.

the **ACE**
TOWN HALL PARADE
BRIXTON
LONDON S.W.2.
737
2886

7 PM – EARLY START!

Sunday 24th October

POISON GIRLS

at the Drill Hall,
Chenies St. W1
WITH

rubella ballet

JOOLZ +

sane but not heard

£2 (£1.50)

POISON GIRLS
· **rubella ballet** ·

BOWES LYON HOUSE
NOVEMBER 1982

Poëzienacht Amsterdam 2

Za. 28 Mei · Paradiso

Zaal Open 21·30u. · Toegang F.10.–+

Presentatie; Jules Deelder

Atilla The Stockbroker · René Stoute
Dave Reeves · Belinda Blanchard
Steef Davidson · Little Brother
Nick Toczek · Herman Brusselmans
Seething Wells · Wim Kaufman
Koos Dalstra · Harry Hoogstraten
Barbara Baumgarten · Jan Kal
Sterrenslag van 15 jonge Ned. Dichters

Muziek; Blue Murder

Zaalontwerp; Peter Gielen

Extra Nachtconcert 02·00u.

Poison Girls

VOORVERKOOP: Nieuwe Muziekhandel, Boudisque, A.U.B.(Cisca) & R.A.K Platen

MEND MEMBERS OF EQUITY FOR NUCLEAR DISARMAMENT

PRESENT

THE DARTS   ROY HARPER
POISON GIRLS   DAVE RAPPAPORT
NATIONAL THEATRE OF BRENT
JIM BARCLAY   ADRIAN MITCHELL
ANDY DE LA TOUR & MORE

PHOENIX THEATRE CHARING CROSS RD

TICKETS £6 £8 £10

SUNDAY 7th AUGUST 7.30pm

BOOKING INFORMATION RING   836 8611   836 2294

NO NUKES MUSIC
'93 PRESENTS
POISON GIRLS
+ RUBELLA BALLET
AT THE BUNKER
SAT. DEC. 4TH
7·30pm   £1·25

Pages 184–85: **North London Poly**, 1 December 1983. A benefit for Greenham Wirecutters, courtesy of Tom Barwood. **1983 Greenham gathering,** courtesy of Rich Cross.
Opposite page: **The Ace**, London, 3 December 1983. **Poison Girls and Rubella Ballet tour poster**, 1982. **Drill Hall,** London, 24 October 1982.
This page, clockwise from top left: **Paradiso**, Amsterdam, 28 May 1983. **Phoenix Theatre**, London, Members of Equity for Nuclear Disarmament benefit, 7 August 1983. **Stonehenge Free Festival**, June 1982. **The Bunker**, Sunderland, 4 December 1982. A benefit for the Campaign for Nuclear Disarmament.

THE ROLLING STONES
MOTORHEAD & ALEXIS KORNER
THE CLASH
THE JAM
JAH. SHAKA   MADNESS ?
RUTS ?
CRASS.   HAWKWIND   HERE & NOW
U2   INNER CITY UNIT   MISTY IN ROOTS
D.J.s POISON GIRLS
B.B.C. REBEL RADIO
JOHN PEEL
JERRY FLOYD   PLUS MANY MORE
STONEHENGE 82
FREE FESTIVAL
16TH TO 29TH JUNE
WILTSHIRE   A303   C.N.D.

Real Woman photoshoot, photo by Chris Lurca, 1984.

6. ARE YOU HAPPY NOW? DID YOU GET WHAT YOU WANTED?

SINGLES 1983-84

In a concerted effort to conduct a successful, and slyly subversive, ram-raid into the cultural mainstream, Poison Girls broker a deal with Illuminated Records. The band release two new singles consciously designed to attract radio play, in the hope of establishing a bridgehead inside (but not reconciled to) the music industry. The muted response to both seven-inches confirms how difficult the attempted incursion will be. The change in direction coincides with some personnel changes, and a conscious recalibration in approach to the practice of live performance. Once again, Poison Girls' reenergised sense of mischievousness is not without risk, while the band's political assertiveness leads to a breach with the one group it had previously cooperated with the most. Taking stock, the band release a retrospective double album as they begin to orient towards a different and more fulfilling future.

Poison Girls now sought to reach a much larger audience—far beyond the frontiers of the cultural underground. The band were considering an audacious plan which would confirm just how far the band were prepared to travel from their original outsider DIY punk roots—or at least give the appearance of having done so. They hoped to put together a raid into the cultural mainstream in which subversive messages could be repackaged to pierce the boundaries of the punk periphery and get injected into previously unreached areas of pop culture. The decision was premised on belief that the band's continued and exclusive reliance on outsider and fringe cultures was preventing their ideas from reaching the people that now needed to hear them.

After the separation with Crass, the band were repeatedly asked if they would ever consider signing to a major label. "I don't see how we can, but nobody's ever asked us," the band told *Subvert* fanzine. "I think the problem with them is that they give you certain facilities and a certain amount of money but for that you've got to give them something and quite often the price you have to pay is too high. It wrecks most bands as they're not allowed to be themselves anymore." Now determined to mount that concerted foray into the commercial world—taking subversive messages inside pop culture, without diluting the radical intent—Poison Girls began to overhaul their own "business" operations. The band decided they would record new material with an accessible pop sensibility sufficient to make an impact on the UK and international singles charts.

"The era of breaking rules, wild experiments, releasing pent up energy and frustration, 'just getting up there and doing it' and a desire to put relevance and meaning back into the music, which the dream rags called 'punk,' is not over," the band explained later. "It is now for us to take ideas that can release imagination beyond the confines of the increasingly comfortable crowd which has raised and inspired us, into the wider world."

Famous stresses the importance of putting the band's aspirations in context. "We were effectively broke," he stresses. "That was why we were trying to find some outside financial support." He suggests a revealing comparison with the position that Crass and Crass Records were in. "We never had a business manager, akin to the role John Loder played in facilitating the Crass organisation, and a history of Crass which doesn't address the huge role he played—his 24-track recording studio, his access to national distribution, his support for their label, and the money it generated to support their band—is flawed." Poison Girls had to navigate their own path, with few similar resources.

In February 1983, Subversa wrote to a contact the band had made at EMI Publishing, enclosing a copy of *Where's the Pleasure* and asking if they'd be willing to "explore a 'deal' on the publishing rights to royalties on our material." Had such an agreement been brokered, Xntrix would have agreed to EMI Publishing making use of songs from the Poison Girls catalogue in return for royalty payments to the cash-strapped band. It would have been a controversial next step, but the fact that Poison Girls were willing to make the pitch was an indication of their determination to break into new cultural territory—*and* settle some of their potentially crippling debts. Yet nothing came of the approach.

A few weeks after sending the letter, Poison Girls approached Martin Goldschmidt—later to become the founder of the independent Cooking Vinyl label—to become the band's manager. "We never really *hired* Martin," Famous says. "But we did agree to work with him. We didn't have anybody who was very good at hustling the business, and looking after the detail of our gigs," says Famous. "So when Martin came along and said, 'Well, you know, I can do this for you,' it seemed like a good idea. And he did it very well." In retrospect, the band acknowledged that the role was "a thankless task." But then Martin was not exactly an industry standard issue when it came to band management, which made him a better fit for the band.

"I met Vi and Poison Girls whilst I was organising antinuclear benefit concerts for No Nukes Music," Goldschmidt recalls. "Poison Girls did some concerts for us and we bonded, and they offered me my first proper job." The band explained to *Peace News* that hiring Goldschmidt was a pragmatic response to rising work pressures. "We're working with an agent because to set up a tour takes something like three weeks' solid work which we just haven't got the time—or the aptitude—to do." His recruitment would also allow them to focus on their musical recalibration. "That doesn't mean that we're rejecting our past by any means, but that we're making music that the people who come, and think they know what we should be doing, don't expect."

"I was a political activist," Goldschmidt reflected later of his outlook at the time. "I never really considered pursuing a career—I never thought in those terms, my agenda was revolution." His work supporting bands began in 1982, when he agreed to act as an unofficial (and unpaid) manager for the political duo Akimbo—an outfit described in a Goldschmidt press release as offering a "heady mix of poetic politics and sensuous spine-stroking soul"—who would later tour with Poison Girls. "No one would put their music out," Goldschmidt remembers, "so I put it out myself." His first 'commercial' release, the band's self-titled debut album was issued on his new Forward Sounds International label in 1982, and secured nationwide distribution courtesy of Rough Trade. At the same time, Goldschmidt was organising benefit shows and supporting a variety of campaigns protesting actions of the Thatcher government. It was the combination of

"Are You Happy Now" lyric sheet for Big Brother Cabaret tour, October 1983.

his experience in working with political artists and his activist credentials that appealed to Poison Girls.

"There were three things," says Goldschmidt, when asked to summarise the reasons for his recruitment to the Poison Girls fold. "They were a DIY-driven band becoming fed up with having to do-it-all-themselves; they thought that my energy and relationships could make a difference; and we were good friends." His harder-edged commercial nous and his interest in reaching out beyond the boundaries of the DIY scene were seen to be in sync with Poison Girls' fast-evolving ambitions. As for a job description? "There wasn't one," he says. "We all made it up as we went along."

When Goldschmidt accepted the position of manager, he was surprised by one request: that he alter his appearance. "I looked every bit like a political activist," he concedes. "They bought me my first suit because they thought I needed to look more like a manager—this from an anarchist punk band!"

"That suit!" Famous recalls with a smile. "We went to Laurence Corner, the legendary theatrical and army surplus store just off the top of the Tottenham Court Rd. The suit was the most garish huge green check one they had in stock, and Martin—who was sartorially challenged—fell upon it with delight," he says. "To be honest, we never thought he would wear it in public—it was more of an affectionate joke than anything. But he did!"

Beginning in 1983, Goldschmidt would work as "all duties" manager for the band for the next couple of years. He accompanied the group out on the road to act as both tour and stage manager. This meant that he found he "did most things" the band needed, including "lying on the stage to hold a dodgy borrowed drum kit together in Washington, DC, at the President's Counter-Inaugural Ball in 1985," he remembers with a smile.

It was a thrilling time for Goldschmidt, "travelling round the world as part of a looney gang trying to change that world," he says. It was also a means to acquire invaluable experience. "Martin wanted to get more involved in the music business—and we were his next step into that, I think," says Famous.

Gig organisers who'd worked with the band before Goldschmidt's recruitment noticed the difference. Alan

Poison Girls' new keyboard player Sian Daniels (aka Cynth Ethics) at the piano, 1985. Courtesy of Pete Fender and Gemma Sansom.

Schofield, who organised gigs in Nottingham with both Crass and Poison Girls under the Taking Liberties banner, was used to dealing with bands directly. Putting together a first Poison Girls gig in the city, the conversation had been "very much along the lines 'can we sleep at your house; can you make us a lentil stew?'" he recalls with a grin. On their return to the city, Goldschmidt had become an unexpected conduit and filter between the promoter and the band. "Working with a manager was obviously something new that they were testing out," says Schofield. This shift changed relationships backstage. "Now it was a case of 'Here's Martin, he's the manager. Do you need to talk to Martin?'"

As he worked alongside them, was it ever challenging to try to manage a group of argumentative, opinionated anarchists? "No," says Goldschmidt. "I was one too—and their expectations were very reasonable . . . most of the time." There was one personal dynamic that he admits was a little more daunting. "It was difficult managing a strong forty-six-year-old woman at the age of twenty-six," he concedes. "The manager is supposed to be the 'adult' in the relationship, and with Poison Girls this clearly wasn't the case."

Even allowing for that, the partnership seemed to work well for everyone involved, as the independent profile of Poison Girls grew. Determined to find ways to release vinyl that might reach audiences beyond the core anarchist scene, Poison Girls were looking to attract the attention of an independent record label—one of a size and scale that could offer the kind of leverage that Xntrix Records, working on its own with a shoestring budget, demonstrably lacked. There were other Poison Girls' personnel changes, inspired by the new approach the band were now adopting.

During the time that Poison Girls toured with Crass, both bands relied upon the sound equipment and engineering services provided by Paul Tandy's impressively compact PA operations. Tandy became a stalwart of British anarcho-punk on tour. Never phased by the cramped, acoustically challenging venues that the bands rolled up at, nor by the sketchy, volatile evenings that sometimes played out in those church halls, community centres or squatted spaces (nor indeed by the sparse to nonexistent budgets), Tandy was the definition of unflappable dependability. "Paul and his colleague Ian were a constant presence at the early gigs," says Famous. "Tandy came from Manchester and thought nothing about travelling the length of the country—for what was basically very little money—to do a one-off gig. They'd also agree take on national and European tours. This was, of course, the time before even music venues had decent sound systems, never mind the hotch-potch of halls we played in." That meant that, for Tandy, "humping round a van load of heavy gear was a necessity."

"His knackered van was legendary," Famous continues. "On one tour round Europe the windscreen wipers were operated by pulling on a piece of string, while two people were needed to change gear—one to pull the clutch cable, the other to move the gearstick!"

At a Poison Girls show at the Rob Fabric in Zurich, Tandy was providing PA services as usual, when the venue and its surroundings became "the scene of a serious riot," Famous recalls. "The tyres of Tandy's van were all slashed. As I recall, he was quietly pleased about the damage. All of them had reached a seriously illegal state of worn tread, and they were replaced, free of charge, by the venue."

Tandy was more than capable of conjuring an impressive live sound mix from his own rig, and had talents in the studio too. "Tandy produced a finished mix of the *Total Exposure* live recordings at Cargo Studios in Rochdale," he adds. "But for some reason it was not used, and the album ended up being mixed at Southern Studios."

Tandy was also generous enough to let others with the know-how make use of his equipment. In the summer of 1982, Pete Fender recorded live sets by Conflict and Omega Tribe at Centro Iberico in London using "outputs from Paul Tandy's mixing desk and a Calrec room mic."

"We did consider him a good friend and a reliable presence in those often difficult and boisterous times," Famous says.

Poison Girls were far from unusual in wanting to have someone on their team attuned to producing as close to their preferred live sound as the local PA system and building allowed. Fender had taken on the role on many occasions, but preferred to focus on developing his skills as a studio engineer and producer. Being able to generate the "right" live sound became all the more important to Poison Girls over time, particularly when touring regularly meant relying on the local 'house PA' or whatever collection of kit local organiser could assemble. Tom Barwood was recruited to take charge of Poison Girls' live sound and join the band on tour.

"I first saw them at a CND rally in Trafalgar Square in London in 1981," he recalls. "They weren't allowed any amplified music at the demo, so they sang 'Take the Toys from the Boys' a cappella. I thought it was great."

"I was also aware of them through Martin Goldschmidt, who was a school friend of mine from way back," he continues. "I met Martin again a couple of years later at a gig. He knew that I was involved with sound, mentioned

that he was managing a band that needed an engineer, and asked if I was interested. And, of course, I was!"

"I was doing live electronics and experimental music, modern classical music, and quite a bit of world music—but not mainstream rock'n'roll," he says. Barwood had helped his mates' bands, by live mixing on a small rig at a few pub gigs—but that was the extent of his experience. "I think that's one of the things that may have warmed Poison Girls to me—the fact that I wasn't coming from that mainstream," he suggests.

"I understood that what they wanted was an *ally* on the other side of the mixing desk, really. Maybe somebody who wasn't part of the rock music scene, but somebody who had a different perspective on it."

"I suppose also not having much music business experience, I maybe didn't quite realise how exceptional they in fact were. I went to meet them and got to know them a bit. In their house in Leytonstone, I sat in on a couple of rehearsals in their basement and absolutely loved it," he says. "It was very exciting. I've never really been in a rehearsal with a band that were that good, that together."

"I quickly became aware that they were something special, for sure. I immediately got on well with them. I was kind of accepted into the fold quickly, which was great for me. I absolutely loved it. You know, I felt like I'd found a bit of a family? I got on very well with Richard and became a very close friend of his and of Vi."

"I learned as I went along. I was given very short notice that they needed somebody to go to Holland with them to do a couple of gigs over a long weekend. And so off we went."

Part of the process of redefining and realigning the band was the recruitment of synth player and backing vocalist Sian Daniels (aka Cynth Ethics) in May 1983. "Sian was another friend of Martin's," Famous says. "She was a very good singer. She'd sung with Kokomo, the British soul band, and had auditioned for Van Morrison." Her vocal talents were the reason to bring her into the band. "Vi wanted to work with a backing singer, a proper backing singer, and explore vocals more. She could also play piano, but she'd never played synth before. So she said, 'Well, I'll play synth.' So that's how that worked. She sort of fell into it. We didn't really say we wanted a keyboard player."

The band were quick to take advantage of the new musicianship in the lineup. "As always, with any band, I think it's the people. You get the right people, and then you find out what they can do. And then you do something with it. That's how we would try to work as a band. And she seemed to fit in, and it did help us change the way that the music was arranged."

Ethics wrote and arranged original keyboard melodies for new Poison Girls songs and provided female backing vocals for songs across the band's live repertoire.

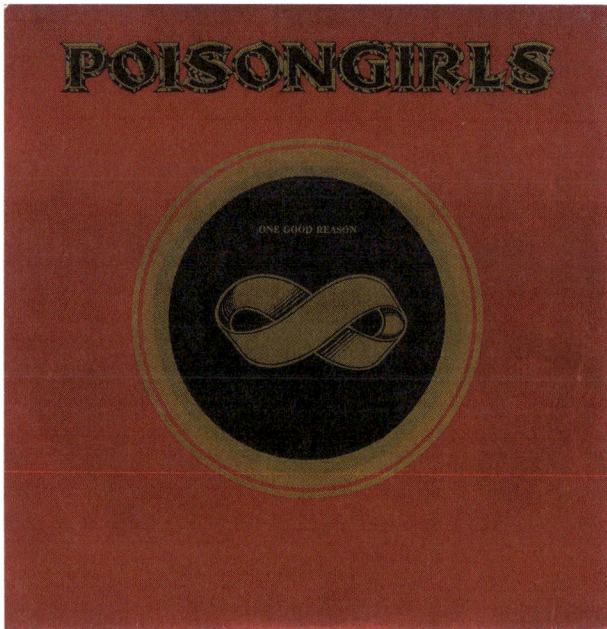

One Good Reason, Illuminated Records, 1983.

"We'd always used the synth in recording," Subversa explained to *Spitting Pretty Pikktures*, "and if we were doing it in recording then it should be part of what we're doing live." With Daniels on board, the band were better equipped to "expand the actual style of music that we were doing," Famous added. "I don't think we'll ever get away from being a 'guitar-based band,' but actually being able to add another instrument and another vocalist just expands the possibilities of sound that we can use."

As she was recruited, Daniels was made aware of the new balancing act that Poison Girls were attempting—weighing continued creative autonomy against increased cultural influence. "I find one of the most exciting things is actually working out how to reconcile how you're going to be real, and progress with your own life, musically and any other way," she explained to *ZigZag* magazine, "but also going to participate in something that is necessarily very manufactured."

Daniels's presence, and her ability to fill out the sound textures and add in punchy chords and catchy flourishes on keys, did allow the band to pull the guitars back slightly in the live mix. Her input comes to the fore on songs like "Too Proud" from *Where's the Pleasure*, the *Are You Happy Now?* single, and the unrecorded "Waiting for the Heat." Famous was keen to stress that the new Cynth Ethics melodies were not part of an attempt to blunt the band's musical edge. "I don't think we've lost the ferocity of our performance," he insisted.

With the band's horizons expanding, a major issue threatened to thwart Poison Girls' ambitious plans: a lack of funds. "Xntrix Records has run out of money and owes money on the projects it has done, chiefly *Where's the*

Pleasure," d'Boyle explained to *Spitting Pretty Pikktures*. This meant the band "had to find some other source of income to carry on doing the kinds of things we were doing—making albums and singles."

Subversa reassured fans anxious that the band might "succumb to any major record companies" that the band remained hostile to the industry mainstream, before immediately making clear that no such approach had ever been made.

Famous recalls that the band's financial position looked grim. "We simply had no money," he says. "We'd been working for seven years by that time and been doing it by 'signing on' and just trying to make ends meet. We were playing for 'petrol and chips' and only occasionally getting a decent fee. Martin was saying, 'Well, let's see if we can get a deal somewhere.'"

Given that the need for "a lot of capital," as d'Boyle put it, was pressing, and major labels were not in play, what was the solution? The band "decided to look around and ask if there was anybody who wants to give us the money," d'Boyle explained. "Illuminated said they would."

On 19 April 1983, Poison Girls signed a recording contract with Illuminated Records, a small label specialising in punk, postpunk, gothic, and industrial artists which had been formed by promoter Keith Bagley in 1980. "The deal with Illuminated, on paper—a big caveat that, 'on paper'—was worth over a quarter of a million quid," Famous reveals. "Of course, we never saw anything like that. It was, in reality, 'fantasy money,' and all of it 'recoverable from earnings.'" As a result, the band got next to nothing—financially speaking—from the experience.

Bagley was an unconventional impresario, with a fondness (it was said by one observer) for holding business meetings "in dusty old daytime drinking clubs" along London's Fulham Road. Alex Turnball, of Illuminated signees 23 Skidoo, praises Bagley's willingness to "take a chance" with unproven artists, but acknowledges that the label had all the hallmarks of a "one man operation" and "was super lo-fi." Illuminated always struggled to raise funds, even as it took on distribution work for other DIY labels and, but was still able to build up an impressive catalogue of more than 150 releases, before the label wound up operations in 1987.

"We knew we could bring out records for our core audience base," Famous continues. "And, according to Rough Trade, we were a 'B-level' sort of band, which meant we could shift something like thirteen to fifteen thousand records. That was sort of the ceiling. The next level jumped your band to selling twenty-five thousand records." That meant the band were striving "to make this next jump, to get to another audience which had not heard of you before—or had heard *of you* but not heard you."

Poison Girls joined forces with Illuminated with the express aim of breaking into the lower reaches of the charts with a series of singles that were consciously crafted to be radio-friendly. In choosing an independent label of that calibre and standing the band were—as with the decision to recruit a manager—seeming to adapt to the norms of the orthodox world of "pop" without moving that far from their DIY outsider roots. Illuminated was a company run on a shoestring budget, and while many similar "indie" labels thrived as platforms for outsider artists suspicious of industry insiders, it was not immediately obvious that Illuminated would be a credible platform for Poison Girls' hoped-for foray into the commercial mainstream.

Despite this, Poison Girls received criticism from some hardline voices in the punk scene who saw the move as an accommodation too far. "People say, 'You've signed to Illuminated—you've sold out.' And they don't even buy our fuckin' records," a clearly irritated d'Boyle complained to *Spitting Pretty Pikktures*. "What are we supposed to do?"

Looking back over a span of more than forty years, Steve Ignorant of Crass is sympathetic. "If I hadn't been in Crass, and I'd been in a band where a record label offered me a load of money to record a bunch of albums, I'd have bitten their fucking arm off," he says.

Ignoring the critics, Poison Girls set about recording their next seven-inch and the first for the new label. *One Good Reason* was an upbeat single, lighter in tenor than anything the band had released before, and with little of the edgy, unsettling ambience of *Where's the Pleasure*.

Famous acknowledged that the band's first single in three years was "superficially a pop song." The band's set out with the clear ambition to "make this next release widely accessible."

Recorded at the Workhouse Studios in south London in April 1983, and produced by Bernie Clarke, the *One Good Reason* single confirmed the gear-shift in Poison Girls' new cultural drive. Clarke was a pianist and keyboard player, who's skills had seen him brought on board by Aztec Camera, Bram Tchaikovsky, The Covers, and Fingerprintz, and who had begun to establish his industry credentials as a producer. "They were quite keen on using Clark," says sound engineer Tom Barwood, "because they thought he might add a kind of commercial and pop credibility to what they were doing."

Wrapped in a sleeve that retained the band's red-and-black colour palette but added gold highlights and a new 'rock' style rendition of the band's name, the design gave few clues as to the band's dissident, anarchist affinities. Only the statement etched into the vinyl of the A-side run-out ("Give me one good reason for voting in the next election") provided a hidden hint. The title track, an upbeat pop-punk number lit up by an impressively strong hook, was an appeal to listeners to break free from the crushing mental constraints imposed by capitalist "common sense," set to an upbeat staccato pop motif:

> Give me one good reason
> For hiding all your sweet desires
> One good reason
> For damping down your forest fires
> Burn it down the wire
> For all to hear
> Tell me what's your reason
> You know you were born to have it
> One good reason
> It's your life so smash and grab it
> Break the locks
> And find the jungle now

The chorus made clear the band's hope that this style of musical mischief making might make it past the industry gatekeepers and secure some mainstream radio play (something which few anarcho-punk bands achieved):

> What's a song like this
> Doing on the radio?
> A song like this
> Playing on the radio
> What's a song like this
> Doing on the radio?

The B-Side, "Cinnamon Garden," a mournful treatise on the anguish of lost love, was a more subdued and reflective affair, with Subversa taking on the persona of the late-night jazz club *chanteuse*. It was a revealing contrast with the more upbeat 'A' side. Both sides of the single were evidence of the band adopting a softer musical timbre, and a less overtly confrontational style. But this first foray into the pop mainstream was neither a commercial success for Illuminated nor a propellent for Poison Girls' visibility. The single received almost no commercial radio play, and did not trouble even the lower reaches of the mainstream charts.

"Illuminated did put their people to work on it," Famous acknowledges. "But the 'pluggers' came back and said they'd never had a single receive less enthusiasm from the BBC and Radio One than for *One Good Reason*," he says glumly. "They didn't even want to listen to it. I think our reputation went before us."

"I think we realised quite early on that it was not going to work, mind you. We got to a much bigger audience by playing live than we ever did by selling records."

Even so, when judged against the band's ambitions for it, the single had not measured up. Of course, the single had to compete for attention amidst the overcrowded conveyor belt of mainstream culture, and on the material's own merits. But the industry's gatekeepers had ensured that Poison Girls had been held up at the perimeter of that production line. In terms of finances, both the band and Illuminated had taken a hit from the single's underperformance. But there were some reputational costs to consider too.

Many of the band's enthusiastic supporters, recognised and supported what the band were attempting. But not everyone following the band understood the mission, the aims of which Poison Girls had not articulated explicitly. To have done so would have given those cultural gatekeepers advance warning of the plan, reducing still further any chance of success. But for some of those enthusiasts for *Persons Unknown*, *Hex*, and *Chappaquiddick Bridge* already disquieted by the direction of *Where's the Pleasure*, the strains of *One Good Reason* sounded a louder alarm. Was it evidence of the band loosening their DIY moorings and blunting their political edge? Poison Girls could not yet convince the sceptics by pointing to the increased political leverage this foray into the enemy's territory had secured. But, for now at least, they remained committed to trying again, even though the odds were clearly stacked against them.

Poison Girls retained a strong fidelity to its underlying principles even as they moved away from its more stringent, "outsider" DIY practices. No longer preoccupied by a need to maintain such subcultural firewalls, Poison Girls were willing to cast their collaborative net far more widely and to be involved in straight commercial punk events. In September 1983, for example, Poison Girls joined the bill of the fifth and final landmark Futurama festival in Leeds, alongside artists such as Death Cult, Killing Joke, and The Three Johns—even though, as Famous's tour diary attests, the experience was miserable.

Poison Girls also decided to play at venues, and at ticket prices, that the band knew might draw the disdain of the most hardline of anarcho-punks. This was not the softening of principles, the band insisted, but another aspect of a concerted effort to reach new audiences. "We never stopped playing the sorts of places we always had played, and at a cost that everybody could afford," Famous clarifies. "But we also decided that we should play more 'upmarket' or 'music business' venues to reach out to an audience that might not go to our more 'streetwise' gigs." It was most definitely "have your cake and eat it time," he concedes.

With greater control of proceedings, Poison Girls were keen to use that freedom to put together "whole packages" of live performance. "I think we got very fed up doing the normal sort of gigs that you did—a band and a support band," Famous says. "And we thought that that approach wasn't particularly good for the sort of audiences that we wanted to connect with." Inspiration came from the new cabaret and alternative comedy scenes that were beginning to attract attention, in London in particu-

lar. Promoters had started to put together a package offer of three to four acts—combining comedy, music, and spoken-word performances. "There were maybe three venues around London that would take that sort of booking," says Famous. "So you could book yourself a Friday, Saturday, and Sunday-night run."

"Myself and Vi had started work on our duo That Famous Subversa to try to tap into that alternative cabaret world, and we got in on that, maybe towards the end of the initial wave." Through Akimbo and his other industry contacts, Martin Goldschmidt knew "a lot of these acts," Famous continues. "He said, 'Well, maybe we can make this work on tour—take three smaller acts out with us, and present the whole thing as a different sort of evening.'"

The band reached out to alternative artists and performers across different styles and genres. Amongst them, Poison Girls approached singer-songwriters Janice Perry and Tymon Dogg (aka Stephen Murray), and poets, ranters, and comics Joolz, Seething Wells, Jenny La Tote, and Mark Miwurdz. Through Goldschmidt's efforts, the band began offering venues an eclectic, and deliberately diverse, all-evening lineup that they would headline. "I remember them being very good events," Famous says, "and the tours being really positive."

A gig at The Venue in London on 28 February 1983, which included Abacush and Fall Out Marching Band alongside Omega Tribe and Tony Allen, gave a good indication of the new approach.

Abacush were a reggae-, jazz-, and gospel-influenced vocal group, who would later join Misty in Roots in studio recording sessions, and release vinyl on their own titular label. Formed in March 1981, Fallout Marching Band were formed "to play music for peace demonstrations as our contribution to the antinuclear struggle." The group included percussionists, saxophonists, tenor horn, clarinet, trumpet, and piccolo players as well as multiple vocalists, and regularly performed their own feminist, antimilitarist song which also took its inspiration and its title from the slogan "take the toys from the boys." When Poison Girls took to the stage as the closing act of the evening, the ambience of the gig would already have been wholly different and more heterodox than a traditional punk event. As for Poison Girls' own ambitions, the aim was explicit: "We want to take punks out of the leather jacket ghetto by playing passionate songs which are subversive because they are real."

On 16 March 1983, Poison Girls appeared at Middlesex Polytechnic in north London, alongside three comedians, poets, and storytellers: Ben Elton, Andy de la Tour, and Benjamin Zephaniah. Performing as a stand-up comic at the time, Elton secured his TV breakthrough in 1986 as the host of Channel 4's *Saturday Live* (in later series retitled *Friday Night Live*, in its new slot). Elton would go on to write the classic British television sitcoms *The Young Ones* and *Blackadder*, before embarking on a successful career

as a novelist, playwright, and director. Unorthodox comedian Andy de la Tour would go on to enjoy a long and varied career as a playwright and director. As an actor, he went on to appear in numerous TV series and big-screen films including *Notting Hill* and *Rogue One: A Star Wars Story*.

Benjamin Zephaniah was then a young Black British poet from Birmingham, who was passionate about performing his published compositions live. "He loved Handsworth, he called it the Jamaican capital of Europe," Zephaniah's official biography says, "but although his work had become popular within the African-Caribbean and Asian community he thought the town was too small, he was not satisfied preaching about the sufferings of Black people to Black people, so he sought a wider mainstream audience." Zephaniah, who had a clear affinity with the rebellious impulses of punk, was a "self-identified anarchist," a vegan, and a committed animal rights activist, regularly performed alongside Poison Girls during this period.

"He'd done one gig with us and Crass down at the 100 Club, I think," says Famous. "It was the first time he'd done a performance gig in front of a punk crowd. And he was really interested in trying to get through to a different sort of audience to the poetry audience, and the Black audiences he'd been working with. I mean, he was brilliant, of course. He had a really good time on the tour, and went down really well."

Zephaniah would go on to become an internationally acclaimed dub poet, political commentator, musician, and author of books for both children and adults. He was awarded honorary doctorates from sixteen universities but turned down offers of accolades handed out by royal prerogative under the Honours System.

The perspective of hindsight confirms how many Poison Girls collaborations were with innovative performers on the political and cultural fringes who would go on to develop high-profile careers, by brokering different types of engagement with the mainstream. It's equally clear just how different a path through dissident and alternative culture Poison Girls were trying to navigate.

During that spring, Poison Girls started to consider how some of these one-off or short-term alliances could be developed into what were effectively touring cabarets: blending spoken word performers, stand-up comics, musical duos, and acoustic combos with traditional bands, but involving artists far from the epicentre of punk. Manager Goldschmidt claims at least some of the credit for "coming up with creative ideas like the Cabaret of Fools." The intention was to subvert the familiar routines of the "rock gig," draw more directly on the traditions of theatre, and so offer an immersive live event hopefully more intriguing to those outside of the core punk milieu.

One of the unusual features of this new approach was the embrace of satire, humour, and self-mockery in the vocabulary and design iconography of those tours. In the bleak political atmosphere in the UK of the summer of 1983, with the reelection of the Thatcher government in the aftermath of the Falklands-Malvinas slaughter, the mindset of British anarchist culture was both downbeat and angry. Poison Girls were clear that revolutionaries needed to equip themselves with more than rage. Rebels had to be able to prick the inflated absurdities of the war state, mock the delusions of those in power, and celebrate the shared alternative spaces that they controlled (even if only temporarily).

As they reconfigured their lyrical, audio, and visual aesthetic, Subversa was clear that the band's harder edges would not be blunted. "I can't imagine that what we're doing could be contained in a softer or easier package," she suggested. "If what it's about is *pain* . . . how can you do it in a comfortable boppy way? But ever since we started we always included a slow, relatively melodious piece. And we do one or two which are on the verge of pop. But I don't think that I could work without that edge of real fear, the real pain, the real panic which is never very far away from the surface of my body."

To kick-start this way of working, the band built on existing collaborations with Akimbo and Tony Allen and reached out to new artists to generate what were intended to be enticing and surprising lineups for what would become the Cabaret of Fools and Big Brother Cabaret tours in the autumn and winter of 1983.

"The first tour that I did with them was the Cabaret of Fools tour," Tom Barwood recalls. "I really liked that cabaret format. It was a 'package of entertainment' with Poison Girls at the top of the bill. They were trying something out, trying to broaden their audience by having different artists involved. And that was great because it was them making an 'event' out of each of these gigs."

There was a wry, witty quality to the way the Cabaret of Fools was choreographed and put together. Poison Girls denunciation of would-be political demagogues was long-standing ("there are no leaders fit to rule, we're all half-saint half bloody fool"). This tour assembled a collection of self-declared fools. But in this usage, "fool" had another meaning, a reflection of the band's knowledge of theatre, both absurdist and Shakespearean. In this reading, the "fool'" was an entertainer, a court jester, a source of amusement but also of the mockery of those in power.

The core lineup of the Cabaret of Fools tour, which got underway in July 1983, was Poison Girls, Benjamin Zephaniah, Tony Allen, and Akimbo. But that lineup was flexible out on the road, depending on location and artist availability. In a further departure from previous anarcho-punk practice, the band arranged promotional photo shoots, in which Poison Girls appeared in themed costumes. These shots were sent out in "press packs" to the mainstream music weeklies, hoping to entice picture editors to include publicity photos of the group in their next edition.

The tour did attract attention from papers including *Sounds* and *NME* and, even when the coverage was not necessarily supportive, there was recognition that Poison Girls were trying something different and distinctive. Attending the Bradford gig, one reviewer noted that Poison Girls appeared "alongside what, at face value, suggests uneasy company." The result was a "moving target of styles" that together "ignite the bill and force the unwieldy concept of 'political cabaret' to work." The whole concept was "elevating stuff . . . for punk audiences," and "the largely favourable reaction" that the artists received was "all the more gratifying" to see.

Not all reviews were as positive, but audiences turned out and the band felt sufficient vindication to plan a follow-on tour that would head out a few months later.

In the closing months of 1983, it was felt inevitable that the imagery and the themes of George Orwell's then-future dystopian classic *1984* would loom large in the aesthetic of anarchist and libertarian activism. Since 1978, the landmark year had been given a particular salience in anarcho-punk culture because of Crass's focus on the countdown to 1984—the year in which the band insisted that they would cease operations. The image of Big Brother—the all-seeing, paternal tyrant leading a system of total control and domination—became totemic and pervasive for a time. Big Brother was always presented as an all-powerful despot, the apotheosis of centralised omniscient power—and an object of fear.

In adopting the moniker of Big Brother for their next tour, Poison Girls were focused on undermining that paralysing perception, treating the tyrant as a figure to be laughed at, scorned, and treated with disdain. As with the Cabaret of Fools shows, this next tour would be organised through independent contacts interested in helping to "create a strong network of creative and uncompromising people who are interested in passion not pap," Poison Girls proclaimed.

The promotional photos for the tour pictured the band, relaxed and at leisure, holding head-sized boxes covered with Big Brother's face. Members of the band could either hold Big Brother in their hands, discard or rip him apart, or place a box over their head to take on his persona. It was a design idea that reflected once again, Poison Girls' interest in offering an absurd and comedic perspective on their politics. The lineup for the Big Brother tour, which began in October 1983, was Poison Girls, Janice Perry, Mark Miwurdz, and Toxic Shock.

Sound engineer Barwood recalls that on this tour even more attention was paid to the stagecraft and visual presentation. "The band adopted stage costumes," he remembers, "and there was a strong artistic continuity between the overall stage design and the costumes that

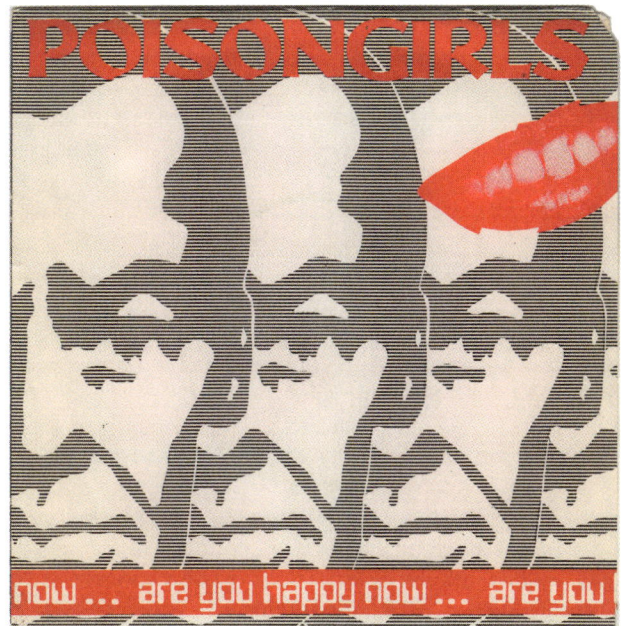

Are You Happy Now?, Illuminated Records, 1983.

they were wearing as they played. I also had a costume, even though I was out there in the audience. I had one as a member of the band, but a member who was out there on the other side of the stage lights."

"We had always embraced a common visual identity as a band," says Famous. "From hand-printed shirts, through the red-and-black period to the later more coordinated costumes. Once you put yourself on stage it is all theatre, after all—and if people think the punk movement was any different, then I beg to differ."

Janice Perry (aka GAL) is an American comedian, musician, and stage artist, nimbly described by *The Independent* newspaper as "a cross between Doris Day and a high-velocity rifle," had begun to tour internationally in 1981. Then in the opening phase of what later developed into a decades long career, solo performer Perry was heralded by US feminist newspaper *Off Our Backs* as "a wild and crazy gal," who was "gusty, intense . . . frenetic, sexual and funny." On the Big Brother tour, Perry would tell stories, blend anecdotes about her personal life with jokes (often at her own expense), and sing a cappella, often using her own body to provide onstage percussion. On the tour, she developed a popular backstage gag, often deployed during pregig mealtimes—a reworking of a song from Poison Girls' *Where's the Pleasure* she retitled "Fear of Vegans."

Mark Miwurdz (aka Mark Hurst) was one of the new wave of "ranting poets" to emerge as part of the proliferation of postpunk performance in Britain. "He was a stand-up comedian who had previously worked the Working Men's Clubs' circuit around Sheffield," Famous adds. Alongside other poets such as Seething Wells and Attila the Stockbroker, these new poets identified as working-class autodidacts with an often intense style of stage presence that combined humour, political vitriol, and leftist social commentary. Miwurdz first took to the stage in the late 1970s. "There was a thriving local band scene, a lot of postpunk electronic stuff and I supported bands like Cabaret Voltaire, and The Comsat Angels," he recalls. Only later did Hurst connect with other active "ranters" as he began to tour more widely, as the opportunities for poets to share a stage with musical acts multiplied. He suggests that the lifespan of the original form of "ranting poetry" was brief, but that "its ripples were felt far and wide for some time after." Through his contacts with Seething Wells, Hurst was put in touch with Tony Allen, and from there was offered live slots on the Alternative Cabaret Tour and at London's Comedy Store. Channel 4 then hired Hurst as a regular on its new youth music show *The Tube*, now recognised as an essential breakthrough platform for many artists, and an exemplar of the new channel's style of brash, upstart "youth programming."

Toxic Shock were a two-piece feminist combo formed in Birmingham in the summer of 1983 by Heather (Joyce) Dean (saxophone and vocals) and Alice (Al) Marsh (bass and vocals). Both women had previously played in punk bands (Dean in Metro Youth and Sanction in Exeter; Marsh in Day Five in Newcastle-under-Lyme), but were now looking for a new musical approach that would allow them to better focus attention on questions of female sexuality, reproductive rights, and the liberation of women from all aspects of their oppression. The catalyst to form Toxic Shock was a Poison Girls gig in Birmingham, an experience that both Marsh and Joyce were hugely inspired by. The two women quickly wrote and arranged their first three songs and approached Poison Girls to ask for a support slot at their next show. They were then offered a slot on the tour. "It was a privilege to be part of it, and I learned so, so much," says Joyce.

The whole ensemble operated as with the dynamic of a touring troupe. "I remember being really good mates with Mark Miwurdz," she adds. "He taught me to play pool, which I was rubbish at. Janice was delightful and as hilarious in real life as on stage. She was *such* a brave performer and so talented. Tony Allen and I stayed mates for years afterwards. He was a genius."

"The thing about being on tour which I learned then, and which has proved true in every other job I've done, is that the gig at the end of the day is only a part of it," she continues. "The dynamics amongst the people you're on the road with is everything. When choosing musicians to work with I'll always pick friends if I can, because basically you're spending far more time in a van trying to keep each other awake or entertained than you are on stage. The coldest, most miserable jobs I've done have been where there's no affection between you. There was

certainly plenty of passion and affection flying around on that tour."

Viewed in retrospect, the Big Brother tour can be seen as a moment of transition, part of the band's preparation for what was an important next phase in their evolving plan. "They had a more sophisticated sound by then as well, with keyboards too, although perhaps I was still too young to appreciate where they were heading," suggests Joyce. "Did the cabaret format work, every night, in every venue?" she asks. "Honestly, not every time. But it was a bold idea and, on those nights it felt like it wasn't working, it was probably because people in the audience had literally never seen anything like it."

"The cabaret format, I really liked," d'Boyle reflected later. "Although it wasn't suitable for large audiences, when people just wanted to go crazy, in the right smaller venues it was a good fit."

"I really liked the way they brought in the feeling of the *commedia dell'arte* into their work, and elements of the circus and the cabaret," says Steve Ignorant. "That was great. Poison Girls could have turned up at a festival and brought in tightrope walkers and fire eaters and people on unicycles, and it would have worked. We couldn't do that as Crass."

With a vacancy for a replacement bass player opening up, Mark Dunn stepped in to take on four-string responsibilities prior to the studio session for the second Illuminated single.

Prior to joining Poison Girls, Dunn had in 1976 been a founder member of inventive County Durham three-piece postpunks Neon. He had immediately shown his bass playing prowess on their *Anytime Anyplace Anywhere* seven-inch (released on Sensible Records in 1978) and even more so on the incendiary follow-up *Don't Eat Bricks/Hanging Off an O* (produced by Martin Rushent, and released on Radar Records later that year).

Recorded at ICC Studios in Eastbourne, Sussex, in August 1983, and produced by Bernie Clarke, *Are You Happy Now?* became Poison Girls' second Illuminated single, and a renewed attempt to prise their way into the British pop charts and mainstream radio playlists. In the hope of reaching audiences further afield, the single was also licensed to Reekus Records in Ireland and, the following year, to Pregnant Records in San Francisco in the US.

Are You Happy Now? saw the band move further away from their punk roots in the attempt to produce a smoother, more radio-friendly sound, this time infused with a percussive dance beat. But the band were incapable of writing bland "pop pap," and the song retained Poison Girls' signature sharp edges and unexpected switches in tone and tempo. Despite its relative lightness, and the pop sensibility that infused it, the song retained an unsettling undercurrent. That was something evident in the single's sleeve design, which mixed comical, grotesque Big Brother and circus clown motifs.

POISONGIRLS

THE OFFENDING ARTICLE

Animal Liberation — A Sexual Issue — or a wank?

For the Donkeys of Port Said.

"He was lonely so we got him a budgie"...."Since my husband died I depend more and more on the cat. Someone to come home to"...."If it wasn't for the fish and Tina (a budgie) I wouldn't talk to a soul for days on end now I can't get out any more"...."my littlest boy was always hanging around the neighbours children till we got him the puppy for company"....
(quotes from a neighbourhood survey on pet ownership)

Substitutes for human love. Less risky than a human relationship. And when the 'affair' is over you can always put your pet 'to sleep'. An affair of convenience. The convenience of the dominent species. Capture, domesticate, exterminate.

Alongside exploitation of animals for laboratory experimentation, the pet and petfood industry is enormous, feeding off our alienation from each other, sentimentalising animals to fit in with our deprivations and need for love, physical contact, and control.

So the prettiest and most appealing pets are fed and pampered in return for companionship and obedience. Where have we heard **that** story before....the Miss World contests? The pretty docile pets of male sexist fantasy? Capture, domesticate, exterminate. A new girl every year? A new wife every seven year itch? And the Nazis who selected the pretty Jewish girls for their brothels in the concentration camps. They murdered the old and ugly. Discarded them and used their bodies for soap, lampshades, and even to feed their guard dogs.

I was a young girl child in the Second World War. All men were soldiers. I couldn't tell from their almost identical khaki uniforms which were 'ours' and which were the 'enemy'. Some of them came home on leave and mingled their tales offighting on the front with snickering stories about the reputed brothels of Port Said, where the prostitutes were on offer side by side with donkeys, who were screwed and abused, just like the women were. Extra extra thrills and treats....I couldn't understand the hot eyed glances and laughter at these stories. I was frightened. I am still frightened.

And of course, male military macho ethics approved of these brothels in Port Said rather than encourage homosexual contact between the ranks. Miltary regimes are terrified of love developing between soldiers. Balls must mean toughness and courage. But the bullet rips through and reveals the vulnerability of the male flesh. Almost as tender as a women? Almost as vulnerable? They dare not admit that possibility.

Listen. 99% of all butchers are **MEN**. The master race. **MAN**ipulators. Tor**MEN**tors. **MALE**factors. **MAN**ufacturers of meat. Think about it. You rape and plunder the entire range of living creatures of all species, even the female and young of your own species. You train the young to follow in your footsteps, if not by word, then certainly by deed.

You must give up your knives. Take instead the vulnerability and tenderness of your own body, your fragile penis. Cherish love between man and man. Learn the tenderness of your own genitals before you so thoughtlessly plunder and penetrate the bodies of young and fertile girls. Learn first the mysteries of contraception, and love, and respect and awe for life of all forms.

In the meantime do not be surprised if the rest of us, women and children, enlightened men, and all the animals, will rise up and turn against you. We can invoke nightmares of revenge, worse than you can imagine. And the women may rise up who will be the other 1% and who will have her knife. And in the name of LIFE she will take up her knife and castrating, will avenge even the least laboratory rat, that, discarded, ends up in the tin of PAL you may feed your pet tomorow morning.

Vi Subversa / Poisongirls / April 1983

This piece was specially written to appear
on the cover of the 'Nation of Animal Lovers'
E.P. ,but deemed unsuitable and omitted by
those who decide what we should or should
not read. Whodunnit?

1.4.83

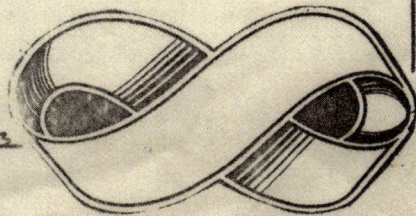

Clipping from *Sounds*, 13 August 1983. Courtesy of Pete Fender and Gemma Sansom.

The message of "Happy Now" echoed the subversive clarion call of "One Good Reason." Once again the band's lyrics urged the listener (albeit in a similarly coded way to the previous single) to take charge of their lives, to be demanding and to refuse to settle for frustration:

> You look so tough, you look so hard,
>   you're cold and uptight
> You talk so rough, you talk so hard,
>   you scare me at night
> But you're frightened boy
> Angry too inside
> Angry . . .
> Frightened too inside
> Well are you happy now?
> Are you satisfied?
> Are you happy now?
> Did you get what you wanted?
> Are you happy now?

In the hope of boosting the single's chart-bound momentum, Illuminated release a remixed twelve-inch version, offering two B side tracks ("Ménage Abattoir" and "Whiskey Voice") rather than the seven-inch version's one ("Cream Dream"). The sleeve of the twelve-inch, designed by Domino (Marie-Dominique Downs), featured photos of the band dressed up as a mash-up of mime artists, circus performers, and street freaks. While it's a striking image, the process of preparing the artwork was fraught. "While I was working, the band's manager harassed me night and day to 'finish it *yesterday*' and caused me so much anxiety that the job took far longer than it should have," she says. "Eventually I delivered the

finished artwork, but when the record came out it was clear that something had gone wrong in the printing." The result was a disappointment to the artist, but was certainly not a cause of the record's underperformance.

The previous year, *Anarchy* magazine had asked the band if they would consider ever appearing on *Top of the Pops*—BBC TV's long-running chart programme, which mixed (what were mostly mimed) in-studio performance with prerecorded promo videos. When Crass were asked the same question by *Tongue in Cheek* fanzine, Pete Wright's precondition for the band's appearance was that Crass "could talk uninterrupted on any subject of our choice for the length of time that the record that got us there took to play." For Poison Girls, Subversa was less absolutist, suggesting that the band were prepared to consider navigating the contradictions: "If we could do it on terms that felt comfortable and appropriate for us. But that's the issue isn't it? It might not be possible, but there's no point trying to avoid the possibility." With the advantage of hindsight, Steve Ignorant now acknowledges, "If Poison Girls *had* got themselves on *Top of the Pops*, I would have been jealous." In the end, that particular dream would remain impossible.

"The idea of us even contemplating *Top of the Pops* is a bit weird," says Famous. "It was always a trick question for any 'serious' DIY band. We always felt that the main 'gatekeeper' for political, indie and alternative music in the UK at the time, was the John Peel show on BBC Radio 1. His show's 'sessions' were a big source of exposure—and cash—for any band invited on. I can't think of any other band that we played with—those that had brought out records at least—who had not had a session, and sometime several, on his show. It was almost a rite of passage. Poison Girls were never offered a session—that exclusion still rankles!"

"We asked several times for a Peel session—a couple of times in person, when we ran into John Peel at events, and a couple times over the phone when we were looking for extra visibility to promote particular record releases. We heard back that his producer John Walters didn't like us, and that was the reason we weren't booked," Famous explains. "It seems to me that was a very convenient excuse, which redirected responsibility."

"We had no particular animosity towards Peel. His show was the only outlet for odd, obscure, 'noncommercial' music—two hours a night, five nights a week, on national radio. We genuinely thought what he was doing for music was tremendous. Our beef with him was that he ignored us."

For many years, Peel's reputation as the British radio broadcaster most dedicated to promoting new, breakthrough, and outsider musical talent, during the genre tumult of the 1970s and 1980s in particular, remained unchallenged. Following his death in October 2004 at the age of sixty-five, many events, awards, and

202

even a stage at the Glastonbury Festival were named in recognition of his contribution to the world of music beyond the mainstream. But in recent years, Peel's personal reputation has been subject to more critical scrutiny as evidence that has long been in the public domain has begun to receive more attention.

Even in the 1970s, his predilections were already known to those in and around the industry. In 1965, aged twenty-five, Peel had married the fifteen-year-old American girl Shirley Anne Milburn (a union that was legal in the state of Texas, despite the age gap and Milburn's youth). Their marriage ended in divorce in 1973. Interviewed by *The Guardian* in 1975, Peel had boasted of his many sexual conquests involving young women. 'All they wanted me to do was abuse them, sexually, which, of course, I was only too happy to do,' he told the journalists. In later years, Peel made many other disclosures about his sexual behaviour involving 'an awful lot' of underage girls. "The very fact that Peel could openly talk about having underage sex, in a national newspaper, with no heed for the PR consequences, speaks volumes about those times," Famous observes.

"Peel often talked on his radio show about two particular women—his wife, 'affectionately' referred to as 'the pig,' and 'Mandy,' the 'simple village maiden.'" he continues. Before relocating to Brighton, the Suffolk cottage Frances (soon to be Vi Subversa) was living in was close to the village of Great Finborough, where 'Peel Acres' (the DJ's family home) was and is located. "Vi knew the parents of 'Mandy.'" Famous recalls, "who were understandably less than impressed by this on-air treatment," he says. "At some point early on in the life of Poison Girls, Vi met with John Peel and mentioned that they had friends in common, on the assumption that this fact might pique his interest. It didn't."

No evidence has yet emerged of any member of Poison Girls challenging Peel directly about his personal behaviour. But there has to have been some reason for Peel—with his eclectic, inclusive, inquisitive musical tastes—to have spurned Poison Girls, while so many of their peers (Crass included) were awarded with a much sought-after Peel Session.

"In retrospect, it's certainly clear that while Peel was extremely important in the alternative music scene, he was nevertheless a seriously flawed character," Famous concludes.

Despite the band's efforts at reinventing themselves, industry gatekeepers declined to embrace these musical interlopers. "It was very difficult to make that sort of judgement," says Zillah Minx. "All this time we're doing this, nobody's making any money, so there's nothing to live on. I think that that affected them. I mean, I think it affected all of us, after years of not really getting paid. I think that Poison Girls made the right decision, doing the music that they did. They wanted to

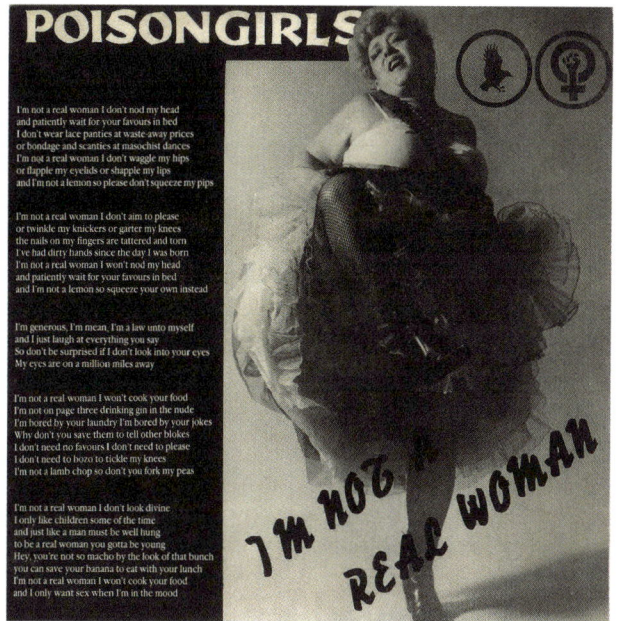

I'm Not a Real Woman, Xntrix, 1984.

be in the mainstream at that point. But it didn't really happen, did it? 'Happy Now' is a great song, but it really didn't help them."

The second Illuminated single was again largely ignored, and excluded from the official playlist of what was the decisive station: BBC Radio 1. The lighter timbre of both Illuminated singles had not found favour with all of Poison Girls' existing followers, and the experiment in entryism had won them few new adherents. The critical reception amongst reviewers was far from effusive, and both singles were widely acknowledged—including by the band—as commercial and artistic underachievers.

"Was I happy with the records? Yeah, for sure," Famous confirms. "Whether they achieved what we wanted, I don't know. I realised that they could quite easily have ruptured the credibility of the band." But Famous strongly defends the band's aspiration and determination to try something different that might reach new audiences. "From 1975 onwards, our stuff had always been really varied," he insists. "We'd never just gone for the political stuff. Everyone likes 'pop music'—let's call it what it is. Wanting to do catchy tunes that people could dance to, I mean, that's the reason why you're in a band!"

As a recent addition to the band, Tom Barwood had a fresh perspective on the experiment. "When I joined them, they'd just done *One Good Reason* and they were hoping for some airplay. I liked the sentiment behind it. But it seemed obvious to me that they weren't really going to get into the mainstream like that," Barwood suggests. "I also wasn't too keen on the production—it didn't really do it for me. It was trying to lay radio-friendly stuff on top of what was fairly niche. I think 'Happy Now'

203

might have stood a chance. But this was when MTV was starting, and everything was becoming hypercommercial. So it was bad timing, I think. They might have had more success doing it in a different period."

Three factors mitigated against the success of Poison Girls' foray into the mainstream: Illuminated's limited resources, the label's relative inexperience and lack of industry connections; suspicion on the part of producers and decision makers that these 'former' anarchist punks were up to something (which they clearly were); and the more widespread industry's disdainful perception that the band were odd and unpresentable (as they were "fronted by a geriatric"). It was arguable too that Illuminated's budget did not stretch to cover the type of studio work that could deliver singles with the requisite radio-friendly quality—ones which did not leave the listener concerned that the band's reach might be exceeding their grasp.

"Poison Girls had many ambitions, and one was commercial success," Goldschmidt argues. "I failed in helping them achieve that. But none of us understood the music business, and in hindsight it was probably unrealistic." Although he saw potential in the band, Illuminated boss Bagley did not share Poison Girls' political and cultural ambitions, and viewed things through the lens of a small business owner who could not keep loss-making acts on the books. "Illuminated were unable to sell either single in the numbers that they required—so we were ditched," Famous says simply.

"Bagley really liked us, and he liked working with Martin," he continues. "But he said that his team didn't, and weren't getting behind us. The record contract, as it was laid out, with all of its ifs-and-buts and whatevers, had promised a lot. We had a half-finished album that we'd begun recording at Foel Studio, and Bagley said 'you can just have the tape for yourselves, and we'll call it a day.' So basically we got two singles and half an album out of Illuminated."

The abrupt end of the relationship meant that Poison Girls again found themselves without a recording contract. At the same time, the lure of the underground was again exerting itself over the band. It seemed the right time to go it alone once more, and without the aid of a manager. "The relationship with Martin had begun to sour after we had worked solidly for a year, doing big gigs all over the shop, but still ending up £5000 in debt," Famous reveals. We thought we needed to do something different, and—being a bit 'up ourselves'—we started to talk, behind Martin's back, with Pete Jenner, who'd been Pink Floyd's manager in the 1960s. Jenner was the only decent person in the straight music business that we ever met." When he found out, Goldschmidt was—understandably—indignant. "Martin then refused to do any more work for us until we signed a formal management contract," Famous continues. "Those negotiations were fraught, although all parties eventually signed." But it was not long before band and manager parted company. "I am not proud of what happened," Famous concedes. "And, in retrospect, I think it was a big mistake for us. But we remained firm friends throughout, despite everything."

"My role with Poison Girls, and with artists in general, has always been to try to enable them to get where they want to go," Goldschmidt says. "We had many, many successes though, and I think I made a strong positive contribution by getting some of my friends to work with them and expanding their live career." After separating, "we always stayed in touch and stayed friends."

Goldschmidt decided to focus his energies on running a new and more outward-looking DIY label, one that remained motivated by the desire to release music at break-even rates. "I didn't understand the concept of profit when we started Cooking Vinyl," he admits. "I was used to doing tours and making sure I could pay my bills." Break-even was always the target. "I never tried to make any money!" As Goldschmidt learned his craft, the Cooking Vinyl label would go on to achieve both critical and commercial success through its releases for artists including Michelle Shocked, Cowboy Junkies, and The Prodigy. In 1985, he revived the Forward Sounds International label to release the *Dig This!* compilation album which celebrated the year-long national miners' strike against the pit closures demanded by the Thatcher government. It featured tracks by Chumbawamba, The Mekons, The Ex, and Omega Tribe—as well as by Akimbo and Poison Girls.

Poison Girls went in search of a new record contract, without success. "We tried," Famous insists. "In the UK, we were met with a wall of indifference—the typical answer was, 'Who's interested in another Poison Girls record?' They may have had a point."

But looking for a 'record deal' was really trying to secure some financial underpinning for the band's work. "Essentially, we were broke," he concedes. "We had been working for eight years and more, had sold half our garden to pay for *Where's the Pleasure* and we still had an overdraft with the bank, when interest rates were at eye-watering levels. We were accused by the 'purer than thou' set that we had 'sold out.' If only!" When it came to Poison Girls, "nobody really wanted to 'buy in.'" he says.

The band now sought for new opportunities to work differently, a rethink that was required, not just by the band's financial position, but by a complex of political developments in the wider world in 1985: the battle over the social wage in the form of municipal socialist councils, the attack on the peace convoy at the Stonehenge Festival, the ratcheting up of cruise missile deployment across the UK, and the end in defeat of the national miners' strike.

Relations with Crass had cooled since Poison Girls had called time on their close collaboration the year before. But the association between the two bands broke

POISON
GIRLS

SEXPOL

FREE CONTRACEPTION/FREE ABORTION/FREE WOMEN/ FREE ABORTION/FREE CONTRACEPTION/FREE WOMEN
FREE CONTRACEPTION/FREE ABORTION/FREE WOMEN/ FREE ABORTION/FREE CONTRACEPTION/FREE WOMEN
FREE CONTRACEPTION/FREE ABORTION/FREE WOMEN/ FREE ABORTION/FREE CONTRACEPTION/FREE WOMEN

THERE CAN BE NO REVOLUTION WITHOUT WOMEN'S REVOLUTION
NO MAN CAN WIN FREEDOM AT THE EXPENSE OF A WOMEN AND PRETEND HE IS REVOLUTIONARY
THERE CAN BE NO REVOLUTION WITHOUT WOMEN'S REVOLUTION

> ....and at the end of the day when he's done his day's work for
> the state; when they chuck him out of the factory at the end of the
> shift; or out of the schools at four o'clock; or on to the dole queue
> when they decide his cheap labour is redundant.........then what ?
> when he's been thrown out of the pub at closing time, when he's
> done brawling with the lads; when your lip is bleeding and his head
> is swimming..........then what ? When the fighting in the battlefield
> is exhausted.......then what ? When even the rich crawl home from their
> executive toy offices, dazed with their expenze account lunches to pat
> the kiddies on their heads.....then what ? When the recession hits even
> them and they too are redundant, loyal, flabby members of the ratrace
> that they were. When even they are cast off as useless.......then what ?
> And when the radical lefties have done shouting at each other about who
> is a wet and who isn't.....when they have outdone each other in machismo
> revolutionary wet dreams and they slam their car doors and get out their
> front door keys.........then what ?

THERE CAN BE NO REVOLUTION WITHOUT WOMEN'S REVOLUTION
FREE YOUR MIND/FREE YOUR BODY/ FREE CONTRACEPTION/FREE ABORTION/FREE WOMEN/FREE WOMEN
THERE CAN BE NO REVOLUTION WITHOUT WOMEN'S REVOLUTION

> ...... then they will reach out their arms and their lips and their sore
> heads.......then they will hold out their broken limbs and their grazed
> knees and their bruised egos.......then they will show their helpless
> hopeless eyes.....
> they will reach out to some woman.....for attention......for care....
> for comfort....for sex

AT THE END OF THE DAY THERE IS THE COMFORT AND SUPPORT AND PATIENCE OF MILLIONS OF WOMEN.
HALF OF THE POPULATION. WHOSE DRAMAS AND WOUNDS RARELY REACH THE HEADLINES OF WHAT IS
CALLED NEWS. THEY PROVIDE DOMESTIC, EMOTIONAL, AND SEXUAL SUPPORT AND COMFORT.
IN ADDITION TO TRYING TO CARE FOR THEMSELVES WOMEN NOW ARE FACING AN INCREASING BURDEN
OF LOOKING AFTER THE MILLIONS OF UNEMPLOYED MEN AND CHILDREN.

THERE CAN BE NO REVOLUTION WITHOUT WOMEN'S REVOLUTION/FREE CONTRACEPTION/FREE ABORTION

WOMEN ARE THE WIVES AND THE MOTHERS OF THE UNEMPLOYED. MOTHERS OF THE BORED AND HOPE
LESS CHILDREN. THE NURSES AND THE DOMESTIC CARETAKERS. BUT WE ARE CHANGING. FREE WOMEN.

WOMEN ARE HALF THE POPULATION. WOMEN HAVE THEIR OWN AMBITIONS AND VISIONS AND DESIRES
WE HAVE OUR OWN VISIONS ANFD AMBITIONS AND DESIRES. VISIONS OF HOW THE WORLD COULD BE.

ISN'T IT AMAZING THAT WITH ALL THE MONEY THEY SPEND ON NUCLEAR BOMBS AND THE DEFENSE
BUDGET......AND OTHER DIRTY FILTHY METHODS OF DESTRUCTION AND POLLUTION............
THERE STILL ISN'T A REALLY SAFE AND RELIABLE CONTRACEPTIVE..........................!

Sex Pol manifesto/Women's Revolution Communique, circa 1982. Courtesy of Pete Fender and Gemma Sansom.

down completely—and, at the time, it appeared irrevocably—in 1983. The unexpected cause of the rupture was a political statement that Vi Subversa was invited to write for the sleeve of Conflict's forthcoming single *To a Nation of Animal Lovers* (a release for which Crass's Steve Ignorant would join Colin Jerwood on vocals).

The single was to be the fourth release on the Corpus Christi label—essentially a spin-off from Crass Records, run and managed by Southern Studios's John Loder. It was Loder who had pitched the idea for Corpus Christi, in response to Crass's insistence that the band would only agree to releases on Crass Records by artists they felt in the closest affinity with. Loder felt that the application of such a high standard was leading to missed opportunities to put out records by deserving bands that were likely to be well received.

Loder wanted to increase Southern Studios' capacity to release material that was either a lower priority for Crass Records's treatment, or was not an immediate fit for that label's openly declared DIY anarchist remit. The first release on the new Corpus Christi label, the *Rising from the Dread* twelve-inch by goth-adjacent post-punks UK Decay (who'd already released vinyl on Fresh Records), confirmed that different calculation. While Penny Rimbaud continued to meticulously supervise all releases on Crass Records, Corpus Christi's parallel operation gave Loder a significant amount of creative latitude. That independence extended to the design of the label's record sleeves, which were not required to adhere to the familiar Crass Records template. It was that relative autonomy, and the extent of the discretion that went with it, that—albeit unintentionally—ensured that the argument about the sleeve of Conflict's single became so explosive.

Ignorant's decision to join Conflict for the single's studio session had been a huge declaration of confidence in the band. Conflict frontman Colin Jerwood was understandably keen to enhance the standing of *To a Nation of Animal Lovers* in the anarchist punk scene still further by involving Poison Girls. Conflict asked Vi Subversa to contribute a statement on any aspect of animal rights that she was motivated to write about. Subversa took the opportunity to be provocative—not simply for the sake of it, but in order to confront some of those people (especially young men) likely to buy an animal liberation themed Conflict single with what she considered to be some uncomfortable truths. Her short but extremely powerful essay set out parallels and interconnections between the exploitation of women and the abuse of animals. It went on to highlight the hypocrisy of those male animal rights activists whose gender politics and personal practice were reactionary, and who ignored the realities of the oppression of women by a social system built on the foundations of capitalism and patriarchy, while rallying in the defence of wild, domesticated, and farm animals. The article ended with an implied 'threat': a warning of the violent consequences that might meet those who, while claiming to be champions of freedom, contribute to the oppression and marginalisation of women.

> We can invoke nightmares of revenge worse than you can imagine. And the woman may rise up who will have her knife. And in the name of life she will take up her knife. And, castrating, will avenge even the least laboratory rat that, discarded, ends up in the tin of Pal you may feed your pet tomorrow morning.

A key consideration was whether Subversa's evocation of ideas of vengeance and bloody revenge were intended as allegory, as symbolism, as metaphor—or as something more direct and literal. "Of course it was not to be taken literally," Famous protests. "It was in the grand tradition of punk rants—of which Crass were past masters—and was, as such, par for the course, we thought. It was a memory of tales of soldiers fucking donkeys, and setting this image against the macho—and increasingly violent—culture of the animal liberation movement at the time, and the treatment of women. The idea of vengeance, or revenge, is posted in the statement as a warning, acknowledging the reality that people are taking notes." The semidetached nature of the Corpus Christi label meant that Crass's Penny Rimbaud was not routinely involved in prerelease approval. When he caught sight of Subversa's essay, he was horrified by the violent imagery (which he considered outrageous and irresponsible), by the ideas drawn from the (in)famous *SCUM Manifesto*, and by what he considered the statement's hostile and divisive intent. "The main objection that we were told by members of Crass was that the statement said 'all men are butchers.' This is a category error. The lyric says 'all butchers are men'—something entirely different," Famous affirms. Rimbaud insisted that the words be removed from the single before its release. Loder acceded to the demand, and the contested essay was replaced before the record sleeves were printed.

No one involved was happy with the outcome. Conflict were irritated by the rebuke from Crass; relations between Loder and Rimbaud became strained, as the semidetached status of Corpus Christi came under awkward scrutiny; and Poison Girls and Crass squared off, viewing each other's behaviour with indignant disbelief.

Appalled at what the band felt was an exercise in political censorship by Crass, Poison Girls went public. The statement "made the connections between animal cruelty, prostitution, militarism—and homosexuality," Subversa explained to the music paper *Sounds*. "This seems to have raised the macho hackles of the Crass organisation," she added, in a statement unlikely to reduce the rancour of the schism.

Crass upped the ante too. "They ended up sending all our tapes, master tapes, all our artwork—everything from Southern Studios—and dumping it on our doorstep whilst we were away on tour, and there was no one in the house." says Famous. It was abrupt confirmation that all support from Crass Records for Poison Girls' work had ended. "They said they wanted nothing to do with us any more."

Poison Girls had no intention of being silenced by Crass. The band first duplicated and distributed print copies of the statement (adorned with the enticement to any potential reader that these were words Crass 'tried to ban'). "After that, we had to make it into a song," he continues. "Mark Dunn, our bass player at the time, had a bit of electronic music that he was playing around, and he thought we could make it fit the words exactly. We worked on it and recorded it in our basement." With Subversa reciting the words, in what was a riveting vocal performance, the impact of the statement was amplified by Dunn's unsettling musical score.

In Conflict's own act of defiance, this audio version of "The Offending Article" was included on the *Who? What? Why? When? Where?* political punk compilation released on the band's own Mortarhate label. "For me, the main beneficiary of the whole affair was Conflict," Famous says. Poison Girls later released the track as part of the band's own *Seven Year Scratch* retrospective double album. The actions of all parties ensured that relations between members of Poison Girls and Crass—and between Subversa and Rimbaud in particular—were not repaired until long after Crass had split up.

Although "The Offending Article" generated a great deal of interest in the work of Poison Girls, the song itself was not a particular favourite of the band. It had not emerged through the group's usual collaborative songwriting methods and had only been recorded as a political rebuttal to Crass. "If I were to choose my twenty best Poison Girls songs, it wouldn't be in there," Famous reveals. "In fact, I think it's probably my least favourite Poison Girls song of all time. I think that 'Statement' or 'Cream Dream' or 'Dirty Work' are all far better political rants. That track is very unrepresentative of what we were doing."

Poison Girls again refocused their attention on live performances and returned to touring for the remainder of the year. What was immediately brought to light by the controversy was the tension that had emerged in Poison Girls' identity. It was hard to reconcile the image of a group hoping to push past the gatekeepers of the cultural mainstream, with that of a band seemingly proselytising in favour of violent retribution against male animal abusers. Famous acknowledges the political tensions that "The Offending Article" revealed—even as he

insists its revenge motifs were rhetorical and cautionary. "As avowed pacifists, leaning in even to the *idea* of violence is problematic. But I don't know if 'revolution' is always possible without some sort of uprising, or that a lifetime of provocation can simply be forgotten."

"The strangest thing about the whole debacle is that—had it not been banned—the words of what became 'The Offending Article' would have remained an insignificant, largely unread and widely ignored statement on the sleeve of an obscure EP," he says. "Hey ho."

Poison Girls' belief in the need to criticise unwelcome aspects of anarcho-punk culture was not blunted by the controversy. New song "White Cream Dream" critiqued different manifestations of machismo, offering a withering account of male domination of social and cultural space. Alongside 'anglo-saxon bully boys' and 'spunky white beauty boys,' young men of a different identity entirely also come under critical scrutiny:

O' my pacifist neochristian, lillywhite bully boys
You cannot stand the sight of blood
You are drenched in the blood of your sisters and
    brothers.
You are drenched in blood

The clear target of Subversa's ire was the moral piousness of those elements within anarcho-punk who considered an 'opposition to violence' as sufficient to excuse its adherents from any culpability for its historic use. Subversa often chose a high-risk approach to delivering the song live, taking herself and her microphone to the front of the stage to eyeball any male mosh-pit or macho enclave within the audience and sing the song inches from their confused faces.

With the band's foray into the pop mainstream proving unsuccessful, Poison Girls swung back sharply in the direction of the punk underground. In the studio, one thing that connected the band's next release with the two previous two vinyl releases was the involvement of producer Bernie Clarke. "He was very much a commercial producer, a part of the music business," Famous says. "He was a strange character, very coarse, and he spoke with an extremely strong Australian accent." In the studio, Clarke was prone to saying outrageous and offensive things. "In a funny way, Vi really liked him *because* of his coarseness, his crassness."

In the uproarious sounds of "I'm Not a Real Woman" there was a sense of joy and of defiance; a reflection of the subject matter itself and of the band's relief at being freed from the restrictions of trying to convince the pop establishment to accept their wily advances.

"I really like 'Real Woman,'" says Famous. "It was a really good track. It is an intentionally funny song, it's got really humorous lyrics. It was a rollicking play when we did it live, as well."

I'm not a real woman, I don't nod my head
And patiently wait for your favours in bed
I don't wear lace panties, at waist away prices
Or bondage and scanties at masochist dances
I'm not a real woman, I don't waggle my hips
Or flapple my eyelids or shapple my lips
And I'm not a lemon, so please don't squeeze my
    pips

The sleeve design reaffirmed the band's sensibilities as outsiders and political satirists. A photo of Subversa, caught in midkick as she solo dances the cancan in a whirl of skirt and petticoats, sits adjacent to the full lyrics of the song. The feminist fist symbol, yin-yang icon, and the carrion crow all make a return, and there's a repeat of Subversa's spoken-word challenge: "Isn't it amazing with all the money they spend on nuclear weapons, there still isn't a safe and reliable contraceptive?" The seven-inch sleeve pushed the political polemic further. On the back cover, beneath anarchist and disarmament logos, and next to the lyrics of "Take the Toys from the Boys," a short statement began:

They play games called Nationalism, Defence,
    Alliances, Religion and Economy.
These games play on our fear and insecurity.
They have rules called The Work Ethic, Right and
Might, Protection, Possession and Profits.
These rules are fixed.

While the record was credited to Xntrix, the release had the backing of Rough Trade. Keen not to repeat the design disappointments of the *Happy Now* twelve-inch, Domino "went to get advice from the record company" before beginning work. "I was happy with the result, and I was very pleased with my design for the back cover," she says.

For the first and only time in the band's history a tie-in video was recorded to promote the single, the costs of which were covered by Rough Trade. Recorded in the back garden of Poison Girls' Leytonstone house, and on the seafront at Southend, the video was produced and shot by Wildtrax women's video collective.

The full Poison Girls lineup (including a cameo from Lance d'Boyle) feature briefly, holding their instruments, in a nod to the expected aesthetic of a "pop promo." But the narrative focuses on an all-woman coach trip to the seaside. Vi Subversa and Gemma Sansom are joined by friends and supporters of the band, on a freewheeling day-out at the beach and funfair as the women enjoy each other's company and echo the song's defiant lyrics. The video concludes back at Poison Girls' house with the image of Subversa gleefully setting fire to washing pegged out on the clothes line—a mischievous metaphor for the rejection of domestic female drudgery, which sees Subversa crack a broad smile.

Anne Robinson of the Wildtrax team happily recalls her memory of "sunny, Southend, subversive, seaside adventures" with the band during the shoot. At that time, video cameras were bulky and cumbersome, lighting and sound equipment prohibitively expensive and editing facilities difficult to access. But the "home movie" qualities of the finished video captured the song's mischievous and defiant tenor. The production costs will have been modest, but the opportunities to screen the video were equally limited. "It did reach the video jukebox in some pubs, so I was told," says Famous.

The fledgling MTV music video channel, which had launched three years earlier, prided itself on its "mainstream music for mall kids" identity, and was completely beyond reach to a British band from the countercultural fringes. In an analogue era, a decade before the launch of platforms like YouTube, direct online video streaming was the stuff of sci-fi. So only a select few were able to watch the video until it resurfaced in digital format years later.

The tensions within the band's evolving political identity were evident, however, in the inclusion on the front cover of not only the lyrics of the title song, but of the return of the crow image and the presence of the classic feminist 'raised fist in the women's symbol' adjacent to the picture of Subversa. It marked something of a retrenchment in terms of presentation.

The year 1984 became "a year that saw a big turning point for the band." As part of that, Poison Girls decided that it was now "a good time to look at our roots."

"At the time, we were trying to work out what we were doing next," says Famous. "The album was really about us just 'holding our ground' for a while," drawing together tracks from the band's back catalogue, "a lot of stuff that never got recorded beyond demo versions— and some live tracks. It was about getting a lot of stuff sorted, really."

The retrospective double album *Seven Year Scratch* brought together the best of their back catalogue. The title of which parodied the concept of the 'seven year itch' (an idea injected into popular consciousness by the 1955 Marilyn Monroe film of the same name) which posited that "happiness in any long-term romantic relationship erodes after around seven years." For a band whose lyrics scrutinised the gender, generational, power, and sexual dynamics of human relationships it was an apt choice for an album title—especially when given a clever Poison Girls' twist, which focused on the reasonable *response* to the irritation ("if it itches, scratch it . . ."). Poison Girls' selection of material reflected the band's own interest in doing more than *scratching the surface* of more than seven years' worth of creative output, and to do so without suggesting that this settling of accounts with the band's past would draw a line beneath it and see them *start from scratch* again.

The album featured three never previously re-leased recordings, and one unreleased song, all from the first two years in the band's life. "Revenge" was a home recording made in November 1977, featuring Bella Donna on bass. "Reality Attack" and "Alienation" were studio demo recordings from April 1978, with Scott Barker on bass. "I Wanted the Moon," featuring Bernhardt Rebours on bass, had been recorded during the studio session for the *Piano Lessons* release. "Piano Lessons" itself was also included, alongside "Statement," the flexi included with *Chappaquiddick Bridge*, "Dirty Work," and "Promenade Immortelle," both sides of the *All Systems Go* single, and—for the first time under the band's own label—"The Offending Article," featuring Mark Dunn on bass.

The two live sides featured tracks from the band's Big Brother Cabaret tour date at Jilly's, Manchester in October 1983. Ten of the twelve tracks were from the *Where's the Pleasure* period, with only "Tension" and "State Control and Rock'n'Roll" from earlier in the band's catalogue. Although the band had arranged in advance to record their set for inclusion on *Seven Year Scratch*, the evening was anything but a high point of the tour. The day before the Manchester show, one of the vehicles the band and family members were travelling in had been involved in a crash, leaving four passengers "shaken up and bruised" and the whole party feeling "really edgy and freaked." Their spirits had been revived somewhat by a "great gig" at the Arts Centre in York that evening (organised by Sue Cooper [Bella Donna]), but the show at Jilly's the following day had been grim. "A horrible gig," Famous's tour diary entry affirms. "No money, no rider, no audience—and generally abusive organisation." Despite considering the gig to have been "the pits," Poison Girls played well, and the energy of their performance more than compensated for the dismal atmosphere in the room. Pete Fender engineered the live four-track recording, and then handled the final mix at Heart and Soul Studios that December, to produce the first official Poison Girls live vinyl release since *Total Exposure*.

The experience of the Cabaret of Fools and Big Brother tour had reignited the interest of different members of the band in other forms of stagecraft and performance art. As part of that process, d'Boyle launched a project aiming to put together a theatrical package that would become known as "The Zany." This was a multimedia revue, with strong echoes of both The Body Show and Poison Girls' recent cabaret-style tours, which drew in the talents of Tony Allen, Pete Fender, Gemma Sansom, members of Poison Girls, and the writer Lee Gibson—who'd interviewed Poison Girls, Crass, poet Andy T, and many other bands for his *Anathema* zine and several others. From the outset, "The Zany" was a collective, inclusive, ensemble effort. Around the same time, individual members of Poison Girls had the

confidence to embrace the risks of exposure that came from independent and solo performance.

"I also remember when Vi performed at a picnic in the garden at the occupied South London Women's Hospital in the summer of 1984," says the "writer, reader, and ranter" Rosanne Rabinowitz. Subversa was accompanied by seventeen-year old guitarist Debbie Smith, who would later play with Curve and Echobelly. "I have a vivid recollection of Vi performing 'Under the Doctor,' very appropriate to the hospital setting: 'What I'm trying to say . . . is you've got to be strong, so strong, because nothing takes the pain away for long!' Sadly, the garden where this took place is now a carpark for the Tesco superstore that replaced part of the hospital."

Poison Girls would find new reserves of energy to continue their collective efforts as a defiant, nonconformist, rebellious alliance—even as the political, social, and cultural environment in which they were working became far more inhospitable.

Opposite: Queen's Walk Community Centre, Nottingham, 1983. Clockwise from top left: Vi, Martin Heath, Richard, Tony Allen, and Cynth Ethics. Photos by Phil Tonge. Above: Vi, Richard, and Max Vol, Berlin Wall, 1987. Below: Vi with Jenny the rat, Berlin, 1987. Photos by Tom Barwood.

PROCEEDS TO RAS + LEWISHAM AGAINST CORRIE

Fight the Corrie Bill

Campaign against the Corrie Bill

Rock against Sexism

S.E. LONDON ROCK AGAINST SEXISM

FIGHT THE CORRIE BILL WITH

PRAG VEC
POISON GIRLS
AU PAIRS CRECHE
LEOPARDS

7~12 FRI 26 OCT bar 7~11
GOLDSMITHS COLLEGE S.U.

Goldsmiths College, London. 26 October 1984. Benefit for Rock Against Sexism and Lewisham Against Corrie.

The Venue

160-162 Victoria Street London SW1 Tel 01-828 9441
Tickets from the Venue box office & Virgin Megastore

THE POISONGIRLS

MONDAY 19TH SEPT

New Single 'HAPPY NOW'

FRANK CHICKENS
NIGHTINGALES
MARK MIWURDZ
TOXIC SHOCK

TICKETS £2.00 AT DOOR

CABARET OF FOOLS PACKAGE

POISON GIRLS
AKIMBO
TONY ALLEN
MARK MIWURDZ

THURS 30th JUNE
£2.00

LEADMILL   LEADMILL ST. SHEFFIELD S1
0742   754500

A BENEFIT GIG FOR THORNTON VIEW HOSPITAL OCCUPATION...

THE BIG BROTHER CABARET featuring

POISON GIRLS
3 L.P.'s + 2 E.P.'s + 4 singles. Present their uncompromising blend of music & politics with more power now than ever before.

+ Mark Miwurdz
Socio-political comedian who has a regular TV slot on 'THE TUBE'...

+ TOXIC SHOCK
tough female/feminist duo on sax + bass + vocals with a unique & innovative style...

+ chumbawumba
Leeds-based band who combine humour & music

COMMUNAL BUILDING, BRADFORD UNIVERSITY
8p.m. TUES. 25 OCT.
£1.50 or £1 with UB40 or student card

IF YOU CAN GIVE TIME TO HELP THE OCCUPATION, PLEASE RING BRADFORD 817574.
Promoter: Nick Toczek (0274) 721061. ALL profit (after very basic expenses only) go to occupation.

Thornton View Hospital, a long-stay geriatric unit is under threat of closure. The staff went into occupation on 5th Aug. '83. A similar hospital, St. Benedicts in London, was closed in '80. Within six months 30% of the patients died! The shock of moving & of a new environment & routine kills very old patients. Does economics matter more than human lives? SUPPORT THE OCCUPATION!

214

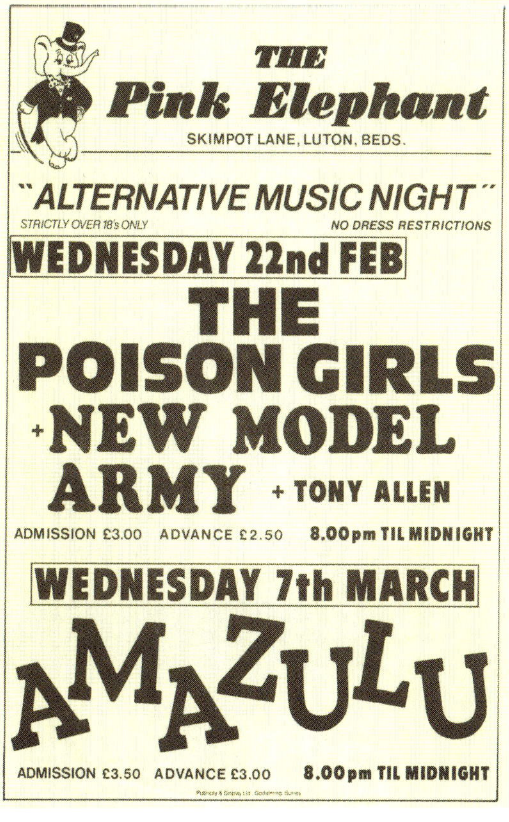

QUEENS WALK COMMUNITY CENTRE
THE MEADOWS · NOTTINGHAM

POISONGIRLS

OMEGA TRIBE

tony allen

£2   7·30pm

sat 25 february

tickets from : mushroom, ouroboros, or on door

TAKING LIBERTIES

SAT 5th MAR

POISON GIRLS

TYMON DOGG

surprise guests

tickets £2·00
doors 7·30pm

ACE

BRIXTON   TOWN HALL PARADE
BRIXTON HILL
TICKETS FROM THE ACE 274 4663 ROUGH TRADE 229 8541
LONDON THEATRE BOOKINGS 439 3371 PREMIER BOX
OFFICE 220 2245

»Artists For Animals   All Proceeds to:
ANIMAL LIBERATION
FRONT

Friday 16th March, 1984

Poison Girls
Annie Whitehall
Ann Clark
Toxic Shock

Theatre
The Polytechnic of North London
Holloway Road
London N7 8DB
£2.50
£2.00 Advance/NUS/Unwaged

0E0032   PNLSU«

THE
Pink Elephant
SKIMPOT LANE, LUTON, BEDS.

"ALTERNATIVE MUSIC NIGHT"
STRICTLY OVER 18's ONLY   NO DRESS RESTRICTIONS

WEDNESDAY 22nd FEB

THE
POISON GIRLS
+NEW MODEL
ARMY + TONY ALLEN

ADMISSION £3.00   ADVANCE £2.50   8.00PM TIL MIDNIGHT

WEDNESDAY 7th MARCH

AMAZULU

ADMISSION £3.50   ADVANCE £3.00   8.00PM TIL MIDNIGHT

Opposite: **The Venue,** London, 19 September 1983. **Communal Building,** Bradford, 25 October 1983. A benefit for the Thornton View Hospital Occupation. **Leadmill,** Sheffield, 30 June 1983.

This page: **Queen's Walk Community Centre,** Nottingham, 25 February 1983. Courtesy of Alan Schofield. **Ace,** Brixton Hill, 5 March 1983. **The Pink Elephant,** 22 February 1984. **North London Polytechnic,** London, 16 March 1984. Benefit for Animal Liberation Front.

Poison Girls' allies. This page: Advert for Rubella Ballet's 1982 single *Ballet Dance*. Promo for Toxic Shock 12" on Vindaloo Records (run by Robert Lloyd from the Nightingales) in 1984. Opposite: Tony Allen promo poster, 1984. Benjamin Zephaniah on the cover of *Traces* magazine, 1985. *Tropical Depression* zine by Annie Anxiety, (Xntrix Publishing,1984). **The Palais**, Nottingham, 27 October 1983. Courtesy of Alan Schofield.

TONY ALLEN'S 1984 'MEANING OF LIFE CRUSADE'

'GOD'S OWN HECKLER'

TRACES

40p

LEAVING NATO
INSIDE AFGHANISTAN

ATTILA

AFRICA
TRAVEL

A SUIVRE

A—Z
META MIX

BENJAMIN ZEPHANIAH

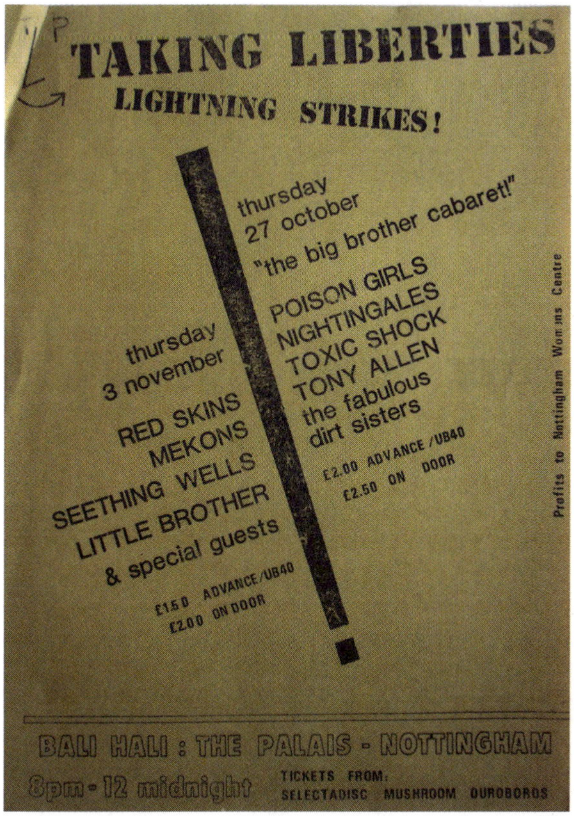

TAKING LIBERTIES

LIGHTNING STRIKES!

thursday
27 october
"the big brother cabaret!"

POISON GIRLS
NIGHTINGALES
TOXIC SHOCK
TONY ALLEN
the fabulous
dirt sisters

£2.00 ADVANCE /UB40
£2.50 ON DOOR

thursday
3 november

RED SKINS
MEKONS
SEETHING WELLS
LITTLE BROTHER
& special guests

£1.50 ADVANCE/UB40
£2.00 ON DOOR

Profits to Nottingham Women's Centre

BALI HALI : THE PALAIS - NOTTINGHAM
8pm - 12 midnight
TICKETS FROM:
SELECTADISC MUSHROOM OUROBOROS

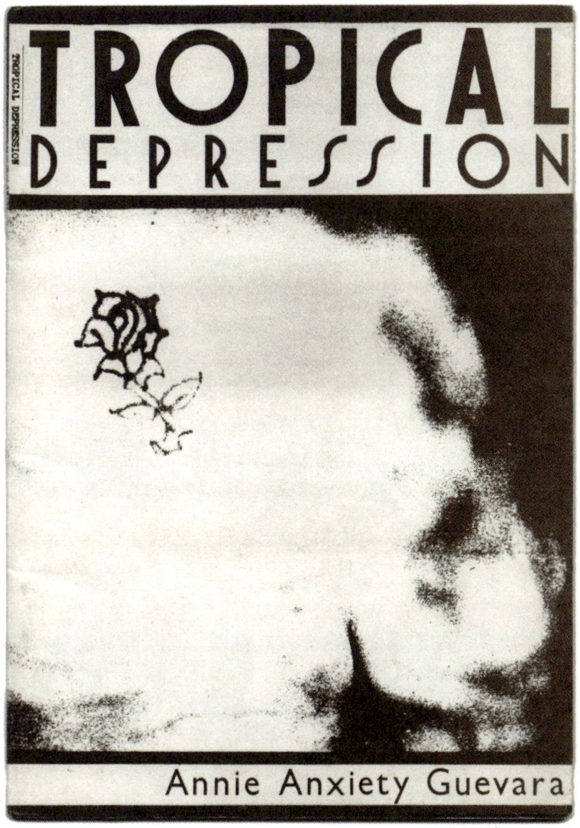

TROPICAL DEPRESSION

Annie Anxiety Guevara

217

The Mermaid, Birmingham, 27 December 1984. Photos by Ming de Nasty.

THE IMPOSSIBLE DREAM #3 1983
POSITIONS OF PRIVILEGE

The release of the third issue was timed to coincide with Poison Girls' acclaimed Big Brother tour, which began in the autumn of 1983. It was the most direct temporal tie-in between *The Impossible Dream* and Poison Girls' other activities.

The front cover design repeated the same stylised icon of Big Brother's face (inspired by George Orwell's dystopian classic *1984*) that was used to promote the tour. This image of the personification of absolute tyranny was immediately undermined by the inclusion of the bright red lipstick "kisses" that overlayed the tyrant's austere face. Absolute power was again being mocked in a response that counterposed humanity and affection—toxic masculinity undercut by feminine assertiveness.

The art of the interior pages illustrated discussions of the representation of male sexuality in American cinema, focusing on the personas of Audie Murphy and Elvis Presley amongst others, and the way that idealised, sexualised masculine behaviour is codified and made aspirational. That notion was transposed to a militarised setting in a two-page comic strip war story using a technique familiar to many Situationist publications produced before and since, *détournement*, which replaced the protagonists' original words with slogans and political statements that make their gung-ho heroism and moral justifications for war making look darkly absurd. The then-current USSR leader Brezhnev and his US contemporary Reagan are referenced directly to complete a critique of male militarism that connects to notions of predatory violence and control.

Two joyous exercises in *détournement* light-up the issue's centre spread and its back cover. That middle image rips the figure of Eve's partner in the Garden of Eden from Michelangelo's *The Creation of Adam* fresco painted on the ceiling of the Sistine Chapel. Rather than reaching for the hand of God, Adam is here preoccupied with a fly infestation and is threatening the insect intruders with an oversized flyswatter. In the background, a pollution-belching industrial vista fills the horizon, while in the foreground two young punks loiter. It's an image stripped of all religious connotations, with Adam dropped into to an uncomfortable contemporary landscape. It's an astonishing and—for those concerned by such things—a *heretical* image which works so well because it's so ridiculous a concept. The inclusion of the slogans 'Pleasure not shame' and 'Desire not jobs' added an affront to religious piety and a mocking anti-work ethic to the presentation.

The double-page war comic *détournement* "The Warrior—he's back" was an uncredited collaboration between Tony Allen and Domino. "Tony wrote the words and I did the artwork," Domino recalls. The back cover collage inserted British prime minister Thatcher into a scene from one of the Nazis' infamous Nuremberg rallies. "Well? You wanted full employment," runs the accusation, in a comedically large speech bubble.

These themes were reinforced by bold visual renderings of lyrics from the *Where's the Pleasure* album. An arresting visual of Vi sat naked in front a large mirror with another oval mirror clamped between her knees, captured in the middle of a silent yell, accompanies the poignant lament "I've Done It All Before." The words from "Tension" are rendered as a suitably fraught word picture, together with a powerful presentation of an early version of the lyrics to "White Cream Dream" (including an excoriating extra verse not used in the final version).

In another innovation it was revealed who had printed the issue: Words Illustrated, based in Thorpe Close in West London. Words Illustrated was the then-latest incarnation of a collectively run, community based printshop first established as Notting Hill Press Ltd during the political tumult of 1968. As the British Library's introduction to the archives of cofounder Beryl Foster explains: "It was the beginning of almost three decades of radical printing in North Kensington and, although the press would change hands and identities over the next decades, its output would remain a consistent and important resource for the neighbourhood until the late 1980s." Words Illustrated produced newsletters, pamphlets, reports, and leaflets for local campaigns and neighbourhood groups, reserving their Rotaprint offset litho for their most advanced and highest quality print work.

For the first time, credits and attribution were handled differently. Issue one had proudly stated that there was "no copyright" on any of the contents. Issue three changed approach, insisting that copyright in all of the material was held by "the writers and artists concerned."

THE IMPOSSIBLE DREAM

POISONGIRLS MAGAZINE

ARE YOU ONE OF THE LUCKY ONES

NO. 3

It is essential that the tree is planted
it is essential that the tree grow
it is essential that the tree be cut down
cut up, mashed up and pulverised to paper.

It is essential that energy be spent
to make paper and more paper
to carry paper and write on paper
to print on paper and sell paper.

These things are essential so that poetry
be appreciated, be criticised
be administered be examined in
be the subject of exams, the subject

of success, the subject of failure
the object of profit and loss
the object of money, the object
for which payment is made.

THE IMPOSSIBLE DREAM No. 3 1983. EDITING, DESIGN AND PHOTOMONTAGE - Lance d'Boyle * POISON GIRLS LYRICS -
Vi Subversa *   'REGARDING POETRY' - Janet Dubé * COMIC STRIP - Tony Allen and Domino * PHOTO - G. *

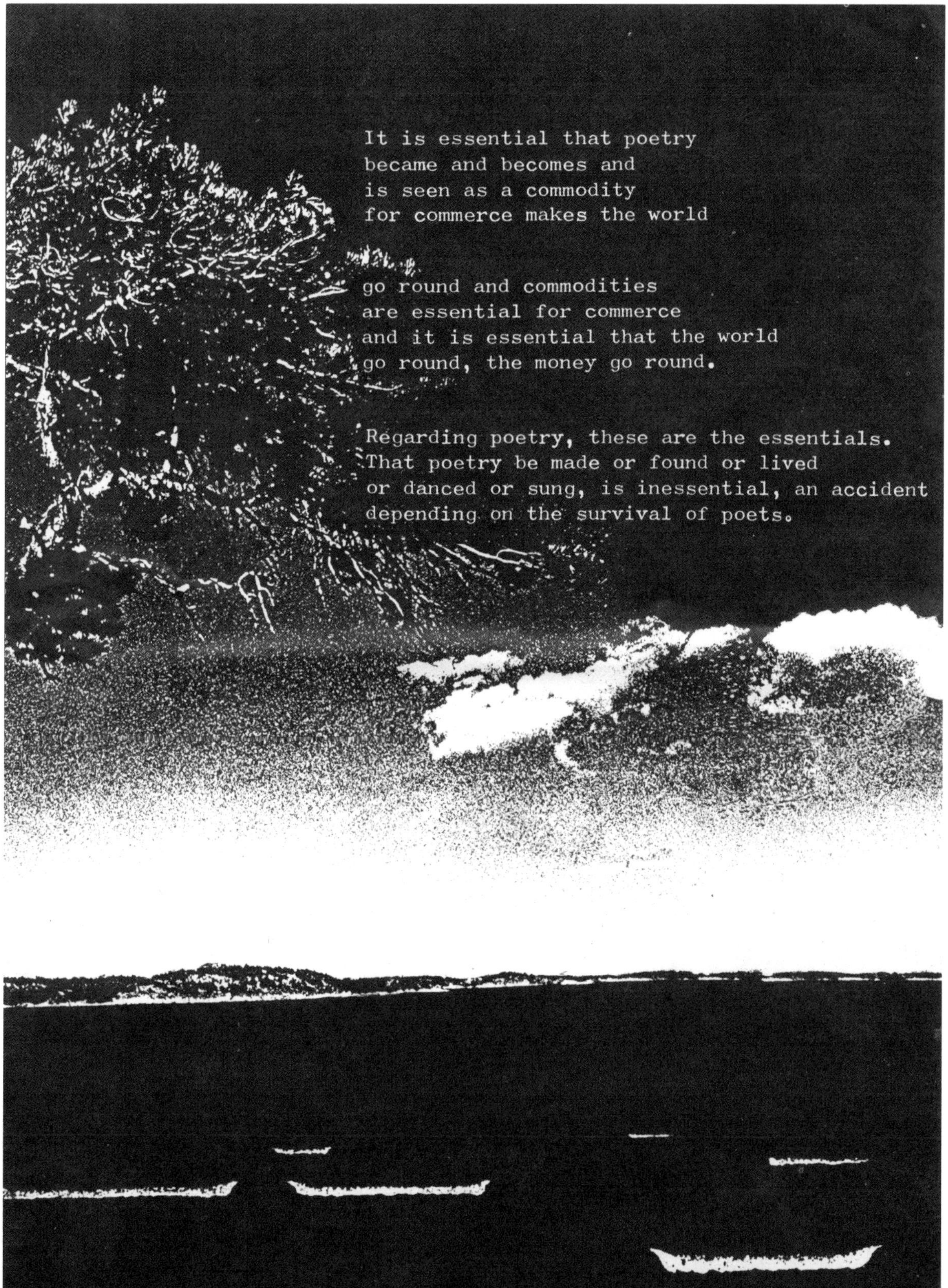

It is essential that poetry
became and becomes and
is seen as a commodity
for commerce makes the world

go round and commodities
are essential for commerce
and it is essential that the world
go round, the money go round.

Regarding poetry, these are the essentials.
That poetry be made or found or lived
or danced or sung, is inessential, an accident
depending on the survival of poets.

Printed by 'Words Illustrated', 1 Thorpe Close, London W10 Tel: 969 1586

I had my first love affair with a star of the silver screen when I was 14. His name was Audie Murphy. He was a young good looking clean cut cowboy. He was always on the side of the law and he always beat the dirty, vicious bad men to the draw. I can remember the moment I was hooked very vividly: The bad men bursting into the saloon where Audie was drinking his sarsaparilla, the full length shot of Audie drawing his gun from the holster, crouched, legs apart, ready for action in his white stetson, blue bandanna, blue shirt, shiny gunbelt and tight white pants. I was a push over. Whatever he did with his gun was O.K. with me. Someone like him had to be right.

Audie was handsome and good. He was the kind of man my mother would have liked me to be. Clean, lawabiding mild mannered, respectful to his elders and betters, kind and protective towards women. He obviously would consider sex only within the confines of marriage and family life. Conventions were never to be questioned or flaunted, only submitted to. He defended his way of life against the ugly and bad, outlaws, indians, mexicans and rebels, with style and confidence. He made lots of B movies and I saw all of them. I got a twin gunbelt and silver guns. We had a gang and had gunfights, died and killed spectacularly.

I was hungry for information about my hero. I found out that in real life Audie Murphy was the most highly decorated soldier of second world war. He had been awarded something like 9 purple hearts and numerous medals for bravery. Now a major event occured in our relationship. They made a film about Audie's life in World War 11. He played himself. He was still the good guy, in fact the goodest guy in the American Army, perhaps the whole war. The scene of the violence had changed from wild west prairie to modern battlefield. Much more close to home. The guns were bigger, the violence more varied and devastating, but inside the rugged uniform and the prick shaped helmet was Audie as handsome as ever. He was on our side, still defending our way of life.

The film left me with such a mixture of pleasure and anxiety that I was in a turmoil for weeks. When Audie was a cowboy, I wanted to be like him, I wanted to BE him. I could cope with the fantasy because there was no way I could actually be a cowboy- the Wild West was in the past. But becoming a soldier, that was possible. Friends of mine were joining the army. I could if I wanted to. But would I? Could I? The awnser was NO I couldn't. I knew I just couldn't face it. Not knowing any better, I interpreted this to mean weakness and cowardice. Well known qualities of outlaws and enemy soldiers. I looked around at my life as teaboy in a carfactory office, settled for what I was, buried my secrets and hated myself.

That is until ELVIS came along. Elvis was the sexual rebel. The dirty bad guy. The mechanic. The greasy kid whose weapon was his body. He obviously respected nothing and could and did have sex whenever he wanted. I fell for it again. This time more secretly because I knew I didn't feel about my body the way he felt about his. His reputation went round the typing pool like, well, wildfire. The junior clerk did imitations of his pelvic thrusts behind the filing cabinets while we all watched admiringly. Girls screamed at the cinema while I sat there silent and smart. My mates were equally disturbed and excited by him, but we never discussed it. Revealing the sources of our sexual identity to each other would have involved a level of intimacy, honesty and trust that we were not prepared to face or that we had any way to deal with. Our fantasies were to do with image and pretence. Some of us fancied ourselves with our good looks and knowledge of sex. The fact that this was a fantasy rather than a reality,   made it more necessary for the pretence to continue. Trying to be the teaboy Elvis was a bit of a joke. Girls didn't exactly fall into our arms, our eyes or our beds.

I was a little relieved but mostly disappointed when it became clear that something had happened to Elvis. His project had been changed, he was cleaned up. The bad boy became the good guy and, oh yes..................... he joined the army.

Audie and Elvis were on the same side, our side. They fought side by side, or their equivalents did, in Korea, Vietnam making the world safe for Cocoa Cola and Levi's. My unquestioning support for what the U.S. Army did in any part of the world was based on my experiences with them at the pictures. What they were doing had to be right. otherwise they wouldn't do it. If it wasn't morally right or cool and hip, they wouldn't be doing it. It took years of seeing contradictory evidence of the actual role of U.S. Army to convince me otherwise and I had help. Think of today's 14 yearolds watching Clint Eastwood progress from cowboy to G.I. to vigilante cop to superspy or Rocky Stallone go from boxer to vigilante and Mad Max I to Mad MaxII and imagine what they are being prepared for.

But that's another story......

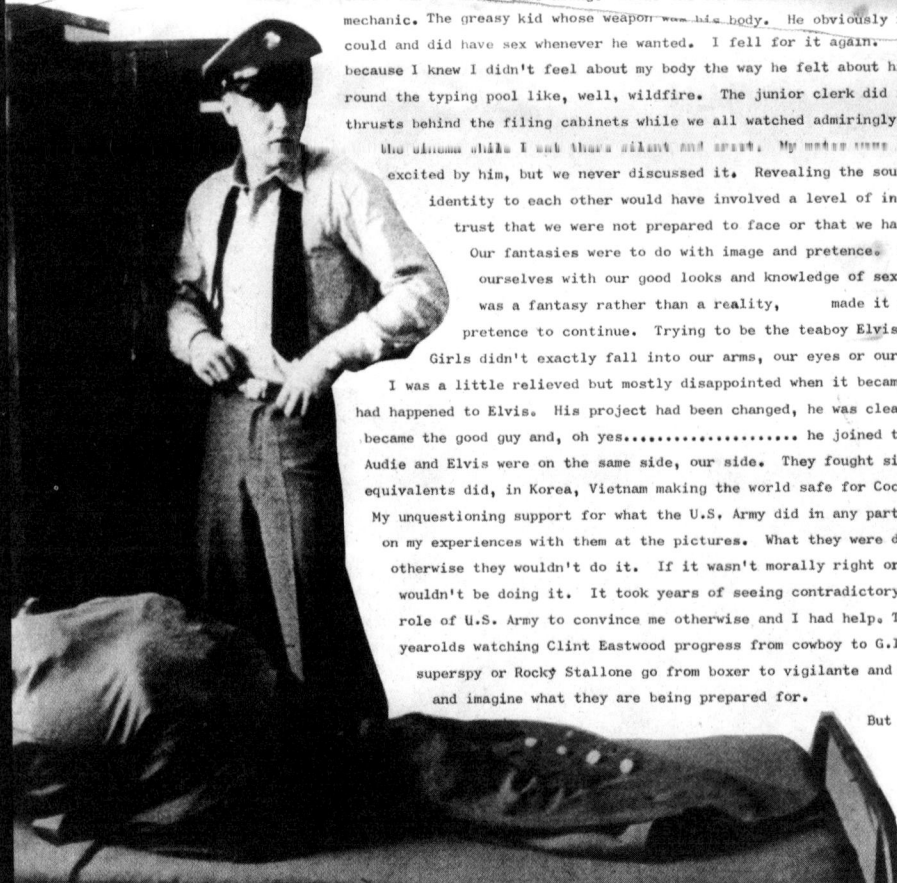

Better Dead than Green

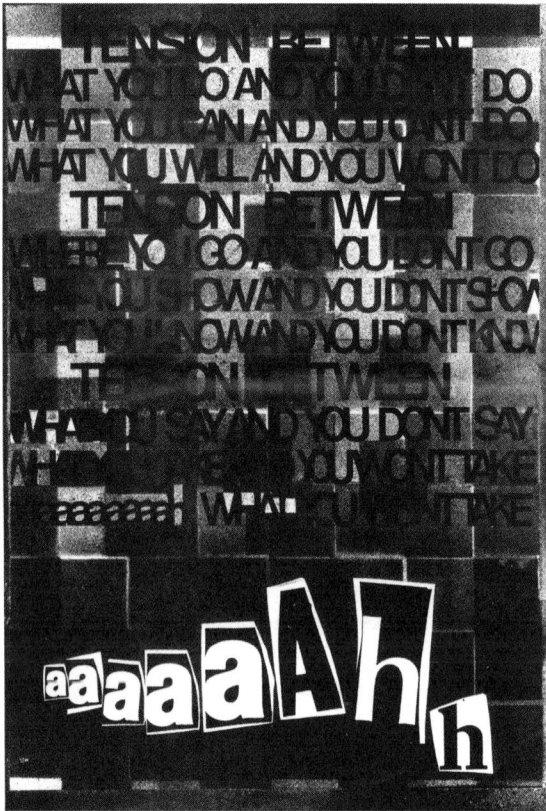

TENSION BETWEEN
WHAT YOU DO AND YOU DON'T DO
WHAT YOU CAN AND YOU CAN'T DO
WHAT YOU WILL AND YOU WON'T DO
TENSION BETWEEN
WHERE YOU GO AND YOU DON'T GO
WHAT YOU SHOW AND YOU DON'T SHOW
WHAT YOU KNOW AND YOU DON'T KNOW
TENSION BETWEEN
WHAT YOU SAY AND YOU DON'T SAY
WHAT YOU TAKE AND YOU WON'T TAKE
aaaaaah WHAT YOU WON'T TAKE

aaaaaAhh

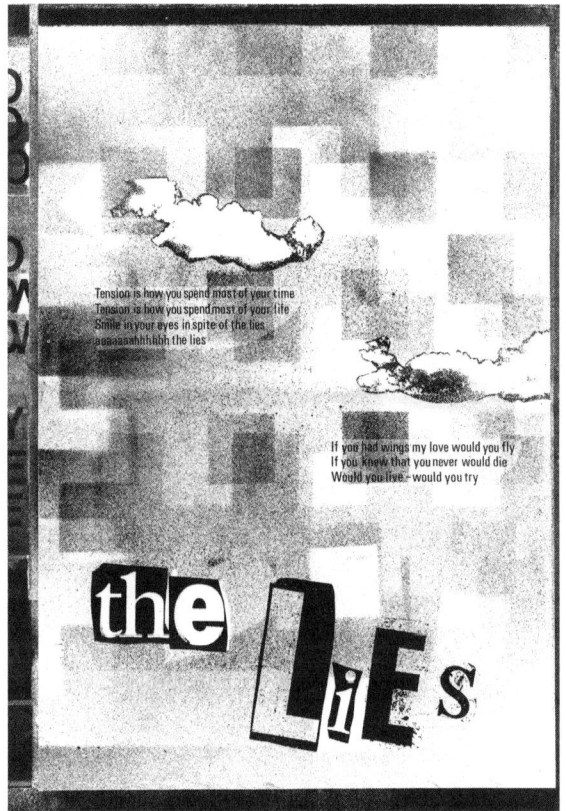

Tension is how you spend most of your time
Tension is how you spend most of your life
Smile in your eyes in spite of the lies
aaaaaaahhhhhh the lies

If you had wings my love would you fly
If you knew that you never would die
Would you live - would you try

the LiEs

PLEASURE NOT SHAME

DESIRES NOT JOBS

OH

MY HONKY WHITE ANGLOSAXON BEAUTY BOYS

YOU ARE SOAKED IN SYRUP LIKE A CHERRY

YOU LEAN AGAINST THE BAR CREAMING AND DREAMING AND THE CHOICEST FRUITS OF THE EARTH ARE ON A PLATE AT YOUR FEET. YOU CAN EAT BANANAS AND SCREW AND PLAY SPACE INVADERS WHENEVER YOU LIKE. AND THOUGH YOU ARE BORED TO DEATH YOU ARE PERMITTED TO WANK IN PUBLIC AS LONG AS YOU KEEP YOUR HANDS IN YOUR POCKETS. OH MY SPUNKY WHITE BEAUTYBOYS. YOU CAN CHEW AND WALLOW AND BITE AND SWALLOW ON GIANT PORNBURGER MANSIZE COWHIDE MEATDREAMS AND STAGGER HOME FLATTERED ON REAL ALE REAL MALE OH YES. THE ONLY SNAG, MY HUNKY PUNKY BOOTBOY BEAUTY BOYS ISWHENYOUHAVETO BE REAL SOLDIERS SQUARE YOUR SHOULDERS SO THAT YOU PAY FOR YOUR BANANAS. YOU PAY WITH YOUR LIVES MY BABY BOYS . YOU PAY WITH THE BLOOD OF YOUR LILLYWHITE LIVES. ITS THE ONLY SNAH IN THE PLAYTIME PLAYGROUND TOP OF THE POPS PARADE GROUND. REAL SOLDIERS. REAL BLOOD. REAL DEAD. OH YES. AND THOUGH YOU STAND IN THE DOLE QUEUE IN THE SHITPILE WITH THE DEAD WEIGHT OF THE QUEEN AND HER COCKTAIL TRAMPLING YOUR SHOULDERS, THOUGH YOU STAND IN THE SHITPILE WITH THE BOOTS OF THE RICH HEELING INTO YOUR MOUTHS, BLINDED BY THE FILTH AND FALLOUT FROM THE BOSSMOB ENTERPRISES INC. BELIEVE ME, BELOW YOU STAND YOUR MOTHERS AND YOUR WIVES AND DAUGHTERS, WHOSE MOUTHS ARE BRUISED BY YOUR HEELS, WHO CHOKE ON YOUR FILTH, FOR SUCH IS THE NATURE OF SHITPILES.

OH MY PACIFIST NEOCHRISTIAN LILLYWHITE BULLYBOYS WHO CANNOT STAND THE SIGHT OF BLOOD. YOU ARE DRENCHED IN THE BLOOD OF YOUR MOTHERS AND BROTHERS. YOU WERE BORN INTO A LUST OF VIOLENCE, PRIVILEDGE, RAMPAGE AND RAPE. YOUR LIPS WERE SUCKERED ON THE DARK TEAT OF PLUMMYMUMMY COALBLACK MAMMY AFRICA INDIA ARABIA EARTH MOTHERS BREAST . YOU SUCKED AND DRAINED THEM AGAIN AND AGAIN AND NOW ITS TIME FOR THE BRUSH OFF BIGBOYS. THEYRE ALL BUTTONING UP THEIR BLOUSES SONNY. NO MORE HONEY SONNY FOR YOURTUMMY SONNY. NO MORE HONEY MUMMY HONEY MUMMY. BRUSHOFF TIME FOR BABBYDADDY GRABBYDADDY. SUCKTHUMB. SUCKTHUMB. BEEBOPDALOOLA BABAMBAMBOOM.

OH MY WHITE DADDYTOY BABBYBOY OI OI BULLYBELLY. OH YOU ARE ALL YOU HAVE GOT OOOOH I BEG YOU TO WAKE FROM THE BAD DREAM WET DREAM CREAMBUN/FUNFAIR. GET YOUR FINGER OUT AND OPEN YOUR EYES. CLOSE THE SUNDAYPAPERS SOMEDAY RAPERS CLOSE THE DREAMRAGS. OPEN YOUR EYES AND EXAMINE YOUR HEARTS AND YOUR BLOOD SUPPLE. YOU WILL NEED THEM BOTH VERY SOON......

i've done it all before
it all be FORe

i've done it all before
losing my head, sharing my bed
love in the bath, love on the floor
i've done it all before

i've done it all before
sharing my head, losing my bed
love by routine, a matter of course
i've said it all before

it always happens again
no need to worry, no need to cry
another face, another time
it always happens again
another chance, another story
another dream to wake up from when we've had our time

but this is now love, it's you and me love
take it easy, let's take it slow
make it last, don't want to lose it
love will die, love will go
i've done it all before
but not with you

YOU

i've done it all before

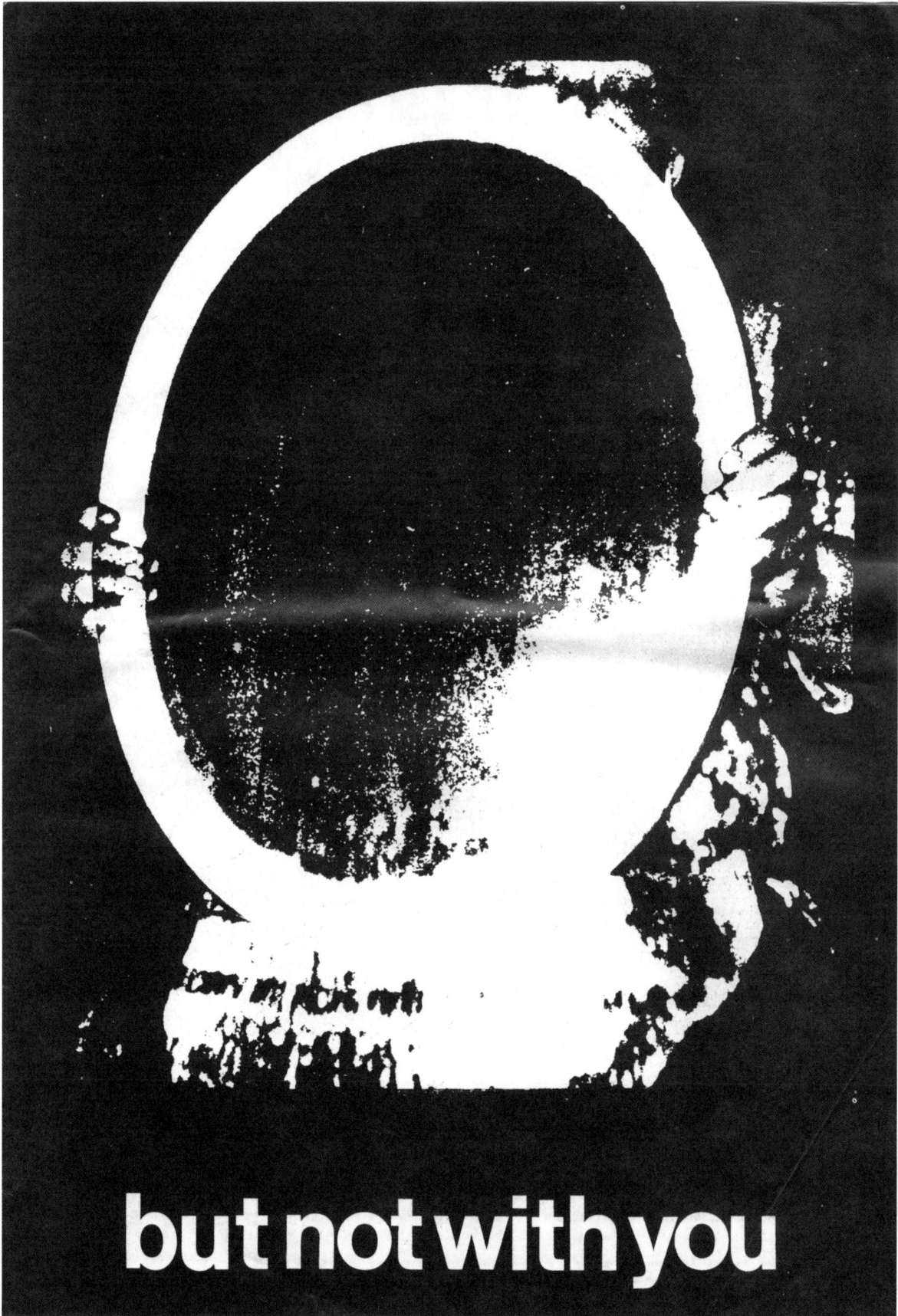

but not with you

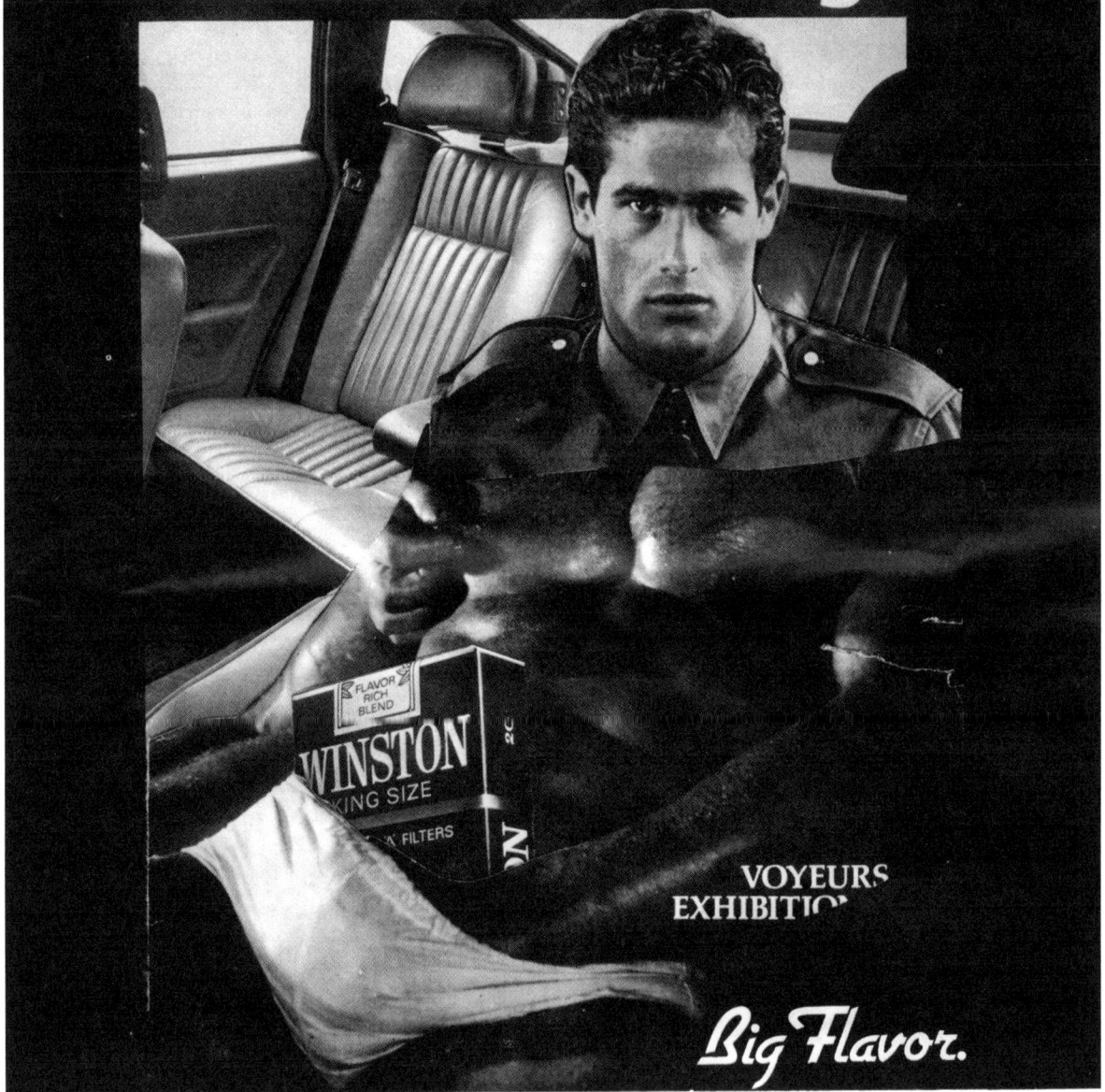

Positions of Privilege.

WINSTON
KING SIZE
FILTERS

VOYEURS
EXHIBITIO

Big Flavor.

IF UGLY BASTARDS LIKE REAGAN AND BREZHNEV CAN FUCK THE WORLD WHENEVER THEY WANT TO – THERES GOTTA BE A CHANCE FOR A GOOD LOOKING GUY LIKE HIM . . . . . .

PREACHING TO THE CONVERTED

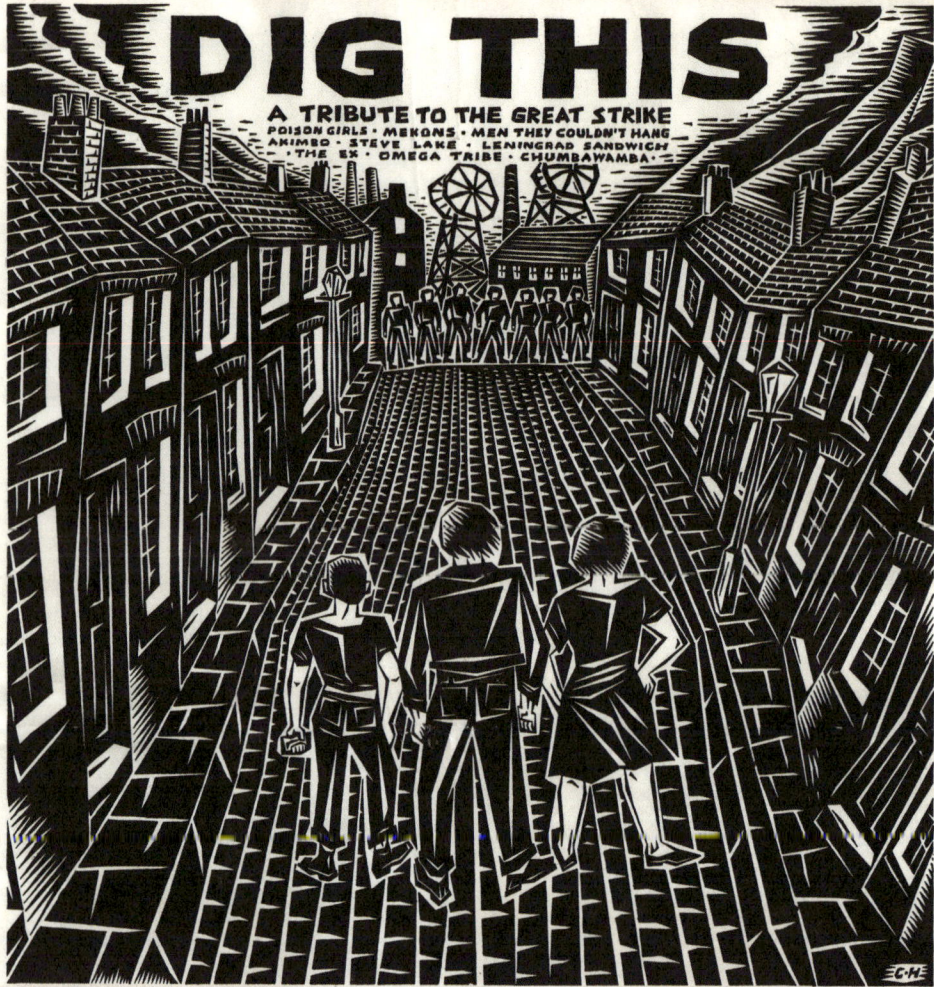

THE EX · **POISON GIRLS** · **STEVE LAKE** · **LENINGRAD SANDWICH**

OMEGA TRIBE · **CHUMBA WAMBA** · **AKIMBO** · **MEKONS**

DIG THIS

A TRIBUTE TO THE GREAT STRIKE

POISON GIRLS · MEKONS · MEN THEY COULDN'T HANG
AKIMBO · STEVE LAKE · LENINGRAD SANDWICH
· THE EX · OMEGA TRIBE · CHUMBAWAMBA ·

MEN THEY COULDN'T HANG

REMEMBER THE 640 VICTIMISED MINERS · **ALL PROCEEDS FROM THIS ALBUM GO TO MINERS SOLIDARITY FUND NATIONAL UNION OF MINERS**

ST. JAMES HOUSE · **VICAR LANE SHEFFIELD** · **S1 2EX**

6. THERE'S A RIOT IN MY MIND– BUT THE STREETS ARE QUIET

SONGS OF PRAISE/ THE PRICE OF BLOOD 1985

Returning to their outsider sensibilities, Poison Girls reassert their anarchist identity in musical and lyrical terms, a process reinforced by the aesthetic of Clifford Harper's graphics. The arrival of new members Max Vol on bass and Agent Orange on drums is confirmed during the recording of the band's final studio album. Celebrations for Vi's fiftieth birthday, and some high-profile gigs, lift the confidence of the band, as side projects and spin-offs expand in earnest. The band's final original twelve-inch EP shows that Poison Girls' sense of righteous anger at the injustices of the world is undimmed.

On 6 March 1984, the National Coal Board which ran the UK's nationalised coal mining industry, under instruction from the British Cabinet, announced a devastating pit closure programme that would begin with the shutting of twenty collieries and the loss of twenty thousand jobs (and hundreds of thousands more in supporting industries). For most of the pits on the target list, the loss of the local mine would lead to the economic evisceration of the local area as its main source of employment was ripped out.

Even when viewed through the absurd prism of free-market capitalist orthodoxy, the pit closure programme made no sense. But through the early 1980s, the Thatcher government had been building the momentum of a renewed class war against organised labour. The miners, who had humiliated previous Conservative governments in the 1970s through their collective industrial muscle, were now in their sights. That same month, a year-long strike began, during which striking miners confronted scabs and strikebreakers, battled with a newly militarised national police force, and mobilised whole communities and supporters to back the strikers, who had to survive more than twelve months without strike pay or state benefits. Amidst that effort, the work of the Women Against Pit Closures group, and the fight waged by "miners' wives" and the women of mining communities was unparalleled and, for many of the women involved, life changing.

For anarcho-punk bands, including Chumbawamba, Flux of Pink Indians, and many others, the social and political questions posed by the strike encouraged a shift in perspective, which saw the culture's strong individualist "antiwork" perspectives now challenged by the imperative to support strikers battling in collective defence of their livelihoods. Poison Girls shared the same rejectionist ideas about "wage slavery," but declared their support for the strike and for the men and women of the mining communities came without the need for political second-guessing.

Compared to previous Poison Girls albums, *Songs of Praise* proved to be a more complicated affair to complete, involving an extended relay of studio sessions and engineers. "We did change our rhythm section during the recordings, but there were no other 'outside' musicians involved this time—a big change from *Where's the Pleasure*," says Famous.

On 12 January 1984, Poison Girls began recording at Foel Studios in Welshpool. Subversa, Famous, d'Boyle and Ethics were joined by new bass player Martin Heath, who would also cover harmonica and steel guitar. Heath had previously played with London-based postpunk art rockers Angletrax, and had recorded with Howard Devoto (of Buzzcocks and Magazine fame). With Bernie Clarke brought in as producer once again, and Brian Foel covering engineering duties, good progress was being made

when the weather turned for the worse. Poison Girls found themselves snowed in at Welshpool, so extended their studio time until the weather eased on 2 February. Even by then, the album was only partly complete.

Rather than return to Welshpool, the band arranged further studio time back in London. A short session at Gooseberry Sound Studios, located in a cellar beneath a dentists' practice in Soho (a compact sound space which had been used by Tubeway Army, Peter and the Test Tube Babies, Killing Joke, and many others), was followed by time at Klockwork Studios, and a wrap-up session at the band's own Xntrix home studio, engineered by Fender. "'No More Lies' and 'Feeling the Pinch' were recorded in our cellar, on the four-track machine," says Famous.

In August 1984, Lance d'Boyle had reluctantly concluded that he could no longer commit to playing with the band, and would have to withdraw from their lineup. "During the mid-1980s I was preoccupied with the illness and death of my mum and dad," he recalled years later. "I went to live with my dad for about a year, and it became clear that I was seriously impeding the progress of the band." He had already recorded drums and percussion tracks for most of the songs on *Songs of Praise*. Despite the decision, d'Boyle would remain an integral member of the Poison Girls family, working on projects including *The Impossible Dream*. "I stayed in touch and carried on working with Xntrix Publishing," he explained, with his usual sense of self-deprecation. The Hippies Now Wear Black offered a more rounded assessment of d'Boyle's contribution to the band: "As one half of the band's rhythm section, Lance embraced the challenge of adjusting to the style and technique of a succession of bass players over the course of eight years, without diluting his own inimitable approach to the business of percussion. In the role of drummer, songwriter, lyricist, poet, artist, graphic designer, propagandist, publisher, and master of ceremonies he was indivisibly and indisputably Poison Girls."

Incoming drummer David Bennett (aka Agent Orange) took over drum duties in Poison Girls after leaving postpunk jazz-Dadaists The Cravats, a band he had joined in 1978. Although these Redditch-based rebels had got together a year earlier, it was with his arrival that "the really productive . . . lineup emerged," The Cravats confirmed later. Bennett played on all of their early singles, including the Crass Records classic seven-inch *Rub Me Out*, and both of the band's studio albums. By the time of the release of *The Colossal Tunes Out* in 1983, The Cravats "had already drifted apart," the band's official history acknowledges, "just at the time when arguably they were producing their best, most adventurous, accomplished material."

Looking for new opportunities with a band who played things differently, Bennett found a conducive new home on the drum stool for Poison Girls. Bennett was "a remarkable and hugely underrated musician, combining

Above: **Portland Ballroom**, Nottingham, miners' strike benefit, 23 November 1984. Below: **The Garage**, Nottingham, 12 December 1986. Page 229: **St James House**, Sheffield, miners' strike benefit in conjunction with release of benefit compilation LP *Dig This!*, 1985. Courtesy of Rich Cross.

the finesse and inventiveness of a jazz drummer with the power of a rock drummer," his former bandmates in The Cravats affirm.

Having joined Poison Girls, one of Bennett's first tasks was to provide the drum tracks for the two still-to-be-recorded tracks of *Songs of Praise*. The different textures and tempos of "Riot on My Mind" and "No More Lies" allowed him to demonstrate just how good a match he was for the evolving Poison Girls' sound.

"I had a great relationship with Dave," says bass player Mick Shenton (aka Max Volume, aka Max Vol). "He was lovely, and great to work with. He owned the biggest drum kit on the planet. It was a classic Ludwig in the largest size possible."

Prior to his departure, outgoing bassist Heath had recorded his tracks for eight of the ten songs. Shenton covered the outstanding bass work for "Riot" and "Feeling the Pinch."

"I saw an advert, I think it was in *Melody Maker*—it was fairly nondescript—a 'band looking for a bassist.'" he says. "I want to audition at their place in Leytonstone. I had been aware of a couple of tracks of theirs in the run-up to that. But above all I was struck by their personalities. They seemed to be generous people, as well as well informed. It was a real pleasure to meet them for the first time."

"We had never done *proper* auditions before and had four or five people round to try out," says Famous.

"They actually chose another bassist over me," Shenton recalls, "but that didn't work out, they didn't get on—so I was their choice number two, and that's how I got the job."

"That first choice was Brian," Famous adds "who did a great audition, but only lasted a couple of weeks and one disastrous gig before it was obvious to one and all that he wasn't right for us. Max Vol had spent his audition with his back to us all, which we found weird, but was a special bass player and, when we contacted him to have a second go, he leapt at the chance. That was our good fortune—and a cautionary lesson about the efficacy of the audition process."

Vol's musical background was in a different tradition to Poison Girls. "My musical knowledge of the punk scene at that time was pretty limited," he admits. "Punk was not really part of my personal musical vocabulary. I'd gone to the University of Warwick and hung out there for a couple of years after graduating. I'd hooked up with the remnants of The Selecter in Coventry, particularly the drummer Charley Aitch."

Politically speaking, Vol's sympathies were with the left. "I would never have considered myself to be an anarchist," he says. "I'd identify as a socialist—with communist leaning tendencies—but a socialist above all. It was only through their introduction to that world that I became familiar with some of the ideas." As well as re-cording bass for the new album, Vol was soon out on the road playing live.

Soon after taking on the role of live sound engineer, Tom Barwood was picking up the extra responsibilities that came from being appointed to the role of Poison Girls' tour manager. "That boils down to one particular moment in time when we were in an airport on tour in the United States," he explains. "Our lovely—but wholly incompetent—manager Martin Goldschmidt was asked to look after my bag for the ten minutes it took to re-arrange our flights out of Washington, DC, back to New York. He took his eyes off it, and the bag was gone. This was the start of the tour, and for the two weeks that we had in the States, I had no clothes," he grimaces. "That prompted me to take more of an interest."

It was in mid-January that Poison Girls returned to the US. The Stateside profile of the band had been boosted by a distribution deal agreed between Xntrix and CD Presents—the company set up the well-known "outsider-culture impresario" David Ferguson. Poison Girls were booked to play at the Counter-Inaugural Ball, a protest gig rallying opposition to the return to the White House of the neocon hawk Ronald Reagan following his reelection to the presidency the previous November. "That was an eye-opener," says Barwood. "It was fantastic getting to go to the States and meet some radicalised people. We were staying with the Yippies in Bleecker Street in New York City, and that was great." The show, a highlight in the continuing efforts of the punk-led "Rock Against Reagan" initiative, was held at the Warner Theatre in Washington, DC, on 20 January 1985, the day before the official inaugural ceremony would confirm Reagan's return to office. Reagan's second-term victory, coming a year after Thatcher's vindication at the 1983 British general election, reaffirmed the resurgence of the neoliberal, free-market, Cold War right on both sides of the Atlantic.

The event promised live sets by D.O.A., Beat the Naked, and "a surprise reggae band" as well as from Poison Girls. The gig was intended as a springboard for the following day's planned series of inauguration protests gathering in thirteen different US cities which, the organisers promised, would "offer a dramatic challenge to the right-wing, racist and sexist policies of the Reagan administration." Interestingly, an early foldout promotional poster, bundled into the radical Yippie-aligned *Overthrow* newspaper, announced that Crass would be making "their only US appearance" at the show—something that might conceivably have been agreed with Dial House before the band's disintegration in the summer of 1984, following their final live show in Aberdare in Wales on 11 July.

While Poison Girls secured several tours in the US, it was not a country in which the band felt particularly at home. "There's a clear distinction to make between

Vi, Max Vol, Agent Orange (Dave Bennett), Cynth, and Richard, 1986. Courtesy of Richard Famous.

the reception we had in Europe and that we had in the States," says bassist Vol. "As Richard always used to say, the fact that the country speaks English just puts you off guard because culturally it is so strangely different from anything in the UK."

"A lot of what I've seen has lived up to my stereotypical image of America, which is kind of brash and big," Agent Orange revealed in a rare interview. "But it's a beautiful country, no doubt about that, and although it's difficult, we've begun to make contacts with some very good people. We thought you were all going to be stereotypical Americans, but that's not so at all." The band's sense of being far from home when in the US was palpable.

"The European venues that we worked with involved people who were consciously on our wavelength. Whereas, for the Americans, punk seemed to be more of a fashion thing," says Vol. There were many "bizarre examples" of the "weird stuff" this brought to light, he says. "I remember doing a gig in Atlanta, where we were confronted by a whole bunch of skinheads who were Black. How does that even work?" Barwood recalls that same show at The Metroplex. "After the gig, we were

looking for a cab to get back to the hotel. These threatening guys arrived and demanded to know, 'Are you the anarchists?' What do you say to a question like that? This Asian cab driver, who was much smaller than these four big guys, had been reluctant to give us and our gear a lift. He clocked what was going on, told us all to get into his car, and just stared down these guys. He rescued us, completely," Barwood acknowledges. "I think we were sometimes unaware of the impact we were having on some of the people who *didn't agree* with our politics."

"There was another particularly ugly moment in Chicago," Vol adds. "We played this hideous club called The Limelight and, on the way out, got attacked by a bunch of thugs, the local fascist youth. It was just never a particularly happy time for us in the States. There was this degree of superficiality, as well as hostility that we encountered there," Vol continues. "I think we all felt it and suffered from it."

One reflection of that was an insincere pitch from within the music industry. "When we were in the US, we were taken under the wing of some big-ass industry agent—who had 'contacts' with Patti Smith, MC5, Frank Zappa, and more," remembers Famous. "She sat us down and told us straight faced, in the way only Americans can, that we were 'worth a million bucks.'" Predictably enough, nothing came of this exercise in flattery.

For Poison Girls, their appearance at the Counter-Inaugural Ball was the start of an intense twelve months of touring. "We then had a hugely busy year," Barwood confirms. "We went to Scandinavia at least twice, and round Europe at least three times, and then back to the States. I can't remember exactly how many gigs we did—something like 100 to 150 gigs, maybe? We were very busy and met some fantastic people. But we couldn't really have done much more than that given that it was not exactly bringing in a lot of money."

That level of activity meant that Barwood had to fully commit to the project. "I realised that I couldn't sustain my full-time job as a tech manager for the electronic music workshops," he says. "So I resigned from that, and cut my income by about two-thirds. On tour, we were all on about £15 a day, and that was it for everything."

As the band could not insist on a particular sound system specification when on tour, Barwood quickly learned to adapt and improvise. "We just worked with what was provided," he says. "Most times, we would have at least a basic PA rig to work with. That said, I think some of the most enjoyable gigs were the ones where I had to put it together from scratch. We did a fantastic gig at a place called the Ultra House in Stockholm. It was a squatted old police station in one of the suburbs, and they had hardly anything there PA-wise. It was very, very basic. Having got over my disbelief that there wasn't going to be any more equipment, we lashed together a sound rig for what was, for me, one of the most memorable gigs that I ever did with them. It was great."

Famous recalls that the experience of touring with the changed lineup confirmed that the new rhythm section "brought together the raw power of our early music with a really solid and funky sound." Poison Girls "were a great live act" in those years. "I think that the work that we did in this period cemented our reputation as a live band, and beyond the confines of the anarcho-punk scene," he says. "And we certainly didn't miss the threat of violence that pervaded a lot of those early gigs."

Songs of Praise was another unusual album title choice by the band—a phrase rife with religious (and specifically Christian) associations. The weekly Christian TV show *Songs of Praise* had become a staple of the BBC Sunday teatime television schedule following its launch in October 1961, filling the "God slot" with a mixture of hymns and religious readings, to become the televisual flagship for the conservative, traditional, hypocritical "family values" of the Church of England.

Punk band The Adicts had released a sixteen-song album of the same name back in 1982 on Fallout Records. In the years since the Poison Girls album was released, artists including A.C. Temple (1987), African Head Charge (1990), God Is My Co-Pilot (1991), Bully-rag (1998), The Golden Virgins (2004), Shame (2018) have all released albums or extended EPs of the same name. By comparison, it's a safe bet that there will only ever be one album with the title *Chappaquiddick Bridge*. "As I remember, we were throwing ideas about, and nothing was feeling right," says Famous. *Songs of Praise* was the only suggestion that stuck. "There was the reference to it in the lyrics of 'Desperate Days,' and we were obviously aware of the TV programme and what was almost sacrilegious in our adoption of the phrase. I agree that it is hardly an original idea. Maybe 'Real Woman' or 'Rockface'—now you're talking—would have been better! Anyway, it's too late to change it now."

Released on the Illuminated label in 1985. *Songs of Praise* announced, in the boldest of terms, a reassertion of Poison Girls' anarchist and outsider instincts. After the temporary foray into the mainstream, in the attempt to inject the subversive into the body politic of pop, the band's final studio album saw them reflecting anew on political and cultural questions in the unprepossessing context of unstoppable Thatcherism and the defeat of the national miners' strike. "The album was put together towards the end of the Thatcher era," Famous recalls. "We'd had quite a battering, politically. We'd been ground down. There was a sense that we—the opposition—had to take a different tack somehow, maybe reflect a bit more." The return to the band's anarchist roots was declared, loud and clear, in the adoption of artwork and design by the acclaimed and much-respected anarchist artist and designer Clifford Harper. Lyrically and musically the record once again saw the band breaking into new territory—blending rage and regret in equal quantities.

"I do like *Songs of Praise*, I'm very proud of it," Famous says. "I don't think we needed to just thrash everything out. I think the songs on that album are very good, and show us maturing as songwriters." *Trouser Press*, the self-styled "bible of alternative rock," declared the record's lyrics as "subtler and more intriguing" than those found on the band's previous releases, and concluded that the album's musical atmosphere landed it "somewhere between Marianne Faithfull, John Cale and Ian Dury."

The album opens with the sublime and sophisticated "Voodoo Pappadollar," a driving, pulsating number that's full of strange and alarming imagery and unsettling lyrical metaphors. Related in the first person, the song is full of references to what might be a battle with addiction, or disconnected frenzy, or a lament for a failed relationship, all mixed in with the evocation of a spellbinding 'voodoo' mojo. Musically, it's confirmation of the continuing evolution of Poison Girls' sound: a song replete with the signatures of dance rhythms and the beats of the pop mainstream. It's a notably upbeat opener for the album, and one of the record's more upbeat numbers

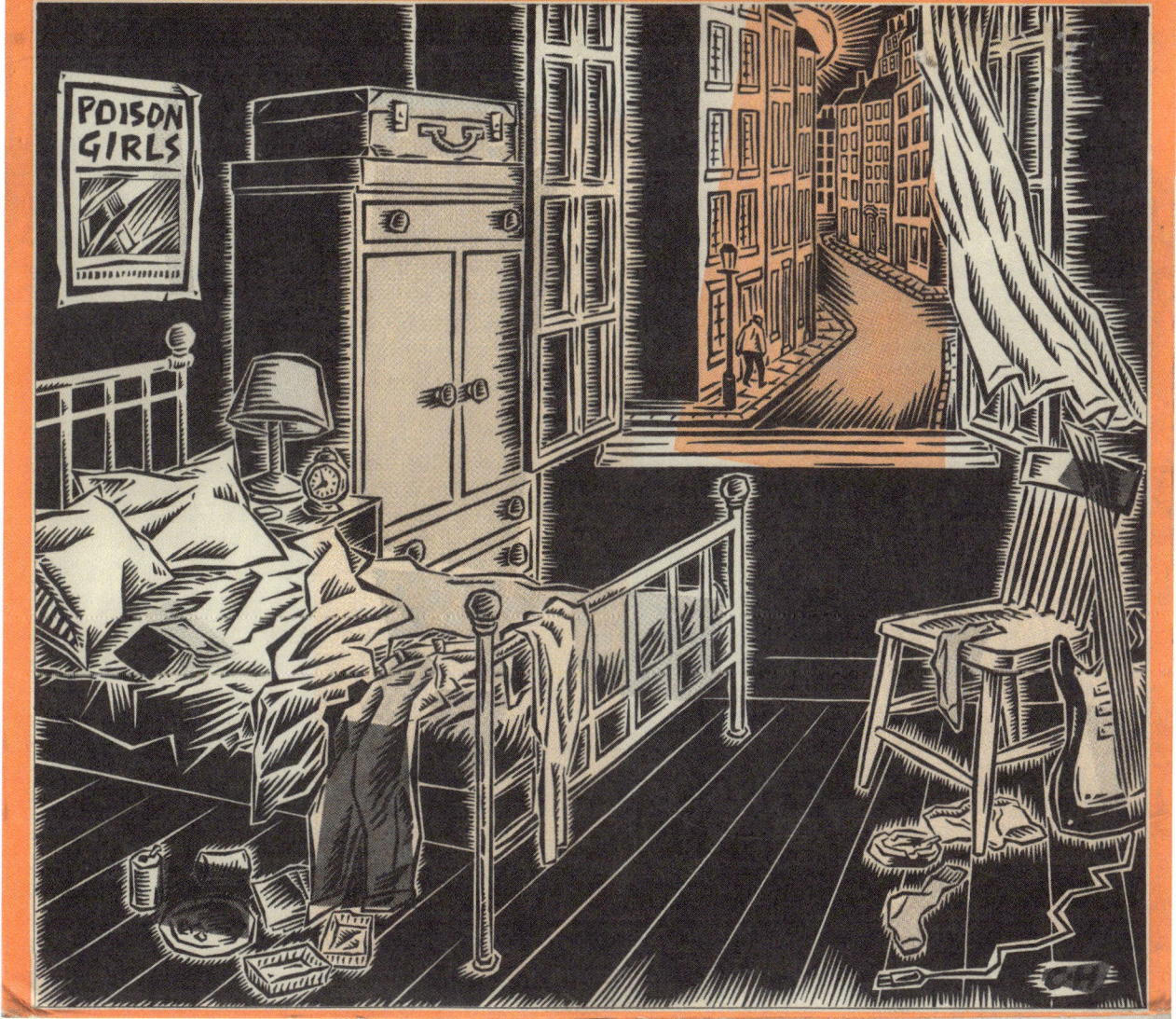

Songs of Praise, Xntrix Records, 1985. Cover by Clifford Harper.

musically; although that breezy tone contrasts sharply with the acerbic, scathing quality of Subversa's words.

Next track "Hot for Love" is a treatise on jealousy and betrayal in a relationship which breaks down when a third party gets involved. There's a strong implication that this is a song with a stronger than usual autobiographical component, as though Subversa is talking about the challenges of an upturned relationship within the band. There's regret in Subversa's words, but also a sense of disbelief at the lack of concern at the new lover's behaviour. It's even closer to the sound of disco than the album's opening track.

There's a return to wider political perspectives with third track, "Riot in My Mind." Lyrically, it's a perceptive evocation of an experience common to many of those identifying as rebels and revolutionaries: the disconnect between the sense of internal rage at the state of the world, and the lack of reaction and the passivity in the world. The running bass line drives the song, investing the song with an edgy, unnerving quality.

"Feeling the Pinch" is the first song on the album to directly address the contemporary issue of the national miners' strike. The oblique imagery of the lyrics pulls together real and metaphorical images from the tumult of the strike—picket lines and strikers and the array of enemy forces that they face (the boss class, strike breakers, and militarised might of the police and the court system). There's a rich sense of melancholy running through the song, which is something of a recurrent theme of the album.

"Desperate Days" is the inverse echo of the themes of "Riot in My Mind," a soulful sense of disbelief at the appalling state of the world and the longing for the resistance that could challenge that awful reality. It's a rolling, sad, soulful ballad which speaks to the desperation of the *chanteuse*.

The mood is immediately lifted with the opening track of side two: the riotous, righteous, uproarious "I'm Not a Real Woman." There's a wickedly humorous tone to Subversa's mocking deconstruction of the idea of proper womanhood. It's joyous and celebratory and defiant, and one of the standout tunes of this later period in Poison Girls' work.

"Too Close for Comfort" is an examination of the challenges of personal intimacy, when that romantic connection with someone else becomes unnerving, even though the embrace that it offers might be yearned for. Lyrically, this concern is mixed in with a wider antipatriarchal critique, in which personal experience is a microcosm for the oppressiveness of societal male power.

There's a thematic dichotomy to *Songs of Praise*, a blend of a retreat into personal reflections on relationship entanglements and the tightrope of intimate connections with others, and a sense that the forces of oppression are in a position where they have gained the upper hand, and the antioppressive forces of freedom are in retrenchment.

Continuing that strong sense of connection between different tracks on the album, "Rockface" is about the experience of being stripped of personal defences and of having no option but to cling on in fear of falling. It circles round to a plea for intimacy, an assertion of belief in the self, and an appeal for openness with others .

"No More Lies" is another lyrical mix of personal and the social, and is the most direct and didactic song on the album, with echoes of the repetitive refrains of "Dirty Work." It's another pulsating, high-energy track, which lets loose Subversa's vocal talents in terms of pitching, phrasing, highlighting, and investing her delivery with all kinds of emotional textures.

The album ends with "Too Proud," a more considered, quieter and reflective number, which again turns the focus inward as Subversa speaks directly to the listener. The lyrics are a personal *mea culpa*, acknowledging that pride can sometimes be an obstacle to making necessary changes or taking responsibility for your life. In the context of the religious overtones of the album's title, the lyrical refrain "just like water that's turned into wine" is especially intriguing. "Too Proud" is a song about resilience, humility, and the strength that comes from a willingness to learn and to adapt.

The album is wrapped up by a brief refrain of "State Control" from *Chappaquiddick Bridge*, this time performed on a banjo—giving it an extra edge of absurdity and incongruousness. Given the experiences the band had been through around the time of "One Good Reason" and "Happy Now," the song's observations on the cynicism of the music industry have added salience.

The sleeve of *Songs of Praise* was designed by the British anarchist illustrator Clifford Harper, whose signature narrative woodcut designs lit up countless anarchist posters, pamphlets, and book covers in the 1970s and 1980s. Harper had produced artwork for anarchist publishers including Cienfuegos Press and

The band according to anarchist illustrator Clifford Harper, 1985.

Freedom Press, and underground magazines such as *Undercurrents*, as well as for many mainstream UK newspapers. In 1987, Harper would publish the acclaimed *Anarchy: A Graphic Guide*, and remained the single most recognised illustrator of the British anarchist movement for many years thereafter.

Commissioning Harper to create the cover art for the album was a first for Poison Girls, and signalled the beginning of a short period of intense collaboration between the two. Choosing to align the band's visual presentation with Harper's work was in itself a public declaration of Poison Girls' reorientation towards anarchist culture.

As well as being a striking illustration, Harper's front cover design is also intriguing. The perspective is looking forward from the doorway of a bed sitting room and out into the street outside. A Poison Girls poster adorns the wall above the bed head. The bed is disordered, with detritus on the floor next to it, and clothes tumbled off the chair against which a guitar rests. A suitcase sits on top of the wardrobe. Outside the street is quiet and empty, aside from a single figure walking along the pavement and passing under the light of a lamppost. It's either sunrise or sunset, and the burst of sunlight through the curtains is rendered in a simple rectangular block of orange (the same colour as the image surround).

It's a very evocative, atmospheric image, and the sense of absence is captured so effectively, as there's no one in the room. It might be the image of a bedroom in Poison Girls' house, a crash space for gaps in the endless cycle of touring (the suitcase readily at hand). Is the person walking in the street the occupier of the bedroom? Are they fleeing their life or heading out in search of connection with others? It's all open to interpretation and, while it is rendered in the classic Harper over style, it's a less didactic image than many of his others. The back cover, which features head portraits of all five members of the band all crafted by Harper, extends the record's ambience of melancholy to include the personas of the band.

While the sleeve, and Harper's work on the follow-up twelve-inch *The Price of Grain*, resulted in some sublime art packaging for the band, neither commission was special for the prolific Harper, who when asked could not recall "anything significant or noteworthy about my making them." As he was handling multiple assignments for different clients at the time, the sleeves were for him "simply another job, which I had to do and do as well and as quickly as I could," he says.

Vi's fiftieth birthday gig flyers. **The Ritzy**, London. 19 June 1985. Courtesy of Ming de Nasty.

The Price of Grain promotional poster by Clifford Harper. Courtesy of Rich Cross.

In 1985, the band undertook "a massive tour of Europe and Scandinavia (Finland, Norway, Sweden, and Denmark for the first time)," as well as arranging two separate "mind-expanding landings in America." As part of a "summer of big festival gigs," Poison Girls played at the Glastonbury Festival, appearing on the 'Other Stage' as part of the Saturday lineup (Toxic Shock, who'd joined the band's Big Brother tour, played the same stage earlier in the day). Glastonbury was not a festival that the band felt naturally in tune with. "We always thought that the festival at Stone-

henge was a holiday for people who didn't have any money—that's what it felt like," Famous suggests. "Glastonbury was so different from that—even then—just so overpriced and commercial." On top of that, that year there had been "torrential rain nonstop for about three days" and when Poison Girls arrived "everyone was completely covered in mud head-to-toe. It was the year of the 'mud people.' It was very weird. But listening to ten thousand people singing happy birthday to Vi when we got on stage was an emotional experience."

The invitation to play Glastonbury was just one reflection of the rising reputation of the band. "There was a time, around 1985, when we seemed to become the 'flavour of the month.'" says Famous. "We did these big GLC festivals, we were on the front pages of magazines, we seemed to be everywhere, you know? That was always something we had tried to avoid. It was always a death knell to any band, to be the flavour of the month. It's great when it's happening, and then it suddenly all falls flat."

In May 1985, synth player and vocalist Cynth Ethics left the band, a few days short of the first anniversary of her joining. "She was very good to begin with, but she got a bit disruptive," Famous explains. Rather than a sacking or a resignation, the arrangement ended "with a mutual 'parting of the ways.'" Poison Girls reviewed their options and, despite accepting that having a second vocalist and a keyboard player gave the band more sound choices, decided not to hire a replacement. "It felt quite liberating to go back to being just four people again," Famous continues. "Every extra person that you had adds a level of complication to anything you do. It was more than welcome to get back to just four people."

After tours in Canada, America, and northern continental Europe, Poison Girls returned to the UK. Poison Girls were back in the business of handling their own business—including booking live shows. "We did, for a while, have a 'proper' agent," says Famous. "We did a couple of short tours that he organised, but they didn't feel right. I think we did still need some sense of connection with the people who were putting on the event rather than just being another act to fill an evening. In the UK especially we were always open to being approached by individuals and organisations that wanted us to play, even on a one-off basis. If we could string these together into a tour, then so much the better."

A gig to mark Vi Subversa's fiftieth birthday was held at The Ritzy club in Brixton, London on 19 June 1985. "If we see the Poison Girls project as an 'arc,' its apex—in the UK at least—was Vi's fiftieth birthday gig," Famous suggests. The show was designed to be a personal celebration for Subversa, a reaffirmation of the binds that held together the Poison Girls' tribe, and a reassertion of the band's defiance of rock and pop's expectations. "All of the bands playing will have worked with Vi & Co over the years," *Sounds* announced. "Entrance on the night will be £1 plus a present for Vi. Easy on the bubble bath and talcum powder please."

The evening brought together an extraordinary lineup of artists, musicians and performers who had connected with Poison Girls redoubtable frontwoman at some point in their creative lives over the previous decade. With Poison Girls headlining, the band were joined by Toxic Shock, Robert Lloyd (The Nightingales), Deb'bora (Akimbo), Lance d'Boyle playing alongside Gemma Sansom, Tony Allen, Mark Miwurdz, producer Bernie Clarke ("and friends"), Sirens, The Marvels, Lurca, and several others.

The make-up of the enthusiastic audience for this landmark gig affirmed the growing shift in those paying attention to Poison Girls. "There was definitely a change to the people that were coming to see us by this point," Famous says. "There were more women for a start, which pleased Vi to no end, and the more arty and less rowdy end of the punk spectrum. I think we were considered a bit passé for the more hard core punks that were left." It was a joyous night and, coming three months on from the end of the national miners' strike and amidst the newly accelerating nuclear arms race, was a brief respite and a recharge for those in the countercultural trenches.

"Honestly, the first thing that comes to mind is lots of anguish about what to wear!," says Toxic Shock's Heather Joyce. "There were some extremely drunken and raucous party antics that I'd rather not share. I remember thinking that Vi suddenly seemed much older. But once she was on stage she hauled out her reserves of laser-bright energy and all was well." For everyone backstage, it was inevitably a long night. "There was a lot of hanging around and of course absolutely everyone who had ever known her wanted to play," she says. "It must've been an absolute nightmare of an evening to organise. But it was wonderful!"

Nightingales frontman Robert Lloyd was eager to be part of the proceedings. "Toxic Shock did a couple of numbers on their own, but then they were my 'backing band' for want of a better way of putting it," he grins.

With the celebrations complete, Poison Girls were again reviewing their options. Following the end of their deal with Illuminated Records, the *Real Woman* single had been released on the band's own Xntrix label. A new contract was now agreed with Upright Records, a small punk, postpunk, and reggae label run by Bill Gilliam, who would go on to head up the UK operations for the Alternative Tentacles label and become the European manager for Dead Kennedys. The Upright label had already released vinyl by The Living Legends, Serious Drinking, The Higsons, and Benjamin Zephaniah amongst other artists. While Poison Girls would not felt out of place amidst such eclectic company, their relationship with Upright only lasted for a single release.

In August 1985, Poison Girls recorded four tracks for what became *The Price of Grain* twelve-inch EP at the studios of Brent Black Music Co-op (BBMC) in London. The BBMC had only opened the month before, after securing the necessary start-up funding. The Greater London Council (GLC) and Brent Council agreed to underwrite the capital's reggae artists by generating "employment, training and other opportunities for the community and its musicians." Poison Girls were amongst the first to make use of the new facilities. It would have escaped no one's attention that Poison Girls contained no Black musicians and were far from being a reggae band.

While Tom Barwood continued to be the band's live sound engineer, others took on the studio role. In the case of *The Price of Grain*, the record was engineered by Sid Bucknor (aka Norman Douglas Bucknor). Bucknor was a Jamaican born sound engineer, as well as a composer and a producer who, after moving to the UK in the mid-1970s, specialised in reggae, ska, and rocksteady, working at Island Studios amongst others and setting up the Third World, Jamaican and Tropical Records labels. The record was once again produced by Bernie Clarke, and managed under the umbrella of Forward Music.

The two tracks on Side A of *The Price of Grain* twelve-inch were direct responses to contemporary political issues that came to preoccupy the British counterculture in 1985 as the consequences of the defeat of the 1984–85 miners' strike continued to reverberate.

When the convoy of vehicles travelling to the long-established free festival at the prehistoric monument site at Stonehenge in Wiltshire was brutally attacked (in what became known as "The Battle of the Beanfield"), Poison Girls' sense of solidarity was instinctive and immediate.

The group penned a song, urging defiance in the face of the authorities' attempts to smother the annual countercultural gathering, and reaffirming the importance of the festival as a nonnegotiable free space. The band were once again asserting their affinity with the outsiders, the deviants and the nonconformists of the British cultural fringe—important allies to stand up with and on behalf of, but not an alliance likely to deliver radio play or to propel the band into the lower reaches of the pop charts.

Recruiting the talents of celebrated anarchist artist Clifford Harper (who would also design the sleeve of the miners' punk benefit album *Dig This!* on which Poison Girls would appear) the sleeve of the *Songs of Praise* album featured a signature 'woodcut' Harper design, shorn of any of the whimsy of *Are You Happy Now?*. Harper also supplied a similarly themed design for the band's final twelve-inch release *The Price of Grain*.

A new and deeply cynical form of 'charity' virtue signalling was on the rise in mainstream pop culture. This new ethos allowed megawealthy musicians to gain the kudos of being seen to 'raise money' for causes such as 'world hunger' through the auspices of televised festivals beginning with Live Aid. "Fucking Live Aid," Famous rages. "The old guard of pop and rock pretending to care. Sticking plaster politics, an event that raises money for a day—but where's the real change."

Organised by a group of musical celebrities, recruited by Bob Geldof (frontman of the pop-punk outfit The Boomtown Rats), Live Aid was a 'global' pop concert, held in venues across the northern, western world, and transmitted to millions of TV viewers across the planet. Its broadcast raised a vast amount of money, mainly in the form of countless small charitable donations made by concert viewers, all of it to be spent on 'tackling world hunger.' But in its determination 'not to be political,' Live Aid assiduously directed attention away from the causes of global inequality, ignoring the inexorable logic of international capitalist competition and the baleful history of imperialism and colonialism—to present poverty and hunger in the Global South as unfortunate events that were not the outcome of historical economic structures and present-day human agency. The Live Aid brand sought to misappropriate popular empathy with the plight of the world's hungry to promote the careers, reputations, and bankability of pop's then aristocracy eager to broadcast their selfless, moral motivations.

The rise of this new charitable ethos in the music business in the mid-1980s was itself confirmation of the impoverishment of protest culture, and its commodification by the controllers of that business.

Other bands in the anarcho-punk firmament targeted their ire at the hypocrisy and self-serving short-sightedness of 'charitable contributions.' On their well-received debut album *Strive to Survive Causing the Least Suffering Possible*, Flux of Pink Indians had torn into such practices in the song "Charity Hilarity." "The money we donate to charity is too small to be of real consequence, but large enough to ease our conscience," the lyrics accuse, before insisting: "Disease, poverty and famine need not to exist, because we let them, they continue to persist—there is enough for all of our need, but not for all of our greed." Chumbawamba had felt so aggrieved by the deception and cynicism of Live Aid that they replaced the entire track listing for their debut LP. "Despite having a big backlog of songs ready to record for this first album, all the lyrics were quickly rewritten and reworked in the light of the 'Live Aid' spectacle which took place a few weeks before recording began," the band explained later. One of a small number of what were effectively the 'concept albums' of anarcho-punk, alongside Crass's *Yes Sir, I Will* (1983) and Flux's *The Fucking Cunts Treat Us Like Pricks* (1984). Chumbawamba's excoriating *Pictures of Starving Children Sell Records* was issued on the band's Agit-Prop label in 1986.

Poison Girls' track "The Price of Grain" addressed many of the same issues, without name-checking Live Aid directly—attacking the moral nihilism of those with wealth and power; the indefensibility of the European Union's 'food mountains' (vast stockpiles of unused foodstuffs warehoused to protect quotas, shore up prices, and ensure profits); and the refusal to recognise the systems of economic exploitation that sustain global ruling-class privilege.

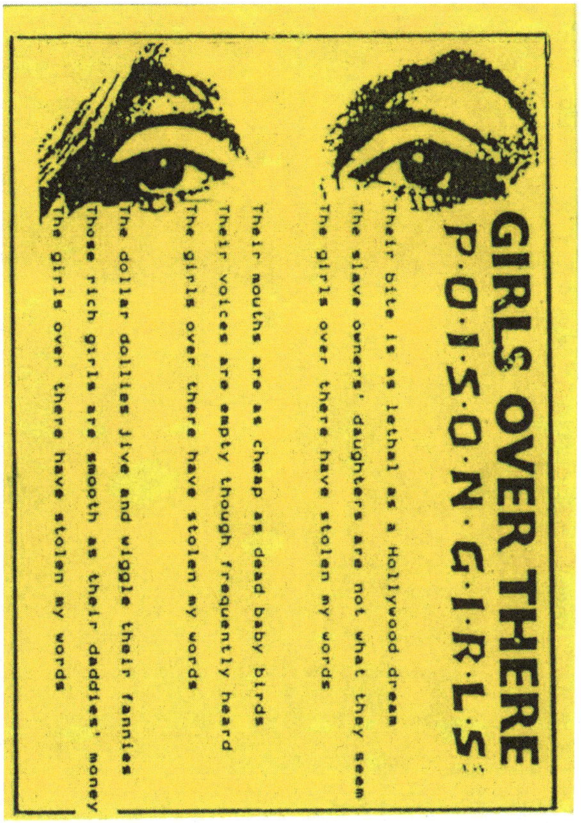

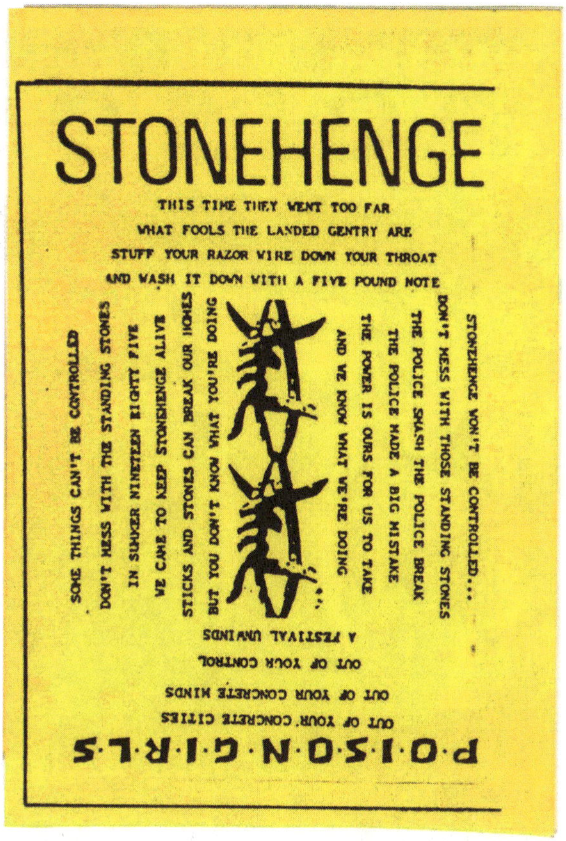

GIRLS OVER THERE
P·O·I·S·O·N·G·I·R·L·S

The girls over there have stolen my words
Those rich girls are smooth as their daddies' money
The dollar dollies jive and wiggle their fannies
The girls over there have stolen my words
Their voices are empty though frequently heard
Their mouths are as cheap as dead baby birds
The girls over there have stolen my words
The slave owners' daughters are not what they seem
Their bite is as lethal as a Hollywood dream
...The girls over there have seen

STONEHENGE

THIS TIME THEY WENT TOO FAR
WHAT FOOLS THE LANDED GENTRY ARE
STUFF YOUR RAZOR WIRE DOWN YOUR THROAT
AND WASH IT DOWN WITH A FIVE POUND NOTE

SOME THINGS CAN'T BE CONTROLLED
DON'T MESS WITH THE STANDING STONES
IN SUMMER NINETEEN EIGHTY FIVE
WE CAME TO KEEP STONEHENGE ALIVE
STICKS AND STONES CAN BREAK OUR HOMES
BUT YOU DON'T KNOW WHAT YOU'RE DOING

STONEHENGE WON'T BE CONTROLLED...
DON'T MESS WITH THOSE STANDING STONES
THE POLICE SMASH THE POLICE BREAK
THE POLICE MADE A BIG MISTAKE
THE POWER IS OURS FOR US TO TAKE
AND WE KNOW WHAT WE'RE DOING

A FESTIVAL UNWINDS
OUT OF YOUR CONTROL
OUT OF YOUR CONCRETE CITIES
OUT OF YOUR CONCRETE MINDS
P·O·I·S·O·N·G·I·R·L·S

POISON GIRLS
DEMONSTRATION

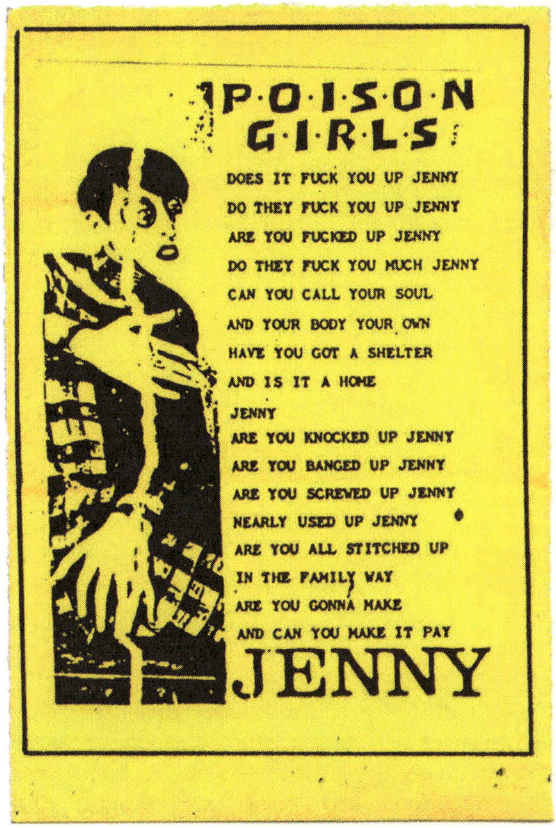

↑P·O·I·S·O·N G·I·R·L·S

DOES IT FUCK YOU UP JENNY
DO THEY FUCK YOU UP JENNY
ARE YOU FUCKED UP JENNY
DO THEY FUCK YOU MUCH JENNY
CAN YOU CALL YOUR SOUL
AND YOUR BODY YOUR OWN
HAVE YOU GOT A SHELTER
AND IS IT A HOME
JENNY
ARE YOU KNOCKED UP JENNY
ARE YOU BANGED UP JENNY
ARE YOU SCREWED UP JENNY
NEARLY USED UP JENNY
ARE YOU ALL STITCHED UP
IN THE FAMILY WAY
ARE YOU GONNA MAKE
AND CAN YOU MAKE IT PAY
JENNY

Stickers, 1985. *Demonstration* [bottom left sticker] was the proposed title for a new Poison Girls studio album that was never recorded. Courtesy of Tom Barwood.

245

Vi, Agent Orange, Richard, and Max Vol with hand-painted shirts.1985 promotional photo for US tour. Photographer unknown.

I asked the well-dressed Eurofarmer
Why do some grow fat
while others starve?
He said "Can't afford to send food to Ethiopia"
Be realistic—this ain't Utopia"
They're dumping potatoes
And burning grain
And pouring fresh milk down the drain
While rich young things
In brand new cars
Play fast and loose like superstars

The sound of *The Price of Grain* combines the feeling of lament and regret running through the tracks of *Songs of Praise* with a sense of controlled but indignant rage. Subversa's edgy vocal delivery is full of scorn and anger, and there's edge and drive in the song's simple but effective refrain.

The year 1985 was also a decisive, disastrous moment in the turbulent history of the Stonehenge Free Music Festival. Organisers of the festival at the site of the neolithic stone circle in Wiltshire had come under increasing pressure from English Heritage, the organ-isation which manages and controls access to the site, to cancel the annual event. Weeks prior to the summer solstice (21 June), the pivotal date in the free festival's calendar, additional restrictions, physical barriers and increased police harassment of those travelling towards the festival site had increased. In an ad hoc response, groups of vehicles had sought to evade police road-blocks and establish a festival site as close to the stones as possible.

But by June 1985, state authorities (fronted by English Heritage) had declared an outright ban on any festival encampment and the introduction of an exclusion zone designed to keep would-be attendees at a distance. Festival supporters insisted that the ban would be openly defied. Following the now familiar cat-and-mouse chase around the Wiltshire countryside, the main convoy of vehicles found themselves corralled and directed into a preselected location in an arable field. At this point, large numbers of tooled-up police officers launched a horrify-ing, violent, and intentionally destructive assault on the trapped convoy. Police smashed up vehicles (many of them people's homes), brutally attacked and injured hundreds of unarmed travellers, including many children, and arrested dozens on spurious and outrageous charges.

In both the mainstream media and the alternative press the attack quickly became referred to as "The Battle of the Beanfield" (simply out of journalistic recourse to alliterative headlines). This was extremely unfortunate, as it implied (as right-wing journalists, at least, fully intended) that a conflict had played out in which two sets of combatants had clashed, and for which culpability had to be shared. What had happened was that one group of assailants, the police, had singled out a group of victims, those travelling to the festival, to attack with impunity. There was no "battle" in the beanfield. There was a brutal, calculated assault carried out with weapons and prejudice by those with power and the immunity of the law and directed against those who had neither.

The Stonehenge Festival, and the community of travellers that were its long-standing supporters (of which the self-styled Peace Convoy were one component) attracted precious little support or empathy from mainstream liberal voices or from either the progressive or partyist left.

As those not in hospital or custody gathered at a makeshift rally point to tend to their wounds, begin repairs and comfort each other, support came from the alternative fringe and from those parts of the anarchist scene prepared to see travellers as part of the coalition of the unwilling. Given their own horrendous experiences at the Stonehenge Festival in 1980, when other festival goers sought to silence them and their supporters with violence, it would have been understandable had Poison Girls' reaction to the attack remained sympathetic but muted. But the band had not turned their back on the festival after that appalling experience. "The last time we played Stonehenge in 1984, just before it got closed down, was really good," Famous affirms.

"We knew the people who organised the Stonehenge festival," he continues. "I remember going to a meeting after 'The Battle of the Beanfield,' at which they were trying to organise things. And we said, 'well, what can we do?' And they said, 'Well, do what you do best—write a song.' So that's where the track 'Stonehenge 1985' came from. I mean, if we hadn't been asked to do it, I don't think we would have written a song quite so specific as that. But it felt very good to do it." The track delivered a full-throated and raucous denunciation of English Heritage and the police, and a passionate defence of the joyous outsider instincts of the festival. The song declared:

The landlords put the fences up a long time ago
They robbed us all as everybody knows
But some things can't be controlled
Don't mess with the standing stones

Stonehenge is alive and strong
It's ain't no ancient ruin

Don't mess with the standing stones
You don't know what you're doing

Out of your concrete cities,
    out of your concrete minds
Out of your control, a festival unwinds
But some things can't be controlled
Don't mess with the standing stones

In summer nineteen eighty-five
We came to keep Stonehenge alive
Stick and stones can break our homes
But they don't know what they're doing

A conscious reassertion of the band's affinities with the underground and the counterculture, "Stonehenge 1985" evoked the atmosphere of a swirling, stomping dance around a firepit out under the stars. It was an ambience enhanced by the spiralling strings of violinist Tymon Dogg (who also recorded a violin part for "The Price of Grain"). In the early 1970s, Dogg had busked with Joe Strummer, and later contributed to The Clash's *Sandinista!* album, joining Joe Strummer and The Mescaleros for a time, as well as enjoying a solo career. Each lilting, singalong verse ends with a moment of respite and anticipation before launching into a driving, riotous chorus—which speeds up as the song spins towards its end, and the imagined dancers collapse in a heap. Although it always made a brilliantly, boisterous number in any Poison Girls' set played in a club, a squat, or a community centre, "Stonehenge 1985" always felt like it was written as a song of the outdoors, of the open air.

The unconstrained rage and defiance of Side A of *The Price of Grain* is balanced by the acerbic, acidic tenor of the ballad of "Jenny" and the poignancy of "The Girls Over There." There is a potency and a power to the way the track "Jenny" unfolds, as Subversa poses questions directly to her titular subject and reflects on the costs of compromise and accommodation. There's a sharper sense of threat to "The Girls Over There," as Subversa turns again to the question of the utility—and the shortcomings—of sisterhood and of feminist politics as tools of analysis and action. Both songs have slower and more complex rhythmic patterns and richer musical textures, revealing their intentions with more of a confident swagger than an anguished shout.

The Price of Grain is another confident, self-assured vinyl release which showcases Poison Girls' evolving songwriting craft and the cohesion and craft that comes from the talented, and now locked in, rhythm section partnership of Max Vol and Agent Orange. It confirms the band's return to the proud outsider status with which they began. Posters to promote the release were printed by (and credited to) Aldgate Press, the anarchist print shop and workers' cooperative spun off from Freedom Press. The bristling agit-prop sensibilities of the record underscore the reality that the cultural ram-raid that Poison Girls first attempted with *One Good Reason* two years earlier has been abandoned. What was not apparent to anyone at the time, least of all the band, was that *The Price of Grain* would be Poison Girls' final original vinyl release.

It had been a demanding year for the band, which had seen them taking advantage of every opportunity to extend their reach and refine their musical identity—both on stage and in the studio. But the effort had taken its toll. Poison Girls acknowledged that they ended the year "exhausted and £5000 in debt!"

The Keep Lying, I Love It single grew out of the collaboration between Poison Girls and The Nightingales, who played many live shows together. "I always had this idea that we would make a record together," says Nightingales frontman Robert Lloyd of Subversa. "Nonetheless, I was quite surprised when I did suggest this to her, and her response straight away was, 'Yeah, let's do it.'"

"I always thought—and I'm not being falsely humble here—that I was a bit of a 'thickie,' really, and I didn't think I was clever enough to be embraced," says Lloyd. "But one of the many beauties of her nature was that sort of open heart and open mind. I just knew there was something very special about her."

"To be completely honest, I wasn't a big fan—and still am not a particularly big fan—of Poison Girls, the band. But I really loved Vi, and I loved her personality, and I loved the sound of her voice. That was the main thing that affected me. I just thought she sounded really good. I really like her singing."

The seven-inch vinyl was a one-off studio collaboration between members of Poison Girls, The Nightingales and Toxic Shock—who were joined by Birmingham based pianist and vocalist Cara Tivey (who would later work with Everything but the Girl and Billy Bragg) and drummer Ron Collins (who would go on to play with the Birmingham-based Noseflutes as well as with The Nightingales).

"I'd written 'Keep Lying, I Love It,' but I hadn't even got an idea for the other side. And, Vi said, 'Oh, me and Richard have got this song that Poison Girls have never got around to recording,' so we agreed to use that," Lloyd says. "Vi came up to Birmingham, stayed at my house for the night, and then we went into the studio the next day."

The 'A' and 'B' sides were recorded at the Zella studios in Birmingham in September 1985, and was engineered by Steve Harris (who would later work with U2, Natalie Imbruglia, Kula Shaker, and many others). Lead vocals were shared between Lloyd and Subversa, while Alice Marsh from Toxic Shock played bass and provided backing vocals.

The front sleeve design consisted of a single staged photo (taken by Anne Parouty) showing Subversa and Lloyd seated at a bistro or café table, awaiting their refreshments, and gazing at each other—seemingly approvingly. "We shot the cover in the cafe of Birmingham Art Gallery," he recalls. "Vi got dolled up in a frock and put her hair up, and with the sepia tone, we just looked like a posh couple having a date over high tea. The humour of that was really strong, I thought. Vi was obviously a very serious person, but was quite happy to take the piss out of herself, and so am I. Maybe that's why we got on—it's probably that more than the music, really!" With everyone's agreement, the finished seven-inch was issued on The Nightingales' Vindaloo Records label, with credit shared between Xntrix Music and Complete Music (previously Cherry Red Music).

"I don't remember any reviews or any radio play. I can't remember if it sold well or not, but certainly neither of us made a penny piece out of it. But I was just as pleased as punch, really," Lloyd beams. "It was one of those amazing moments. 'I've made a record with Vi Subversa,' you know!"

Subversa's fiftieth birthday celebrations could only be a time of reflection and of taking stock for the whole band, as Poison Girls considered their next moves. The release of *Keep Lying, I Love It* was just one of a series of spin-off and side projects that would involve different members of the band. Even as the momentum surrounding the band continued to push Poison Girls forward, new—parallel and competing—interests would begin to draw their energy and attention.

Top: Poison Girls on their US tour in Phoenix, Arizona, 1985. Bottom: Agent Orange (Dave Bennett), Vi, and Richard, somewhere in Scandinavia, 1985. Photos by Tom Barwood.

Vi's fiftieth Birthday, 19 June 1985, Ritzy, London. This page: Toxic Shock (Alice Marsh and Heather Joyce) with Robert Lloyd of The Nightingales. Vi and Gemma Sansom.

Top: Vi with Vi with Michael Coates and Adrian Grey-Turner, both old friends from The Dandies from the Brighton days. Below: The Marvels with Pete Fender on vocals and Daryl Hardcastle on the left. Photos by Ming de Nasty.

FORWARD MUSIC. 96 TAPES. WILF WALKER   present

P·O·I·S·O·N · G·I·R·L·S

the **EX** FROM HOLLAND   THE **NiGHTiNGALES**

BLYTH POWER

design by FANG

clarendon hotel
ballroom.
hammersmith
broadway w6.

Compere: TONY ALLEN.

POISON GIRLS NEW ALBUM SONGS OF PRAISE

friday 10th may
doors open 7·15
music starts 7·45
tickets: 2·20 concs./3·00
(PREMIER, L.T.B. ROUGH TRADE, CAGE (GREAT GEAR MARKET)

ROSTITUTES RIGHTS ORGANIS

• BENEFIT CONCERT •

ONDON's

POISON GIRLS.

Birmingham's

Nightingales

from HOLLAND

BUNKER

and if theres time, the local

GBH

THIS SATURDAY·· MAY 10·· DIGBETH CIVIC HALL ·£1·· 7

VANCE TICKETS FROM INFERNO RECORDS. DALE END.

Brambles Farm—

peace festival

torpedo town..... WATERLOOVILLE   HAMPSHIRE.

AUGUST 9th 10th 11th

bring tents and sleeping bags

admission
free

Kids
Shows

PEACE LIFE JUSTICE FREEDOM LOVE EQUALITY

STALLS
MUSIC
poetry
food
bands
theatre

camping starts on AUGUST 6th

· WITH ·   **POISON GIRLS** ·

ROY HARPER   DAVID EGGLETON ·
(The Mad Kiwi Ranter)

KANALL SYNDIKATET [from NORWAY] · · ·
Red Flag ·   WEDDING PRESENT ·   THE REDS ·

subhumans - new jazz aliens
- secret corners -

general belgrano · D.I.R.T. · ANTI-SECT ·
· dennis gould · fools of nature · THE BRAMBLES SHAMBLES
PRINCE BOOHOO & THE SMUTS · dog to dogma · the spell ·
· FREAK OUT ETHEL · THE POOR BACHELORS · TERRY SCHULMAN ·
ANOTHER GREEN WORLD · The Starlings · waldo carvajal ·
STEVE GINN · ALIBI · CIRCUS BONG · KAYAK ·
TASHKENT · Uncle Ian · the probes · Mike Hobson ·
· the sewers of oblivion · pish · DAMIEN BODEN ·
the rivers street band · & ? ∆∆ ? && ? ∆∆ ? & ·

· · Plus – ATTIC THEATRE – from Winchester
BRAMBLES FOR PEACE – TEL: torpedo town 252887.

NOT CANCELLED   Definitely Going Ahead

252

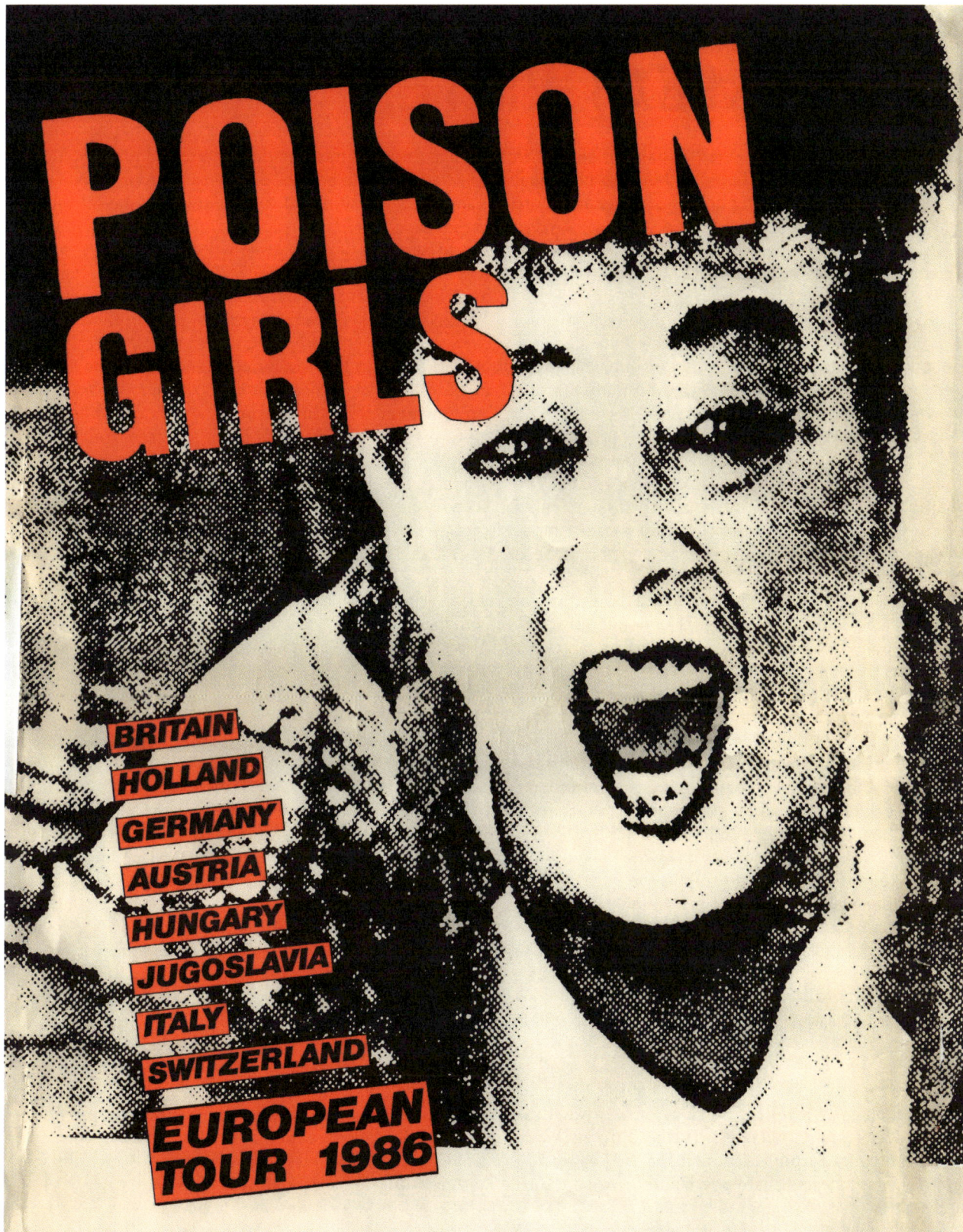

POISON GIRLS

BRITAIN
HOLLAND
GERMANY
AUSTRIA
HUNGARY
JUGOSLAVIA
ITALY
SWITZERLAND
EUROPEAN
TOUR 1986

Opposite: **Clarendon Hotel Ballroom,** London, 10 May 1985. **Brambles Farm Peace Festival**, Hampshire, 9–11 August 1985. The Peace Camp occupied the land for ten weeks before being evicted. **Digbeth Civic Hall,** Birmingham, 10 May 1986. Benefit for Prostitutes Rights Organisation. This page, 1986 European tour poster courtesy of Pete Fender and Gemma Sansom.

THE IMPOSSIBLE DREAM #4 1985
LET THEM EAT VINYL

Published in 1986, the fourth and final edition of *The Impossible Dream* showed d'Boyle extending his visual experiments with the construction of collages and more complex cases of *détournement*. Every bit as striking as the previous issues, it was though the issue which steered most closely in the direction of Gee Vaucher's own style of artistry.

By this point, d'Boyle had surrendered the drum stool in the Poison Girls lineup, but the magazine, together with the other activities of Xntrix Publishing, ensured his continuing connection with everything that the band was doing.

Work in the issue highlights the links between capital's focus on the acquisition of money and power and the deployment of military and economic leverage. The visual shorthand of the pyramid of power was a repeated motif in several visuals. The opposition to western imperialism manifest by Native peoples around the globe is explored in depth, a focus that echoed the band's growing hostility to the exploitative, ruinous activities of rapacious mining company Rio Tinto Zinc. Rendered across different high-concept images and visual set pieces is the refusal of commodity culture and the rejection of vacuous, conspicuous consumption.

The issue turns its thematic scrutiny to questions of consumerism, cultural imperialism, and structural racism—here presented as the manifestation of an unfortunate and all too "possible dream." A wider international focus is in evidence too, partly as a response to the worsening position in the nuclear Cold War standoff, and also in reaction to the emergence of the Live Aid charitable brand, linked to the ideas expressed in *The Price of Grain* vinyl, and presented in these pages through the "deification" of the figure of Bob Geldof of The Boomtown Rats and public figurehead of the Live Aid phenomenon. It's clear that the contents of each issue of *The Impossible Dream* were shaped in large part by the political concerns that d'Boyle was preoccupied by at the time of its production.

At the time that issue four was being put together, it clear that d'Boyle had immersed himself (or, more likely, reconnected with) the writings of two American authors, both staunch "outsiders" in their different ways: the radical feminist Andrea Dworkin and the Beat movement icon, satirist, and postmodern author William Burroughs.

While uncredited, d'Boyle also reproduces the work of prolific British travel writer Norman Lewis, drawing extensively on material he wrote about the pernicious work of Christian missionaries determined to "bring God" (in other words to enforce obedience to an imagined and exploitation-blind deity) to remote and "undiscovered" native peoples.

The words of those other writers dominate the textual elements of the issue: Lewis's reflections on the fate awaiting the Panare tribe he observed in Venezuela in 1983 (later published in *A Voyage by Dhow*); Burroughs's searing indictment of "junk culture" from *Naked Lunch*; and Dworkin's highly contentious analysis of the "nexus of sex and race" outlined in *Pornography: Men Possessing Women*. Poison Girls' words and political sentiments *are* present, but the band's ideas are decentred by the attention afforded to these other competing voices. It's arguable that the social and cultural analyses illustrated in the issue are less persuasive—and less tied to the perspectives of the band—as a result.

This time the artwork is credited to "Domino" as well as to Lance d'Boyle. Domino was the pseudonym used by Marie-Dominique Downs, an artist living and working in West London and "a respected artistic figure in her own right," Famous recalls. "She was a very striking person, and a well-known personality around the Notting Hill area."

"My friend Tony Allen was working with Poison Girls and he introduced me to Gary [Lance] in 1982," Domino recalls. "I was already embedded in the counterculture and left-wing politics, and I immediately felt at home in that milieu. I was working with printers and making zines and posters." Her affinity with Lance embraced both the personal and the creative. "Gary and I were on the same page with our artistic practises and swiftly began working together—as well as starting a relationship that lasted for about three years. I didn't live with the band but usually spent time with him at their house in Walthamstow at weekends. Gary and I discussed the overall themes of this issue and then worked on our images separately." Domino would go on to provide sleeve designs for Poison Girls' releases including *Happy Now*, *One Good Reason*, and *Seven Year Scratch*. "I was excited to be asked to do record covers for them and keen to do a good job," she says "In the end I produced a mixed bag."

The text in issue four of *The Impossible Dream* was provided by Vi Subversa, Dworkin, and Burroughs together with "anonymous journalists and copywriters" whose words were borrowed. Copyright was again asserted as belonging to the "artists and writers involved" although there was no indication on the page as to who printed the issue. "Issue four was printed with the help of Housmans bookshop, or through Freedom Press, if I remember correctly," Famous suggests.

While issue four signalled the end of *The Impossible Dream*, it's important to recognise that print was not the only medium outside music that interested d'Boyle—he was also an enthusiastic (if not exactly a prolific) film-maker. "He worked in 8mm film," recalls Pete Fender, "memorably producing a couple of short surrealist films with Mark Easton, Neil Mouat (Moet the Poet) and Lee Gibson, one of which involved stop-frame animation."

D'Boyle "understood the power of images more than anyone I had ever met," says Mark Easton, who collaborated with him on the 8mm film project *Do You Love Me?* in the early 1980s. The central theme of this work (subtitled *The Cult of Sex and Death*) was the representation of masculinity in advertising, "a subject which dominated much of his collage work too of course," says Fender.

"Although I had more technical knowledge of film-making it was Gary [Lance] who really directed the film," Easton explains. "For some of the film he suggested we refilm adverts off the TV screen with the Super-8 camera, I would get it processed then cycle the twelve miles to Poison Girls house in Leytonstone where we would watch the rushes," he adds. "Weeks later I would cycle back and he would settle us down with cups of tea and then explain what he had found through viewing the material."

"The film was a journey for me into exploring what it was to be a man, he helped me understand sexual politics and was always mentioning people or movements I should look up," he says. "But just as much he taught me to laugh at myself and others, he was never too serious, always demanding that things be looked at with stunning clarity, never accepting what they tell you is true."

Do You Love Me? became a labour of love for the pair, although few people got the opportunity to see the completed work. "In the end the film took seven years to make and only lasted fifteen minutes," says Easton. "I remember it being shown at CopyArt, a community arts project in London's Kings Cross, to a good crowd, but this was before the internet and it never found an audience."

Even in the realm of political action, d'Boyle preferred the ridiculous, the absurd, and the impractical over the doctrinaire or the formulaic. The abortive efforts of his troupe of "Kamikaze Kultural Warriors" to close down the operation of all record stores on London's Oxford Street (during the pre-Xmas rush) through the deployment of stink bombs gives a "whiff" of his self-mocking Situationist style. That contrast between such "childish pranks" and the seriousness and sophistication of Lance's own political worldview was, of course, another exercise in deliberate Dadaist misdirection.

There were moments when the desire to provoke a reaction could end up with unintended consequences. "One of Lance's other pranks was to publicise the entirely fictitious single 'Michael Jackson's Brain Is Missing.'" Famous recalls. "We needed a band name that was as controversial in Britain as 'Dead Kennedys' was in the US, and plumped for 'Thatcher's Cunt.' It soon misfired as Rough Trade distribution promoted the nonexistent single, got a shed load of orders, and then were less than impressed—in fact *furious* with us—that it did not exist."

"His flights of fancy—his impossible dreams—seemed at times if not absurd then just plain weird," Famous suggests. "But when they came to fruition, it proved what a special take on reality he had."

THE ImPOSSIBLE dREAM

Way In

POISON GIRLS

MAGAZINE

NUMBER

4

THE BEST

REMEMBER·WHEN·CIGARETTES·WERE·ONLY·KING SIZE

JUNK
JUNK

JUNK.
is the ideal
product · the
ultimate
merchandise. No
sales talk necessary.
The client will crawl
through a sewer and beg to
buy . . . . The junk merchant
does not sell his product to the
consumer, he sells the consumer to
his product. He does not improve and
simplify his merchandise. He degrades
and simplifies the client.

The possible dream.

The Panare

were good examples of a people described as incredibly impervious to Western influence,

A long ancestry of nomadism had shaped them, and by comparison their nearest white neighbours, who spent their lives on horseback or in cars, seemed awkwardly put together, a little misshapen even, and inclined to fat. The Panare could run and walk 50 miles a day across the savannah if put to it,

The Indians' physique was superior to that of the local whites, and now it seemed likely that they enjoyed better health in general. A number of families had produced six or more children, all of whom seemed lively and intelligent.

The Panare claim that before introduced diseases such as influenza, measles and malaria took their toll, they suffered from no illnesses at all. Their mental health appeared equally robust. The close-knit communal life of the Panare protects them from most of the pressures familiar in our society, and the crime-rate is nil.

In Guanama their round-houses were masterpieces of stone-age architecture, built for all weather. Only one thing seemed out of place in this calm and confiding atmosphere – the new barbed-wire fence.

New Tribes Mission had moved in. Members of this organisation are the standard-bearers in Venezuela of the new computerised, airborne evangelism that insists not only on conversion, but on the demolition of all those ceremonies and beliefs by which an indigenous culture is defined.

Evangelists rush to cover the unclothed human form, and the spectacle of Indians dressed in shapeless and often grubby Western cast-offs is frequently a glum reminder of their presence. Apart from the barbed-wire fence Guanama was free from the ugliness too often associated with the disruption of belief.

From time to time *Brown Gold*, house magazine of the New Tribes Mission, prints a jubilant notice of a tribe that has been persuaded to change loincloths for trousers, "The first time we entered the village they were wearing loincloths and very primitive

"See how they have grown in the LORD"

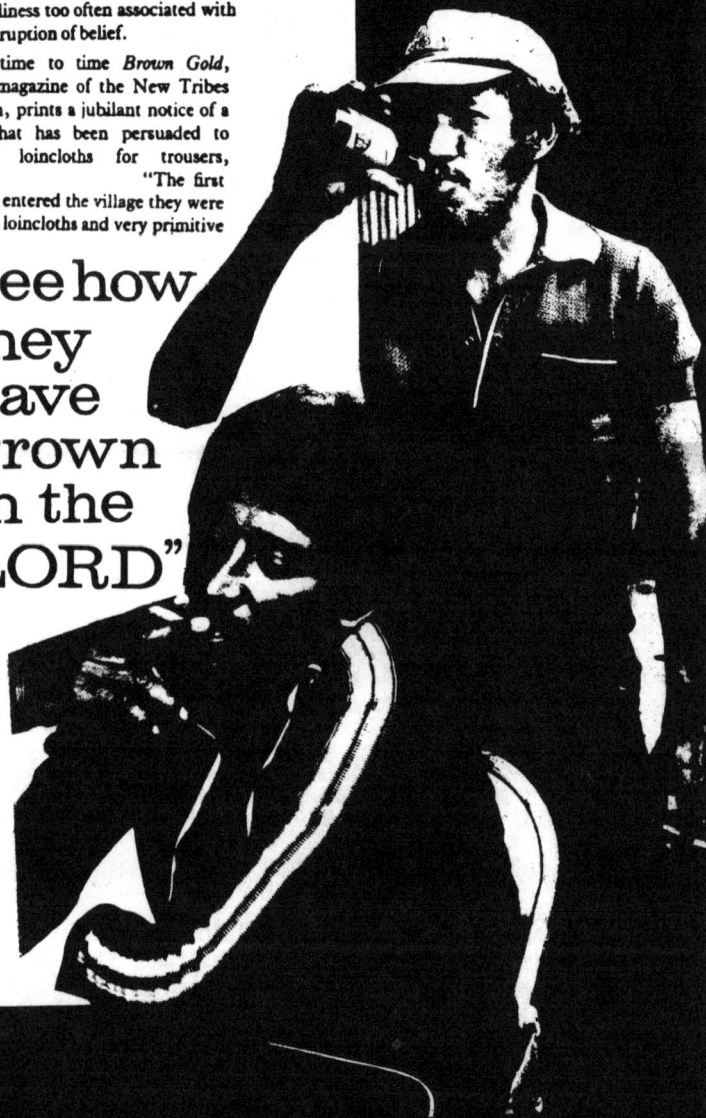

The Pyramid

of junk, one level eating the level below (it is no
accident that junk higher -ups are always fat and
the addict in the street is always thin)
right up to the top or tops since there
are many junk pyramids feeding
on peoples of the world and all
built on basic principles of
monopoly:

1—Never give anything away
for nothing. 2—Never give
more than you have to give
(always catch the buyer
hungry and always make him wait).

3—Always take every thing back if you possibly can.

The Pusher always gets it all back. The addict needs more and more junk to maintain a human form .

WE NEED
YOUR COUNTRY

The New Tribes Mission, now continuing its implacable advance in those parts of the world where "uncontacted" tribal people remain to be swept into the evangelical net, was founded in 1941 in El Chico, California, and now has some 1500 missionaries working with 125 tribes in 16 countries. In South America, which it has divided up with its missionary rival, the Summer Institute of Linguistics, and where it is represented in Venezuela, Bolivia, Brazil and Paraguay, it has rolled over the Catholic opposition. The Catholic Fathers, sometimes reproaching their flock with desertion, are discouraged by the reply, "You have no aeroplanes. You are not in touch with God by radio."

Mission finances, according to its prospectus, depend upon public donations. These do not necessarily take the form of cash. Survival International (1980) reports an offering of 2500 hectares of land by ⟫⟫→ the Government of Paraguay, and in 1975 a missionary spoke to me of "a heck of a piece of land given to the Mission by a company in the Paraguayan Gran Chaco engaged in the extraction of tannin.

Military dictatorships are the natural supporters of the New Tribes Mission, with whom they share similar views.

It was useful for Indians in remote jungle areas to be under the control of people who were so far politically to the right that they classified all their opponents, archaeologists, journalists, army officers, the Apostolic Vicar of Puerto Ayacucho alike, as communists,

The Mission does not hold itself aloof from engaging in commerce, acting frequently as middleman in the supply of goods to the Indians or the resale of their artefacts. Survival International mentions that they are in the fur trade in Paraguay, dealing in jaguar skins which fetch high prices since the jaguar elsewhere is an internationally protected animal.

Impressive technical equipment and abundant funds give the New Tribes Mission more than a head start in the race for souls.

Naval Captain Marino Blanco, charged with keeping an eye on the doings of foreigners in the country's remote regions, spoke of scientific espionage. He noted that the missionaries inevitably installed themselves in areas known to contain strategic minerals such as cobalt and uranium, and claimed to have proved that they were in the pay of American multinationals, naming two of them as Westinghouse and General Dynamics. He noted that the Mission had been in trouble in Colombia, suffering expulsion for "damage to national interests and for having assisted illicit explorations carried out by transnational companies in areas likely to contain deposits of strategic materials". The captain had found missionary baggage labelled "combustible materials" to contain military uniforms and "other articles" – this being taken by the press to refer to geiger counters. The uniforms were explained away by the missionaries as intended to impress the Indians. Captain Blanco said that the head of the New Tribes Mission had tried to bribe him. He gave his opinion that the missionaries' involvement with the Indians was only a cover for their other activities.

Shortly afterwards, pressure had been brought to bear resulting in Blanco's dismissal from the service.

The Mission proclaims with fervour and enthusiasm the imminent Second Coming of Christ and the destruction of this world, and its doctrinal statement includes the belief in the "unending punishment of the unsaved", thus committing to the flames of Hell all adherents of Judaism, Hinduism, Buddhism and Islam, besides several thousand minor religious faiths and all the great and good men of all races whose misfortune it was to be born before the coming of Christ.

Two thousand tribes remain to be contacted, all of them under a threat of everlasting fire, so conversion is a task of utmost urgency. It is this sense of time being so short that tends to outweigh all considerations of the convert's welfare in this life, provided that his soul is saved for eternity. "He saves the souls of men," runs the New Tribes Mission doctrine, "not that they might continue to live in the world, but that they might live forever with Him, in the world to come."

Here is a missionary speaking: "We leave gifts . . . knives, axes, mirrors, the kind of things Indians can't resist . . . After a while the relationship develops. We have to break their dependence on us next. Naturally they want to go on receiving all these desirable things we've been giving them, and sometimes it comes as a surprise when we explain that from now on if they want to possess them they must work for money . . . We can usually fix them up with something on the local farms. They settle down to it when they realise that there's no going back."

The manoeuvre never fails to work, accomplishing in the end the inevitable tragic result. There's no going back. The trap baited with the fatal gifts is sprung and conversion follows with its long catalogue of prohibitions. The evangelised Indian is forbidden to drink, sing, dance, wear traditional ornaments, paint his body, take part in any of the old ceremonies, marry a non-believing wife. A stern and pleasure-hating deity speaking through the missionary's mouth lists his embargoes, backed by awful descriptions of the lake brimming with fire and brimstone. Too often, "something on the local farms", whose owners may themselves be close to the poverty line, is hardly distinguishable from slavery, and in the end the detribalised Indian drifts away to his last refuge, the slums of a town where his wife's prostitution provides the money to buy rum and oblivion.

there's no going back

In the words of total need: "*Wouldn't you?*" Yes you would. You would lie, cheat, inform on your friends, steal, do *anything* to satisfy total need.

FOR U

THE IMPOSSIBLE DREAM #4 1986. Do You Know Your Junk? Edited and Designed by Laura Boyle. Writing by ... Andrea Lewicki, William Burroughs. Published by ARTECH Publishing 1986. Address for correspondence: P.O. Box 209 LONDON E11 1BF.

Junk yields a basic formula of "evil" virus: *The Algebra of Need.* The face of "evil" is always the face of total need.

MIDDLE TAR As defined by H.M.Government

IT'S A PIECE OF CAKE!

Because you would be in a state of total sickness, total possession and not in a position to act in any other way. Dope fiends are sick people who cannot act other than they do.

The sexuality of the racially degraded male is depicted as superior in terms of brute sexual force: his alleged sexual nature, being brute and thus bestial, is precisely what licenses violence against him in a racist value system. His sexuality is a savage masculinity, while the phallus of the white carries civilization to the dark places. amount to nothing, are worth nothing, then the conquest of them—except for the momentary pleasure of it—means nothing. proves

something important for his sexuality of which the racially praise in the insult, so much praise, racially degraded male is masculinity, mesmerized into force of his sex as his identity, on the women of the racially relations or he will take back his against them. He cannot see his

complicity: an acknowledgment of a superior male is envious. There is or such essential praise, that the mesmerized by the myth of his own accepting the ideology that posits the even though this myth often costs superior group through taboo sexual own women using his sexuality way clear to making an alliance

with women—even the women of his peer group—based on sexual justice because he has accepted the bribe: masculinity belongs to him; he brings it to its purest expression; to contaminate it through empathy with the female would mean weakening or losing it; the one thing he has, masculinity. The bribe, once accepted by the racially degraded male of any group, insures that if the racially masculinity is realized in the triumph of male over male, whether

"Light my Lucky."

LUCKY STRIKE LIGHTS ONLY 8mg TAR

VEILS

nothing. It is not sustaining. It cannot sustain a sense of masculine superiority because the conquest of nothing is nothing. But the conquest of other men, especially men with a more massive, more brute sexuality, does amount to something. It is sustaining because the conquest of bigger, better cock is the ultimate conquest. And here one finds the bribe. The racially degraded male collaborates in the degradation of women—all women—because he is offered

the sphere of conflict for dominance is intraracial or interracial. The genius of the bribe is in the fact that, metaphorically speaking, no matter which gang wins the battle, the white man wins the war. The sexuality of the racially degraded male—the only capacity allowed him—becomes both justification for taming or colonizing or castrating him and the mechanism by which he destroys himself, because he honors masculinity as authentic identity.

LONDON'S BIGGEST SELLING GUIDE TO NIGHTLIFE·DANCE·FILM·THEATRE·MUSIC

PLUS

FAR OUT

MILLIONS DYING OF SPIRITUAL STARVATION

LET THEM EAT VINYL

7. I'VE DONE IT ALL BEFORE- BUT NOT WITH YOU

ENDGAME AND AFTER 1986 AND ON

Poison Girls decide the time has come to wind up operations. There's a renewed focus on appraising the band's work, releasing retrospective collections, celebrating birthday milestones and exploring new opportunities for performance and presentation—much of it outside and beyond the confines of the band, and involving several extraordinarily audacious stage musicals. Decades later, the outpouring of respect and recognition that followed the deaths of Vi Subversa and Lance d'Boyle confirms the esteem in which the band were held and the strength of Poison Girls' legacy.

Poison Girls continued to mix gigs in the UK with live appearances in continental Europe—often returning to venues that the band felt a special affinity with. "We just kept playing," Famous says. "We did a lot of work in the mid to late 1980s on the European continent. We went around Scandinavia several times, and Germany—and got big audiences. Those were good, big gigs over there." The band could be confident that crowds would turn out for their shows, to hear material drawn from across Poison Girls' decade-and-more of writing, together with the new and unreleased songs the band were perfecting live.

"Quite often those gigs were arranged by people who really wanted to see the band," Barwood adds. "So we were given a great welcome. We met some lovely people who were really motivated and very grateful that we'd come to collaborate on a cause that they were raising funds for. A lot of those shows were benefits for women's refuges and different kinds of notable causes. We made some really good friends at The Kob in Berlin, and we did some absolutely scorching gigs there—so good, so fun."

Playing in Berlin could involve hopping between different venues across the city. "We could, in the space of a week, do three or four gigs at different capacity spaces and absolutely pack them out," says Barwood. "Even if we played a second night at the same venue, everyone came back! It was really exciting to be able to do that, and it made you feel that the wind was behind you as a band."

"The Kob was a special venue for us," Famous agrees. "Typical of Berlin, it was a big square slab of a building built around an internal courtyard, and was run as a squat. The organisers had physically fought the council when threatened with eviction and eventually got a big grant to renovate the whole place. There were lots of people living there, and there was a café and a small cinema room. We made good friends with several of the people that were instrumental in organising the whole complex. We played there several times including the 1995 reunion final Poison Girls' gig."

"In Holland, Scandinavia, and Germany we met some really clued-up and radical people working like this," he adds. "The Blitz Café in Oslo was another great venue with wonderful people—apparently situated in Edvard Munch's old house."

"Generally, the later European gigs were put on by activists of one sort or another," he continues. "We seemed to have the knack of arriving at a place where 'the action' was about to kick off, or had just happened, or—in the case of the Rote Fabric in Zurich—even while we were playing!" The social unrest of the Opernhausk-rawalle (the Opera House riots) in the city in May 1980, had signalled the birth of a new politicised youth scene in Switzerland, which led to clashes between punks, protesters, and other dissidents and the Swiss authorities for years after.

"It was easier in Europe because there seemed to be much more support for small venues—often art centres and the like. It was definitely the norm to be well looked after. We actually got beds to sleep in, and decent food to eat, which made the hours in the back of a crap van a tad more manageable."

But things were not as buoyant back in the UK. "Playing live in Britain, it felt that our arc was downward," Famous says. "We'd go back to places and get a smaller audience than we'd had before. I mean, we were still getting people turning out. We were still meeting people all the time who said how important we'd been to them, and we still were to them." Yet there were fewer of them—which fuelled the concern that interest in the band in their home country might have peaked.

Poison Girls were also uncomfortably aware of a change in the correlation between the type of show that they played and the experience that they had. "When we started as a band, by far the best gigs to play—and the ones where you were treated with the most respect—were the benefit gigs that we did for free. If we were ever playing for money, generally the experience was grubby." But as the poison of Thatcherism leached into every aspect of British culture, things changed. "By the mid-1980s, if we did a gig for free, we were treated—at best—poorly, and, the more that we charged, the better the experience we had. This was a tough lesson for us to learn."

Further studio sessions followed the recording of The *Price of Grain*. Three tracks from those sessions, "Mirrors and Glass," "Abort the System," and "Let It Go," were included on the band's *Statement* retrospective. "Cupid" ("Got a restless feeling, like I'm grieving for something that I never had") appeared in the 1995 *Real Woman* compilation issued by Cooking Vinyl. But several other new songs in the band's evolving repertoire went unrecorded—aside from raw live versions sneaked from venue mixing desks. Poison Girls' New Year press release in 1986 reported that the band were "presently stockpiling material for a new studio album provisionally titled 'Demonstration' for release later this year," but the project never progressed.

The result is a frustrating gap in the band's history of recorded material which makes it difficult to fully appreciate the creative and political worth of Poison Girls' later work. "There's a whole set full of songs that we played in the last three or four years that never

Triple Concert

IRHA
DES ARMES
ITALIE

Poison Girls
POUR LE
GRANDE BRETAGNE

DogFacedHermans
SALVADOR
ECOSSE

DIMANCHE 30 AVRIL DES 20 H

CITÉ UNIVERSITAIRE NE

HORS GABARIT

coll: centre culturel

got recorded—it must be twenty-plus tracks," says Famous. "A few were done in a basic eight-track studio and were included in the *Statement* CD box set. "All the Way" and one or two others that were written for *AIDS: The Musical*, but most never reached the studio." Several new songs from that era stand out, showing the different ways the band were continuing to push against the boundaries of other people's expectations.

"Hot Slots" is a driving, pulsing critique of Las Vegas's blend of selling sex, money, wealth, and tacky wedding chapels, all of it a conjured up illusion of "fun," managed by gatekeepers competing to promote the "hottest slots in town." It doesn't take much imagination to pinpoint the metaphor in Subversa's attack on wealth and sexual exploitation. "'Hot Slots' was written after a road trip from San Francisco through to Phoenix, taking in Death Valley and Las Vegas," Famous says. "On driving out of Death Valley, having spent the night in a hotel in the valley, we arrived at the Nevada border to see a motel with the word 'Brothel' painted in huge letters on the roof. Prostitution is legal in Nevada. That was a culture shock."

"Stranger" is a song that revisits one of the band's recurrent themes, the challenge of the "otherness" of those with whom you might have a romantic entanglement. That sense that this person is someone about which you know little, and whose intrusion on your own independent life is something you might ultimately resent.

Built upon some sassy dance motifs, "The Money's Not Real" is a witty, acerbic attack on the ridiculousness of wealth and its pursuit. Other songs included "Waiting for the Heat," "Oh, Boy—It's a Girl," "I Hate the West," "Seducer," and "The Force." This new material showed there was no blunting of Poison Girls' creative edge, as the band's songwriting efforts continued to steer them further away from their raucous punk origins. Richard Famous remains unconvinced by the suggestion. "I question this assertion," he says. "'Hot Slots,' 'The Money's Not Real,' or 'Mirrors and Glass' would not have been out of place on *Hex*." But there's a richness, a mischievous warmth and a self-aware pop sensibility to those later songs that is hard to discern on Poison Girls' earliest vinyl releases. In any case, the strength of the new material was matched by the sense of resilience and commitment that continued to surround the band—all of it genuine and heartfelt.

As to the future activity of Poison Girls, Subversa explained to the *NME*, "We've got a lot of new stuff that we want to bring out but it's a matter of doing things right. We don't want to make the same old mistakes. Maybe we'll make some new ones, but we don't want to make the old ones all over again."

But it was far from clear what Poison Girls' next steps should be, if they were to avoid settling into a repeating cycle of break-even-at-best touring, especially when their artistic and cultural reach did not seem to be extending. That sense of uncertainty exacerbated other latent personal tensions within the band and also made innovative spin-offs and side projects even more appealing.

"I think the band that we toured Europe with during that time—Mick, Dave, Vi, and me—the lineup that was the longest lasting—was a really, really good live outfit. We worked really well together," Famous says. When Mick announced that he was leaving, it proved to be a lineup change that was much harder for the band to adapt to than it had been on many previous occasions.. "He was working as a promoter and liaison officer with an arts venue in Hackney, London, and he wanted to commit to that."

The last gig that Poison Girls played with Mick Shenton on bass, at The Kob in Berlin, was captured on a 16-track recording for a planned vinyl release. "It was a cracking night," says Famous. "I remember it being a really great gig." The set was also recorded in a three-camera video shoot. "Unfortunately, all three cameras used different recording formats. Typical of the anarchist scene in Berlin at the time!" It was going to be a complicated and expensive technical process to standardise and then stitch together the footage. "We couldn't afford it at the time—and no one seemed interested in financing a live Poison Girls video—so the project got sidelined, never to be seen again."

After Shenton left, Poison Girls recruited Andy Demetriou to replace him. It was a process the band had been through many times before, but this time everything felt that much harder. "It just seemed like a lot of work," Famous sighs. "We'd had so many bloody bass players. Every time you get another member of the band, the whole dynamic changes. We'd had such a good dynamic with Mick and Dave working together. When Andy came along, it was good, but it was different." It was no reflection on Demetriou's abilities, but the change in momentum his arrival signalled contributed to the sense that the band had "just run out of steam," Famous acknowledges.

As is usually the case with bands that have written, performed, and recorded together for more than a decade, the end of Poison Girls was not the result of a single determinant, but rather the collision of several factors. Yet it was hardly coincidental that Poison Girls' endgame played out in a political and cultural context that bore little comparison to the groundbreaking, empowering, and fast-replicating subversive environment in which the band had begun. The sharp retrenchment of the DIY punk scene, especially in the UK, reduced the spaces in which Poison Girls could operate.

"It seemed to us that a lot of energy had been syphoned out of the anarcho-punk side of things by left-wing organisations around the miners' strike and the subsequent prominence of Red Wedge," Famous

That Famous Subversa, photo by Jill Posener, 1987.

suggests. "We did of course support the miners, but were very wary of behind-the-scenes organisations that were intent on co-opting 'the youth,' and syphoning their energy into party politics. For us, it seemed very reminiscent of the old cynical politicos of the Socialist Workers Party using Rock Against Racism—with whom we had had many a run in in the late '70s."

The righteous rage that animated political punk had been diluted by the music industry's nullification of that radical temper and its displacement by cynical moral posturing and the manoeuvrings of the hard left. Increasingly subterranean punk scenes battled on, many splintering into ever smaller niches, but the sounds of the underground were being remixed by the emergence of the free party scene, and the surge of rave culture. "Everyone's given up and just wants to go dancing," one student insisted to an unconvinced US academic researching the phenomenon. Even if that sweeping comment greatly oversells the shift, there was still a growing recognition that, in these changed times, there was now little prospect of the band secur-

ing the kind of breakthrough that had previously eluded them—politically, culturally, or artistically.

The centre of political gravity inside the wider British anarchist movement was also shifting. Anarcho-punk's original sharp edge had been blunted over time and by the mid-1980s it was no longer the disruptive interloper of British anarchism. New organisations, many of them keen to refocus the movement's attention on class-based forms of collective struggle, began to attract attention. The Class War newspaper made much of the tabloid notoriety it actively sought, but in truth it was only one of several new or resurgent anarchist organisations now vocally advocating combative class politics. Over the next few years, the advocacy syndicalist Direct Action Movement, the Anarchist Communist Federation, the Anarchist Workers Group, and several other national, regional, and local organisations would cumulatively eclipse the earlier preoccupations of political punk—in the UK at least.

The prepunk anarchist experiences of Poison Girls meant that this shift was less of a culture shock than it would otherwise have been. But that political recalibration did mean that far less attention was being paid to DIY punk gigs, zines, and vinyl releases than before.

That fact can only have added to the cumulative sense of exhaustion that inevitably came from relentless touring. But there were key personal considerations too. "The end of the band was also very much to do with a change in my relationship with Vi," says Famous. "I don't think it's a coincidence. The band actually broke up at the same time as we broke up. Our relationship had changed, which meant that the band wasn't really viable anymore."

Still eager to share the benefits which accrued from autonomy, Poison Girls spoke of their plans to expand the Xntrix family of artists. Doubtless reflecting on the band's own recent experiences, Subversa suggested in 1988: "If you just make a record and put it out now, it goes into a big garbage heap of records. Seventy, eighty, a hundred records come out every week, and it's like you're nothing. So we're trying to make a label which will be like a collective of bands who would otherwise have no chance."

Such ambitions, which echoed so strongly the ethos of many other anarcho-punk and independent punk labels like Crass Records, Spiderleg, Bluurg, and Mortarhate, quickly came to naught. By the close of 1988, Xntrix Records had been wound up, taking most of the Poison Girls back-catalogue with it, as members of the band increasingly focused on various side projects.

In the spring of 1989, Poison Girls were invited to join a "Weapons for El Salvador" ("Waffen für El Salvador") tour across Germany and Switzerland, alongside the Dog Faced Hermans from Scotland and Italian punks Irha. The tour included dates in Zürich, Fribourg, Munich, Hamburg, and West Berlin in April and May.

Following the right-wing military coup in El Salvador in 1979, a coalition of left-wing guerrilla groups battled murderous government forces (backed by the Carter and Reagan presidencies in the US) in a grinding civil war. Support for the critique of the antigovernment rebels was common across the international left—although explicit backing for the guerillas' paramilitary campaign was less widespread.

"We were asked to do the tour through our good friends in Berlin," says Famous. The tour's explicit theme was quite a political departure for the band. "We were all avowed pacifists and the idea of supporting a weapons drive was weird, to say the least," he acknowledges. "There was a lot of discussion and argument about whether we should even consider it." Max Vol agrees that "everyone was very unsure about doing it." The band "did a lot of reading about the situation in El Salvador," Famous continues, "and came to the decision that we should at least add our weight to the effort to highlight the struggle happening there."

A key consideration for the band was the recognition that the impact of the tour would be more rhetorical than practical. "Touring around Germany in a hired bus, covering subsistence living costs for nearly twenty people, was not really financially viable in itself given the size of venues we were playing," he adds. "It was pretty obvious that no significant amount of money—if any at all—would be raised to pay for weapons."

"The tour itself was quite controversial, and several gigs got cancelled en route. I am glad we did it, but it still leaves a peculiar taste," Famous acknowledges.

It was at the end of a short European tour in 1989, that Poison Girls decided to wind up operations, signing matters off with a final gig in what Famous remembers was a "very tense" Zagreb in November. As the fracture lines in the edifice of the USSR accelerated in the era of *glasnost* and *perestroika*, the pressures that would soon tear apart Yugoslavia in a brutal civil war (in the aftermath of the Soviet Union's collapse in 1991) were palpable. It was a strange and unsettling context for the band's final live show.

Poison Girls' decision to cease operations was met with a wave of "industrial strength indifference," the band reflected later. Although no one in the band opposed the act of dissolution, it was still a huge wrench for everyone involved.

"We'd been going for thirteen years as Poison Girls," Vi Subversa explained to feminist newspaper *Bad Attitude*. "Vi Subversa was a very strong persona . . . and when that came to an end I needed to find out who I still was—apart from Vi Subversa," she continued. For all members of the band, whose existence in Poison Girls had shaped their lives through years of intense and closely collaborative work, contemplating life *after* the band meant trying to reconnect with the identity of the "person unknown" who was not a Poison Girl.

In the years that followed, Poison Girls' profile dimmed, in part because of band members' reluctance to be drawn back into the public realm to discuss their work. But the end of the band did not mean that its members scattered in centrifugal response. Former Poison Girls turned their attention to new collaborative endeavours.

In the last years of Poison Girls' existence, attention being paid to side projects and spin-offs from the band's core work had already been increasing. In terms of musical activities, Richard Famous and Vi Subversa had begun to perform as a live duo under the name "That Famous Subversa." The two-piece were a natural fit for the kind of cabaret and club nights that had been a key part of the inspiration for the Cabaret of Fools and the Big Brother tours.

"It was myself and Vi doing a stripped down version of our songs," Famous explains. "I was playing raw electric guitar at punk volume, backing Vi's extraordinary

The Lenya Hobnoobs Theatre Company, 1987. Courtesy of Pete Fender and Gemma Sansom.

vocals. There was no one else doing anything like it at the time. It proved to be a really tight and efficient format—minimal gear, turn up in a car an hour or so before performance, and end with a quick get out."

"We also used That Famous Subversa as a way of playing a selection of our older songs as a support act for a full Poison Girls' set," Famous says. "This was another way of streamlining the whole gig process." Subversa also performed as a solo artist, focusing on spoken word and poetry. There were larger collaborative projects too.

The Lenya Hobnoobs Theatre Company was a left-wing, libertarian, "and unapologetically gay" theatre group brought together in 1987 to create what became the scathingly satirical *AIDS: The Musical* through a series of collaborative improvisation workshops.

The initiative of David Bunnett, a London-based gay artist, writer, and activist, the group attracted radical musicians, vocalists, and actors—including several members of the Poison Girls family. Bunnett named the group after a fictional lesbian writer and artist, for whom he devised a made-up life story. He chose the name "Lenya" as it evoked the idea of a "persecuted Russian radical" and "Hobnoobs" after tweaking the name of "a well-known UK brand of biscuits" to produce an identity for his troupe which he hoped "sounded vaguely exotic."

The same sense of mischievous provocation that had fired up the work of The Body Show a decade earlier

ignited the narrative of *AIDS: The Musical*. By the mid-1980s, HIV infections were spreading with devastating impact across the globe, spread by unprotected sexual practices and needle sharing by injection drug users. In the UK, government health warnings declared that HIV would automatically lead to full-blown AIDS and certain death. Public Information Films on TV and in cinemas finished with the image of a tombstone falling in a graveyard, amidst swirls of mist, and inscribed with the words 'Don't Die of Ignorance.' Public hostility towards groups and communities seen to be at risk was rife. Open admission of HIV infection could lead to ostracism, loss of employment, eviction, and financial penury. AIDS began to decimate creative, musical, and artistic scenes across Europe and the US.

To write, rehearse and tour a satirical, subversive theatrical production addressing the challenge of AIDS was an extraordinary decision. To make it a musical was a step further. To give it the title *AIDS: The Musical* was, in the context of the time, an intentionally incendiary provocation. Very "punk," in its own way. The actors and musicians knew that many of those hearing the *title* of the show would be appalled, outraged, and repelled. They also knew that many of those in the eye of the AIDS firestorm would have viewed the audacity with joy, wry humour, and a righteous sense of solidarity.

AIDS: The Musical posters. Left: **Chat's Palace,** London, 1988. Right: **Melkweg,** Amsterdam, 1989.

The music and lyrics for *AIDS: The Musical* were written by Subversa and Famous, with one exception. The song "Body Positive" featured the music of Buzzcocks (credited to Pete Shelley), with lyrics provided by Famous and Gemma Sansom. The live band included Poison Girls members Max Volume, Tom Barwood, and Pete Fender, alongside Famous (who also acted as musical director). As a piece of musical theatre, the performance required the cast to act as well as sing. "And as an actor, who can forget Lance's outstanding performance as the demented Dr Killdaring?," asks Famous.

The creative team summarised the plot of *AIDS: The Musical* as follows:

Set in 1985, the plot revolves around Peter, gay and apolitical; Paul, a liberal manual worker; and Mary, a "radfem" socialist. Despite watching the glitzy and appalling Cilla Diamonte Show reduce the AIDS issue to sexual titillation, Paul decides to take "the test." He is told he is HIV positive, and, as a result of telling his workmates, he is sacked. In an attempt to lift his mood, Pete, Paul, and Mary retire to a gay bar. Paul leaves by himself and gets "queerbashed" waiting for a bus. He does not survive. Mary is interviewed by the police, who seem more interested in her sex life than in Paul's death. They presume that Mary has AIDS and her name is added to the "AIDS Carrier Register." At the funeral, it is revealed that a mistake had been made on Paul's test result. He was HIV negative. Fast forward to 1994. The Prime Minister agrees to help Dr Killdaring set up self-financing "AIDS hospices," special camps, actually, to rid the country of "undesirables." May is recruited as her name is on the "AIDS Carriers Register." She is forcibly removed, and soon finds out the truth behind voluntary euthanasia. Another body on the stage. Enter Peter to find Mary. He realises that there is murder in the air, and the penny drops. With the help of the inmates, Killdaring is dispatched, the hospice is liberated and the seeds of a popular revolution are sown.

The last Poison Girls show, 3 June 1995. **K.O.B.**, Berlin. Photo courtesy of Richard Famous.

Enthused by the response to *AIDS: The Musical* the company agreed to continue their collaboration, developing two further stage productions—*Desert Storm* and *Mother Russia* (aka *Mother Russia Was a Lesbian*)—both of which also featured members of Poison Girls.

Three recordings were made of Lenya Hobnoobs Theatre Company productions, all of which were released in cassette format under Poison Girls' Xntrix imprint, albeit in very limited quantities. A live version of *AIDS: The Musical* was recorded at a performance at The Melkweg in Amsterdam on 5 April 1989. That recording was produced by Famous, engineered by Dan Sansom (Pete), and mixed back at Xntrix basement studio back in London. A studio-based performance of *Desert Storm* was completed in 1991; and a version of *Mother Russia* combined music recorded live at London's Chats Palace in 1991 with vocals recorded back in the studio the following year.

In the late 1980s, Lance d'Boyle had left the UK to move to the Andalucian mountains of southern Spain where he would live and work for the last third of his life. Eager to channel his creative energies in new di-rections, d'Boyle revived his formative career as an artist, this time building physical, three-dimensional artworks. Being an independent ex-pat artist quickly became a rewarding occupation, and generated suffi-cient income to sustain a modest lifestyle. D'Boyle rev-elled in the rustic, frugal artisan life, and the clement climate Spain offered. He continued to make music and occasionally to perform live. But it was sculpture that became the recurring outlet for his artistic talents. "He worked mostly in plaster and wood, as well as found objects, including wire and scrap metal," Pete Fender recalls. "A well-known series that he did in later years, *The Life and Death of the Pomegranate*, depicted the fruit itself in various stages of decay and was recorded in a series of photographs."

With other projects in the UK winding down, in 1994 Vi Subversa also decided to begin a new life chapter by relocating to Spain close to where d'Boyle had settled. She found a new creative community in that area, regularly hosting visitors from across Europe and working with other local musicians. She performed live with local bands and built recognition for her vocal

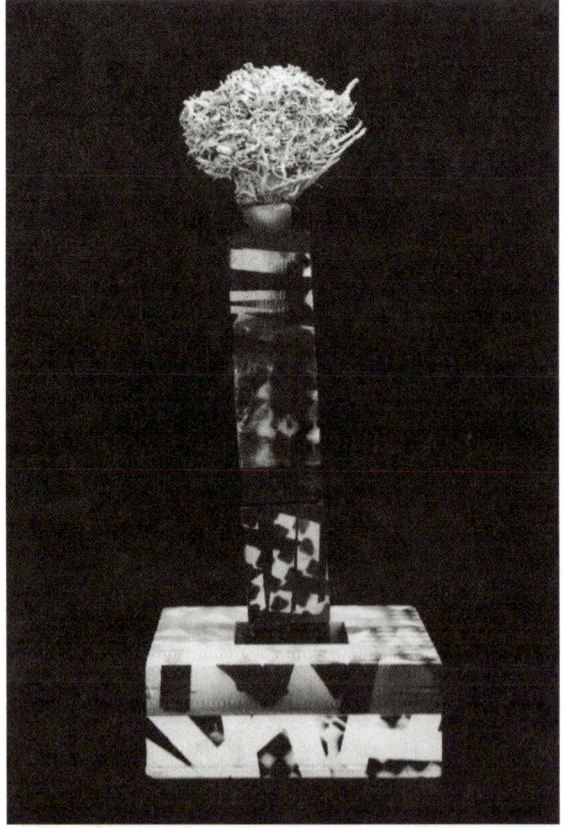

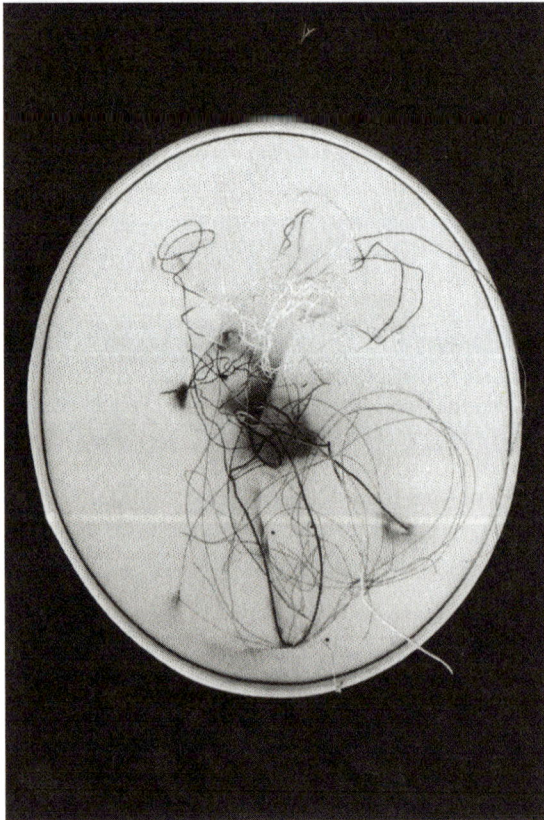

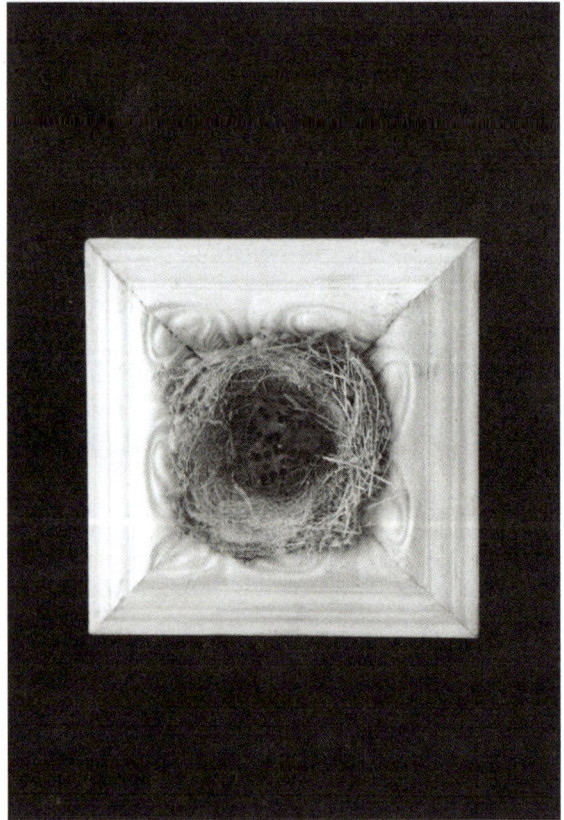

Lance d' Boyle (as Gary Garrett, assisted by Tomas Loco), *Black and White Series*, 2015.

Lance in Spain, 2015. Photo by Nikki Gibbs.

talents in particular. Lance relished the opportunity to have Vi in his life once again, and the pair once more shared a great deal of warm, companionable, and creative time in each other's company. One of the bands that they both played together in, "The Rooms," began to pick up a following in the local area. Richard Famous later relocated to Shetland, an archipelago off the Scotland mainline positioned between Orkney, the Faroe Islands, and Norway, and the northernmost region of the UK, to work as a painter and installer and to continue to write and record new music.

Six years after the band had split up (and perhaps in response to the approach of another 'seven year itch') Martin Goldschmidt's Cooking Vinyl label agreed to release a retrospective CD box set. *Statement* brought together the band's back catalogue of studio and live releases across four discs, accompanied by a detailed illustrated history of the band written by Robin Gibson. A rare advocate for the band amongst the fraternity of music journalists, Gibson was an astute choice. "The band I was always happiest to get something in on was Poison Girls," he explained later. "Because I felt that they were really *challenging*—virtually everything they played, by the existence, by the makeup of the group, by the sub-

ject matter of the songs, and by the fact that they gradually made the music more and more accessible."

As well as bringing together versions of *Hex*, *Chappaquiddick Bridge*, *Where's the Pleasure*, and *Songs of Praise* on CD, the collection also included selected early demo tracks, singles from the Crass Records era, and later previously unreleased studio recordings. Although the lyrics of "Abort the System" and the striking designs that accompanied them had all been crafted during the band's formative years, *Statement* contained previously unreleased musical interpretation of that pro-choice statement. Subversa had written the words back in 1979, during the surge of extraparliamentary opposition to the Corrie Bill. Motivated by right-wing religious fervour, Tory MP John Corrie had launched a Private Members Bill which aimed to sharply restrict women's reproductive rights. The intention was to curtail time limits and reduce the grounds for abortions. Although it progressed through various parliamentary stages, Corrie ultimately admitted defeat and dropped the bill. Eight years later, MP John Alton, a Liberal, launched another bill intended to annex women's control of their bodies. The Alton Bill triggered another wave of protest and was also abandoned before becoming law.

Statement: The Complete Recordings, retrospective 4 CD box set, Cooking Vinyl, 1995. *Statement* included two booklets: lyrics and the first compiled history of the band.

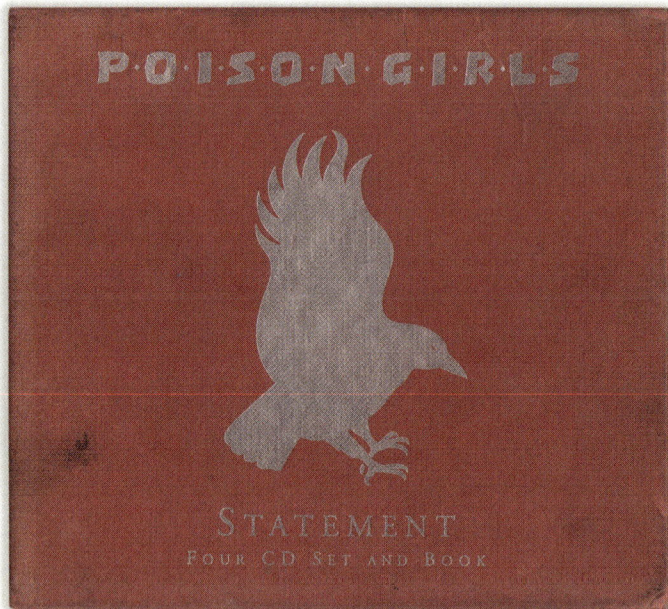

"'Abort the System' came up at a time when the John Corrie Bill was trying to stop a women's right to have abortions—and so it's a reminder of that," Subversa told *Realities of Society*. "It got defeated, so a lot of people stopped thinking about it, but it's still important to women to be able to choose whether they become parents." But Subversa wanted to frame the struggle for reproductive rights in the context of the wider struggle against state power. "That's partly why we use the word *abort*," she continued, "and, well, the *system* is . . . the *system* oppressing you." She was mindful that "there's a kind of abstract system that after a while can mean nothing—because it becomes too abstract. So I think the actual question is to ask what *actual* system is oppressing you and get rid of it, burst out of it—and that is what it means to me."

Beautifully packaged and presented, *Statement* once again lifted the profile of the band, and drew a fresh wave of attention to Poison Girls' work.

To tie in with the release of *Statement*, Poison Girls reformed for one-off performances to celebrate Vi Subversa's sixtieth birthday at the Astoria II in London on 3 June 1995 and at The Kob in Berlin on 10 June. Poison Girls described the two dates as a "brief reprise." Vi Subversa and Richard Famous were joined on stage by bassists Bernhardt Rebours, Bella Donna, Chris Grace, and drummers Lance d'Boyle and Agent Orange in a variety of combinations.

In 1995, resistance to the Criminal Justice Act (CJA), the then-latest effort by the Conservative government to criminalise and eradicate opposition to its increasingly authoritarian rule, was growing in protest groups across Britain. It was exactly the kind of attempted clampdown on the freedom to be different guaranteed to raise the hackles of any ex-Poison Girls. It was entirely fitting then that the gig was a benefit show for those resisting the CJA, raising money for Liberty (previously the National Council for Civil Liberties) a pressure group leading the mainstream, moderate strand of opposition to the Act.

The turnout was impressive, "a big crowd—over 1,000," Famous's tour diary notes, "and a great atmosphere" in the venue. Also on the bill for the evening longtime friends and allies Zounds and Omega Tribe, together with Penny Rimbaud and Eve Libertine (formerly members of Crass), with Tony Allen acting as master of ceremonies, and Mick Shenton handling stage management. The presence of Libertine and of Rimbaud marked the beginning of an overdue public rapprochement

between members of the two bands more than a decade on from the rupture that followed the controversy over "The Offending Article."

Poison Girls' last ever live set in the UK opened with "Statement," "Persons Unknown," and "Old Tart"—for which Rebours and d'Boyle joined Famous and Subversa. At the midpoint, Bella Donna took over from Rebours to perform "Revenge"—recreating an even earlier Poison Girls lineup. Chris Grace then stepped in to play "Where's the Pleasure" and "Cry No More," before d'Boyle handed the drum stool to Agent Orange for the remainder of the set. The encore of "I've Done It All Before" was completed with a final reprise of "Persons Unknown."

The evening was "a very emotional time for all, with lots of reunions and reminiscences," Famous's tour diary notes. "We all go on to Smithy's Wine Bar to have a chill out party," to round off a "very successful and emotive gig."

A week later, the band were back in Berlin for "more cake and kisses," with Chris Grace and Agent Orange in the last ever four-piece lineup. "Despite the drizzle, we get to see a bit of Wall-less Berlin and the changes it has made," Famous records. "We met lots of people that we know, and stayed at The Kob—of course."

The gig itself "though hard work—and not as full as it should have been—is great," he continues. "We get lots of applause and—after two encores—we get ten minutes of continuous stamping and clapping and have to go back for more." And with that, Poison Girls' final "brief respite" came to an end at one of the band's best loved venues.

Individually, and as a collective, after the band's dissolution, former members of Poison Girls tended to be reticent and self-deprecating about the group's work. In contrast to some other well-known political punk bands who shared the same anarcho-punk milieu, who's members were rarely shy about singing their own praises, Poison Girls could appear diffident. Members of the band had sometimes to be coaxed into discussing what, to many others, was the simple fact of Poison Girls' importance and influence. That reluctance, when combined with some slow responses from the band to approaches by punk historian Ian Glasper led to Poison Girls' omission from Glasper's milestone participant history of British anarcho-punk *The Day the Country Died*, first published by Cherry Red in 2006.

Former Poison Girls did agree to occasional interviews, including those sit-downs that Subversa offered to Zillah Minx for the *She Is a Punk Rocker* documentary, the editors of the book *The Truth of Revolution*, and the writers for *Maximum Rocknroll* and *Zero Tolerance* magazines, but such encounters were infrequent.

In 2002, as opposition to the impending inva-sion of Iraq became the catalyst for the largest antiwar demonstrations ever seen in the UK, former members of Crass arranged an evening of performances by artists opposed to the war at Queen Elizabeth Hall. Eve Libertine performed alongside Crass rhythm guitarist Andy Palmer; while Crass bassist Pete Wright, lead vocalist Steve Ignorant, and drummer Penny Rimbaud all contributed their own musical and poetic pieces. Vi Subversa delivered a passionate antimilitarist statement via prerecorded video, but was not joined by any other members of the band.

The visibility of Poison Girls was given a fillip by the decision of Richard Famous and Lance d'Boyle in 2011 to launch an official band website. Alongside a short history of the band, and selected photos from their personal archives, an honesty-box download platform for the band's musical back catalogue offered access to releases long since deleted on vinyl, cassette, and CD.

Concerned by a number of health issues, and keen to be closer to her children and grandchildren, Subversa decided to return to live in the UK in 2012 at the age of seventy-seven. She settled in Hove, in Sussex, just a few miles from the Brighton locations where Poison Girls had originally lived, rehearsed and performed thirty-five years earlier. She arrived back in Britain in resilient mood, and proud of her Spanish life experiences.

In June 2015, family and friends, organised an eightieth birthday party for her, at which Subversa sang accompanied on acoustic guitar by Michael Coates, an old friend and colleague from the band's earliest Brighton days. The formation of the new duo—which took the name 'Vi Subversa's Naughty Thoughts'—represented "a new start," Subversa explained. "That is, I think, about the most punk thing you can do," she explained. "Make a new start that reflects the way you are now." Her last public performance was a sell-out Naughty Thoughts gig at The Green Door club, in Brighton, on 5 December 2015.

Subversa opened her brief set with "I've Done It All Before," following up with renditions of classics by Bertolt Brecht and Kurt Weil and new song "Whistleblower"—the result of a renewed creative collaboration between herself and Richard Famous. "The words are taken from a poem by Vi named 'Whistleblower' and were not intended as the lyrics to a song," Famous explains. "Coincidently, I had been working on a song also called "Whistleblower," and it seemed too good an idea not to bring the music and lyrics together. She loved the result, and it became the first Famous-Subversa composition for twenty-five years." Another highlight was the memorable pared-back version of "Persons Unknown" (rereleased on vinyl in its original studio version by All the Madmen Records, and launched at the gig). She then signed off with arguably the most fitting song

Vi, Orgiva, Spain, 2013. Photo courtesy of Richard Famous.

possible. "Her set finished with the uproarious 'Old Tart's Song,' a withering denunciation of exclusion based on generation and gender, which concludes with the memorable assertion: 'Everybody has their price. Up yours!'" The review on *The Hippies Now Wear Black* site noted, "Sharp, incisive and marvellously defiant, without any accommodation to the privations of age. A pretty good metaphor for Vi Subversa herself." The reception for her, in a small DIY Brighton venue—close to the location of The Vault, where Poison Girls made their live debut—was rapturous.

"Her voice was perfect for Brecht," attendee Rosanne Rabinowitz recalled later. "'I've Done It All Before' (just about the only love song I can stomach) acquired even more resonance when sung by an eighty-year-old woman. I especially liked the little polyamorous flourish she added at the end: 'I've done it all before, but not with you . . . and you . . . and you.'" There was, as The Shend from headliners The Cravats observed from the stage, "a huge amount of love in the room" that evening.

After a short illness, Francis Sokolov died on 19 February 2016, aged eighty. "The word inspiration doesn't do her justice," insists her former Brighton musical compatriot Helen McCookery. "She was incredibly kind, and I clearly remember her being the first adult I spoke to in my life up till then who actually listened to what I said and seemed to value my opinions." Steve Ignorant of Crass was equally effusive. "Vi Subversa from Poison Girls was one of the most wonderful people you could have ever had the fortune to meet and I miss her dreadfully," he says.

A sense of the esteem in which Vi Subversa was held by those in the UK's punk and alternative scene was provided by the 2017 Another Winter of Discontent (AWOD) festival held in London. Having run for several years as a platform for artists in outsider and DIY punk circles, the second day of the AWOD 2017 was designated 'Vi Day'—a "charity event celebrating the life of Vi Subversa" with all profits (which totalled at £1,155) given to the antidomestic violence charity Refuge.

The all-day lineup comprised "all female front-ed bands paying tribute to and playing the music of Vi

Subversa and the Poison Girls," and included Omega Tribe, Dirt, Rubella Ballet, Hagar the Womb, Dub the Earth, Lost Cherrees, The Pukes, Lab Rats, Dogshite, Refuse All, and Bratakus.

Huge vinyl prints of the gig poster, featuring a smiling and defiantly self-assured portrait of Subversa framed the stage, and the sounds of Poison Girls' back catalogue provided a fitting audio soundtrack in between each of the live acts. All the artists on the bill were, simply by appearing, clearly acknowledging the significance of Subversa's inspirational influence on the original (and present-day) punk and countercultural scenes. In addition, most bands met the challenge of delivering a credible cover of a Poison Girls song, and each band at some point made direct reference to the impact that Subversa's words, music, practice, or presence had had on them and their contemporaries. Those verbal contributions ranged from the short and direct (such as the observation by the two-piece Lab Rats that Subversa's life showed it was possible "at whatever age, at whatever time of life" to be motivated to "grab a mic and shout" and demand your voice is heard) to the extended personal recollections of Gary from Dirt of meeting Subversa during his first bewildering encounter with the vagaries of the early anarchist punk scene. Hagar the Womb reminisced about meeting Subversa at the Wapping Anarchy Centre, when she coached singer Karen through handling period pain ahead of the band's first gig. Zillah and Sid from Rubella Ballet acknowledged directly their debt to Poison Girls: without their encouragement and support, they would never have had the confidence or access to the resources necessary to form a band.

Throughout the day, artists performed songs from amongst the extensive Poison Girls' repertoire, some making unexpected selections. Pete Fender praised "some astonishingly good covers . . . not all of them were obvious choices that were at all easy to pull off." Dogshite delivered a stripped-down and energetic punk reading of "Crisis" from *Hex*, Bratakus offered an edgy reworking of "Jump Mama Jump," while Refuse-all revisited and reimagined "Lovers Are They Worth It" to impressive effect. Bolshy produced an almost unrecognisable pop and funk-infused reading of "No More Lies," while Dub the Earth delivered a vibrant rendition of "The Price of Grain."

Lost Cherrees and Omega Tribe both offered spirited and raucous versions of "State Control," and in the latter case were joined by Fender on guitar and backing vocals. Lost Cherrees also provided a committed and moving performance of "Cry No More," while Hagar the Womb bounced through a suitably chaotic interpretation of "Old Tart's Song," with both again assisted by Fender. Especially arresting was The Pukes' passionate multivocalist performance of "Persons Unknown" ("all six minutes of it," as they observed with some pride); and

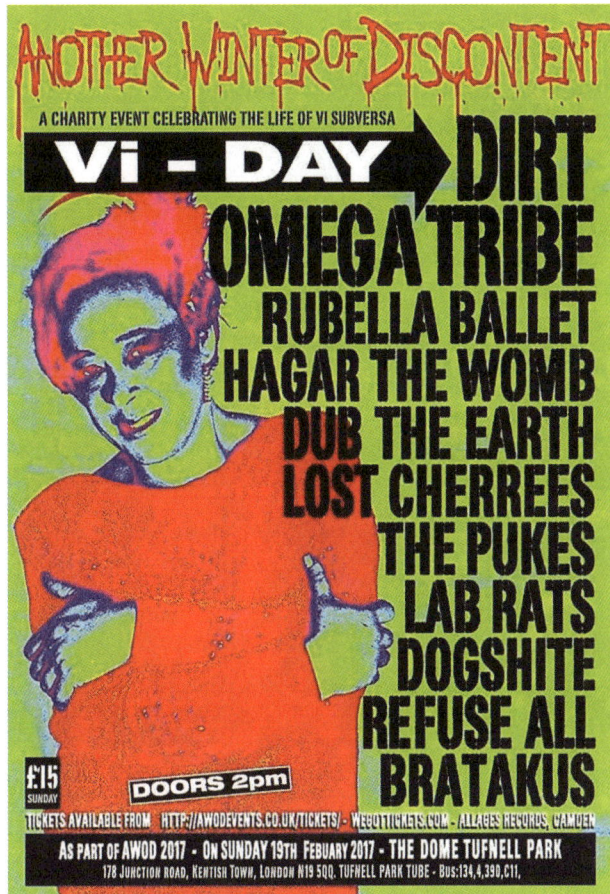

Dome Tufnell Park, London, 19 February 2017.

Dirt's electrifying delivery of "Crisis" which segued into an equally chilling exposition of "Bremen Song."

The evening was brought to a close by a triumphant festival "debut" from the now reformed Omega Tribe, a band who, like Rubella Ballet, had shared a stage with Poison Girls many times back in the early 1980s. They ended an assured and textured set in fine style as former member Fender joined the band on stage for their closing numbers.

The following day Fender thanked the organizers for hosting such a "tremendous event," one that ensured that "a fine day was had by all" and which left everyone who was there with memories of "a wondrous night to look back on."

The event was given even greater poignancy by the fact that Poison Girls' drummer Lance d'Boyle, a lifelong friend, associate, and close collaborator with Subversa, died on 16 January 2017 at the age of seventy-six, after a short illness—a further sad loss of a key figure from the formative years of anarcho-punk's first wave, and one that several bands commented on directly from the stage.

Vi's eightieth birthday gig, 19 June 2015, **Hove.** With longtime Brighton friend Michael Coates, who'd played with The Dandies and was part of the Lenya Hobnoobs Theatre Company. Photos courtesy of Ming de Nasty.

A series of vinyl rerelease revived the reputation of the band, and encouraged a reappraisal of the band's creative, musical, and political output. Waterwing Records rereleased *Hex* and *Chappaquiddick Bridge* in 2014, followed in 2016 by *Where's the Pleasure*. For Record Store Day 2023 in the UK, *Hex* was repackaged for rerelease with design and creative direction by Bernard Rebours.

The Nightingales album *The Last Laugh*, released in 2022, included the track "Frances Sokolov," an appreciation and a celebration of the life of Vi Subversa. "I think it was impulsive, really," says songwriter and singer Robert Lloyd. "I've no idea where it came from—why it felt like that was the moment. I didn't have any kind of epiphany, but once I thought of Vi, then it just seemed like a really natural thing to do. I mean, what a subject!"

"It's not the greatest lyric in the world," he continues, "but it's truthful and sincere—she actually did make her heart a home for a lot of people. I think she's worth much more credit, certainly as a human being, and as an artist as well. She did enough top-notch stuff that she should be recognized more highly as an artist. But as a human being? One of the best I've met."

Poison Girls were often frustrated that they did not secure the attention they felt the band deserved and had worked hard to earn. In the decades that followed, former members of the band came to doubt that the group would ever receive proper recognition or acknowledgement. But the band is far more valued and appreciated than its members realised. "If you're writing about alienation, gender roles, love, and sex . . . in a punk band without being familiar with her work, you're doing yourself an insane disservice," suggests Shannon Thompson of the present-day Boston peace-punk band Pandemix of Subversa's influence down the decades. "One of the greats."

Subversa summarised her personal manifesto succinctly in an interview with *New Youth* zine in 1983. "The basic thing that I want to say is don't let anyone push you off the rails. You've gotta keep going and do what you believe is right. You should live your own life, not what you're told to do by stupid conditioning. Don't stop when you're twenty-four or twenty-five, keep pushing forward and as you get older and older that's when you become a threat, because they don't expect it. Don't give in to their stereotypes, you don't have to be what you're expected to be, you just be yourself and live your own life."

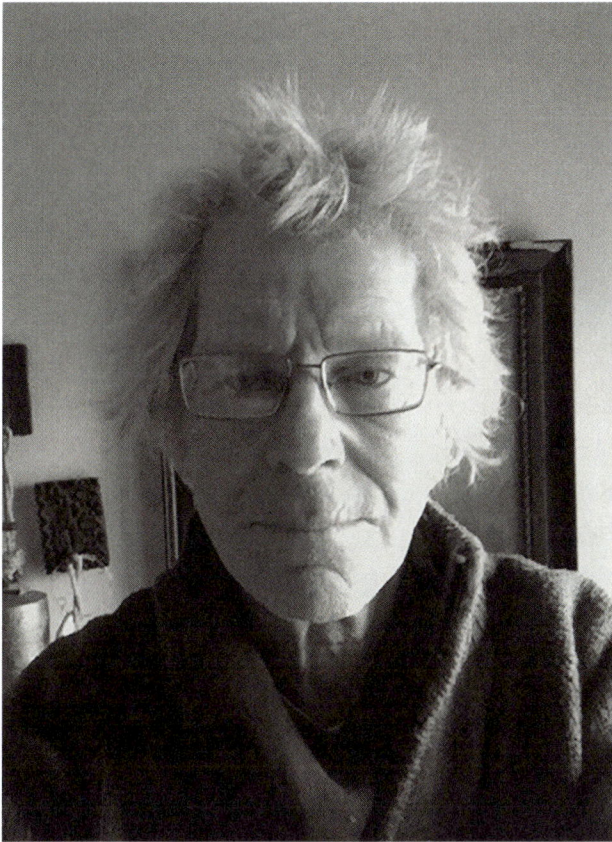

Richard Famous, Shetland, 2021.

"Poison Girls started as a group of people who wanted to play music together," says Richard Famous. At the beginning, the aim was not to try to change the world but "just to make a racket and have a voice." The band's politics came into sharper focus "when we found a kindred spirit and started the collaboration with Crass," he continues. "It was never in our makeup to be preachy, certainly not to tell anyone what to do. We just wanted to have our voice recognised—Vi especially wanted to shout her experiences loud and clear. We found our most receptive audience in what could loosely be called punk."

"As those joint Crass and Poison Girls gigs got traction, it became clear that we were being labelled as 'leaders' of the anarchist and feminist punk movement. This was difficult for us. If our politics meant anything, it was that you should think for yourself, and not follow leaders, but follow your instincts. We thought that Crass were too prescriptive in their attitudes, which was one of the reasons for us breaking away from that alliance."

"There was always a deep vein of anarchist politics running through all of Poison Girls' work. But the driving force behind the music is the recognition that it is the personal that is important and that politics is embedded in who we are," he continues.

"The later work of the band attempted to engage with an audience that had missed out on punk—either by being too old or too young—and to reengage with the punks, especially the women, who had grown out of the more laddish and sometimes violent punk gigs. In a way we were rediscovering 'music for music's sake.'" The goal was to reconnect with the idea that "gigs could be both thought provoking and fun," Famous says. "You didn't need to wear black at a Poison Girls gig!"

"Did we have any impact on the political landscape?" Famous asks. "I know that we got—and still get—feedback from people all over the world, who told us we helped shape their opinions on life," he says. But the band never adopted a finger-wagging, censorious approach, in which they handed out instructions. "I hope that Poison Girls never told anyone what they *should* think or do," he clarifies. The intention was always to give those who listened to the band's work "the confidence and support to think for themselves—which, as far as I am concerned, is the defining feature of anarchism."

Subversa never lost sight of the challenge that those opposed to the existing order of things were confronted by. "The owners of the territories, the people who own the property, the big companies. The whole package is dominantly white, dominantly male, and by definition dominantly rich, and they don't like losing control," she insisted. "They don't want to hear from us . . . [and] it's hard for us to hear each other because the mass communication is owned by them as well."

Poison Girls encouraged those who heard their messages to break out of their isolation and disconnection, and refute the feelings of powerlessness that those in positions of authority sought to impose upon them. "Invisible people, show yourselves," they urged. "People in hiding, come out." It was a message that many, who recognised the irresistible power of that idea, embraced.

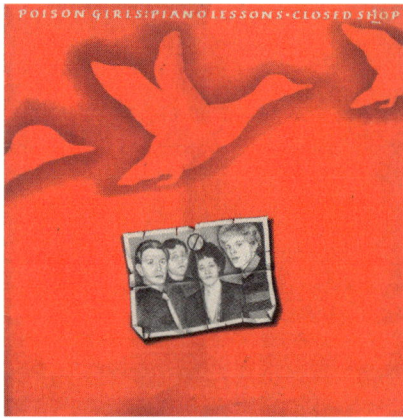

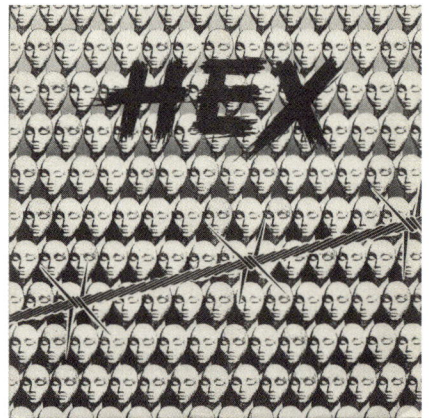

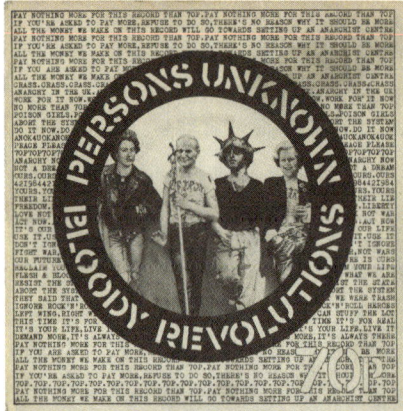

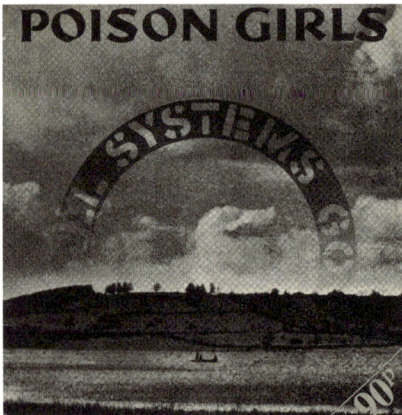

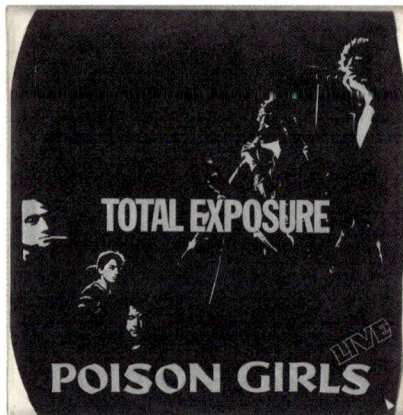

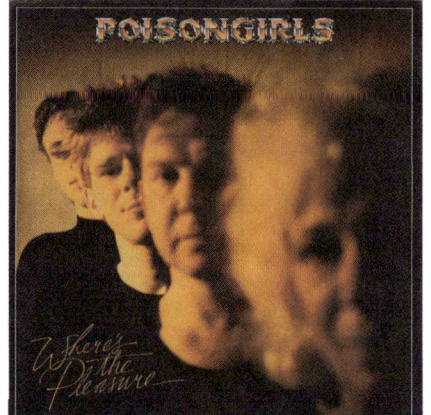

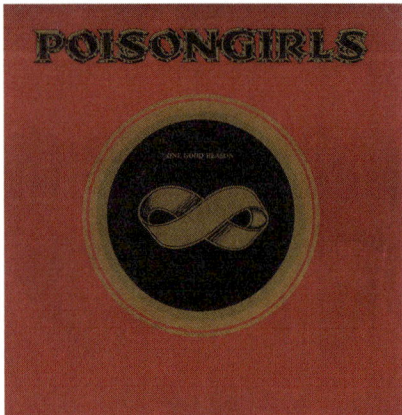

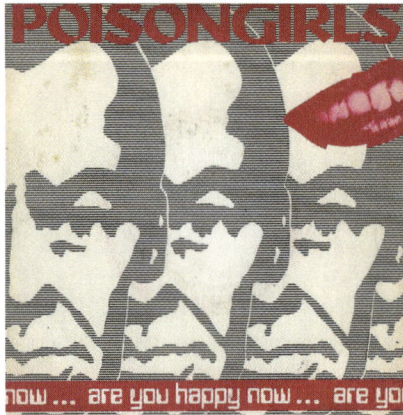

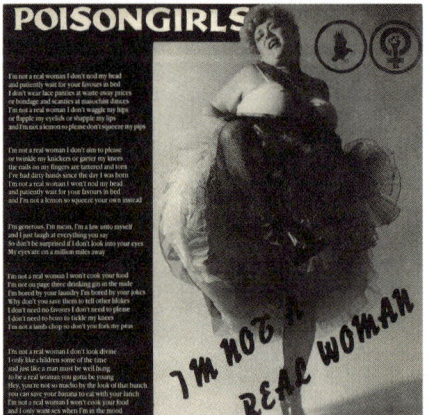

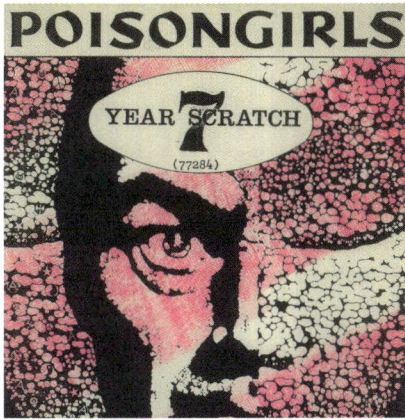

POISONGIRLS — YEAR 7 SCRATCH (77284)

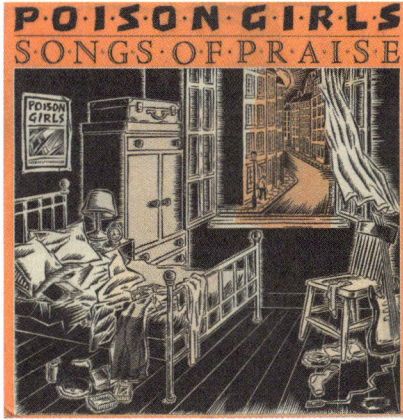

POISON GIRLS — SONGS OF PRAISE

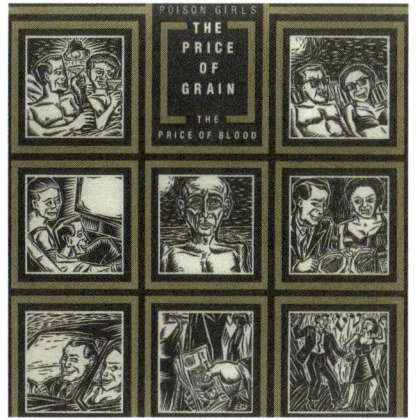

POISON GIRLS — THE PRICE OF GRAIN / THE PRICE OF BLOOD

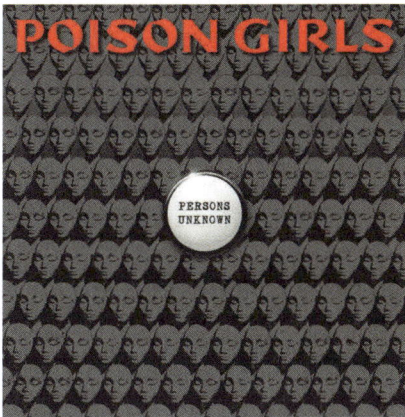

POISON GIRLS — PERSONS UNKNOWN

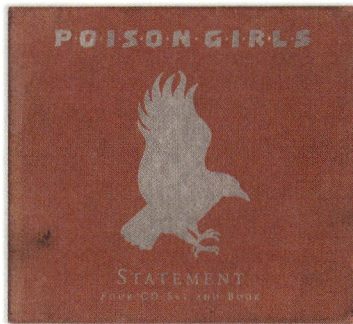

POISON GIRLS — STATEMENT

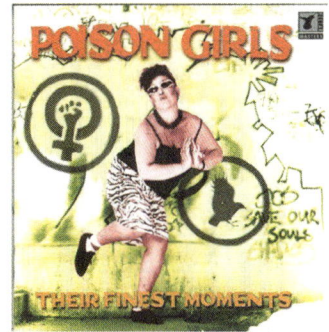

POISON GIRLS — THEIR FINEST MOMENTS / SAVE OUR SOULS

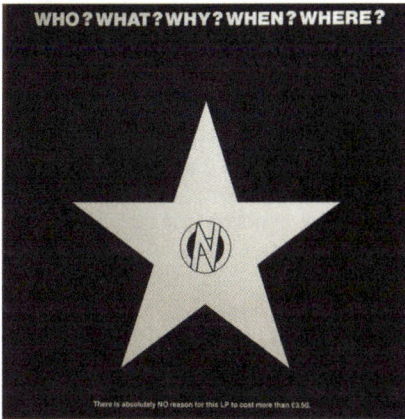

WHO? WHAT? WHY? WHEN? WHERE?

There is absolutely NO reason for this LP to cost more than £3.50.

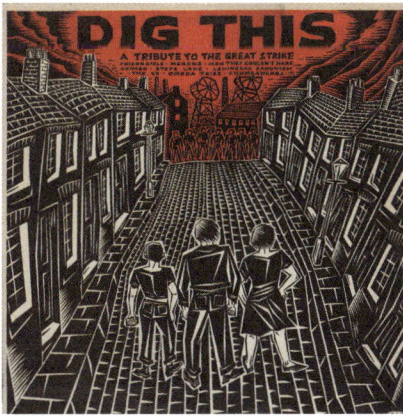

DIG THIS — A TRIBUTE TO THE GREAT STRIKE

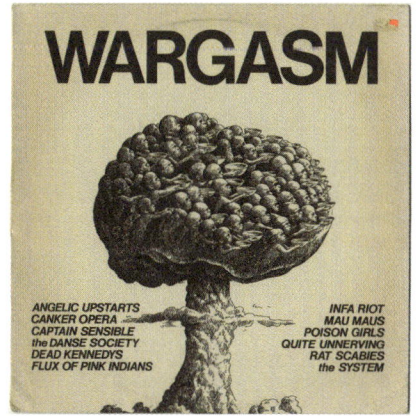

WARGASM

ANGELIC UPSTARTS
CANKER OPERA
CAPTAIN SENSIBLE
the DANSE SOCIETY
DEAD KENNEDYS
FLUX OF PINK INDIANS

INFA RIOT
MAU MAUS
POISON GIRLS
QUITE UNNERVING
RAT SCABIES
the SYSTEM

THIS IS THE A.L.F

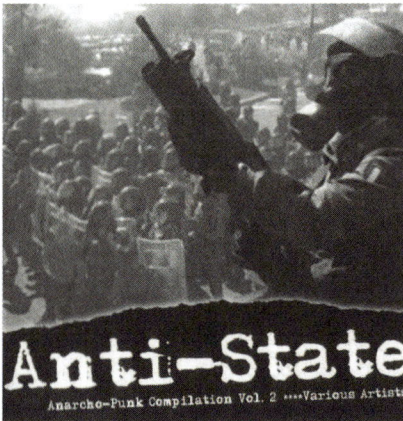

Anti-State — Anarcho-Punk Compilation Vol. 2 .....Various Artists

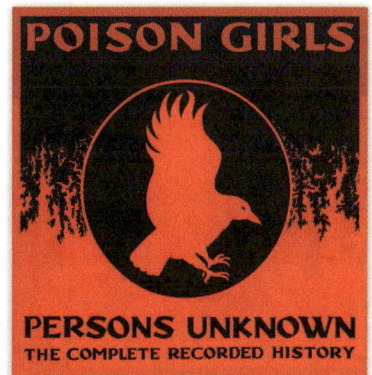

POISON GIRLS — PERSONS UNKNOWN — THE COMPLETE RECORDED HISTORY

RELEASES:

Closed Shop/Violence Grows
Split with Fatal Microbes

Xntrix/Small Wonder Records, 1979 –
12" EP – Weeny 3, ▽E IB

Closed Shop
Piano Lessons

Vi Subversa (guitar, vocals)
Richard Famous (guitar, vocals)
Lance d'Boyle (drums)
Bernhardt Rebours (bass)

Cover design: Bernhardt Rebours
Recording: Adrian Grey-Turner & Poison
Girls at Spaceward Studios, Cambridge.

Hex
Xntrix/Small Wonder Records, 1979 –
12" – Weeny 4
Crass Records, 1980 – 12" – 421984/9
Xntrix, 1989 – cassette – SCUM 1
Water Wing Records, 2014 –12" –
  WW010
Cooking Vinyl, 2023 –12" COOKLP636

Old Tart's Song
Crisis
Ideologically Unsound
Bremen Song
Political Love
Jump Mama Jump
Under The Doctor
Reality Attack

Vi Subversa (guitar, vocals)
Richard Famous (guitar, vocals)
Lance d'Boyle (drums)
Bernhardt Rebours (bass)
Eve Libertine (backup vocals)

Cover design: Bernhardt Rebours &
Lance d'Boyle. Recording: Penny Rim-
baud & John Loder at Southern Studios,
London.

Bloody Revolutions/Persons Unknown
Split single with Crass
Crass Records, 1980 – 7" – 421984/1

Persons Unknown

Vi Subversa (guitar, vocals)
Richard Famous (guitar, vocals)
Lance d'Boyle (drums)
Bernhardt Rebours (bass, synth)
Nil

Cover design: Gee Vaucher. Recording:
Penny Rimbaud & John Loder at Southern Studios, London.

Chappaquiddick Bridge

Crass Records, 1980 – 12" LP plus

"Statement" flexi disc – 421984/2PG,
421984/2
Xntrix, 1989 – cassette – Scum 2
Water Wing Records, 2014 – LP –
WW011
Cooking Vinyl, 2016 – LP – none

State Control
Another Hero
Hole In The Wall (Thisbe's Song)
Underbitch
Alienation
Pretty Polly
Good Time (I Didn't Know Sartre Played
Piano)
Other
Daughters And Sons
Tender Lover
Statement

Vi Subversa (guitar, vocals)
Richard Famous (guitar, vocals)
Lance d'Boyle (drums)
Bernhardt Rebours (bass, synth)
Nil (electric violin)
Gem Stone (backing vocals)

Cover design: Bernhardt Rebours Recording: John Loder at Southern Studios,
London.

Bully Boys/Pretty Polly
Flexi disc included with In the City #15
In The City, 1980 – 7" flexi – None

Bully Boys (live 18/6/80)
Pretty Polly

Recording: Pretty Polly by John Loder at
Southern Studios, London.

All Systems Go
Crass Records, 1980 – 7" – 421984/1

Promenade Immortelle
Dirty Work

Vi Subversa (guitar, vocals)
Richard Famous (guitar, vocals)
Lance d'Boyle (drums)
Bernhardt Rebours (bass, synth)

Cover design: Bernhardt Rebours
Recording: Penny Rimbaud & John Loder
at Southern Studios, London.

Total Exposure
Xntrix, 1981 – LP – XN2003

Persons Unknown
State Control
Old Tart's Song
Bully Boys
Tension
Hero
Don't Go Home Tonight
SS Snoopers
Other

Daughters And Sons
Fucking Mother
Dirty Work
Alienation

Vi Subversa (guitar, vocals)
Richard Famous (guitar, vocals)
Lance d'Boyle (drums)
Bernhardt Rebours (bass)

Recorded live at the Lasswade Centre,
Edinburgh, Sunday, 5 July 1981.
Cover design based on a photo by Jill
Posener. Live sound: Ian Hinckley & Paul
Tandy. Engineering: Simaen Skolfield,
Colin Richardson, Ian Blackburn, & John
Brierley.

Where's The Pleasure
Xntrix, 1982 – LP – XN2006
Water Wing Records, 2016 – LP – WW16

Where's The Pleasure
Lovers Are They Worth It
I've Done It All Before
Whisky Voice
Ménage Abattoir
Take The Toys
Soft Touch
Take The Toys (Reprise)
Velvet Launderette
Rio Disco Stink
Cry No More
Mandy Is Having A Baby
Fear Of Freedom

Vi Subversa (guitar, vocals)
Richard Famous (guitar, vocals)
Lance d'Boyle (drums)
Pete Fender (bass)
Chris Grace (bass)

Typography: Bernhardt Rebours. Pho-
tography: Gwyn Kirk. Production by:
Poison Girls, Simaen Skolfield, & Stuart
James. Engineering: Simaen Skolfield &
Keith Hancock.

One Good Reason
Illuminated Records, 1983 – 7" – ILL 23

One Good Reason
Cinnamon Garden

Vi Subversa (guitar, vocals)
Richard Famous (guitar, vocals)
Lance d'Boyle (drums)
Chris Grace (bass)
Cynth Ethics (synth)

Cover design: Domino. Recording: Bernie
Clark at the Workhouse Studios, London.

Are You Happy Now?
Illuminated Records, 1983 – 12" – ILL 3112
Illuminated Records, 1983 – 7" – ILL 25
Reekus Records, 1983 – 7" – RKS 011
Pregnant Records, 1984 – 7" – RUPG 13

Are You Happy Now
Ménage Abattoir
Whiskey Voice

Vi Subversa (guitar, vocals)
Richard Famous (guitar, vocals)
Lance d'Boyle (drums)
Chris Grace (bass)
Cynth Ethics (synth)

Cover design: Domino. Producer: Bernie Clark at the Workhouse Studios, London.

I'm Not A Real Woman
Xntrix, 1984 – 12" – XN2010
Xntrix, 1984 – 7" – XN2009

I'm Not A Real Woman
Perfect Crime (Rebels Or Hooligans)
Take The Toys From The Boys
Tension

Cover design: Domino. Producer: Bernie Clark

7 Year Scratch
Rerelease of studio tracks, two previously unreleased songs, and live versions from the Big Brother Cabaret tour.

Xntrix, 1984

Revenge
Reality Attack
Alienation
Piano Lessons
I Wanted The Moon
Jump Mama Jump
Statement
Promenade Immortelle
Dirty Work
Cry No More
Offending Article
Fear Of Freedom
Where's The Pleasure?
Too Close For Comfort
Real Woman
Rio Disco Stink
Are You Happy Now?
Too Proud
Tell The Children
White Cream Dream
State Control And Rock'n Roll
Tension
I've Done It All Before

Cover design: Domino. Engineering: Robyn Banks, Jeff Muir, Pete Fender.

Songs Of Praise
Xntrix, 1985 – LP – XN 2008
CD Presents, 1985 – LP – CD 033, △9439

Voodoo Pappadollar
Hot For Love
Riot In My Mind
Feeling The Pinch

Desperate Days
Real Woman
Too Close For Comfort
Rockface
No More Lies
Too Proud

Vi Subversa (guitar, vocals)
Richard Famous (guitar, vocals)
Lance d'Boyle (drums)
Agent Orange (drums)
Martin Heath (bass)
Max Volume (bass)
Cynth Ethics (synth, vocals)

Cover design: Clifford Harper. Production: Bernie Clark. Engineering: Bob Broglia, John Brand, Brian Foel & Pete Fender.

The Price Of Grain And The Price Of Blood
Upright Records, 1985 – 12" – UPT 12

The Price Of Grain And The Price Of Blood
Stonehenge 1985
Jenny
The Girls Over There

Vi Subversa (guitar, vocals)
Richard Famous (guitar, vocals)
Agent Orange (drums)
Max Volume (bass, vocals)
Tymon Dogg (violin)

Cover design: Clifford Harper. Production: Bernie Clark. Engineering: Tom Barwood & Sid Bucknor.

Persons Unknown/Statement
All the Madmen Records, 2015 – 12" – MAD35

Persons Unknown
Statement (Orchestral version)

Vi Subversa (guitar, vocals)
Richard Famous (guitar, vocals)
Lance d'Boyle (drums)
Bernhardt Rebours (bass)
with Member of the National Youth Orchestra

Production and conducting: Jason Osborn. Orchestral score: Barney Unwin Engineering: Tony Cook. Recording: Southern Studios, London. Design: Bernhardt Rebours

COMPILATIONS:

Statement – The Complete Recordings
Cooking Vinyl, 1985 – CD Box Set – COOK CD 087, B6747, B6748, B6749, B6750
Cooking Vinyl, 2004 – CD Box Set – COOK CD 309, 3110724, 3110723, 3110721, 3110722, 45804, 45805, 45807, 45810

72 track, 4 CD retrospective. Includes a history of the band and lyric booklet.

Real Woman
Cooking Vinyl, 1995 – COOK CD 086
Cooking Vinyl, 1997 – COOK CD 086, B6413

12 song greatest hits compilation, includes 4 live tracks.

Their Finest Moments
Nectar Masters, 1997 – CD – NTMCD541
Reactive Records, 1998 – CD – REM-CD503

18 song greatest hits compilation.

Poisonous
Snapper, 1998 – CD – SMCD 137
Recall 2cs, 1998 – CD – SMCD 137

30 song, 2 CD, greatest hits.

Persons Unknown - The Complete Recorded History
PM Press, Cooking Vinyl, Free Dirt, and Active Distribution, 2025

7 CD box set

SELECTED APPEARANCES:

Wargasm
Antiwar themed benefit compilation, multiple beneficiaries. (Pax Records, 1982)

Who? What? Why? When? Where?
(Mortarhate Records, 1984)

Dig This! (A Tribute To The Great Strike)
A benefit for the Miners' Solidarity Fund. (Forward Sounds International, 1985)

This Is The A.L.F
A benefit for the Animal Liberation Front. (Mortarhate Records, 1989)

A Sides (Part One. 1979–1982)
Collection of singles released on the Crass Records label. (Crass Records, 1992)

Anti-State (Anarcho-Punk Compilation Vol. 2)
Part of three volume anarchist punk compilation. (Overground Records, 2005)

Action Time Vision—A Story Of Independent UK Punk 1976–1979
Diverse collection of British punk and postpunk artists. (Cherry Red, 2016)

APPENDIX 2.1: SPOTLIGHTS- BAND MEMBERS

VI SUBVERSA

Guitarist, redoubtable frontwoman, singer, and main lyricist for Poison Girls, Frances Sokolov (aka Vi Subversa, aka Vi Squad) found the confidence to take to the stage—and make herself heard—at the age of forty as the storm clouds of punk gathered.

"Most of my life, I've felt like Alice in Wonderland, lost down one rabbit hole or another," Vi Subversa reflected, at the age of eighty. "And now, looking back, it's beginning to make sense." Her perspectives on fronting a punk band as a fortysomething mother now have an additional salience. "What I've realised now is that, in those days, I was addressing *children*. The audiences were children, basically," she suggests. "And I didn't know what they were taking in and what they weren't taking in. I just had to speak what was on my mind. My grandmother used to say, 'What is on your lung should be on your tongue.'" An epithet, long out of popular use, which encourages someone to voice their thoughts and articulate their convictions without succumbing to self-censorship."

"And that's what I was doing," she says. "And I got very little feedback at the time. And now I get a lot of positive feedback from those same young people. They've grown up, and they're now parents, and they tell me they know what I was talking about at the time. I can appreciate that I wasn't just blabbing into nothingness, which it felt a bit like at the time."

It was a blend of anarchist and feminist impulses which led Subversa to demand her right to be seen and heard on stage as the new sounds of punk exploded. "I had an anarchist background, and had been in touch with the London Anarchist Group, sold *Freedom* in the streets, left home and become another sort of wild kid," Subversa recalls of her formative years. In the 1960s, and through her involvement in the peace movement, Subversa found a strand of political thinking that made most sense to her. "I didn't like what anarchists in those days were arguing about—because it was all about Lenin and Trotsky and the Russian Revolution, and things that didn't really mean very much to me," she acknowledges. "The women's movement put more life into our politics"—and, in the process, uncovered new concerns (social, cultural, and personal) that felt more immedi-ately relevant to a defiant young mother of two.

Once Poison Girls had formed, Subversa's earlier political experiences meant that she recognised in the approach of her new allies Crass things that she warmed to and things that left her unsure.

"I trusted their energy, and I trusted Crass's message—but I was quite wary," she admits. "Lance and Richard were both more sensible in seeing that here was an opportunity for us. And I trusted that instinct too, and did come to see it was an opportunity, a mutual give-and-take arrangement. We were given a higher profile, we were given the attention—although I had to fight every inch of the way to keep my sanity."

"There were some moments when we were really very good friends. Lots of good things happened. Some of it was crap, and some of it was brilliant. I suppose that's true of any relationship—cut it down the middle and you get a bit of both. But I was always scared of them. I didn't like the regalia—all that black and the heavy boots." As for the music that Crass made, it was not a soundscape that excited her. "It didn't come anywhere close to me," she says.

Despite the benefits of the alliance, Subversa recognised when the time had come to break away. "We all knew that we had to leave by then—the point that we were becoming 'Mrs. Crass.' That wasn't what we were in it for. It didn't matter that we would no longer have the support that they gave us. We had learned to fend for ourselves—and we did." Subversa saw that the context in which the band was working was changing too. The original punk wave had "more-or-less played out by then," she suggests, "and we were never a 'punk band,' properly—we were 'too old,' we were 'too melodic.'" Keen to follow a new path, Poison Girls showed that "we still had something of that spirit of 'get up and go,' which took us on a new journey," she continues. "We did, I think, some very good albums after we left Crass. *Where's the Pleasure* was one of my favourites."

Subversa concedes that her role as lyricist, singer, and frontwoman in Poison Girls could be unsettling—even challenging—for her two children. "They didn't want this woman who was ranting about this, that, and the other," she says. "They didn't know why I was writing this heavy stuff—not really. They wanted a mum at home, you know? There's a normality to that." Even when being that "normal" mum, Subversa would stand out. "I used to go to parent evenings at their school with pink hair," she recalls.

"Some of my songs were quite heavy about the male psyche. My son Dan was copping all the anger about the patriarchy, wasn't he? He was a little boy, and that wasn't very helpful for him, I don't think. But he's turned out to be a really great guy, and his relationship with me is fantastic. With my daughter Gemma too, we've gone through it, and I've explained things. I went to Spain, and left them alone for a bit. You have to trust the process with children. It's a fucking horrible, hostile world out there, and while children pick things up within the family, they have to make their own meaning. You have to trust that they will sort it out. We've healed a lot of that pain, and their anger about stuff they didn't understand."

The last years of Subversa's life coincided with a resurgence of interest in the work of Poison Girls, and in the persona of "Vi Subversa"—something that she found gratifying, if not entirely comfortable. "This sudden interest in myself is quite overwhelming," she conceded. "There's an interview with me in *Maximum Rocknroll*. In that, I said that 'our intention as Poison Girls was to communicate authentically, fuelled by love and passion.' And that's about right."

LANCE D'BOYLE

Percussionist, artist, illustrator, graphic designer, film-maker, and political prankster Gary Robins (aka Lance d'Boyle) was a founder member of Poison Girls. He was the group's drummer from 1977 until 1984, after which he remained closely entangled with the band's work.

Born in 1940, d'Boyle grew up relying on the radio as his window on the world. "I was very taken with a band called Spike Jones and the City Slickers, a comedy jazz combo, who did piss takes of pop and classical works," he recalled. In the studio, the band blended lots of weird sound samples into their music. "What appealed to me was the chaotic—one might say anarchic—effect of mixing two or more realities."

D'Boyle first hands-on experience with making music came at the instigation of his parents. As a child, he found himself having piano lessons. It was a tightly controlled introduction to musicianship. "My piano teacher Miss Bunne was very stuck in her ways and liked her pupils to play old-fashioned classical music," he remembered. "My friend, who was taking piano lessons from somebody else, was playing Little Richard and boogie-woogie tunes from sheet music. She wouldn't let me play that kind of stuff. I had to play Brahms's 'Lullaby' and 'Little Tin Soldier.'" It was, at least, a good training ground for his later "escape into punk."

Another of his audio interests developed into "an obsession with SFX," d'Boyle admits, which led to him collecting the entire series of sound effects records released by the BBC Radiophonic Workshop, including the perennially popular *Out of This World*.

"That interest came to fruition when we were recording *Hex* with Penny Rimbaud," he explained. "I dis-

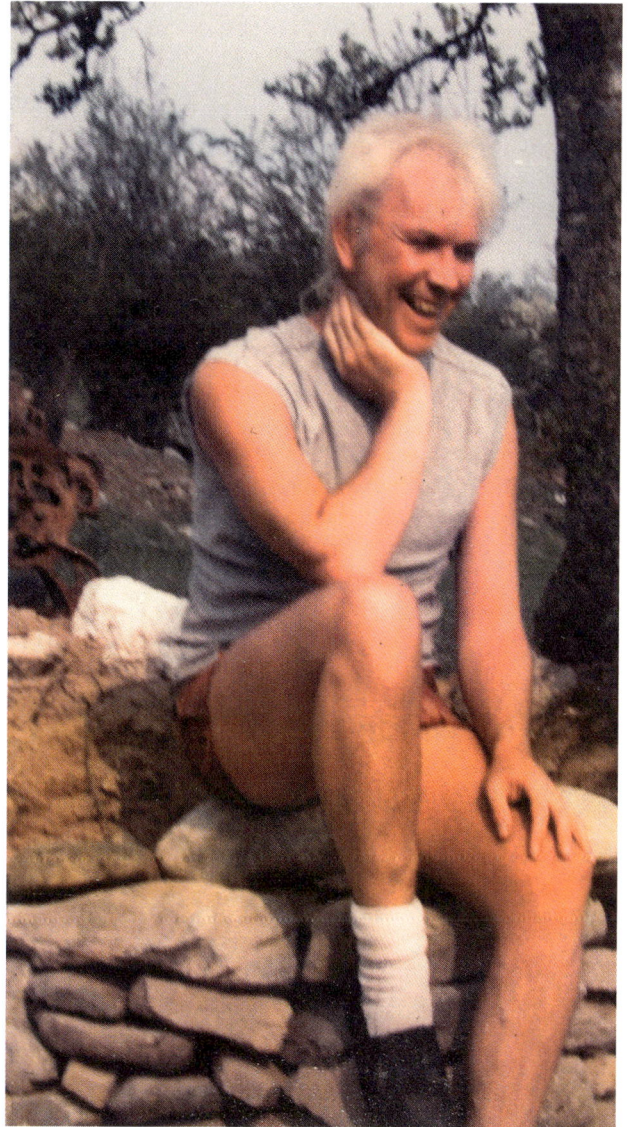

Lance at home in Spain, 1985. Photo by Domino.

covered that he was into SFX too, so we made some extra sound tracks especially for the record. If you listen closely to 'Bremen Song,' you can hear the Burleigh House cockerel Gladys announcing the arrival of dawn."

"Listening to *Hex* again, I'm gobsmacked by how good it sounds," he continued. "It's timeless and strange, and deep with violent poetry that I think is even more relevant now than then, given the current state of things. Vi's voice and her poetry were awesome weapons of 'love and hate,' and the rest of us were able to respond perfectly to the atmospheres she created, all of us making it up as we went along." Keen to acknowledge Rimbaud's inspired work as producer—"adding in other layers into the collage to make the whole album one continuous piece"—d'Boyle suggested that *Hex* had to be recognised as "an anarcho-punk anthem"—before adding, "but then, I would say that, wouldn't I?"

D'Boyle always enjoyed those spontaneous moments of creative inspiration that punctuated Poison Girls' studio work. But he was keen to acknowledge that much of the process was "very unglamorous." As any rock drummer will attest, it's the percussion tracks that get set down first in the studio. "I'd spend several days doing my bits, if we'd got time—or half a day if we hadn't. And then I'd kind of done then, really. Maybe backing vocals or something else later on," he said. After that there was a lot of "sitting around for hours and hours and hours, listening to tracks over and over again." It was always enjoyable, but "very tiring—you end up completely knackered." Studio days were always long. "Although you go in during the daytime, you end up working at night. Somehow the nighttime is more conducive to concentration."

Someone who enjoyed the experience of performing live, d'Boyle had particularly vivid memories of the Edinburgh gig recorded for the *Total Exposure* album. "I remember that gig very well. A nice place to play. A big hall, and a lot of people came," he recalled. "But because we were recording it live, everyone was on edge. We recorded the whole set in the afternoon, with nobody in the hall watching, as a backup, just in case we fucked up later." That evening, as the last seconds of tape spooled their way through the closing song, tensions at the mixing desk rose. "We were doing that long ending to "Alienation"—that cycling repetition of 'What'cha gonna do about it? What'cha going to do about it?' And then that fades out, and I'm left powering through this solo snare beat to finish out the song. And I just got to the end of it before the tape ran out. And backstage they were so relieved, saying, 'Oh, my god, we did it, we got the whole thing.' I thought it was a fantastic gig, and that we played really well."

D'Boyle also loved the theatricality of Poison Girls' visual aesthetic—on and off stage. He recalled how the costume design for the twelve-inch sleeve of *Are You Happy Now?* came about. "We went to the local fancy dress shop in Leytonstone looking for some inspiration. And there were these clown costumes—four of them. We thought that they would be perfect."

"Vi loved that kind of thing, as you can see from her poses. While we were working as Poison Girls, she trained for some time with a movement coach. She was really good at 'making shapes' on the stage. And you can see that in the way she is able to pose for photographs. It's brilliant."

Vi and Richard. Photo taken by Bernhardt Rebours during his tryout for Poison Girls in 1978.

RICHARD FAMOUS

Guitarist, singer, and songwriter for Poison Girls, Richard Swales (aka Richard Famous) grew up in the 1950s and politically came of age in the tumult of the late 1960s amidst a new generation of protestors.

"Politically I was a 1960s 'rebel,'" he says—a teenager in a world that felt perilously unstable. "I remember the Bay of Pigs incident—the US backed and funded attempt to invade Cuba in 1961—as a day the world very nearly ended; the assassination of JFK and the so-called death of hope."

Although "slightly too young" to fully understand the seismic shifts unfolding in society, Swales was "aware of the huge cultural changes that were going on." Instinctively antiwar, Swales became politically active at school. "The Schools Action Union was active in Leeds, and in our school, highlighting the teachers that still used corporal punishment on a regular basis," he says. "Naming and shaming in that way was considered very subversive. I avoided being expelled, but others didn't. This was my first introduction to more organised and more radical politics, and my first experiences of the way that leftist groups like Socialist Workers Party operated."

"I was also involved with actions by the Campaign for Nuclear Disarmament (CND) in the 1960s. I joined demos in Leeds and even travelled down to London—quite a big deal in the days before the M1 had been built—to take part in a sit-down protest outside the US embassy in Grosvenor Square alongside Pat Arrowsmith, who was legendary within CND circles."

Student politics were another draw. "In 1970, with long hair and those ubiquitous patched jeans, I went to the University of East Anglia in Norwich," Swales recalls. "UEA was one of the new universities built in the late 1960s, and I was involved with the occupation and sit-in at the Arts Block, which lasted over a fortnight, and was only resolved when the Computer Building—there was a dedicated building for the computer—was also threatened."

It was during Swales's time at UEA that he had his first encounter with future members of Crass. "Coincidentally, at around the same time, I went along to a live performance by an experimental group named EXIT—which both Penny Rimbaud and Gee Vaucher of Crass were involved with. I only twigged the connection much later," he admits. "I had an EXIT poster on my wall for years."

"For me, the early 1970s were also a time of deep disenchantment with the mainstream politics of the Wilson and Heath governments," he says. "There seemed no depths that politicians wouldn't stoop to. Looking back from today, of course, that seems very naïve—we were enjoying the fruits of twenty-odd years of progressive politics. As a generation, we seemed to have it all. It would turn to shit soon enough, though."

"As the 1970s progressed, things got bleak really quickly," he continues. "I left university and went travelling round North Africa for a while." Back in the UK, Swales was forced to accept brief periods of "soul destroying employment" as a clerical assistant in the Department of Health and Social Security. "It was the lowest clerical level, and staffed entirely by graduates dragged off the dole." The interview process was memorable. "I was asked, 'Are you British, were your grandparents British, have you ever been in any trouble with the law?' [and told,] 'OK, you start on Monday—or your money is stopped.'"

"That was followed by six gruelling months in a Dickensian factory in Brighton—feeding huge baths of ammonium bifluoride and concentrated nitric acid," he says. It was an experience that focused the mind as well as challenged the body. "I decided that I might be better off trying to take the band seriously, than risking my life in what was a health and safety horror show." At that moment, the city's new Resources Centre beckoned and "things took off."

Sue Cooper playing bass in No Fit State, 1979. Photo by Seamus (Nick James).

BELLA DONNA

Taking on the persona of Bella Donna—the name of the toxic herbaceous plant otherwise known as 'deadly nightshade'—Sue Cooper became Poison Girls' bass player while living in Brighton and moved to Epping with the band in 1977.

"Our parents met through the Communist Party in the 1930s," Cooper explains. "Our mother died when me and my twin sister Adi were very young, and our dad—who brought us up—was a member of the Communist Party all his life. So we grew up in this North London, Jewish, left-wing communist tradition. I wouldn't have said this at the time, but looking back—although we never were in the party—there was a really strong sense of political activism running through our lives."

"My involvement in the Anti-Apartheid Movement started around 1965–66," she says. While still teenagers, both Adi and Sue became active in peace campaigning and "going on all of the anti–Vietnam War protests." By the late 1960s, both were involved in school student activism. At the turn of the 1970s, Adi and Sue became more explicitly involved in the women's liberation movement, and joined 'consciousness-raising' groups.

The influence of the hippy-infused counterculture, combined with a strong affinity with libertarianism, encouraged a rejection of the strictures and discipline of the pair's familial Communist Party background. "We were not into that sort of 'organized' stuff," she explains, "but we were politically engaged and very active."

"We'd been on CND marches with our father when we were children, and we continued to march as young adults. I first met Richard Famous's brother in Trafalgar Square on the Easter CND march in 1968, and through that I eventually met Richard." After the pair's travels through North Africa (Morocco, Tunisia, and Algeria), Cooper arrived in Brighton to begin a course at the university, where Adi was already studying. "We were part of a group that organised a national women's conference on women's sexuality at Sussex University," she recalls. "We also set up a women's therapy group around that time."

Cooper got involved in The Body Show and then in the work of Poison Girls. "The Body Show had involved a mix of students and nonstudents, which was quite unusual at that time," she recalls. "After returning from the Edinburgh Fringe, we got much more involved with stuff happening in the town and at the Resources Centre and then The Vault."

Amidst the excitement of the early gigs in The Vault, Cooper experienced patronising gender assumptions that some in the early punk scene still clung to. "I can remember somebody coming up to me after a gig in Brighton saying, 'You play quite well, you know, *for a woman*.'" she says. "For some men, it just wasn't expected. I grew up with few women musicians to look to. There weren't that many role models of women musicians playing in rock bands." For Cooper, being in Poison Girls was an expression of the insistence many young women in the punk movement were making to be heard and taken seriously.

Managing parental expectation was another factor. "A common experience of immigrant families is a focus on upward mobility, and getting good jobs and establishing yourselves—my parents had that sort of focus." This meant that acceptance of their daughter's life choices had its limits. "They felt that there was a time and place when me being in a punk band was fine—while I was a student, and when it was just for fun—but the idea of me doing it 'for a career' was a step too far."

While rehearsing and performing with Poison Girls, Cooper became involved with Buzzcocks and the release of their first DIY EP. "Howard Devoto got in touch with us—I think he was getting in touch with everyone he knew—to see if we could help raise the money to fund their first vinyl release."

"I was part-funded for my degree, with my parents having to cover the rest of the fees. But instead of paying the university, I lent that money to Devoto to help pay for the pressing of *Spiral Scratch*," she reveals. "When they paid me back, I settled the outstanding fees."

By the time Buzzcocks made their one appearance at The Vault months later, Devoto had left and Pete Shelley was fronting the four-piece, but Cooper's associations with the band continued. When she arrived back from a trip to India, and decided she could not return to the Poison Girls fold, Cooper considered her next steps.

"I wondered if I should go back to university and do more academic stuff—it was much easier to get grants back them—but I didn't really fancy that," she says. "And then Richard Boon got in touch with me and asked if I wanted to come and help him. So I moved to Manchester and worked with Richard for two and a half years, setting up an office for him and supporting his work managing Buzzcocks."

"We had the New Hormones record label, and we ran a nightclub called The Beach Club. The Manchester scene at that point—1978–1980—was really exciting, with New Order and everything else that was going on."

"I went on from that to work in an art centre in York. I'd kept in touch with Poison Girls, and would arrange gigs for them when they were on tour and promote their work," she explains. "I still went to loads of their gigs."

Despite the personal issues that led Cooper to break with the band, the connections between her and the other founder members of Poison Girls remained strong. "Frances and I were good friends—Gary too. Richard remains my oldest friend. Every couple of years, me and my partner Nick go to visit him in Shetland. To me, Poison Girls were a family—a family by choice."

Bernhardt Rebours, Poison Girls European tour, 1981.

BERNHARDT REBOURS

A member of Poison Girls from 1978 to 1981, Bernard Chandler (aka Bernhardt Rebours) was a bass player, a designer, and a graphic artist for bands in the scene, and someone who turned down the chance to play bass with Crass.

Rebours's connections to the founder members of Crass and to Dial House stretch back to the 1960s. "The first contact I had was at the art department of my local further education college in 1965, straight out of secondary school," he says.

Penny Rimbaud and Gee Vaucher were teachers at the college, and Eve Libertine enrolled the following year. "I found Gee and Penny engaging, and relatively easy to relate to." Rebours enjoyed how the pair dispensed with conventional art teaching methods. "They encouraged us to explore our own curiosity about how we relate to the world." Not every art experiment was a success "but it always felt like it was an adventure," he says.

"Working in the college in close contact with Gee, Penny, and later Eve, drew me among others to Dial House." He was immediately struck by the ambience of the place. "Dial House in the summer was idyllic," he re-calls. "The atmosphere was welcoming, trusting, and inviting. Its physical setting, how everything was cared for in the house, the blissful garden—the resulting positive mental impact was something I had not experienced in quite the same way before."

In that conducive setting, a new musical endeavour began to form—Ceres Confusion. "Talking of it as a 'band' isn't strictly accurate," he says. "It was three of us—Penny, me and a guy called Pete [not the Crass Pete] who was the brother of a school mate. We 'played' or hit musical instruments and made a lot of noise." The project began as a relaxing "detox at the end of the working week—just noodling around, letting our stress out." Over time things firmed up "and the energy skyrocketed," he recalls. "Eventually, we were doing three- or four-hour sessions every Friday evening. It was nuts. But creative nuts. At times it was rather beautiful." Never reaching the stage of studio recording or playing live, Ceres Confusion ground to a halt. "It only lasted a year or two," Rebours recalls. "We just stopped. It felt that it had run its course."

Soon after, the first two-piece Crass rehearsals began, but Rebours's connections with the residents of Dial House continued. Months later, "Crass had just started getting gigs," he remembers. "I saw them a few times at the White Lion, Putney, and once at Action Space, just off Tottenham Court Road."

After one early gig, Crass made an unexpected offer to Rebours, asking him to join the band as a second bassist. "I was taken by surprise," he admits, "as Pete Wright was already playing bass with Crass." The intention seemed to be to experiment further with Crass's evolving sound, and to reinforce the power of the rhythmic low end by having two bass players bounce off each other. "The offer came completely out of the blue, and at that time I had no particular interest in being in a band. I didn't play bass guitar—which isn't an excuse not to join a 'punk' band! But I wasn't in the right space to trust myself to be involved."

"It was only later that Penny made contact with Poison Girls, who had recently moved to Burleigh House in Epping, a few miles down the road. They were on the lookout for a replacement bassist and he gave me their phone number. I arranged to meet up with them for a chat and a play, without thinking that I'd actually be *joining*."

"I borrowed a short scale Burns bass strung right-handed from Dial House," he explains. "Not having played a bass before, I had no means of comparison—so the fact that the strings were the wrong way round for a left-hander like me wasn't an issue."

At Burleigh House, Rebours took part in a rehearsal—which became a de facto audition—with encouragement from Famous, Subversa, and d'Boyle to improvise in response to the music. "That first audition, working with people I hadn't known or met before, with such different personalities was an odd experience—because it *didn't* seem unfamiliar. It was easy to relax in that sort of chemistry. I wasn't embarrassed about not being able to 'play' the bass. Ceres Confusion had given me this outlook."

"I went all over the fretboard, just trying to fit in," he says. Inspired by the approach of Ceres Confusion, Rebours "just waggled my fingers up and down the neck with no idea what I was playing or how, but responding to the mood and the commitment they so obviously showed."

"Despite my playing skills being pretty lame, I trusted the music would guide me. It was very spontaneous—bonkers, really! My attempts must have been so unexpected to them." Rebours focused on trying to complement and augment the musical prowess Poison Girls clearly already possessed. "It was something that the band took to," he says. "I hazard a guess that they found it refreshing."

But it was not technical ability that won him the spot, he suggests. "I felt they were more interested in me as a person than somebody who could play 'properly'—but without any soul," he suggests. "This was why I was hired, I guess."

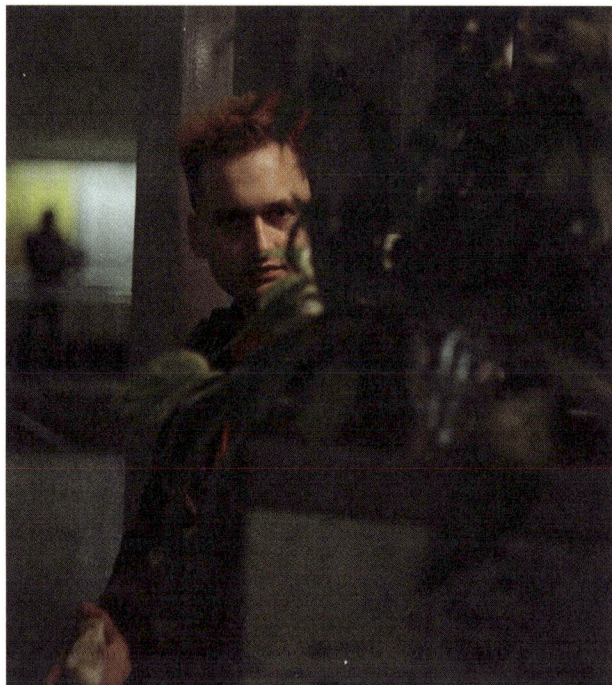

Max Vol, 1985. Photo by Tom Barwood.

MAX VOL

Adopting the stage moniker Max Vol, bassist Mick Shenton joined the Poison Girls lineup in October 1984—and played with the band for the next five years, forming the rhythm powerhouse alongside drummer Agent Orange, and becoming the de facto tour manager.

"In my twenties, I could think of nothing finer—particularly the touring," says Vol of his time in Poison Girls. "I thought it was amazing, I utterly loved it."

Vol's memories of playing in Europe are particularly warm. "We had a great relationship with a place in Berlin called The Kob. And that really did stick out. It was a gigantic, sort of semilegalised squat. On one of the main drags out of West Berlin. The people there were amazing and really engaged. We went back there many times over the years. There was certainly a ready audience in all of the German cities that we went to. I mean, it was still a niche kind of appeal—we played clubs, not stadiums. But people came out to see us in the places we toured."

Before joining Poison Girls, Vol had been part of the music scene in Coventry, the birthplace of the British ska and 2-Tone revival at the turn of the 1980s. "I'd graduated from the University of Warwick (on the outskirts of Coventry) and hung out around there for a couple of years after. I'd hooked up with the remnants of The Selecter after they first split, particularly the drummer Charley 'Aitch' Bembridge. We were kind of the 'Sly and Robbie of Leamington' before I moved down to London," he jokes.

As he looked for new musical opportunities, Vol was not particularly cognisant of the political punk scene in and around the capital. "My musical knowledge of that area at that time was pretty limited," he concedes. "I'd heard of Crass, for instance. But I could not have placed Crass and their various acolytes in any kind of framework. It just wasn't part of my background."

Before auditioning for Poison Girls, Vol was only "faintly aware" of their work. "I had heard a couple of their tracks before I tried out. Funnily enough, one of the tracks I knew best had no bass on it—so wasn't much help in applying for the post of bassist."

Vol was though tuned in to the political opposition to the actions of western governments that was fast fermenting in the 1980s. "Thatcher and Thatcherism was, in many ways, a boon to the counterculture, because it angered such a lot of people and pushed them into rejecting everything it stood for." This meant that the dividing lines on either side of the argument became clear cut. "Life became hard for a lot of people as a result, but the political landscape was a lot easier to decipher, I would say, than it became later."

Politically and personally, Vol came to appreciate Vi Subversa "as a force to be reckoned with." She was someone who "never minced her words on stage or off," he recalls. "Clearly, she was an amazing lyricist. She was also very funny and was super bright. It was a real privilege to be around her."

When it came to organising tours for the band, the methods remained DIY and low budget. "I don't know how we did it, really," he says—especially in an entirely analogue era. "Gigs were set up on the basis of a couple of phone calls. I think fax machines had arrived by that point, so maybe a few of those too. But it was amazing that you could tour Europe, and indeed the States, on the back of a few pieces of paper and little else."

Direct person–to–person contacts remained key. "Often new promoters that we found were friends of existing friends, or contacts of contacts we had made at other gigs. I soon discovered that there was an amazing network of like-minded people out there, across Europe certainly, who knew our work and were overjoyed to welcome us."

Vol is keen to stress that the experience, while inspiring, was rarely glamorous. "In practical terms, it could be extremely scrappy, and at times downright rough," he recalls. "We spent a lot of time sleeping on people's floors, and the pay was nonexistent."

One thing Vol is clear was absent from Poison Girls gigs during this time was crowd trouble that had marred too many early shows. "Vi and Richard told me about that—about the initial years of Poison Girls when, in fact, violence was rife at quite a lot of their gigs," he says. "I never saw any of that in the UK or Europe."

During that period, the band had kept up an intensive gigging schedule. "For several years, we were doing one hundred plus gigs annually, which was, with hindsight, stupidly exhausting," Vol suggests. That tempo began to slow in the band's final years as different side projects demanded more attention. "As the gig bookings slowed down, I started doing other stuff. I had to pay bills and had to keep my head above water." Vol had already begun to establish some physical and creative distance. "I had lived with them in Leytonstone for a couple of years, and I'd extricated myself from that, as my other interests developed."

What accelerated Vol's departure in May 1989 was Poison Girls' growing interest in theatrical performance, and the focus on *AIDS: The Musical*. "I just have an aversion to 'luvvies,' even if they're of an alternative flavour," he acknowledges. "That type of thing just didn't suit my 'style' at the time. From a musical perspective, I'd wanted to explore something new and, slowly but surely, my attention had turned elsewhere. It was not an unfriendly parting, by any means. I just thought it was time to do something else."

TOM BARWOOD

Brought in to ensure that Poison Girls' live sound consistently captured the band's aspirations, Tom Barwood toured with the band across the UK, Europe, and the US, becoming a fixture behind the mixing desk of hundreds of the band's gigs.

"I think we were all exploring new territory together," sound engineer Tom Barwood reflects on his work with

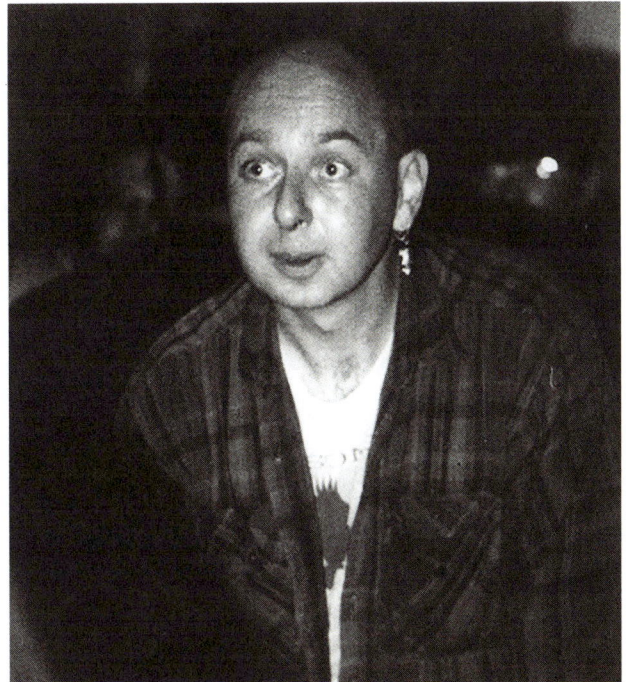

Tom Barwood at the soundboard, Berlin, 1995.

Poison Girls. "That was what was great for me."

Barwood's entry into sound work came through university. "I got a fairly middling general arts degree, and was very uninspired by the kind of opportunities being offered to me," he says. "Having obliged my parents by getting a degree, I thought, 'Fuck it—I'll do something that I want to do now.' I was already a musician, I was doing very left-field stuff, experimental things. I managed to get a postgrad diploma in electronic sound at Cardiff University."

"There was a punk scene in Cardiff when I was there, but it wasn't huge. I went to a few gigs, but I didn't get that involved. I was involved in left-wing politics and stuff as a student, in various kinds of niches. And so I was aware of that sort of politics. Also, I'd been quite involved in sexual politics, being part of the antisexist men's movement—for better or worse."

Once qualified, Barwood "fairly quickly walked into a job," becoming the technical manager of an electronic music workshop at Morley College in London. His focus remained on nontraditional and experimental styles of music making. "Now I look back on it, 'rock music' is the most formal music that I've ever been involved with—and I didn't really warm to it very much. At that time, I was not really involved in the 'music business' as such."

It was at the 1981 CND rally in London that Barwood first heard Poison Girls—as they defied the authorities' music ban with an a cappella version of "Take the Toys from the Boys." "I was there with a lot of like-minded people, and the sense of defiance that came from them doing that was great." But while the performance was memorable, it was not in itself a life-changing moment. "The scales didn't fall from my eyes," Barwood says with a smile. "But it made me aware of them, and I appreciated their agit-prop style."

A couple of years later, following an approach from old friend Martin Goldschmidt, Barwood found himself drawn into the Poison Girls fold. "It was immediately clear that there was a lot of energy in and around the band. I remember talking to Vi early on about what her influences were as a performer. That was very interesting, very exciting."

"Not having experience of the mainstream music business as such, maybe I didn't quite realise how exceptional they might have been. Because they weren't trying to conform to the pursuit of commercial success. I soon became aware that they were something special, for sure."

That sense of Poison Girls' distinctiveness was apparent from Barwood's first experiences out on the road with the band, viewed from his position behind the mixing desk. "One of the things that I really liked about them was that it seemed that each of their gigs was a singular event," he says. "Each one of their concerts felt unique, as far as I was concerned. Usually, the gigs were arranged through direct personal contacts, on a grassroots level. It wasn't like a commercial gig. The 'specialness' of each night really appealed to me."

"They always seemed to have a lot of new ideas, and there were some different 'phases' during the time I worked with the band. The first tour that I did with them was the Cabaret of Fools. That was them trying out some different angles, and trying to broaden their audience having different acts involved. I really like that cabaret format."

"They'd have comedians like Tony Allen and poets like Benjamin Zephaniah," he recalls. It was a sort of 'package' of entertainment, with Poison Girls at the top of the bill. They were making an event out of each of these gigs, and broadening their own horizons. I missed out on part of the Big Brother tour, the following year, because I had other work commitments, when they were trying yet another way to present themselves in a distinctive manner."

Part of the pursuit of a new identity, Barwood was aware, came from a determination to move on from the band's past associations. "Crass were not really spoken about very much," he remembers. "They were very much in the past tense, when I joined them. I never came across any of them in person until Vi's sixtieth birthday gig at The Astoria in 1995."

"I didn't know anything about Crass, really," he concedes. "The only thing that I did know was that they were bitterly upset by the rift with Crass, and the fact that they'd come back from a tour and found all their master tapes in the porch. They felt betrayed and very angry about that."

When it came to mixing the band's sound, Barwood felt very much in tune with Poison Girls' evolving style.

"When I first joined, they had Chris Grace playing wonderful fretless bass, and the keyboards and female backing vocals of Cynth Ethics. And that was a hugely different sound. They never had that kind of sound again. And I think they could have moved in a different direction if they'd stayed with that kind of lineup."

"In terms of mixing, I really liked some of the slower, more elegiac material. Big songs like 'I've Done it All Before' were ones where I could let rip with some delay and reverb and pump things up a bit. I always thought that that style worked really well, and suited what they were saying. I certainly found that easier to work with than some of the more angular stuff."

Touring with the band, in the UK and Europe in particular, Barwood enjoyed many extraordinary nights. "Some of those gigs were just absolutely superb, you know? They could not have been better. There's nothing like it—that sense of everybody coming together, this loyally supportive crowd. The energy that can flow from that is exceptional. Being part of that experience has remained my yardstick for judging exceptional live gigs ever since then."

PETE FENDER

Dan Sansom (aka Pete Fender) is the son of Frances Sokolov and Philip Sansom, and the brother of Gemma Samson. After playing bass with Poison Girls as a young teenager, he became a member of Fatal Microbes, Rubella Ballet, and then Omega Tribe. An accomplished sound engineer, he also recorded live and studio sessions by different punk and postpunk artists.

"I think it was the sudden change, after all that medium-style, medium-tempo music in the 1970s," says Dan, about his attraction to the punk explosion. "It had become so predictable. You suddenly had this faster, heavier, growly music and people were cutting their hair and jumping up and down—it was irresistible, really."

"I was still only twelve years old . . . so I was transfixed by the allure of it all being just kind of out of reach to me. I loved the sound of Buzzcocks, the attitude of Poly Styrene and Johnny Rotten. It connected with the same part of me that loved Alice Cooper and Marc Bolan. But I could tell there was another layer of angst about the way things were changing in the world. It was just so exciting, coming when it did."

The child of two committed anarchists, Dan learned about political activism from an early age, aware of his parents' involvement in protests like "the CND march from Aldermaston and all that," he says. It was a set of experiences which left him predisposed to the activist anarchist current that emerged within the punk scene. "I didn't make a conscious effort towards anarcho-punk," he says. "It happened around me and I took part. There just wasn't any question—it felt more like a sort of family loyalty than anything else."

What was a clear, conscious choice for Dan was becoming a musician and grabbing the opportunity to play with others. "There just wasn't anything else I wanted to do," he continues. "It offered everything: a means of expression, a social group—you can get really close in a band, it really is special when it works well." He quickly realised that he had a natural aptitude as a musician.

One of the first bands that Dan played in was the fledgling Poison Girls, becoming part of an early lineup of the new group fronted by his mother—"what an immense talent," he says, with evident pride. "I did a couple of stints playing bass with Poison Girls, the first was in '78 before they were widely known," he explains. Despite having the ability to hold his own alongside others in the group, and enjoying the experience, Dan knew that he needed to make his own independent musical mark.

"I think it spurred me to seek people of a similar calibre to work with and to try to produce good material. There was some personal cost—the family life that we compromised to make all this stuff happen was not in any way normal. But I tried not to feel under too much pressure as an artist because of my mum's success with the band. Maybe a little."

Dan has positive memories about his time playing with different bands. "The first record I did, *Violence Grows* with Fatal Microbes, is probably the single most important thing that I've done," he suggests. "I listen to it now and I am still amazed at the rhythm part I played on that. It's so simple, almost infantile in its simplicity, but it just couldn't be more effective. That song is probably the most powerful piece I have done and I can't find anything wrong with it—thanks in part to great production from Richard Famous and, of course, the superb vocal and lyrics from Honey Bane."

"The Peel session with Rubella Ballet was definitely a special moment. That was like, 'OK, we've arrived' . . . Playing the Stonehenge Free Festival with Omega Tribe in 1983 was a really thrilling experience—going on at five o'clock in the morning as the sun was rising after waiting all night to play," he recalls. "It was quite magical . . . you can't replicate something like that."

Over time, Dan's sense of distance from the anarchist and DIY punk scenes grew. "It did become too rigidly defined," he suggests, "but the scene was under attack from the police, and at the same time the benefit reforms were having an impact on people's social freedom . . . As well as this, the natural waning of enthusiasm in the face of toughening odds was setting in."

Dan recognised the need to take a different direction. "I started very young. I hadn't had much experience of the world outside the scene, apart from at school," he

Pete Fender performing at Vi's eightieth birthday celebration. Photo by Ming de Nasty.

says. "It was important for me to develop as a person away from all that attention and to see what I could do about earning a living and growing up and having a family and all that stuff. I dabbled around the trip-hop scene in the mid-1990s, played in a couple of cover bands, got a few producer gigs, that sort of thing, but essentially became quite domesticated and inured to regular work."

Dan also put his talents in music production and studio engineering to good use. "I was involved in a few cabaret projects, some theatrical work and that sort of thing, for a short while," he explains. "Political in a broader sense, you know? It was another avenue to explore after the energy of punk began to fade, and quite civilised after being drenched in beer at every gig."

Adapted with permission from an interview with Pete Fender in *Street Voice UK*, originally published in 2014.

APPENDIX 2.2: SPOTLIGHTS- FAMILY AND FRIENDS:

GEMMA SANSOM

The daughter of Frances Sokolov (Vi Subversa) and Philip Sansom, and the sister of Dan Sansom (Pete Fender), Gemma grew up in Poison Girls' shared houses and played in both Fatal Microbes and Rubella Ballet.

For Gemma, her parents' experience in the postwar British anarchist movement became a form of political education by osmosis. "It's hard to say when I became aware of it," she says, "but from a young age I knew about anarchy and that my father had been a writer and illustrator for *Freedom*, that he'd gone to prison for his beliefs. I kind of absorbed the ideas from material lying around his flat and tried to understand words like 'syndicalist.'"

"I liked the concept of a barter system where nobody would be rich—that was easy to understand too," she continues. "I was aware that the general population thought of anarchy as chaos and bomb-throwing terrorists, but I knew different. My folks were pacifists to the core."

"As I got older, I was really proud of that stuff," she says. "I realised my father was well respected in the movement with an important history. But it did feel like it was a politics from a different time. He was imprisoned for inciting disaffection of the troops during World War II, amongst other things. His comrades were fighting for the end of the state, and for the workers to rise up. So were the punks of the 1980s. But I feel like the anarchist politics of my youth was more about creating alternative ways to live now, not waiting for a revolution that may never come."

"I think my father saw aspects of the women's movement as unnecessarily divisive and that we should all work together, women and men, to bring about change," she continues. "This was at odds with the feminist movement that my mother was so closely involved in, which was so clearly saying that women had stuff to do on their own."

"But politics aside, he was my dad too, and when I was young and went to stay with him in London we just hung out and had fun."

Once Gemma, Dan, and Frances had moved to the Sussex coast, they connected with the local alternative and underground scenes. "There were a few other hippy families in Brighton in the 1970s, of course," she recalls. At the age of seven, Gemma was enrolled in a local Free School for a year, "where the idea was to teach kids what they wanted to learn about, find the people that had the skills and knowledge, and not just teach the usual stuff," she says.

A few years later, Gemma's awareness of the new phenomenon of "punk" began when her mum began work in the city's Resources Centre. "Dan was a punk by then as well and was really into Buzzcocks, who played at The Vault," she recalls. Younger than her brother, Gemma's involvement started a little later. "It wasn't until we moved to Epping and formed Fatal Microbes that I started to get actively involved in the punk thing."

Gemma and her brother were in the unusual—if not unique—position, beginning before either were teenagers, of having a mother who fronted a political punk band. How did it feel to be in that position? "That's a difficult question because there are different answers," she begins. "On the one hand, it was cool and I was really proud. She was an amazing performer and as the band got bigger I enjoyed some of the reflected limelight. If it hadn't been for her doing the music, none of it would have happened. But it set in motion a change in all of us that had deep repercussions. Her lyrics were so powerful that sometimes they scared me. She dealt with such heavy stuff in her writing and things became heavy around us without much protection."

"But I think the hardest thing in the long term," she continues, "was that she stopped being a mum. She'd been drifting off for years but, when the band fully took off, she was on a journey that became all-encompassing for her and took her focus far away—sometimes physically too, when Poison Girls were on tour. I was left to get on with it. So I got on with it."

There were opportunities to be a part of things, Gemma suggests. "I loved Poison Girls' music and went to most of their gigs over the years," she says. "I went on some of the tours abroad with them, and often Rubella Ballet was on the bill—so, of course, I was there. I sold merchandise at their gigs and I did the mail order and fan mail with Gary—for which they paid me! I sang on a few recorded tracks too."

But there were clear personal costs too. "At the time I accepted the situation and joined in," Gemma says. "It wasn't until later that I became more aware of the loss."

Teenage defiance against a punk mum would have posed its challenges too. "If I was going to rebel I would have needed to become a successful banker or something," she suggests. "Maybe I just delayed it for when I became a mum myself? I'm a very different

pic by Caroline McfadIe Marwhad

Rubella Ballet (Gemma, Sid, Sean, and Zillah), 1983.

mum to my kids, and have brought them up in relative-ly conventional surroundings."

"That said, my politics are still the same, and my two daughters would definitely make my mum proud if she could see what amazingly strong women they have become."

ZILLA MINX AND SID TRUELOVE

Members of Rubella Ballet, whose early lineups included Gem Sansom and Pete Fender, Zillah Minx and Sid True-love were involved with the work of Poison Girls for many years, joining the band on tour, living at Poison Girls' house and releasing material through the Xntrix label.

"The first time we met Poison Girls was at a gig, at the Conway Hall in Holborn," Zillah Minx recalls. "I was there with Sid." By that time a then-homeless Sid Truelove had

already been invited to move into Poison Girls house. "It wasn't actually a house. It was more like . . . a mansion," says Minx. "It was huge," Truelove agrees. "It had two staircases up either side to go upstairs. It was massive."

Relieved to have somewhere to live, Truelove also knew that he was part of a very different way of living. "When I moved in, I kind of moved into a commune," he says. "I was part of a commune." It also came with another key benefit—proximity to Minx. "When I first met Zillah, she was living in East Ham and it was a long way across London for me to reach her. Living so much closer to her in Epping, that changed."

"But Poison Girls' house in Epping had already been marked for demolition, because of the plan to build the M25 through the area," he continues, and the building was already showing signs of dilapidation. "Burleigh House was something like five floors," Minx says. "And the top two floors were falling apart, really," Minx says. "It was the time that Sid and me were getting to know each other," Minx says. "And we were both allowed to live there."

It was an extraordinary opportunity for the pair. "It was a really good space, not least because it had so many

297

rooms," she continues. "One of the rooms was a rehearsal studio, and Poison Girls would set up their PA system and had all of their equipment in there." That meant that anyone in and around the house had the chance to experiment with making music. "Poison Girls were generous enough to let us use it, and that's really why Rubella Ballet formed. Before that, it had been one of the reasons why Dan [Pete Fender] and Gemma [Gem Stone] were able to start Fatal Microbes, with Honey Bane, so quickly."

Both bands began with fluid and changing lineups. "At first, there were a lot of different people trying out in Rubella Ballet." One of the earliest lead singers was Annie Anxiety. "When Annie left, I ended up being the singer," Minx explains.

"On the way to a gig, Annie just decided, 'Right, that's it. I'm not doing any more,'" Sid recalls "I'd heard Zillah singing all the time, and knew she could do it. Before we arrived at the gig I just said, 'Do you want to sing?'"

As well as living and rehearsal space, Poison Girls also gave Rubella Ballet some early exposure. "We were playing support slots with them straight away for our first few gigs," Minx says. "They were always so helpful with getting us live shows, and offering advice on how we might do certain things."

But life at Burleigh House was not without its downsides. "There were some quite difficult times there as well," she acknowledges. "There were these violent skinheads around who used to attack people," she says. "And because Poison Girls had an open-house policy, sometimes some very violent people would turn up and try to scare us all. One day a skinhead named Animal burst into the house when only me, Sid, Gemma, and Dan were there, and was threatening to kill everyone. But I come from East London, and I was used to standing up to skinheads, and I was able to get him out of there."

"And, of course, everyone living in the house was poor," Minx says. "We were living communally but also very cheaply. We would have one meal together in the evenings." There were also house meetings to discuss and share out work, which could be challenging because of the mix of family, parental and cross-generational relationships involved. "Dan was around fourteen. Gemma was about twelve," Minx recalls, and living in a shared house with their mother, other band members and family friends. Not always the easiest of situations for any fledgling teenager.

By the time that BBC TV cameras arranged to visit Poison Girls to record a segment for 'youth programme' Oxford Road Show, the band had relocated to a new residence in Leytonstone. "We used to go there a lot, we used to rehearse there and they had set up a new studio in the cellar," Minx recalls.

With Poison Girls' support, Rubella Ballet has begun work on their Ballet Bag cassette release. "We must have been one of the first bands to release a cassette tape in a bag that had all these other things with it— like a 'lucky bag.'" she says. "The whole thing was Lance d'Boyle's idea. So we recorded a nine-track cassette, packaged it with a poster, a badge, and a lyric book in a zip bag. We printed the booklet on Poison Girls' drum roll printer, and the badges were made at Better Badges, by my sister's husband. We were able to do this ourselves, because we had access to the facilities where we could produce all this stuff."

"I remember turning up in Leytonstone one day, and Vi saying that Oxford Road Show was coming to film. 'Well, we can show you working on your Ballet lyric book,' she said. I ended up appearing in the film just because it was a day I was working with Vi on the release. It wasn't anything we'd planned," says Minx.

The footage captured a moment early in the collaboration between Rubella Ballet and Poison Girls that would develop and evolve over the course of many years. Both Minx and Truelove recognise how pivotal that relationship was. "Without Poison Girls, my involvement with Flux of Pink Indians would never have happened," says Truelove. "Rubella Ballet wouldn't have happened. It really is down to Poison Girls—all of that. We planted the seeds of what we hoped to do. But it was Poison Girls that helped those seeds blossom into so many different, amazing things."

HEATHER JOYCE

One half of the feminist duo Toxic Shock, a band directly inspired by the work of Poison Girls, Heather Joyce and Alice Marsh joined the 1983 Big Brother tour within weeks of writing their first songs.

A face-to-face zine interview at the Exeter gig on the 1981 Total Exposure tour was Heather's first in-person encounter with Poison Girls. "It was life changing and life affirming," she recalls. "I had a lot of conflict going on within my family, and I'd just never, ever met anyone like them. Vi was mesmerising and Richard was so cool and clear. They were both so warm and funny and generous with their time in front of the three scrappy kids interviewing them. I had no idea it was possible to grow up and be an adult like that," she says. "It gave me hope!"

Two years later, Heather (known as Heff at the time) was living in Birmingham, and active in the women's peace and feminist circles in the city. Seeing Poison Girls perform at The Mermaid changed the direction of her life and that of her close collaborator Alice Marsh. "We were just genuinely thrilled by them," she says.

"That Birmingham gig had affirmed everything about the choices I'd made in my short life." In Heff's flat, the pair quickly put together their first songs—with Heff on saxophone, Al on bass, with both sharing vocals.

Their excitement was palpable, but there was little by way of a plan for the new band. "I was eighteen, possibly just nineteen by then, but still really young and naïve," she concedes. "Al was a few years older than me—but there honestly wasn't any agenda." The duo wanted to share their work with Poison Girls at the next date on the tour. "We didn't have much money, so hitching to the gig to show them our songs meant we might at least get in at the door for free!"

"We didn't pitch to play alongside them, we just turned up at their gig," Heather continues. After Poison Girls watched the new duo perform for them after their own soundcheck, they immediately gave Toxic Shock a slot on the bill. "I never thought they'd let us play with them that night," says Heather. "And the idea that they might take us on tour was like living in a dream." But Toxic Shock were soon signed up for upcoming Poison Girls dates that would take them across the country.

Heading out on the road on the Big Brother tour in the autumn of 1983 was a revelation. "The first shock was the money," Heather admits. "The deal was that we would be paid £15 a night each. Al and I were still signing on the dole and had never earned any money playing music—unless you count my teenage job as an assistant in a record shop and the whopping £3 an hour I earned giving clarinet lessons."

"My dole money was about £23 a week, if I remember rightly. So it seemed like a fortune. Perhaps not such a good deal for the solo acts, on reflection, as we were paid per person. There was a lot of sleeping on people's floors and eating chips and beans," she recalls. "As vegans on the road, Al and I weren't eating properly and kept getting sick. I stopped drinking alcohol and started taking pint glasses of herb tea on stage which helped a bit and at least looked like beer."

"The best moment of the night was always Poison Girls' set, when—whatever else was going on—Al and I would just push our way to the front and manically dance, singing along to every song. It was all very cathartic. They had a fantastic sense of theatre, of the whole show, of colour and light. Vi was magnetic, of course, but the whole experience was often more like being taken on a journey than going to a gig."

"My impression was that Richard was very much the composition, musical arrangements, and business guy and the general motor behind the band—a job he did with relentless skill and energy. He was a brilliant musician. I was very in awe of him. He was a bit more distant and reserved—faced with the relentless flow of people coming through the Leytonstone house."

Cover of Toxic Shock's *Just Another Day* EP (Vindaloo Records, 1985)

"Some of Vi's most intimate—and sexy—lyrics were obviously about their relationship. That made him something of a mysterious figure."

"Lance was more amiable and open. He was a lovely bloke, originally from Birmingham. Long after Toxic Shock split, he was regularly in town visiting his dad and he often came to stay at my place for some respite," she remembers. "We got on really well, and he had wonderfully varied musical tastes."

"Out of all the bands at that time, I think Poison Girls were not only the most extraordinary—in that they were fronted by a singer-guitarist, and also had a drummer, who were each a generation older than everyone else in the room. But they were also the cheekiest, the most original musically, and the most innovative—as well as the most interesting, politically."

"I'm both humbled and honoured to have grown up from my midteens onwards knowing them so well and to have started my career as a musician by gigging alongside them."

Robert Lloyd performing with Toxic Shock on Vi's fiftieth birthday, 1985. Photo by Ming de Nasty.

ROBERT LLOYD

Frontman, lyricist, singer, and songwriter for break-through Birmingham punk band The Prefects (formed in 1976) and experimental postpunk nonconformists The Nightingales (launched in 1979), Robert Lloyd shared the stage with Poison Girls at many gigs—and recorded a single with Vi Subversa.

Robert Lloyd's first encounter with Poison Girls was in his home city of Birmingham. "There were a bunch of characters in the city that called themselves the '021 Anarchists'—021 being the area code for Birmingham," he recalls. "They were organising a benefit gig for a mental health patients' advocacy group called PROMPT and, for whatever reason, they thought that The Nightingales would be a good match to join the bill alongside Poison Girls."

"I don't know why this anarchist group took to The Prefects and then to The Nightingales, because I never thought that we were a particularly political kind of band. But other people seemed to think so." Lloyd does recognise that The Nightingales were in sympathy with the outsider and DIY impulses of the political punk scene. "I don't want to get pretentious about it, but I have got a sort of

anarchist streak in me. I just don't 'wear the badges,' if that makes sense. The Nightingales were never part of, and never joined, any kind of 'gang.'" he says. "But, as far as I can recall, that's the first time I would have come across Poison Girls—playing together at Digbeth Civic Hall."

For Lloyd it was not a moment of epiphany—at least, not in relation to the music, lyrics, or presentation of Poison Girls. But he was immediately struck by the personality, presence, and talent of Vi Subversa. "That was the main thing that affected me," he confirms. "I immediately just knew that there was something very special about her."

"It was at the time that Martin Goldschmidt was their manager, and pretty soon after that, we were invited to join a little tour with them—a bit of a package of us, Omega Tribe, and Toxic Shock joining Poison Girls. It was very much bands from the anarchist punk side of things and The Nightingales. I thought we were a bit of an anomaly, really."

"People were definitely there to see Poison Girls—so to include us made it an odd bill," says Lloyd. "But I liked—and I still like to this day—playing to people who don't know who you are."

"That's when I got to speak to Vi properly, on those dates. And I don't know what it was, but she obviously came to like me well enough for us to keep working together, to make the single together that we did and for me to perform with the women from Toxic Shock at her fiftieth birthday gig."

"To me, Vi was open-minded, loving, funny, and nonjudgemental. I felt that she passed on a great deal of wisdom. I was a fairly thick young man, really. I didn't think I was clever enough to be embraced. But that was one of the many beauties of her—her open heart and her open mind. I can't speak on her behalf, as to what she thought of me. But, immediately, I knew. I just knew there was something very special about her."

"And she talked to me about things, like contraception, that I wouldn't normally have thought about. She spoke with me about what you would call 'feminist issues.' I was from Cannock in the West Midlands, and that was not the kind of stuff that people were talking about."

One element of the *Keep Lying, I Love It* single that the pair produced together in 1985 that Lloyd is keen to emphasise is Vi's humour and wit. "That single is full of funny gags and clever insinuations about sexuality," he says. "Her humour was a very strong part of who she was. She was obviously a very serious person, but she was quite happy to muck about and to take the piss out of herself—and so am I. So maybe that's part of why we got on so well."

"I'm not going to lie and say I'm a Poison Girls fan. I mean, I think 'Persons Unknown' is fantastic, a genuinely fantastic piece of work—but that's probably their most popular song. They did have a few other songs that I quite liked, but not loads," Lloyd concedes. "I think that Vi would have said the same about my music. I don't think you'd have found any Nightingales records in her vinyl collection."

"I think the *Keep Lying* single was only ever intended to be a one-off. It wasn't like we were going to be collaborating on a regular basis. And, by this stage, The Nightingales had got a bit of its own audience, and Poison Girls had got their own audience. We'd toured together once or twice, and that's enough. You don't want to just do the same thing over and over again."

Months before the recording session for *Keep Lying*, Lloyd had accepted an invitation from Goldschmidt to appear at the gig to celebrate Vi Subversa's fiftieth birthday, and was backed on stage by Heather Joyce and Alice Marsh of Toxic Shock. "I performed at that gig, and then after that I didn't see her again," he says, with a clear sense of sadness. Ten years later, "they got in touch with me and asked me to play at her sixtieth birthday party—and I was going to be in America at that time, so I couldn't do it."

Years later, Lloyd felt inspired to write a song in Vi's memory. "Apart from one song about my mum, I've never written a song about or for someone like that. I think Vi is worth so much more credit, certainly as a human being—and as an artist she did enough top notch stuff that she should be recognised more highly." The track "Frances Sokolov" appeared on the 2022 Nightingales album *The Last Laugh*. "By my standards, it is a bit soppy, I suppose," Lloyd says. "But it is genuine, and it expresses a very sincere feeling."

"Poison Girls were all good souls, as well," he concludes. "I very much liked them all. They were a pleasure to tour with. They were a band of good people."

STEVE IGNORANT

Founder member, songwriter, and vocalist for the band Crass, Steve Williams (Steve Ignorant) shared a stage with Poison Girls for almost a hundred gigs between 1979 and 1981. He also developed a close personal bond with the musicians of Poison Girls, particularly with Vi Subversa and Lance d'Boyle.

Although Steve Ignorant would come to hold the work of Poison Girls in the highest esteem, he was not immediately won over by seeing them play. "Pete Wright came back to Dial House and said, 'I've just seen this band play, they live in Epping, and I think that they're worth checking out,'" Ignorant recalls. "So me, Pete, and Phil Free went along to the next Poison Girls gig. That was the first time I ever saw them—and, I have to admit, I really didn't like them," he concedes. "The music wasn't 'punk' enough for me. It was also Vi Subversa's voice. It sounded a bit like Eartha Kitt to me, which I wasn't expecting."

"But as time went on, I put me sensible head on, and I thought, 'No, she's singing about issues that no one else is, you know? She's doing songs about being a single mother, and other really important personal things, you know? No-one else is doing that.'" But that recognition took time. "That understanding of what they were about did come, but afterwards."

What made the key difference was the opportunity for Crass and Poison Girls to spend some time in each other's company. Both bands recognised the many things they had in common, but for Ignorant it was the personalities of Poison Girls that made their alliance so straightforward. "For me, it was just the open friendliness and easiness of them that clinched it," he says. "Vi was just so interesting to talk to and to listen to her speak about what she'd been through in her life. And Lance d'Boyle as well. You couldn't help but warm to Lance instantly, the minute you met him. He was such a great bloke, you know—they were all just lovely people."

The affinity between the two bands evolved quickly, Ignorant recalls. "That just happened as time went on and we saw each other more," he says. "And then the first time that the two bands played together—that gig, that night, really gelled things."

The experience of sharing a stage together became a pivotal moment for both groups. "As well as being good

Vi and Steve Ignorant, 1980.
Photo courtesy of Bernhardt Rebours.

people, they were such a good band," Ignorant says. "I remember standing in front of the stage watching the Poison Girls at one of our early shared gigs—it might have been in Manchester—and they played 'Bremen Song.' And maybe for the first time I really listened, and I realised in that moment, 'Fuck me—this really is good.' That's when my heart really warmed to them. I realised, even back then, what an underrated band they were. Even by people like me. I'd underrated them," he admits.

The agreement with Crass opened up the potential of a larger and growing audience for Poison Girls. But it was not necessarily an immediately engaged one. "I'd say that, at the beginning, Poison Girls got quite a cold reception from the audience, because so many of the punks were waiting to see Crass," Ignorant says. "Then the ice began to break, and then they started to get a few people coming along regularly to see them, who would want to talk to them afterwards."

"So it took a bit of time. But I think once their albums and singles circulated more widely—and people were able to read their brilliant lyrics—that changed," he suggests. "And a lot of young women started coming to gigs as well."

Away from the intensity of gigging, Ignorant's personal connections with Vi and Lance also grew. "I used to go around to Burleigh House quite a lot on my own. I remember one morning, when it was just me and Vi there, me sitting at the kitchen table with a cuppa she made me, and she was at the sink, with her back to me, washing up. And she said, 'I've got this new song—now, how does it go?' And she just sang these lyrics to me—just me—as she worked," he recalls. "I remember thinking,

'This is fucking great—she's seeing me as an equal, and she's not treating me like a young kid.' For a while I was worried that maybe she would, but she never did. She was always full on, straight on, but she was never patronising. And she was such a strong person that, as time went on, you saw that she could do anything, really."

"I remember saying to her once, 'Vi, I just wish I could write songs like you.' And, because she was so supportive, she said, 'Well, you do alright?'" Ignorant continued: "'No, there's a *poetry* in your lyrics, Vi, that I can't match.' I mean, the songs she wrote—'Cry No More,' 'Stonehenge 1985'—were just fantastic. How fucking brilliant do you have to be to write something like 'Persons Unknown'? This was a woman and a writer who's not gonna hold back on what she thinks."

As for Poison Girls' decision to end the close collaboration with Crass, "It was the right thing to do," says Ignorant. "The good thing to come out of it for them was that they proved that they could make a name for themselves, on their own terms and in their own way. And there's so many people that I meet today who come up to me and say, 'Steve, I always loved Crass. But I think Poison Girls are better.' And quite often I'll say, 'Do you know what? I'm sort of with you there.'"

"Where Poison Girls really excelled was their ability to reach people very easily with what they were saying," he concludes. "Vi's writing about feminism, about single parenthood, it wasn't 'intellectual'—the way she said things. I could read it and understand it, and that let me in so I could connect with those ideas."

APPENDIX 3: BAND MEMBERS

The 'cast' of Poison Girls, from 1977 to 1989 (and there-after)—as recalled by Richard Famous.

Vi Subversa (aka Frances Sokolov) (1975–89)
From the first rehearsal to the last encore. Singer, guitarist, and primary lyricist—the beating heart of the band.

Richard Famous (aka Richard Swales) (1975–89)
From the start to the finish—guitar, occasional vocals, and Vi's songwriting partner.

Lance d'Boyle (aka Gary Lance Robins) (1975–84)
Drummer, percussionist, occasional songwriter, singer and, visual artist.

Drummers

Lance d'Boyle (1975–August 1984)

Agent Orange (aka David Bennett) (21 August 1984–November 1989)
We had met him several times when he was playing drums with The Cravats, and got on well. We heard he had relocated to London and, when Lance had to leave, got in touch, and persuaded him that he should not give up playing. A longtime vegetarian, who didn't eat vegetables, he seemed to exist on cigarettes and cake! A great drummer though.

Scheebo Pampillonia (20 January 1985)
Longtime drummer with The Stilettos (the precursor to Blondie), and a stalwart of the New York City music scene. He stepped in to cover the drums for our appearance at the Counter Inaugural Ball in Washington, DC, after Dave Bennett was refused a US visa.

Bass players

Bella Donna (aka Sue Cooper) (1975–October 1977)
Part of The Body Show. Left Brighton to travel to India and eventually work for New Hormones. Briefly managed Linder. Played in different groups, and formed a klezmer band, playing double bass and gigging in and around Manchester. Subsequently became a board member of International Greenpeace.

Chlorine (aka Jaqui) (1977–early 1978)
Friend of the band Jaqui joined after Bella left. A good bassist who played several early gigs. But Jaqui had a job which took up too much of her time, and the band wanted to rehearse every day.

Scotty 'Boy' Barker (22 April–17 June 1978)
An Epping local. A solid, no-nonsense bass player. Through him we met Honey Bane. He played bass with Pete Fender and Gemma Sansom on the Fatal Microbes' *Violence Grows* twelve-inch, the flip side of Poison Girls' *Piano Lessons*.

Pete Fender (aka Dan Sansom) (4 August–24 August 1978)
Had already played several gigs with Poison Girls between Bella Donna leaving and Scotty 'Boy' Barker joining. A wonderful musician who was able to fill in brilliantly when we found ourselves between bass players. Went on to play with Rubella Ballet and Omega Tribe, amongst other bands. He also set up and ran a studio as both engineer and producer.

Bernhardt Rebours (aka Bernard Chandler) (October 1978–5 July 1981)
Recommended to Poison Girls by Crass, even though he didn't play bass! He arrived, dived right in, and earned the nickname 'Thunderbugger Rebours.' He played throughout the time the band played alongside Crass, leaving to have a baby with Mandy (of "Mandy Is Having a Baby" fame). After leaving the band, he continued to play—developing an interest in improvised jazz, and becoming an exquisite graphic designer.

Nil (aka Neil Wright) (28 September–20 December 1981)
With the band from the beginning, he was an essential presence throughout the early years. The label "roadie" does not do him justice. He was our driver, sound engineer, fabricator, inspiration, and the offstage fifth member of the band—before taking up bass duties. He did everything with a quiet efficiency, including playing a self-built 'skeleton' electric violin on *Chappaquiddick Bridge*.

Chris Grace (19 June 1982–15 July 1983)
Joined us from Sheffield after connecting with the band through the *Wargasm* project, arriving as we were sorting out the songs for recording *Where's the Pleasure*. He brought a fretless bass with him, which features on several tracks. Went on to become an in-demand session bass player in several big London studios. In 2006, he set up the Bluebarn recording and rehearsal facility in Ely, Cambridgeshire, becoming a skilled studio music producer.

Mark Dunn (7 August–15 December 1983)
Came recommended through a contact at Southern Studios. He was the bass player on the live set recorded for

Seven Year Scratch, and his synth backing track formed the basis for "The Offending Article."

Martin Heath (24 January–10 August 1984)
He had played with Howard Devoto, amongst others. A great funky bass player who contributed to all the Illuminated period records, two singles, and the *Songs of Praise* album.

Pete Fender (10 August–27 August 1984)

Brian (September 1984)
Delivered a stunning audition, and played one terrible gig (at The Klub Foot in London's Hammersmith on 15 September). Talented and capable, but not right for the band. We finally realised that personality was far more important than technique!

Pete Fender (29 September 1984)

Max Vol (aka Mick Shenton) (24 October 1984–13 May 1989)
He answered an advert as part of the same audition process that led us to Brian, but spent the whole audition with his back to us! He was asked if he wanted to join after the disaster of Brian's brief tenure, and thankfully said yes. A great bass player and a perfect fit for us. Alongside drummer Agent Orange, he formed the rhythm section that powered Poison Girls' final five years. He was also effectively the tour manager for the band and eventually left to became a production manager at London's Southbank.

Andy Demetriou (30 July—15 November 1989)
He met Vi when she was a student at East London University. A solid rock bass player and a good bloke.

Keyboards

Cynth Ethics (aka Sian Daniels) (27 May 1984–10 May 1985)
Martin Goldschmidt introduced Sian to us. She was an excellent and experienced singer, having worked with Kokomo, and 'nearly' (her word) with Van Morrison. She was also a pianist and piano tuner and took to the synth with relish. A great addition to the more sophisticated sound of the band for the time she was with us.

Sound

Tom 'Tom' Barwood (May 1984–November 1989)
Also introduced to us by Martin Goldschmidt. He had been working in West Square Electronic Music Studio which was part of Morley College. He had a good musical ear and became a key member of Poison Girls setup right until the end. Went on to be the resident sound engineer at the Bass Clef—the most hip jazz club in London's Shoreditch in the 1990s.

Management

Simon Johnson (1975–78)
The director and energy behind The Body Show, the precursor of the band. He was also the instigator of Xntrix Records, and played a big part in early Poison Girls. He bowed out when we started working with Crass.

Martin Goldschmidt (1983–85)
Became Poison Girls' "all duties" manager before and throughout the time that Poison Girls were working with Illuminated Records. While he remained a close associate and supporter of the band, he left to focus on setting up the Cooking Vinyl label.

Line-ups for the 1995 reunion gigs

The Astoria II, London, 3 June 1995
Vi Subversa (guitar, lead vocals); Richard Famous (guitar, vocals); Bernhardt Rebours, Bella Donna and Chris Grace (bass); Lance d'Boyle and Agent Orange (drums).

The Kob, Berlin, 10 June 1995
Vi Subversa (guitar, lead vocals); Richard Famous (guitar, vocals); Chris Grace (bass); Agent Orange (drums).

APPENDIX 4: RICHARD FAMOUS'S GIG DIARIES

Beginning in 1978, Richard Famous began to keep a hand-written 'gig diary,' recording details of every live show the band—and its spin-offs and side-projects—played in the UK, the US, and across continental Europe. The following extracts from the three volumes in the series offer a revealing (and unromanticised) picture of the band's experiences out on the road.

1978

16 January, The Vortex, London
First on, in a bill of four (The Art Attacks headlined). Gig went well—slow start, good ending—audience cold. What do you expect for the first one at The Vortex? Got return gig. Paid £10 plus six guest tickets.

27 January, Centrepoint, London
Good evening, including fire eating, poems and Bum Notes disco. Did the same set as at The Vortex, faster and with more continuity. Played well, small stage. Met Crass.

11 February, Polytechnic, Brighton
A prestigious one. Support to Siouxsie and the Banshees. Good audience, good gig, slick and efficient. We pulled it off really well with our biggest crowd yet (400–500 people). Got paid £10. Siouxsie is a stuck-up snob.

9 May, The Triad, Bishop Stortford
Nice hall, and stage. We played two sets (a mistake—last time we do that). We drove 200 people away, ended up with about fifteen left. Great. No door money, just a whip round. We got £8.14. Van expenses for the night £11.10. All good clean fun. The bastards will regret it next time.

17 June, The Factory, Manchester
Nice new place, big stage and dance floor, clear sound and a good, big audience. We played for around an hour—fast and well—with everyone dancing. Last gig with Scott.

1979

18 January, University, Bradford
Start of a short northern tour. We played with Crass and Mick Duffield's film *Autopsy*. The Epileptics [later renamed Flux of Pink Indians] didn't turn up until it was all over. Our playing was a bit flabby—still, the audience didn't help. Paid £30 expenses.

9 April, Moonlight Club, London
With Crass. Nice club, respectful 'punk elite' audience. So much dyed hair. Used our own PA, which was a bit of a strain. Played well, and the evening seemed fine—usual response.

26 May, Conway Hall, London
With Crass and The Epileptics. A really good gig, and nice to go back to the same hall. New set order really worked. Big audience—attentive and receptive. Benefit for *Peace News*. Met three fanzine people who wanted to do interviews.

14 July, Hope & Anchor, London
Very hot, very full and very, very sweaty. Small stage, good PA and a great atmosphere. Played very fast and very well. Paid £10.

18 August, Resources Centre, Brighton
One of those important nights—the first real headlining gig without Crass and a return to Brighton and the Resource Centre. A good evening all round. We played with a few technical slips, but generated a lot of energy.

4 October, Village Hall, Orton, Sevenoaks
Nice country hall—very plush area (and audience), and we freaked them out a bit, I think. First gig using our ambulance for transport. Played really well with the new set. Paid £20. The benefit was for the youth club and we raised about £100.

28 October, Theatre Royal, Stratford
The one that got broken up by the National Front/British Movement. 'Sieg Heils' and abuse through Rubella Ballet's set, and then stopping our set outright. Much confusion. Vi got felled by a can; Lance hit over the head; and [manager] Simon [Johnson] beaten up quite badly. Bad organisation by the Theatre, and—I suppose—by us. We were very shaken up—almost to breaking point.

1980

31 January, The Warehouse, Preston
We did the 'new' set—taking risks and generally revitalised ourselves. A nice attentive and appreciative audience, and lots of good feedback. We played really well. Stayed at Sue's [Cooper], used Tandy PA. Paid £43. A good one—the best for ages, in fact.

14 March, Centro Iberico, London
No real audience. The Centro was good, but a bit dispersed in terms of energy to work from. It cost us money—we lost about £20, hey-fuckin'-ho—but thought it was worth doing.

29 March, Nijmegen, Holland

The last night of the Dutch tour—a huge old school building. We played really confidently, taking liberties with arrangements and generally tightening everything up. A relaxed, easy atmosphere. Drove straight back to the Hoek van Holland for the boat ride home. Amazing tour. After paying Paul Tandy for PA, we split the money. We lost about £50 overall.

26 April, Digbeth Civil Hall, Birmingham

Same chanting skinheads and punks as last time mob us—but there's more of them tonight. We got gobbed on again (disgusting). Broken strings added to the restrained mood of the set—mainly because of the bad feeling in the room.

19 June, Civic Hall, Totnes

A tin can of sound in an echoey building and relatively empty. The small crowd was receptive and appreciative. It was light relief after the last few heavy gigs. We played well.

9 October, Institute for the Blind, Hull

Nice hall, but the stage was too low—Vi had to stand on a box! Very young audience, who went bananas. The giving out of the badges afterwards got out of hand, with kids scrabbling like hens for corn. It leaves a sense that they're desperate for anything they can get their hands on.

11 October, Rock Garden, Middlesborough

Totally barbaric audience. Chanting and gobbing throughout the evening; fights sporadic but constant. Attempts to clamber onto our stage. Vi and Dave both hit. We played well, though it was more out of a determination to assert ourselves than anything else. Guitar broken, either in the fights or stage trouble. Should we do gigs like this?

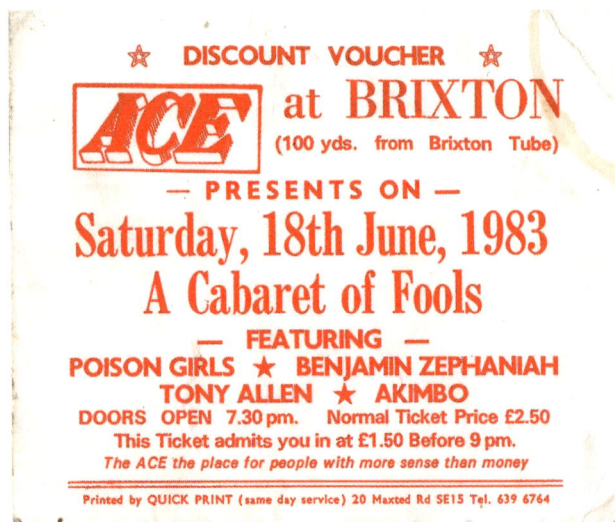

1981

31 March, Music Hall, Berlin

Smallish club in the centre of Berlin, with a small stage. Very 'poseur punk' audience, who didn't know what to make of us. We played well, I think, and the audience was confronted and a bit frightened by our performance.

9 June, 100 Club, London

The first Crass gig in London for an ages. Nice place, apart from the pillar in the centre of the stage. Full. Good atmosphere. No trouble. Things seemed a bit *too* safe—comfortable and gratuitous. Where's the edge? Crass recorded it for their album.

28 September, Moonlight Club, London

New era! Nil on bass. *Total Exposure* on the verge of release. Busy and exhausting time. We used the house PA—adequate, but we all missed Paul [Tandy]. Good audience. Lots of exposure—*The Leveller*, Radio 1, *NME*, *Sounds*. New set—new rules, OK!

24 October, South Bank Polytechnic, London

Day of the national CND march. Venue packed out. Whole host of technical problems—but the atmosphere was really good.

19 December, Anarchy Centre, Belfast

Small square, black hall—straw bale stage—good audience—fantastic atmosphere. We played really well. One of the best gigs that we're done—in terms of the whole event. Something special. Walked back to the flat in the rain—party with the Belfast punks.

1982

20 June, Anarchist Squatting Centre, Den Haag

Good energy, good organisation and a nice atmosphere. We played well—more party than gig. As it was Vi's birthday, she got a cake at the end.

27 June, Gigant, Apeldoorn

Small, smelly punk style venue, which ended up being really good. Played well and got very drunk afterwards. This gig was going to be cancelled due to the organisers' doubts about the audience, but we attracted quite a crowd. Everyone happy.

19 December, Zig-Zag squat gig, London

Quite an event, as it turned out. We asked to play early, and did a short set with borrowed guitars and amps. We were all glad we were not in this area any more. *All* the Crass-type bands played—about 19 in all. This is the first gig with the Big C since the bust up. They haven't changed at all. We have.

1983

18 June, Ace, Brixton, London

A big gig, and really successful, with 700–800 people and a really mixed audience—punks, lefties and others. A good gig and a pointer to the future.

2 September, Radio Sheffield Show, Sheffield

A Big Top on a windswept and wet showground, we were amongst the flowers and massive vegetables on display. Played a short set, then back to the BBC for a two-hour radio interview. Strange gig. Aren't they all, these days?

18 September, Futurama Festival, Queen's Hall, Leeds

Concrete floors, tram shed iron girders and the ambience of a factory farm crossed with a prison. Efficient, but deadly. Dozens of bands and a derelict atmosphere. Why are we here? Who knows, but here we are. We play—no reaction, apart from a stunned silence.

19 September, The Venue, London

Promo gig for the Big Brother Cabaret. Big posters, good publicity, lots of people and a great atmosphere. We got a lot more concessions from the management of the place than last time we played. Lots of business interest and general business buzz.

19 October, Brannigans, Leeds

Stayed at Chumbawamba's house before and after. Couldn't get into the venue until late, and so everything was rushed as usual. The gig was recorded on the four-track, but not the right desk to do it the way we wanted. Small audience.

1984

24 February, Pavillion Theatre, Brighton

At last! A good gig. Nice stage, nice place and back in Brighton again. We played well, despite broken strings and walking bass drum.

8 June, Ambulance Station squat, London

After two months with only one rehearsal with the whole band, we were all a bit wary of this one. But there were lots of people and an amazing reception—like a party. Ended with a shambolic version of "Persons Unknown", but great.

21 August, The Leadmill, Sheffield

50p on-the-door price—400 people paid to get in! A great gig, with no major disasters and an energetic feeling all round.

19 December, ULU, London

Miners' benefit. Playing support for the first time in years. Good gig though. Lots of publicity—lots of people, and a great set from us. Having intense rehearsals and recording for the new album all seems to have paid off.

1985

21 January, Warner Theatre, Washington DC

What a way to start a year and end a holiday—the Counter Inaugural Ball, in the freezing cold and with shambolic organisation. Still a weird and wonderful gig, relying on our stand-in drummer after Dave [Bennett] was refused a visa. The audience left after our set.

10 March, Bakke Bydelshus, Trondheim

A strangely quiet gig. We played well, but a bit restrained—though the audience seemed to love it all. Lovely people and a totally respectful audience.

30 March, The KOB, Berlin

Packed out and really hot and steamy. Trouble with broken strings, but we played tight and well. Lots of people left outside as the venue was full. Hastily arranged a second gig for the following night.

★ FEATURING ★ WAYNE KRAMER & TOMMY FLANDERS
FORMERLY OF MC-5 PLUS
PLUS ROCKABILLY beat the naked
FEATURING THE HIT: "NOBODY I KNOW LIKES THIS GOVERNMENT"
REGGAE MOJA NYA
PLUS AKIMBO FROM ENGLAND
PLUS-STAND-UP COMEDIANS & MORE!
PLUS POISON GIRLS FROM ENGLAND
FILM BORN IN FLAMES
FEMINIST S.F. ★★★★
WARNER THEATRE
513 G. St., NW
MOVIE AT 6:00 MUSIC AT 8:00 ADM: $10.00
TICKETS AT TICKETRON (D.C.) AND AT YOUR LOCAL RECORD SHOP

21 April, Old Profanity Showboat, Bristol

Playing on a boat! Great space and a great gig. Packed out. We had technical problems, and That Famous Subversa stepped into the breach again. Lovely venue, nice people and quite an experience.

13 October, Lone Star, New York

A weird venue. We were playing support. No sound check, and a peculiar vibe for our first set—but we wowed them with the second. We ended up in a Lower East Side bar.

14 November, Music Theatre, Hanover

An old swimming baths—nice place, and lovely people. Really well looked after. No people at the gig though (well, 38 actually). We played well, despite the lack of audience—and those who were there thought it wonderful.

12 December, The Garage, Nottingham

No PA, we find as we get there. Panic and eventually get a 500 watt job down six flights of stairs at 7pm. Nice club, and we do wonders with the equipment at hand. The gig is great, though we are all exhausted. We play well, and get a great response.

1986
22 March, The Greyhound, London

First Poison Girls gig for ages—and a batch of new songs to brighten our spirits. Seems strangely unconnected times with us working on a new set (*hard* work too) with no visible way out of the corner we find ourselves in. Quite a good evening, but a mixed response on the critics' grapevine

7 August, International Club, Manchester

Long drive north, but a nice place—big. We are treated really well. The place looked empty, though the crowd was really enthusiastic. Where are the people!? Longer drive back and a 5am touchdown.

28 August, The Ritz, Trondheim

Nice club, but expensive to get in. No audience—due to no advertising? Felt it was a bit of a waste of energy for us, though we play well and tight.

1 September, Club 77, Helsinki

The same club that we played last time we were here. Although we were tired, the gig was really good and the crowd went crazy. Spent a nice morning looking over the older part of the town—first time we've been 'rogue' in Finland!

22 November, York Arts Centre, York

A sold out concert—but no PA, due to a misunderstanding. Much panic, many phone calls and cliffhanger drama later, we end up doing a soundcheck at 10:30 and playing straight after. Good gig at the end of it all, but why does this stuff happen!

5 December, The KOB, Berlin

The on-off European tour lurches from crisis to completion, with a certain amount of trepidation all round and a lot of hard work. The KOB is a wonderful place, and Berlin is a good city for us. The place is full, and we play well.

1987
1 August, festival, Nuremberg

Well paid and exciting jaunt into Frankfurt—a hire car and two nights in Nuremberg. We play in a moat! Lots of people. We all feel a bit down after the gig—just rusty. Hey ho. The European tour is sorted out, and a jolly good time is had by all!

15 September, squat gig, Groningen

Huge squat and a very punky atmosphere. But the gig is good, if not particularly well attended. We get asked a lot about hardcore punk—where do we fit into that? A fast fierce set!

30 September, unrecorded venue, Zurich

Organised at three days' notice, and a gig at the 'politically sound' venue in Zurich. A great gig it was too. Terrible acoustics in the hall, but 400+ people turned up. Followed up with an hour interview on local alternative radio. Stayed with great people in an old house by the river. A thirteen hour drive back to the KOB in Berlin the next day.

19 November, New Hall, Tiverton

A big stage, but less time to set up and a smaller audience than the Exeter gig the night before. Those that were there enjoyed themselves! We play a short set and beat the acoustics of the place. Vi develops an abscess from toothache, and ends up in hospital. We have to cancel the next gig—for the first time ever.

1988
12–13 January, Chats Palace, London

After lots of work, *AIDS: The Musical* at last gets an airing. The show benefitted from being performed and will get better still. Full houses and generally well received. Review in *The Guardian*.

9 July, Black Horse, Shedfield

A big country pub located between Portsmouth and Southampton, and a really good gig at last. Lots of people, convoy buses and a great atmosphere.

17 November, Tunnel Club, London

Why? Terrible place, terrible promoter and terrible support bands. Argument about the guest list. The bastards pulled the plug on us at the end.

3 December, West End Centre, Aldershot

A nice place—an arts centre with theatre, restaurant, bar and more—like Chats Palace, but with money. Good gig for us, we play really well.

1989

28 April, Heuried, Zürich

Start of the much-discussed and on-and-off Arms for El Salvador tour. The place is a concrete cross between a swimming baths and an amphitheatre. Horrible. All the bands are unhappy with their performance. The drums fall apart, and we play as badly as we can. However, the gig seems somehow to work. It can only get better—or so they say.

1 May, Reithalle, Bern

Huge squat in old stables buildings. The concert is 'open entrance' with people paying what they want to get in. Seems like home-from-home for us. We play well—fast and furious—for the first time this tour. We stay in a lovely squatted courtyard.

8 May, KOB, Berlin

The KOB is nearly finished, and looking great. The band room now has a flat, shower, cooker and all. We are playing by ourselves and it feels so good. Nervous about whether there will be anyone there, but the place is packed and we have a good time. A brief That Famous Subversa set too!

10 November, Duchess of York, Leeds

Long drive through traffic jams and the rain, and we arrive late. Trouble with the sound and lots of broken strings and chord rearrangements as we go. Not as many people here as last time. Something's gotta change.

15 November, 'Spider Hall,' University, Zagreb

Big concrete hall and, though there were 300 people there, the audience didn't get properly involved. We play well and are told they enjoyed it. Tiring day off in Zagreb, waiting for interviews that didn't happen. A 6am start for the journey home. Exhausted.

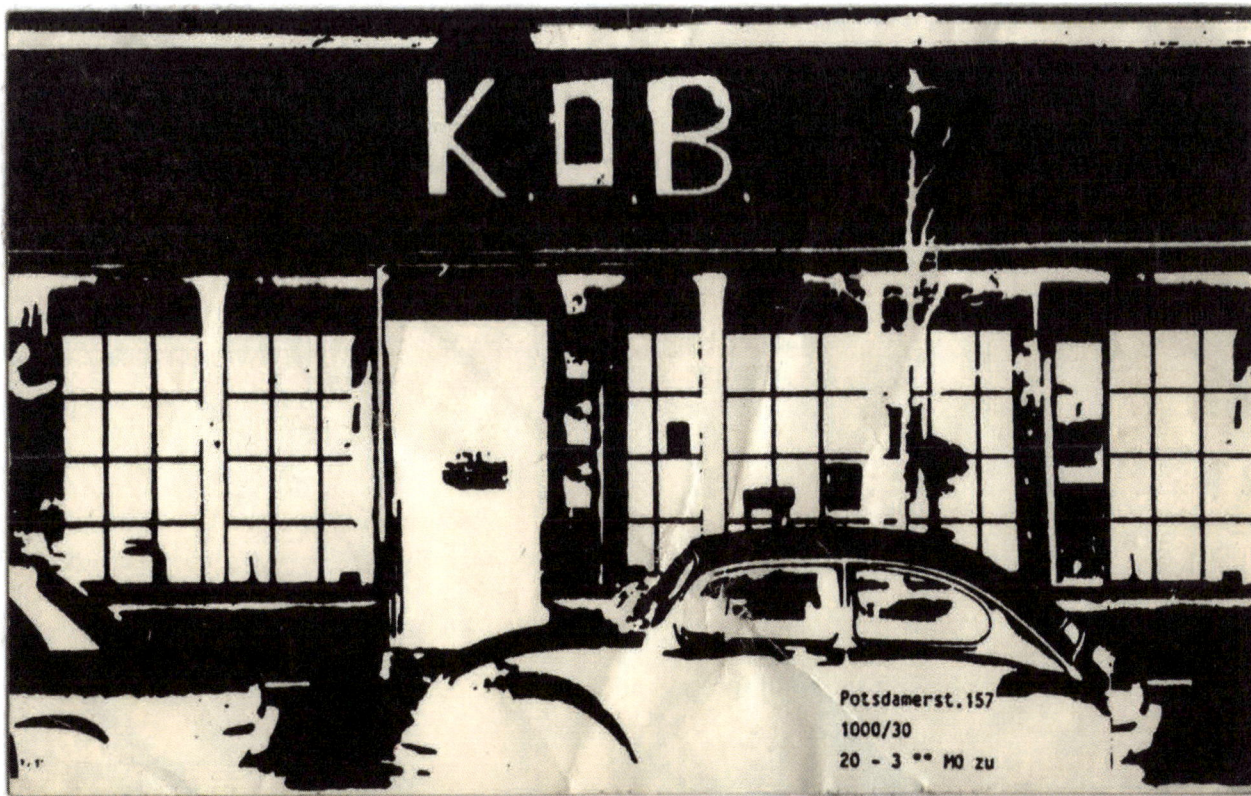

Potsdamerst.157
1000/30
20 - 3 ** MO zu

SPITTING PRETTY PIKKTURES

30p

NEW YOUTH

ADULTS & ELEPHANTS ONLY

WE AIN'T DEAD YET!

YOUTH IS AN ATTITUDE NOT AN AGE.

No. 6

DON'T ASK FOR FREEDOM TAKE IT!

Guanabatz | Sid Presley Experience | 3 Johns
Neurotics | Housemartins | 3 action! | Jesus Christ
live aid is no aid | S.Africa | N.Ireland | Redskins

30p

Anarchy 50p

"The problems that you
suffer from/are problems
that you make
The shit we have to climb
through/is the shit we
choose to take"

POISON GIRLS, CRASS QUESTIONED

KICK IT OVER

No. 9 • HEALTH ISSUE • DECEMBER 1983 • 75 cents

THIS ISSUE:
● Art of War
● Illegal Herbs?
● Women and Therapy
● Peace Movement
● Native Spiritual Struggle

BLACK FLAG

Vol. V. No. 10 SEPTEMBER 1979 20p

Organ of the Anarchist Black Cross

HAVE YOU CONSPIRED WITH PERSONS UNKNOWN?

Ronan Bennett

Iris Mills

Trevor Dawton

Vince Stevenson

TRIAL DATE SEPTEMBER 17th

Taff Ladd

ZERO

16 page issue 25p

Anarchist / Anarcha-feminist Newsmagazine ZERO 6 May / June 78

spare Rib

women's liberation magazine
issue 113 december 1981
50p

Choosing life over nuclear death — Women in Clydebank, Suffolk and Cumbria reclaim the future

Self-help therapy

Scots rape law

Vi Subversion on Poison Girls

PRODUCED INDEPENDENTLY BY ANARCHA-FEMINISTS
ISSUE 2 May 1984

Gaining Ground

OUTTA CONTROL
ANARCHA-FEMINIST NEWS

CAUSE LABOUR HOPE OF THE WORLD

peace news

for nonviolent revolution

No 2150 Friday July 24 1981
FORTNIGHTLY

25p

COMMENT ON RIOTS * TOTALITARIANISM * CO-OPS REPORT
BRITISH DETERRENCE * REVIEWS

APPENDIX 5: SELECT BIBLIOGRAPHY

Interviews
Tom Barwood (10 May 2023)
Lance d'Boyle (March 2014 [interviewer Simon Nolan])
Adi Cooper (5 March 2025)
Sue Cooper (16 October 2024)
Dominique Downs (30 December 2024)
Richard Famous (May 2023–May 2025)
Martin Goldschmidt (22 November 2022)
Steve Ignorant (8 July 2025)
Heather Joyce (7 July 2024)
Andy Lee (21 June 2025)
Robert Lloyd (19 August 2024)
Zillah Minx (25 August 2024)
Bernhardt Rebours (March–May 2024)
Gemma Sansom (3 October 2024)
Alan Schofield (8 July 2003)
Mick Shenton (26 May 2023)
Vi Subversa (July 2014 [interviewer Simon Nolan])
Sid Truelove (25 August 2024)

Correspondence
Scott Barker (November 2024)
Adi Cooper (March 2025)
Pete Fender (February 2023–June 2025)
Clifford Harper (April 2024)
Penny Rimbaud (June–July 2025)

UK Zines and Fanzines
Acts of Defiance
Widely respected anarcho-punk zine produced in Sunderland by an editorial group involved with the Sunderland Musicians Collective and The Bunker venue.

Exposure
Photocopied A5 punk zine solo produced by 'Jabbs' out of Southwell in Nottinghamshire, UK.

In the City
Bridging the divide between fanzine and magazine, *In the City* mixed mainstream and fringe punk and postpunk culture with coverage of fashion, politics, and lifestyle. It was sufficiently commercial in outlook to attract and carry advertising.

Obnoxious
Hardcore anarcho-punk zine, published in Exeter by then fourteen-year-old Clem, three issues, 1980–82.

Heather Dean and Rich Cross of Metro Youth (and *Catalyst* zine) helped out with printing and editorial work.

New Youth
Eclectic punk and postpunk zine, based in Hull, UK, and edited by Swift Nick and associates. "Youth is an attitude, not an age," its front page banner declared.

Positive Creed
Present-day punk zine, written and published in Exeter, Devon, UK, by Rob Stone. Issues have included extensive original interviews with Lance d'Boyle and Bernhardt Rebours

Realities of Society
Punk zine produced by Daryl Hardcastle of Omega Tribe. Gary Robins (Lance d'Boyle) of Poison Girls helped to arrange printing.

Self-Destruct
Photocopied A5 punk zine put together by a group of punk friends living in Buckie, Banffshire, Scotland.

Spitting Pretty Pikktures
Punk zine edited by Lee Gibson, who also published *Anathema* amongst several other zine titles. The zine's contact address was on Brougham Road, Hackney in London, a famous stretch of punk squats in the capital in the 1980s.

Anarchist newspapers and magazines
Anarchy
First published in the UK in the 1960s, the initial series of *Anarchy* magazine brought together extended essays, reviews, and think pieces by prominent writers and thinkers in the British anarchist and libertarian traditions, under the aegis of Colin Ward and Freedom Press. Relaunched in 1971, the second series of *Anarchy* adopted a different and independent guise prioritising class struggles in the workplace, in prisons, and in inner-city communities. In the early 1980s, the magazine's coverage of anarchist punk bordered on the disdainful. As membership of the editorial committee fluctuated, later issues veered off to document the activities of European paramilitary groupings.

Black Flag
Having begun life as the *Bulletin of the Anarchist Black Cross* (a support organisation for anarchist prisoners the world over) in 1968, *Black Flag* developed into a militant anarchist newspaper closely aligned with the combative, class struggle, and insurrectionist strands of the movement. Stuart Christie and Albert Meltzer were prominent figures in the editorial group. Its coverage of political punk was fitful but not consistently hostile. The final newspaper format edition was published in November 1991. A magazine format relaunch began in 1993, which later morphed into an online review.

Freedom

Longest-running British anarchist newspaper, first published in London in 1886. Vi Subversa's partner Philip Samson was a member of the editorial group during the Second World War. Although its political centre of gravity was regularly in contest, in the 1970s and early 1980s it was most clearly aligned with the artistic, cultural and philosophical strands of the British anarchist tradition, with a recurring focus on individualism and antimilitarism. The paper traced the evolution of anarchist punk attentively. *Freedom* ceased regular print publication in 2014 and is now online but still producing irregular print issues.

Gaining Ground

Produced 'independently by anarcha-feminists' in Belfast, *Gaining Ground* was sold as a self-contained component of *Outta Control*. The magazine focused on women's struggles, reproductive rights, sexual health and legal battles in the Six Counties of the north of Ireland.

Green Anarchist

First published in 1984, editors Alan Albon, Richard Hunt, and Marcus Christo hoped to combine the countercultural activism of punk and hippy with a militant form of eco politics. The mix proved unstable, and led to splits and recriminations as the magazine was shunned by the mainstream anarchist movement as *Green Anarchist* adopted increasingly reactionary and oddball editorial positions. Two rival versions both wound down in the early 2000s.

Kick It Over

Canadian anarchist journal, published by the anonymous Kick It Over collective based in Toronto between 1982 and 1994. Taking its name from a song by The Clash released on the B-side of "London Calling," the collective sought to combine the rebellious impulses of punk with a focus on feminist, ecological, and new forms of dissident and radical cultural politics.

Outta Control

Launched in 1980, *Outta Control* was a monthly newsletter produced from the Just Book bookshop offering the 'news and views' of Belfast Anarchist Collective. Forty-two issues, focusing on struggles in the Six Counties of Northern Ireland, in the Irish Republic, and beyond, before the title was wound down in 1984. The following year, the Collective began publishing the new 'Belfast anarchist bi-monthly' *Ainriail* (1985–87).

Zero

A short-lived, London-based anarchist newspaper whose editorial group sought to 'realise the links between anarchism and feminism' to prosecute a 'sexual-social revolution' that would deliver the 'simultaneous overthrow of capital, patriarchy and state.' Launched in June 1977, the final issue was published the following August.

Political and campaigning publications

The Leveller

A libertarian infused radical left news magazine, sympathetic to nondoctrinaire far-left and anarchist ideas, but proudly editorially nonaligned with any one group on the British left. First published in 1976, the monthly attracted an eclectic mix of progressive professional journalists and activist writers until its closure in 1985.

No Nukes

Occasional zine-style magazine of the No Nukes Music group, principally covering bands who played under its banner in the early 1980s.

Peace News

Pacifist newspaper and magazine launched in 1936. By the late 1970s, it had relocated from London to Nottingham. Published fortnightly, it was run by an editorial collective and had adopted the subtitle 'for nonviolent revolution.' In the 1980s, it was the voice of the radical activist wing of the disarmament and antimilitarist movements. It continued to publish in different formats—most recently appearing as a bimonthly newspaper—until suspending print and online publication in 2024.

Sanity

The moderate and mainstream monthly house magazine of the Campaign for Nuclear Disarmament (CND). Launched during CND's first surge in 1961, *Sanity* was closed down in 1991.

Spare Rib

Independent feminist monthly magazine, launched in 1972, covering politics, culture, and history from a variety of feminist perspectives, from mainstream to radical to separatist. The final issue was published in 1993.

Music press and publications

The so-called trinity of British music press weeklies (sometimes referred to as the 'inkies') dominated and defined mainstream coverage of rock and pop, throughout the 1970s and 1980s, before the proliferation of rival culture and lifestyle magazines—and then the decline of the analogue press—sealed their fate. At their peak, their circulation was in the hundreds of thousands of copies per week, with actual readership far higher. Coverage in these publications would reach an audience vastly larger than the most widely circulated fanzine. For anarchist and outsider artists, the price of inclusion was compromise, the antithetical context and the risk of journalistic hostility.

Melody Maker

Long-running British weekly music newspaper, first published in 1926. Initially willing to champion breakthrough musical genres, by the time punk arrived *Melody Maker* was widely seen as the most conservative and risk averse of its contemporaries. With a few exceptions, its writers seemed more bemused by than hostile towards anarchist punk. In 2001, it was merged into the *New Musical Express*.

New Musical Express

Most often referred to by the acronym of its title, the *NME* was launched as a weekly music paper in Britain in 1952. In the 1980s, it was both praised and derided as the most cerebral of the three music weeklies, the *NME*'s coverage was iconoclastic and diverse. Writings by Paul Du Noyer, Graham Lock, and others provided some of the British music press's most attentive and considered coverage of DIY and dissident punk. *NME*'s existence as a weekly print publication ended in 1991.

Sounds

The relative newcomer of the three, having launched in October 1970. By the time that punk broke, *Sounds* had crystalised its identity as an upstart, becoming far more willing than its competitors to embrace new (and sometimes seemingly 'unfashionable') genres, like UK82 punk, Oi! and the New Wave of British Heavy Metal. Writer Garry Bushell channelled widespread music journalist antipathy towards anarcho-punk, but others at the paper, including Winston Smith (a pen name for Richard Newson) and Johnny Waller, were more intrigued by the scene's aspirations. *Sounds* closed in April 1991.

Articles, Chapters, and Books

Allen, Tony. *Attitude – Wanna Make Something of It: The Secret of Stand-up Comedy*. Glastonbury: Gothic Image Publications, 2002.

Bayton, Mavis. *Frock Rock: Women Performing Popular Music*. Oxford: Oxford University Press, 1998.

Cross, Rich. "'Take the Toys from the Boys': Gender, Generation and Anarchist Intent in the Work of Poison Girls." *Punk & Post-Punk* 3, no. 2 (2014): 117–145. https://doi.org/10.1386/punk.3.2.117_1.

Cross, Rich. "Why Do You Think That They Are Laughing?" In *'Some of Us Scream Some of Us Shout': Myths, Folklore and Epic Tales of the Anarcho*, edited by Greg Bull and Mike Dines. Portsmouth: Itchy Monkey Press, 2016.

Ensminger, David A. *Punk Women: 40 Years of Musicians Who Built Punk Rock*. Portland: Microcosm Publishing, 2021.

Harper, Clifford, Dennis Gould, and Jeff Cloves, eds. *Visions of Poesy: An Anthology of Twentieth Century Anarchist Poetry*. London: Freedom Press, 1994.

McGuirk, Niall, and Michael Murphy, eds. *Great Gig Memories: from Punks and Friends*. Hope Publications, 2021.

Minx, Zillah, director. *She's a Punk Rocker UK: A Film Documentary by and About Punk Women*. Ultra Violet Punk Productions, 2010.

O'Neill, Sean, and Guy Trelford. *It Makes You Want to Spit: The Definitive Guide to Punk in Northern Ireland*, 1977–1982. Dublin: Reekus, 2003.

O'Sullivan, Sue, ed. *Turning the Tables: Recipes and Reflections from Women*. London: Sheba Feminist Press, 1987.

Reddington, Helen. *The Lost Women of Rock: Female Musicians of the Punk Era*. Sheffield: Equinox Publishing, 2012.

Sofianos, Lisa, Robin Ryde, and Charlie Waterhouse. *The Truth of Revolution, Brother: An Exploration of Punk Philosophy*. London: Situation Press, 2014.

AUTHOR BIOS

Rich Cross is a researcher and writer on British and European protest movements and counter cultural resistance, particularly from the anarchist and libertarian traditions, Cross has published and presented extensively about the UK's original anarcho-punk scene. He has edited the website The Hippies Now Wear Black website for well over a decade, documenting both the history and the continuing creative dissidence of that scene's most resilient troublemakers.

Alec Dunn (layout) is a designer, printer, and nurse. He co-edits *Signal: A Journal of International Political Graphics & Culture* and coauthored *It Did Happen Here: An Antifascist People's History*. He is a member of the Justseeds Artists' Cooperative.

Erin Yanke (editor) is a self-taught documentarian with thirty-five years of projects. She regularly publishes zines and occasionally produces podcasts and films. She was a coauthor of *It Did Happen Here: An Antifascist People's History*.

Boff Whalley (foreword) is a musician, a cofounder of Chumbawamba, and a writer. His most recent book is *But: Life Isn't Like that, Is It? Stories of Disruption and Digression*.

Poison Girls in late 1982: Nil, Vi, Richard, and Lance. Photo courtesy of Richard Famous.

About PM

PM Press is an independent, radical publisher of critically necessary books for our tumultuous times. Our aim is to deliver bold political ideas and vital stories to all walks of life and arm the dreamers to demand the impossible. Founded in 2007 by a small group of people with decades of publishing, media, and organizing experience, we have sold millions of copies of our books, most often one at a time, face to face. We're old enough to know what we're doing and young enough to know what's at stake. Join us to create a better world.

PM Press
PO Box 23912
Oakland, CA 94623
www.pmpress.org

PM Press in Europe
europe@pmpress.org
www.pmpress.org/uk

Friends of PM Press

In the eighteen years since its founding – and on a mere shoestring – PM Press has risen to the formidable challenge of publishing and distributing knowledge and entertainment for the struggles ahead. With over 500 releases to date, we have published an impressive and stimulating array of literature, art, music, politics, history, and culture. Using every available medium, we've succeeded in connecting those hungry for ideas and information to those putting them into practice.

Friends of PM allows you to directly help impact, amplify, and revitalize the discourse and actions of radical writers, filmmakers, and artists. It provides us with a stable foundation from which we can build upon our early successes and provides a much-needed subsidy for the materials that can't necessarily pay their own way. You can help make that happen – and receive every new title automatically delivered to your door once a month – by joining as a Friend of PM Press.

Here are your options:

- **$15 a month:** Get 3 e-Books emailed to you plus 50% discount on all webstore purchases.
- **$30 a month:** Get all books and pamphlets plus 50% discount on all webstore purchases
- **$40 a month:** Get all PM Press releases (books, pamphlets, and e-Books) plus 50% discount on all webstore purchases
- **$100 a month:** Superstar - Everything plus PM shirt, PM hoodie, free downloads, and 50% discount on all webstore purchases

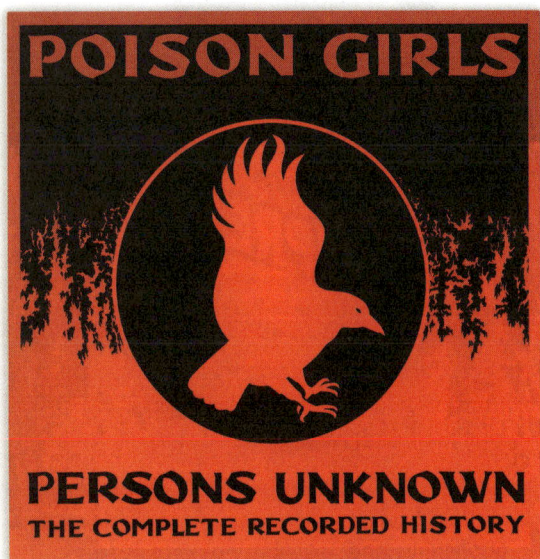

PERSONS UNKNOWN:
THE COMPLETE RECORDED HISTORY

This seven CD box set brings together all of Poison Girls studio and live albums, plus all of the band's singles released on the Xntrix, Small Wonder, Crass Records, Illuminated, and Upright labels.

Also included are demo recordings of unreleased tracks from early in the band's career, songs by spin-off duo That Famous Subversa, and live and home recordings from the final years of the band's life—material that has never been released before.

The box set includes a fully illustrated, full-colour 96-page booklet that contains an exhaustive set of song lyrics and a succinct history of the band.

Poison Girls. Persons Unknown: The Complete Recorded History
PM Press, Cooking Vinyl, Free Dirt, and Active Distribution, 2025.

DISC ONE:
- "Persons Unknown" single
- *Ilex* twelve-inch
- *Piano Lessons* single
- Demo recordings 1978-79

DISC TWO:
- "Statement" flexi
- *Chappaquiddick Bridge* LP
- *All Systems Go* single

DISC THREE:
- *Total Exposure* LP, live 1981
- "The Offending Article"

DISC FOUR:
- *Where's the Pleasure* LP
- "Statement" (orchestral version)

DISC FIVE:
- *One Good Reason* single
- *Not a Real Woman* single
- *Seven Year Scratch* LP—live tracks, 1983

DISC SIX:
- *Songs of Praise* LP
- *Happy Now* single
- live tracks 1984-85

DISC SEVEN:
- *Price of Grain* twelve-inch
- Leytonstone studio recordings
- Unreleased live recordings, 1987
- Songs by That Famous Subversa
- "Statement," live 1995
- "Persons Unknown," live 2015

Available from PM Press—$70.00

POISON GIRLS MERCH AVAILABLE FROM PM PRESS

Poison Girls red crow on black tee– $35.00

Take the Toys from the Boys black ink on cream tee– $35.00

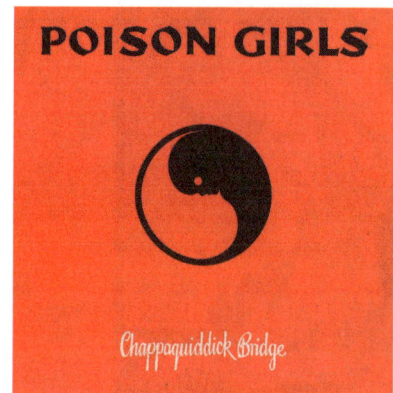

Chappaquiddick Bridge
12" vinyl 11 song LP
Originally released in 1982. Re-released by Water Wing Records in 2016. $25.00

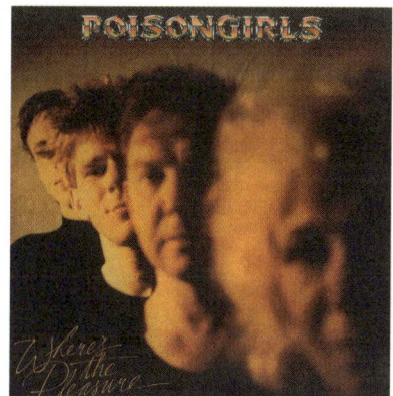

Where's the Pleasure
12" vinyl 13 song LP
Originally released in 1982. Re-released by Water Wing Records in 2016. $22.95

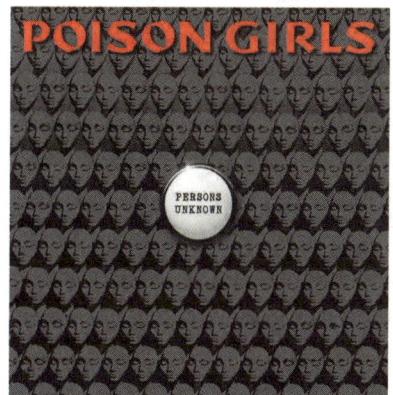

Persons Unknown/Statement
12" vinyl 2 song EP
Both songs from 1980, includes the orchestral version of "Statement." Re-released by All the Madmen Records in 2015. $16.99

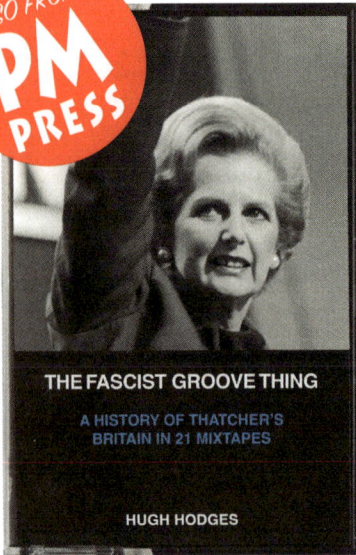

The Fascist Groove Thing: A History of Thatcher's Britain in 21 Mixtapes
Author: Hugh Hodges
Preface: Dick Lucas • Foreword: Boff Whalley
ISBN: 9781629638843
384 Pages
$22.95
A furious, sardonic history of Thatcher's Britain told through the rebellious pop of the late '70s and '80s—when hundreds of bands turned music into protest and resistance.

Various Artists – The Fascist Groove Thing cassette
SKU: TFGTcassette2nd
Various Artists
63 minute audio cassette
$10.99
This soundtrack compilation to Hugh Hodges's brilliant book *The Fascist Groove Thing: A History of Thatcher's Britain in 21 Mixtapes* features 20 tracks of classic punk, anarcho-punk, and folk from Margaret Thatcher's reign and eventual demise (some quite rare).

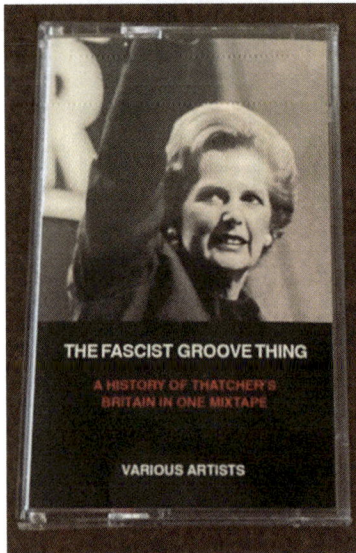

The Last of the Hippies: An Hysterical Romance
Author: Penny Rimbaud
ISBN: 9781629631035
128 Pages
$12.00
First published in 1982 as part of the Crass album *Christ: The Album*, Penny Rimbaud's *The Last of the Hippies* is a fiery anarchist polemic centered on the story of his friend, Phil Russell (aka Wally Hope), who was murdered by the State while incarcerated in a mental institution.

The Story of Crass
Author: George Berger
ISBN: 9781604860375
304 Pages
$22.00
Crass wasn't just a band—they were a radical collective who turned punk into a way of life, fusing music, politics, and art into a defiant challenge to authority and culture. In *The Story of Crass* they have collaborated with the author on telling the whole Crass story.

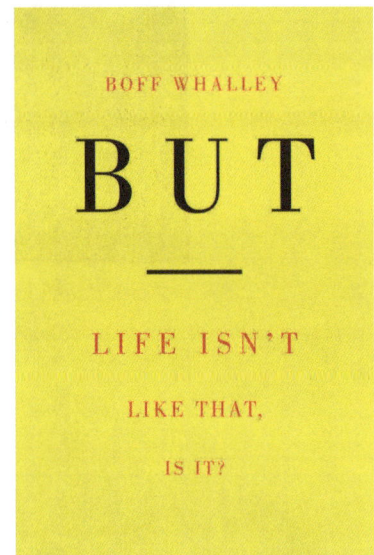

But: Life Isn't Like That, Is It?
Author: Boff Whalley
ISBN: 9798887440897
288 Pages
$19.95
A collection of wayward, disruptive stories that refuse the tidy beginning–middle–end, *But* captures real life in all its stuttering, funny, unfinished, and unpredictable messiness.

The Day the Country Died: A History of Anarcho Punk 1980-1984
Author: Ian Glasper
ISBN: 9781604865165
496 Pages
$27.95
An in-depth history of the UK anarcho-punk explosion of the early '80s, *The Day the Country Died* captures the bands, politics, and DIY spirit that turned punk into a revolutionary movement.

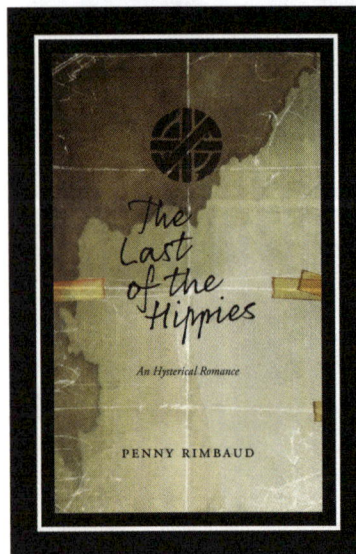

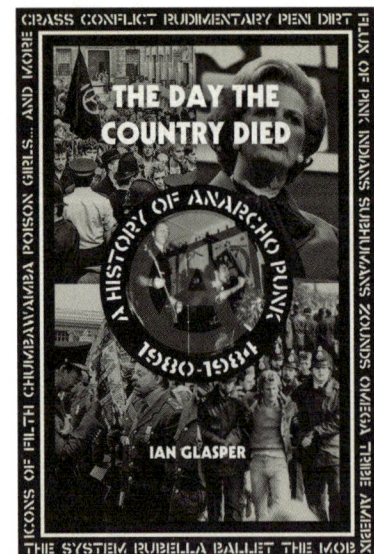

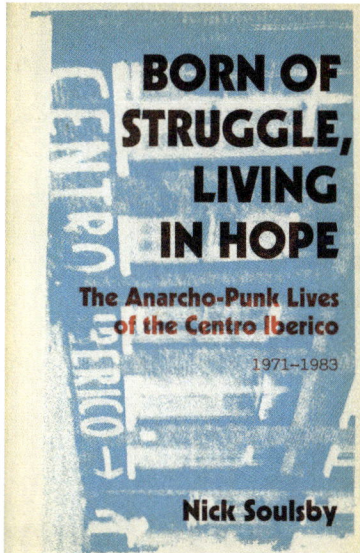

Born of Struggle, Living in Hope: The Anarcho-Punk Lives of the Centro Iberico, 1971–83
Author: Nick Soulsby
ISBN: 9798887441221
208 Pages
$19.95

Born of Struggle, Living in Hope tells the story of the Centro Iberico, the legendary UK music venue and self-managed support centre. Centro Iberico grew out of the anarchist prisoners' aid organization Anarchist Black Cross and functioned as both a political centre and a creative venue.

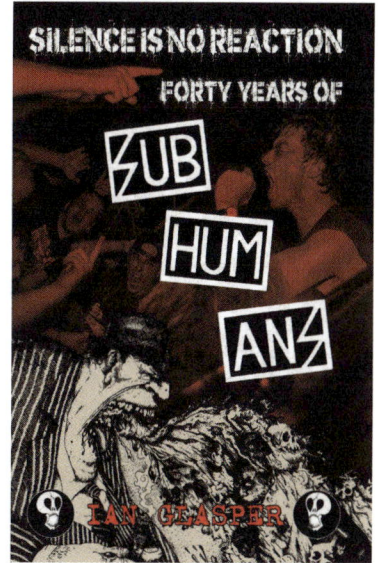

Silence Is No Reaction: Forty Years of Subhumans
Author: Ian Glasper
ISBN: 9781629635507
640 Pages
$25.00

The Subhumans are rightly regarded as one of the best punk bands to ever hail from the UK. *Silence Is No Reaction* tells their whole story straight from the memories of every band member and many of their closest friends and peers, along with hundreds of flyers and exclusive photos.

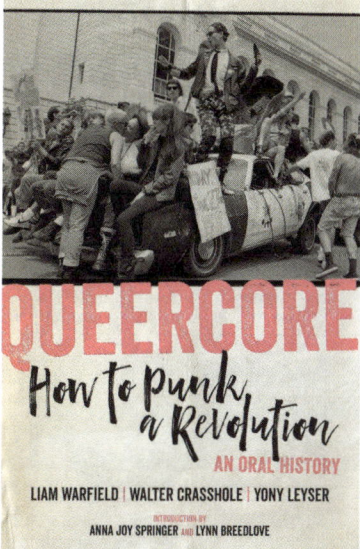

Queercore: How to Punk a Revolution: An Oral History
Authors: Warfield, Crasshole, and Leyser
ISBN: 9781629637969
208 Pages
$20.00

Queercore is a firsthand account of a movement by the people that lived it—from punk's early queerness to Toronto kids' decision to create a scene that didn't exist to the emergence of riot grrrl, as well as the zines, art, film, styles, and music that made this movement an incitement to both mainstream gay and straight society.

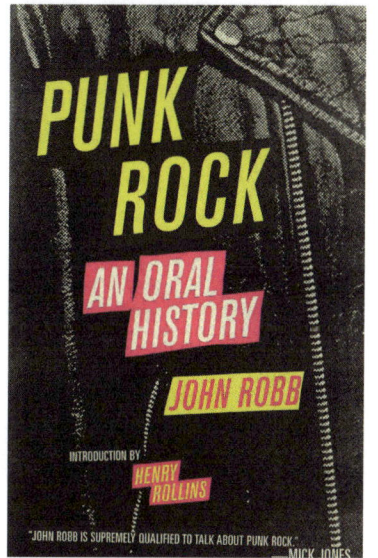

Punk Rock: An Oral History
Author: John Robb
ISBN: 9781604860054
584 Pages
$24.95

John Robb weaves together interviews in this oral history of UK punk: from the Clash to Crass, the Sex Pistols to the Stranglers, the UK Subs to Buzzcocks, and many more. Over 150 interviews capture the excitement of one of the most thrilling waves of music and cultural change ever.

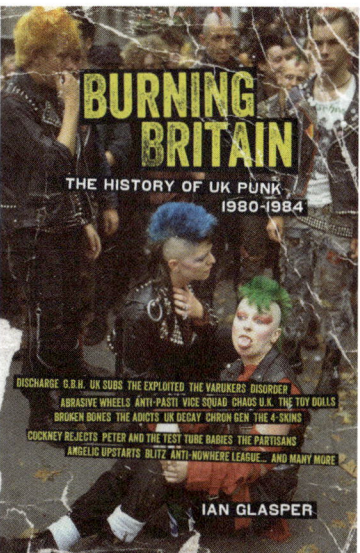

Burning Britain: The History of UK Punk 1980-1984
Author: Ian Glasper
ISBN: 9781604867480
456 Pages
$24.95

As the media declared punk dead, a new breed was emerging from the gutter, more aggressive and political than their predecessors. Featuring hundreds of interviews and photographs, this is the true story of punk in Thatcher's Britain.

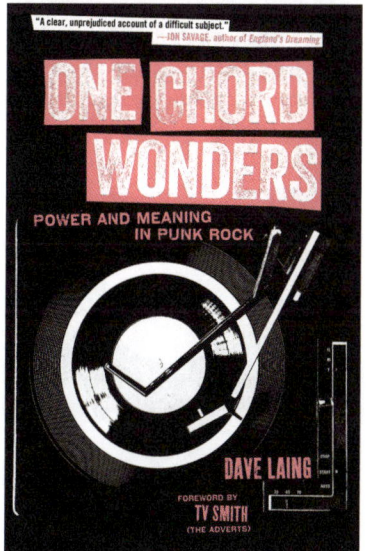

One Chord Wonders: Power and Meaning in Punk Rock
Author: Dave Laing
ISBN: 9781629630335
224 Pages
$17.95

Originally published in 1985, *One Chord Wonders* was the first full-length study of British punk rock and the ways it exposed the workings of power in the entertainment industries.

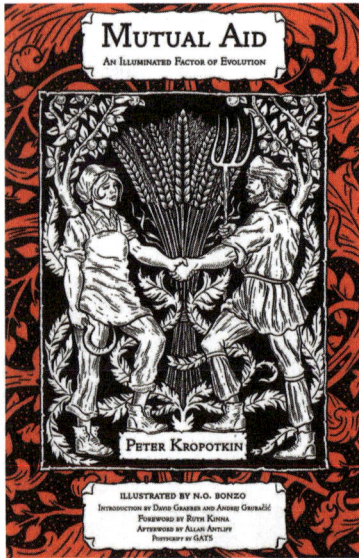

Mutual Aid: An Illuminated Factor of Evolution
Author: Peter Kropotkin • Illustrated by N.O. Bonzo
Introduction by David Graeber & Andrej Grubacic
ISBN: 9781629638744
336 Pages
$30.00
In *Mutual Aid*, Peter Kropotkin, still one of the most inspirational figures of the anarchist movement, presented a seminal critique of the hypothesis of competition promoted by social Darwinism and helped revolutionize modern evolutionary theory. Beautifully illustrated by N.O. Bonzo.

Anarchy and the Sex Question: Essays on Women and Emancipation, 1896-1926
Author: Emma Goldman • Editor: Shawn P. Wilbur
ISBN: 9781629631448
160 Pages
$14.95
For Emma Goldman, sex constituted "the most elemental force in human life." As this diverse collection of her writings reveals, it was subject that touched on politics, economy, morality, and social relations.

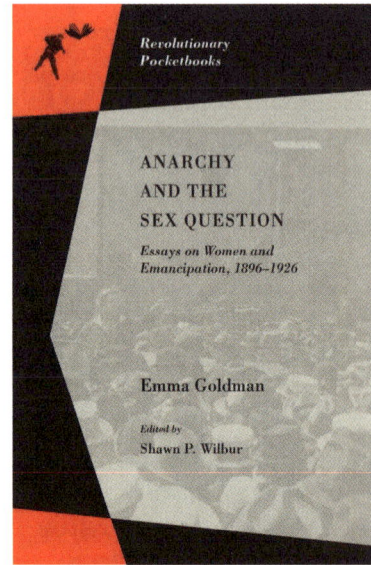

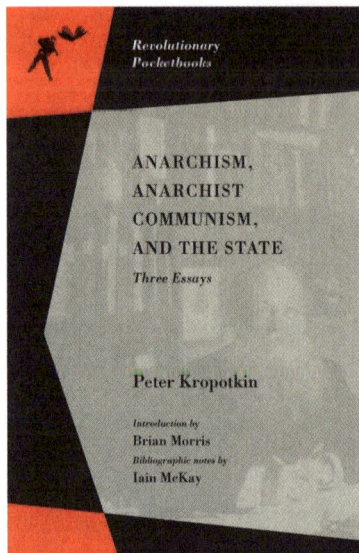

Anarchism, Anarchist Communism, and The State: Three Essays
Author: Peter Kropotkin
ISBN: 9781629635750
160 Pages
$14.95
Peter Kropotkin, the eloquent and passionate advocate of a world without kings or bosses or borders, attempted to distill his many insights into these brief but brilliant essays on the state, anarchism, and the ideology for which he became a founding name—anarchist communism.

Anarchy Comics: The Complete Collection
Author: Jay Kinney
ISBN: 9781604865318
224 Pages
$24.95
Compiles the legendary four issues of *Anarchy Comics* (1978–1986), the underground comic that melded anarchist politics with a punk sensibility, producing a riveting mix of satire, revolt, and artistic experimentation.

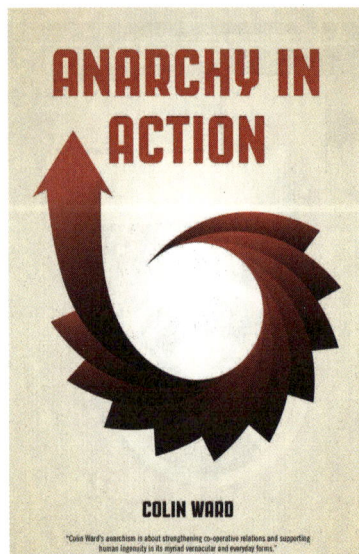

Anarchy in Action
Author: Colin Ward
ISBN: 9781629632384
192 Pages
$15.95
Through a wide-ranging analysis—drawing on examples from education, urban planning, welfare, housing, the environment, the workplace, and the family—Colin Ward shows that the roots of anarchist practice lie precisely in the ways that people have always tended to organize themselves when left alone to do so.

Wildcat Anarchist Comics
Author: Donald Rooum • Colorist: Jayne Clementson
ISBN: 9781629631271
128 Pages
$14.95
Collects the drawings of Donald Rooum, mostly from the long-running *Wildcat*, an anarchist comic strip that has been published in *Freedom* newspaper since 1980.

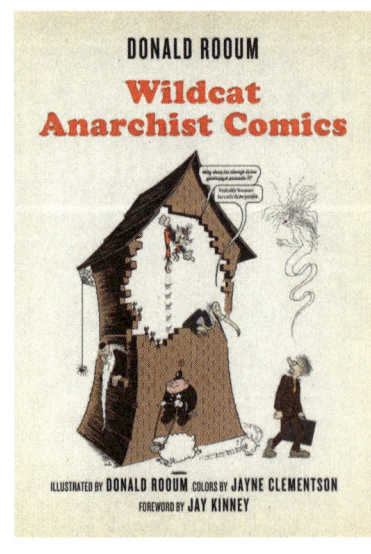